T0262977

DIGITIZATION OF ECONOMY AND SOCIETY

Emerging Paradigms

DIGITIZATION OF ECONOMY AND SOCIETY

Emerging Paradigms

Edited by
Sudeshna Basu Mukherjee, PhD
Saheli Guha Neogi Ghatak, PhD
Nilanjan Ray, PhD

First edition published 2022

Apple Academic Press Inc.
1265 Goldenrod Circle, NE,
Palm Bay, FL 32905 USA

4164 Lakeshore Road, Burlington,
ON, L7L 1A4 Canada

CRC Press
6000 Broken Sound Parkway NW,
Suite 300, Boca Raton, FL 33487-2742 USA

2 Park Square, Milton Park,
Abingdon, Oxon, OX14 4RN UK

Library and Archives Canada Cataloguing in Publication

Title: Digitization of economy and society : emerging paradigms / edited by Sudeshna Basu Mukherjee, PhD, Saheli Guha Neogi Ghatak, PhD, Nilanjan Ray, PhD.
Names: Mukherjee, Sudeshna Basu, editor. | Ghatak, Saheli Guha Neogi, editor. | Ray, Nilanjan, 1984- editor.
Description: First edition. | Includes bibliographical references and index.
Identifiers: Canadiana (print) 20210191082 | Canadiana (ebook) 20210191228 | ISBN 9781774630280 (hardcover) | ISBN 9781774639108 (softcover) | ISBN 9781003187479 (ebook)
Subjects: LCSH: Technology—Social aspects. | LCSH: Technology—Economic aspects. | LCSH: Information society.
Classification: LCC T14.5 .D57 2022 | DDC 303.48/3—dc23

Library of Congress Cataloging-in-Publication Data

Names: Mukherjee, Sudeshna Basu, editor. | Ghatak, Saheli Guha Neogi, editor. | Ray, Nilanjan, 1984- editor.
Title: Digitization of economy and society : emerging paradigms / edited by Sudeshna Basu Mukherjee, PhD, Saheli Guha Neogi Ghatak, PhD, Nilanjan Ray, PhD.
Description: 1st edition. | Palm Bay : Apple Academic Press, 2021. | Includes bibliographical references and index. | Summary: "This new volume looks at a selection of important issues resulting from the digitization of society, which has fundamentally transformed organizations, with the pace of technological change exacerbating the challenges. New technological innovations are creating new opportunities as well as new challenges. Digitization of Economy and Society: Emerging Paradigms considers the emerging paradigms of digitization in economy and society, which covers a wide spectrum of digitization processes and consequences, accelerated by the current COVID-19 pandemic, the lockdown scenario, and the increase in digitization by individuals, businesses, and governments. The book explores digital social trends, digital marketing and the service industry as well as the societal consequences of technologies and solutions to those problems. The diverse topics include the societal impact of digitization on gender issues, virtual relationships, e-government, online privacy, the gig economy (using Uber as an example), work life changes, online education, online media health public service advertisements, loneliness of the elderly, and more. This book is essential reading for students and faculty of social sciences, economics, and management technology to understand the broad dimensions of digitization in our everyday life and the theoretical and practical utilization and outcome of digitization. The chapters in this book will surely provide valuable understanding to both social scientists and policymakers interested in the subject"-- Provided by publisher.
Identifiers: LCCN 2021017471 (print) | LCCN 2021017472 (ebook) | ISBN 9781774630280 (hardback) | ISBN 9781774639108 (paperback) | ISBN 9781003187479 (ebook)
Subjects: LCSH: Social networks. | Gender identity--Social aspects. | Interpersonal relations. | Electronic commerce. | Customer relations--Management. | Organizational change. | Work-life balance.
Classification: LCC HM742 .D5446 2021 (print) | LCC HM742 (ebook) | DDC 302.3--dc23
LC record available at https://lccn.loc.gov/2021017471
LC ebook record available at https://lccn.loc.gov/2021017472

ISBN: 978-1-77463-028-0 (hbk)
ISBN: 978-1-77463-910-8 (pbk)
ISBN: 978-1-00318-747-9 (ebk)

About the Editors

Sudeshna Basu Mukherjee, PhD
Professor, Department of Sociology, University of Calcutta,
West Bengal, India

Sudeshna Basu Mukherjee, PhD, is a Professor and an alumnus of the Department of Sociology at the University of Calcutta, India. She has been associated with the academic field for over three decades. She has been teaching in the department since 1995. Her fields of knowledge dissemination are sociological theory, research methodology, sociology of organization, and sociology of aging. Her areas of research interest are aging; intergenerational alliances; stress of the sandwich generation; women's empowerment; micro, small, and medium enterprises (MSMEs); and health-seeking behavior, among others. She completed an interdisciplinary PhD at the University of Calcutta in Applied Psychology and has experience of research and completion of major projects under aegis of the University Grants Commission of India, Indian Council of Social Science Research, and Asiatic Society. Her ongoing research concerns are related to socio-economic and cultural transformations among women and youth; state diaspora formation and integrative assimilation through self-help group initiatives; sustainable economic, social, and political empowerment of women through MSMEs; strategic learning from South and Southeast Asia; and tribal reproductive health behavior and health seeking activities of tribes. Dr. Basu Mukherjee has to her credit several papers in both national and international publications and a book titled *Innovative Work Behavior and Global Challenges for Managers: Innovative Work Behaviour and the Role of Human Resource.* Her chapter "Family, Marriage, and Sexuality: Valuable Insights on 21st Century Youth" was published in the *Handbook of the Sociology of Youth in BRICS Countries.* Her recent publication "*Elderly* Health Care: Diverse Cultural Implication" appeared in the journal *Asian Ethnicity.* She has also been associated as a reviewer with *Sage Open* for a long time.

Saheli Guha Neogi Ghatak, PhD

Assistant Professor, Department of Sociology, Adamas University, Kolkata, India

Saheli Guha Neogi Ghatak, PhD, is an Assistant Professor and HOD of the Department of Sociology, School of Liberal Arts and Culture Studies at Adamas University, West Bengal, India. Her degrees include PhD, MA (Sociology), MSW, and MLIS. She has six years of teaching experience at the under- and postgraduate levels and five years of research experience. She is presently guiding several research scholars. She has published over 12 research papers in national and international peer-reviewed journals and book chapters, and she has presented research papers at more than 25 national and international seminars/conferences. She was invited as a guest researcher by the University of Copenhagen, Denmark, and invited as chairperson of an international conference in Bangladesh. Dr. Ghatak is a life member of the Indian Sociological Society.

Nilanjan Ray, PhD

Associate Professor, School of Management, Adamas University, West Bengal, India

Nilanjan Ray, PhD, is an Associate Professor of Marketing Management at Adamas University in the School of Management, West Bengal, India. Dr. Ray has obtained a certified Accredited Management Teacher Award from All India Management Association, New Delhi, India. He has obtained his PhD (Mkt); MCom (Mkt); MBA (Mkt), STC FMRM (IIT-Kgp). He has 10 years of teaching experience in BBA, MBA, BCom, and six years of research experience and has guided around 56 postgraduate students' projects. Dr. Ray has contributed over 60 research papers in reputed national and international, peer-reviewed journals, proceedings, and has edited eight research handbooks from Springer, IGI-Global USA, and Apple Academic Publisher, CRC Press (a Taylor and Francis Group), USA. He has also associated himself as a reviewer of *Tourism*

Management, Journal of Service Marketing, Journal of Business and Economics, Research Journal of Business and Management Accounting and as an editorial board member of several refereed journals. He has also chaired in a technical session at the IJAS Conference 2012 at Harvard University, Boston, USA. Dr. Ray is a life member of the International Business Studies Academia, and a fellow member of the Institute of Research Engineers and Doctors Universal Association of Arts and Management Professionals (UAAMP) New York, USA.

Contents

Contributors

Trisha Bakshi
Research Scholar, Department of Sociology, Vidyasagar University, West Bengal, India,
Phone: 9088735571, E-mail: trishabksh@gmail.com

Jayanta Kumar Behera
Assistant Professor, Department of Sociology, I.G.N. Tribal University, Amarkantak, Anuppur,
Madhya Pradesh–484886, India, E-mail: jkbigntu@gmail.com

Ananya Chatterjee
Assistant Professor, Department of Sociology, Haldia Government College, Haldia, Purba
Medinipur–721657, West Bengal, India

Pujasree Chatterjee
Assistant Professor, Department of Sociology, Vidyasagar University, Midnapore,
and PhD Research Scholar, Department of Sociology, University of Calcutta, West Bengal, India,
Phone: 9432928107/8240343902, E-mail: pujasree.chatterjee@gmail.com

Debastuti Dasgupta
Assistant Professor, Department of Journalism and Mass Communication. Asutosh College, Kolkata,
West Bengal, India

Madhurima Dasgupta
Assistant Professor, Department of Sociology, Adamas University and PhD Scholar,
Department of Sociology, Kolkata, Jadavpur University, West Bengal, India

Sanchari De
Assistant Professor of Sociology (W.B.E.S.), Government General Degree College Mangalkote,
Burdwan, West Bengal, India

Sharmila Kayal
Associate Professor, Department of Communication Management. Adamas University, Kolkata,
West Bengal, India, E-mail: sharmilakayal@gmail.com

Sayak Pal
Assistant Professor, Department of Communication Management. Adamas University,
Kolkata and PhD Research Scholar, Symbiosis International (Deemed) University, Pune, India,
E-mail: palsayak01@gmail.com

Sukanya Pal
PhD Research Scholar, Department of Sociology, Jadavpur University, West Bengal, India

Tanmoy Putatunda
Assistant Professor, School of Languages, KIIT Deemed to be University, Bhubaneswar, Odisha, India

Debanjali Roy
Assistant Professor, School of Languages, KIIT Deemed to be University, Bhubaneswar, Odisha, India

Ruma Saha
PhD Research Scholar, Manipal University Jaipur, Rajasthan, India,
E-mail: ruma.saha.kolkata@gmail.com

Alok Kumar Sahai
Associate Professor, Faculty of Management Studies, Sri University, Cuttack, Odisha, India

Rahul Singh
Assistant Professor, St. Xavier's College, Burdwan, and PhD Research Scholar, Adamas University,
Kolkata, West Bengal, India

Chaitali Guha Sinha
Assistant Professor, Amity Institute of Social Sciences, Amity University Kolkata, West Bengal, India

José G. Vargas-Hernández
Research Professor, Department of Administration, University Center for Economic and Managerial
Sciences, University of Guadalajara, México,
E-mails: Jvargas2006@gmail.com; jgvh0811@yahoo.com; josevargas@cucea.udg.mx

Abbreviations

B2B	business-to-business
BPO	business process outsourcing
CABE	Central Advisory Board of Education
CALL	computer-assisted language learning
CBCS	choice-based credit system
CLV	customer lifetime value
CMC	computer-mediated communication
CPFR	collaborative planning, forecasting, and replenishment
CRM	customer relationship management
DDoS	distributed denial of service
DESA	Department of Economic and Social Affairs
DMA	direct market association
eCRM	electronic customer relationship management
ELT	English language teaching
EMR	electronic medical record
GDPR	general data protection regulation
GDS	geriatric depression scale
GMGA	good morning/good evening
HBM	health belief model
HIV	human immunodeficiency virus
ICT	information and communication technology
IT	information technology
ITAP	IFPS technical assistance project
MALL	mobile assisted language learning
MMPs	mission mode projects
MPS	mail preference service
MSN	Microsoft Network
NCF	National curriculum framework
OECD	Organization of Economic Co-Operation Development
OPS	open profiling standard
P2P	person-to-person
P3	platform for privacy preference
RE	Royal Enfield

RPA	robotic process automation
RTE	right to education
SAT	tax administration service
SCM	supply chain management
SCOR	supply chain operations reference
sCRM	social customer relationship management
SNSs	social networking sites
SSA	Sarva Shiksha Abhiyan
SSL	secure sockets layer
TELL	technology-enhanced language learning
TNC	transportation network companies
TPS	telephone preference service
TWh	terawatt hour
UCLA	University of California Los Angeles
W3C	world-wide-web consortium
WWW	world wide web

Foreword

It gives me immense pleasure to write the foreword to this book, *Digitization of Economy and Society: Emerging Paradigms*. The publication of this book assumes added significance in the aftermath of the nationwide lockdown that was imposed by the Government of India by the end of March 2020 and which was only eased a bit by the beginning of June 2020. The pandemic and the lockdown brought some important but unpalatable facts to all of us. This is the first time in the history of our nation that we find a great majority of the population spending time indoors, not because of their free sweet will but forced by Government order. The young and the old, the working and the superannuated, the children, adolescents, and youths belonging to all age groups, were decreed to spend the days and the nights indoors. Even with newspapers not being printed and distributed during the early period, the only mode of communication, information, and entertainment were smartphones and computers. This is, of course, the story of the middle class and the upper-middle class.

During this period, people began to communicate through smartphones, take part and produce programs of recitation, musical extravaganza, cinematic exercises, etc., indoors in a variety of innovative ways. A new experiment in indoor living started and, frankly speaking, most of the populace could compensate for the absence of the outside world with the virtual world of the internet.

On the other hand, a sizable section of the population residing in urban slums were forced to huddle together within the confines of the four walls of their unhygienic living space, mostly without the benefit of the internet. Rural India was predominantly outside this forced indoor trauma.

Another significant development also took place in the wake of the pandemic lockdown. Thousands of our own countrymen who went far and wide during normal times to eke out a living in various parts of our vast country were left high and dry by their employers and the authorities of our central and state governments. They trudged hundreds of kilometers to reach their homes. A veritable stream of humanity was on the highways and railway tracks. Their only connections with their near and dear ones were through mobile phones. Some very ingenious among them used the google map to find their way through the maze of the railway tracks.

The above facts do suggest that our economy and society are now integrally connected with digitization. Therefore, the study of our society and economy in the era of digitization is not only necessary but essential if we want to understand the impact of it on our people. The whole cross-section of our population, from children belonging to 3 years of age and above, adolescents, youths, middle-aged, and old people, male, and female, are all connected by WhatsApp, Facebook, Messenger, and Twitter and various other connecting devices. The most significant aspect of these devices is that they are interactive. Unlike the radio and television, these apps offer a platform to all and sundry to express themselves and be heard and commented upon.

Previously, with the advent of telephone, radio, and television, we used to say that the whole world has become a village: Basudhaiba Kutumbakam. Today the whole world is reduced to a smartphone, a tablet, a laptop or a computer. Literally, the world is on our fingertips. Printed encyclopedias have disappeared because the information they provide, is no longer updated. No gurus are sacrosanct today because the fact is available instantly on the smartphone. Textbooks and reference books are available on the asking. The world literature with connotations and references in multiple languages are available on the internet. Any topic like the last world war or the latest information about COVID-19 is available on the cell phone. Fiji or Chile, Vietnam or Madagascar, their scenic beauty and political or social conditions can be found out with a click. This multifaceted, multi-layered device which can be kept in your pocket or held in your palm, is nothing but the sixth wonder of the world though we do not consider it a wonder anymore because of its ready availability.

While volumes could be written about the efficacy of this wonderful device, its negative impact is also giving rise to not so salubrious consequences. Gullible young people are very often duped by unscrupulous men and women using false identities. False hopes are generated through unethical advertisements. Even suicides are enacted online. All sorts of pornographic materials are available to both children and adolescents. Various mating and adult sites have the potential to cause havoc in the mental and physical hygiene of the uninitiated. The road to hell is slippery and near. Since the real and the virtual world have interpenetrated each other, neither the real nor the virtual one can be studied in isolation. The present book is such an attempt to understand this phenomenon.

Thirteen chapters dealing with important topics have sought to illuminate the area under consideration: There are chapters on management sciences, essays relating to human behavior and gender studies, an essay relating to mass communication, and then there are essays dealing with the professional life of a teacher in the digital age, an essay on career choice in the age of digitalization, on e-governance, last but not the least, an essay on English language learning.

We welcome the publication of this book. We hope that other books dealing with many other aspects of the digital world will also be published. An important area of concern is the digital divide. How this could be reduced to the minimum should also be studied thoroughly. The future world will be both real and virtual.

—Asoke Bhattacharya
Director, Bangladesh Institute of Lifelong Learning, Dhaka, Bangladesh;
Formerly Professor and Head, Adult, Continuing Education and Extension
Department, Jadavpur University, Kolkata, West Bengal, India;
Erasmus Mundus Scholar of the European Union,
Recipient of the UNESCO-NLM Award for
Outstanding Contribution in the Field of Literacy

Preface

Digitization has fundamentally transformed organizations, with the pace of technological change exacerbating the challenge. We are moving towards a digital society. Digitization is actually accelerated through the COVID-19 pandemic and the lockdown scenario. We all are becoming more used to the digital economy and society. This book is an attempt to understand the emerging paradigms of digitization in the economy and society, which covers a wide spectrum of digitization processes and consequences. In 2020, the pandemic situation compelled us to move towards more digitization in terms of every aspect of our life, ranging from communication, relationship, education, shopping, banking to health services. Thus, this book is essential to read for the students of social sciences, economics, and management, technology to understand broad dimensions of digitization in our everyday life and the theoretical and practical utilization and outcome of digitization. The chapters of this book will surely provide valuable understanding to both social scientists and policymakers interested in the subject.

Acknowledgments

This book has come to fruition due to the vision and collective effort of the members of the editorial advisory board and technical reviewers of this volume. This book is the group endeavor of an interdisciplinary team investigation of the paradigm shift in technological operations and the challenges having an impact on the varied population worldwide. We acknowledge indebtedness to all the members.

We are thankful to all the authors for their valued contributions that have enriched the volume with a thought-provoking analysis of different areas of digitization. We express our gratitude and thank the officials at Apple Academic Press for their invaluable efforts, great support, and valuable advice for this project towards the successful publication of this book.

—*Editors*

Introduction

Digitization is the big-scale adoption of connecting digital services by customers, companies, and governments. In recent years it has performed as the significant economic engine that speeds up knowledge growth, helps easy-paced stress-free living, and creates new roles while serving as a catalyst for occupational growth in the comprehensive economy. It has changed companies radically, with the accelerated usage of digital technology.

Digitization, per se, is the route of transforming corresponding information to a digital format. Digitization, as a social process, denotes the changes in the technological impacts on the economic environment and resolving social and institutional processes by the use of digitized communications and applications. Unlike other technological innovations, it builds on the evolution of network access technologies. The digital age has arrived with a number of huge tests, new audiences, linear to hypertext interactivity, innovative languages and a new grammar used to communicate. Not only has this transition changed the media landscape for the normal performers, but most critically, it opens the mass communication network to a large variety of fresh and digitally produced participants.

Organizations currently need a cohesive strategy that involves a plan to retrain workers; the bound of digital transformation is leading to the quick transfer of companies; the challenge is equally persistent for governments as it is to the wider society. The rate and extent of change is reaching unprecedented levels. This poses unique challenges for society's future, day-to-day, quality of life, industry, governance, and economy.

With the emergence of new and incipient paradigms, exciting technologies and challenges due to resource scarcity, big implications for climate and environment, rising fluidity of physical and digital borders, growing decentralization of industries, exponential growth, and many more global drivers-all leading to a future of digital trends.

Digital enablers of demographics, connectivity, and convergence, consumers, and expectations in the digital revolution referred to as the advancement of the Information Era started during the 1980s and is ongoing; is at times referred to as the Third Industrial Revolution. This is today the backbone of economic, technological, and social prosperity after the industrial revolution. The medium of communication has changed rapidly, and digital communication has become an inevitable part of life as digital devices enable easy and faster connectivity. This is bringing a paradigm shift in the way of life people behave or act as now we are getting into the era of the internet of things and augmented reality.

Digital reliability and dependability are rampant. The abundance of knowledge among all and the integration among nanotechnology, genetics, economics, banking, information technology (IT) along with the social and cognitive sciences create an exponential development that accelerates both. Our visions for the future are now too conformist. According to UNESCO's "Diversity of Cultural Expressions in the Digital Age" (2015), it is suggested that this transition has primarily transformed the manner in which cultural goods and services are created, transmitted, and accessed; has accelerated the expansion of social networks and content provided by users (UGC), and the explosion of accessible data via cloud computing and the multiplying obtainability of connecting multimedia devices like smartphones, tablets, e-readers in the hands of the consumers, has had a colossal bearing on the cultural scene globally. Technological advances have prompted new players to emerge, new logics, new patterns, new boons, and banes.

Digitalization causes wide-ranging socio-economic transition, setting the stage for a complete technological revolution. The shifts represent societal tastes and the evolving role of technology in everyday life. As digitalization moves toward a more tailored approach, new trends are beginning to emerge. Shifting to these modern paradigms is in today's digital world are exceptional windows into the personal world of every consumer, i.e., customizing vs. mass. Today, people don't advertise—they win over customers through stories and content marketing; advertisement needs a customizable way to promote. Mobile use for communication is the existential necessity and new normal today; it represents a major paradigm shift in 'time for others' and 'time for self.' Shifting to these emerging new paradigms in the digital world can be effectively customized to consumer demographics. In social life, the role of Digital media, and the way they relate to behavior, human relationships, and identity, can be documented as playing a central role in all aspects of our lives now.

This book has three sections. Part I: "Digital Social Trends": The world has witnessed many changes and advancements in the industry with a much faster pace, and all this has been conceivable and attainable due to the introduction and usage of information and communication technology (ICT). The use of ICT by government to provide innumerable governmental facilities to people at a click is called e-government. Digital India is an umbrella under which the government targets to makeover India into an information and knowledge economy. Nowadays, there are online platforms for direct government-public contact. These are included in services provided by e-government mechanisms that venture to make it participative, transparent, and give responsive interaction. Social media is an important player in the forum, being used to shape politics, business, world culture, education, careers, innovation, and more. Social media affects society in both constructively and destructively. It provides a genre for people to interact, keep in touch with family and friends, share fun, and engage with interesting and insightful content. Fundamentally, social networking changes the way we connect, chat, coordinate, and form opinions and even shop. The blurred borders, increased clarity and mutability in everything we do. Given the thorough union of social media into the lives of people and the role it plays in connecting teens to old and new friends as for contemporary youth very often friendship starts digitally; allowing family that is far and wide to connect virtually; a clutch that the elderly use to take support and get over their loneliness as these platforms aid one and all to get connected.

Part I consists of five chapters, that is, Chapters 1–5. Chapter 1 titled "Impact of Social Networking Sites in the Construction of Masculinity: A Sociological Study of High School Boys of Kolkata," explores and analyzes how adolescent boys' practice and construct their notions of masculinity by using and being engrossed in social networking sites (WhatsApp, Facebook, Instagram, and Twitter). Social networking sites helps the adolescent boys build friendships and interact with strangers in order to reduce loneliness. They enjoy flaunting their bodies in social networking sites like Facebook and Instagram, all in a bid to increase their reputation among their peers for enhancing their self-esteem and reputation among female peers resulting in the formation or construction of masculine identity. The social media also provides a solace for the adolescent boys since it helps them to escape from the mundane life and remain engrossed in a different sphere of entertainment which helps in developing notions of masculinity. Chapter 2 titled "Digital Transformation and Its Impact: An Analytical Study" assesses the Digital India program that aims to develop the IT interface to achieve full coverage through e-Governance and e-Service in the world. The key focus of this arrangement is that the Indian government is concentrating on empowering digitally. This chapter provides an understanding of the concept, types of service launched, scope, and effect of digital transformation and its future benefits in the creation of technology applications that contribute significantly to our quality of life. Chapter 3 titled "Virtual Connections: Friendship Relationships in the Cyber Age," reconnoiters the impact of information-communication technologies (ICTs) on the friendship relationships of adolescents. This chapter examines from a critical angle the magnitude to which the social networking sites (SNSs) aid in increasing and sustaining friendship relationships and how do these modify the quality of these relationships, especially for teens and young adults. The Internet is becoming another location to come across and socialize; relations created there also tend to transfer to other settings. Chapter 4 titled "Digital Self: Men and Women Motorcyclists 'Doing Gender' Through Social Networking Sites," attempts to comprehend the meaning set forth by enthusiastic' motorcyclists' of both gender through photos/videos that they often post on their social media pages. Here the focus is on how people use these interactive networking sites to fulfil gender roles. The study section begins by showing how motorcycling is gendered, while the second half delineated how women are compelled not to do gender in motorcycling. Chapter 5 titled "E-Governance- Impact on Society," is concerned with metamorphosis that is caused by the use of information technology in the society that has gone Digital. It stresses the mutations that information technology has brought to the nation's government services that includes transparency and accountability that is important for electronic governance. E-Government is regarded as a critical component of revolutionary growth.

Part II: "Digital Marketing and the Service Industry": The key corner stone of business growth is technology be it for increasing efficiency, new resources for generating a professional network, or innovative ways to influence the potential customers; digital marketing is a boon for business of all kinds. It has proven specifically beneficial for the service industries that are using different digitized promotion schemes. Each of these strategies serves a discrete reason, even though they have a common objective. Well-structured digital promotion drives like the App cabs can be used an integrated way to achieve the objective, e.g., easing travel, making it transparent and traceable. Digital marketing campaign requires a considerable time and effort market enquiry, identify the audience, content creation, customer retention strategies versus prospect conversion program, and site protection also need to be addressed. Neglecting this factor could entail risks for both company and customers. Part II has two chapters, that is, Chapters 6 and 7. Chapter 6 titled "Digital Marketing in Today's Privacy-Conscious World," explores the area of digital marketing, which has been influenced and limited by customer privacy issues, with protection related to the regulation of individual data advancement. It addresses the issue of judicious usage of personal information and tries to explain customer privacy concerns regarding Internet marketing, and provide awareness and solutions. It was found that an effective advanced marketing campaign necessitated considerable time and effort speculations. Building a good system was important for success in computerized marketing, while ignoring could risk both entrepreneurs and clients. Chapter 7 titled "A Strategic Analysis of the Rise and Fall of Uber in the Private Urban Transport Business in the Metropolitan Area of Guadalajara," analyzes the strategies for entering the private urban transport services market managed by the multinational company Uber in the Metropolitan Region of Guadalajara, the conditions of increase in coverage and its effect on urban mobility movements and the decline due to competition and finally to the 2020 pandemic.

Part III: "Societal Consequences of Technologies and Solutions": The promise of information and communications technology (ICT) to provide transformation is inviting. Today, digital technological innovations are having far-reaching paraphernalia across various domains of society, and policy creators are performing on concerns regarding viable productivity, intellectual property, confidentiality fortification, and affordability of and starter to information. It is social media campaigns and guidelines, advertisements on the television, daily news bulletins and newspaper columns that are arguably this was the most concerted attempt to bring the message across about the importance of grooming to preserve good health and wellbeing. Contextualizing the framework to a specific strategy with implementation plans to achieve by creating a culture of social sanctions that challenge the acceptance of critical sanitation and hygiene behaviors at large scale is achievable to a certain extent. The impact of information technology on pedagogical innovations and material content for teaching, dispersing, and sharing knowledge; making a choice from varied range of careers, the methodology of realization and accessibility are rampantly available on web today. Changing teaching-learning modalities are highly influenced by ICT. Career choices made have long lasting significances, and attention must be rewarded to their economic, social, and personal impacts. Information technology is gratifying for the elderly population with all the mediums of connectivity, socially, and physically and as a supportive pillar to rely on. Technology has significantly driven linguistic change in the last two decades; a revolutionized onset of technology has offered a better pattern to explore the new teaching exemplars by using its unique advantages. Part III comprises six chapters, that is, Chapters 8–13. Chapter 8 titled "Impact of Digitalization on Pedagogical Innovation and Changing Work Life of a University Teaching Professional in West Bengal," discusses about the impact of digital technology in education sector. Effective use of digital technology to innovate curriculum, teaching-learning method would lead to better learning outcomes and would match the global requirements. It seeks to understand the changing work-life of a teaching professional by focusing on issues ranging from innovation in pedagogy to changes in teaching-learning methods and introduction and use of ICT in the teaching and learning process and the accompanying changes in the role of a teacher from being a teacher to a mentor as well as the perception of the faculties regarding the nature of teaching job. Chapter 9 titled "Career Choice: A Critical Study in the Age of Digitalization," ascertains how digital India with its global vision on education and technology-based e-learning curriculum, affecting urban secondary and higher secondary school students (both male and female) while making the career choices both positively and negatively. Chapter 10 titled "Analyzing Digital Media Public Service Advertisements on Health and Hygiene: A Rural Indian Scenario," extensively analyzed and debated, helped government and non-government advertising practitioners to develop their potential offerings for better performance. PSAs are narratives focusing on emerging problems that need immediate attention and treatment in order to be eliminated from society. The bulk of these PSAs are concerned with making positive and beneficial behavioural changes through proper awareness campaigns on subjects such as smoking, menstrual health, family planning, AIDS, sanitization, and so on. These commercials are deliberately tailored for a wider audience and rely heavily on subject-matter research. The study examines the content of these public service ads on the digital platform in India to determine the motivation for message formation while emphasizing mass health benefits. Chapter 11 titled "Technology Usage and Loneliness Among Older Adults," demonstrated that technical interventions and usage of the internet has had a significant impact on the physical and psychological well-being of older adults. Since they are a digitally disadvantaged, and little research has been done till date on the impact and efficacy of various technologies in reducing isolation among the older adults, this study ventured to comprehend and analyse through the current empirical studies the role of technology in reducing feelings of social exclusion and methods that help achieve senior digital inclusion. The importance of taking a holistic view of the elderly user's condition was stressed. Chapter 12 titled "Technology in Language Classrooms of India: Decoding Digital Learning and Dynamics of Context and Curriculum," with the advent of enhanced language learning technologies, attempts are made to delve into the complexities of Indian socio-cultural contexts and language education. There was a rapid reconstruction of teaching methodology and principles associated with a classroom as technology foraged into the language curriculum.' The nation's urban areas were quickly adapting to online learning through Web 2.0 resources. The nation's digital divide, on the other hand, resulted in an asymmetrical distribution of technical and thus educational resources to rural and underprivileged areas. Chapter 13 titled "Electronic Customer Relationship Management (eCRM)," the electronic CRM (eCRM) uses IT to reach and serve attractive consumers in order to maximize the value of the relationship and explains the essence and method of e-commerce in business. Amazon is able to understand the different micro-segments of customers, forecast their long-term value to the business, and service them with speed and enhanced quality thanks to technology-based eCRM. Electronic customer relationship management is a business method for attracting, maintaining, and increasing profitable customers. There are two major categories of eCRM: organizational and analytical. eCRM operations entail direct communication with customers through electronic means such as the internet. Analytical eCRM analyzes the data obtained by operational eCRM. The utility of operational and analytical eCRM has increased exponentially as a result of fourth-generation mobile networks. The potential of sCRM is tremendous, assuming that consumers can be convinced to give up their personal information, which can then be used as tags in predictive analysis of consumer behaviour, resulting in shared benefit.

Digitization can discover, ascertain, and transform life, and professionals agree that the internet is one of the biggest boons to humanity a person can reach out to other people for all possible purposes. It offers us flexibility and endless choices on how we wish to invest our time and it has given us an interconnected global village. Digital life has had its impact over the last few decades; it has changed and opened analytical possibilities and countless interpretative gazes arousing diverse perspectives on the subjective dimension of science and technology's use and development. The themes in the book conclude the concerned questions of ontological character related to e-governance, social networking, competitive advantages of industries, changing life perspectives of teaching community, youth, and elderly, digital learning dynamics, online customer relationship through the subjective relationship between people and the technology. Logically the ICT's deconstruct our practice and skills, but lend it a new nature at the same time. The rising possibilities of online living in the last decade world has increased the possibilities and raises the question about new ways of living together, a new way of being shaping the world.

PART I
Digital Social Trends

CHAPTER 1

Impact of Social Networking Sites in the Construction of Masculinity: A Sociological Study of High School Boys of Kolkata

MADHURIMA DASGUPTA

Assistant Professor, Department of Sociology, Adamas University and PhD Scholar, Department of Sociology, Kolkata, Jadavpur University, West Bengal, India

ABSTRACT

Adolescence is an age when boys spend most of their leisure time in accessing and frequent using of social networking sites (SNSs). Social media produces a profound impact on the lifestyle of adolescent boys, which helps in the construction of masculine identity. The present chapter explores and analyzes how adolescent boys' practice and construct their notions of masculinity by using and being engrossed in SNSs (WhatsApp, Facebook, Instagram, and Twitter). The present research uses a mixed methodology in order to study 50 boys (aged 16–17 years) who studies in XI and XII standards of high school in North Kolkata. The research is carried out by non-probability purposive and snowball sampling techniques. The majority of adolescent boys affirmed in spending their leisure time in frequent usage of SNSs (WhatsApp, Facebook, Instagram, and Twitter) for the purpose of interacting with their peers and their closed ones on issues of intimacy followed by sexuality. They also build friendships and interact with strangers in order to reduce loneliness. All boys affirmed that they enjoy flaunting their bodies in SNSs like Facebook and Instagram, all in a bid to increase their reputation among their peers, which will not only enhance their self-esteem but also will increase their reputation among female peers resulting in the formation or construction of masculine identity. The social media also provides a solace for the adolescent boys since it helps them to escape from the mundane life and remain engrossed in a different sphere of entertainment which helps in developing notions of masculinity.

1.1 INTRODUCTION

It was during the 1990s that research initiated on men and masculinity in academia in the West due to the significant impact of the feminist movement, which challenged the stereotypical representation of masculinity as a gendered category. As a result of this, the social construction of masculinity was highly challenged not only to understand about men and multiple forms of masculinities but also to understand how gender identities are formed. Certain changes had also taken place following this in traditional gender roles during the twentieth century which resulted in the social construction of masculinity[1].

With the onset of technology, the Internet also emerged, which not only provided various forms of information ranging from news to facts and events but also helped users to use it for official purposes. Social networking sites (SNSs) are one such platform in the virtual world which has emerged so that users can stay connected with their family and friends globally for a better means of communication and entertainment purpose.

Social network possesses a unique aspect to help the users to articulate their networks on a global forum which results in a global connection between the users. Some participants, however, communicate over social media like WhatsApp, Facebook, Instagram, and Twitter in order to increase their social network without much interest in making friendships with strangers. For this reason of networking as an important attribute of the sites, social media is also known as social network sites[2].

Though social media is used mostly by youngsters, its popularity has increased significantly among adolescents in society. The period of adolescence is a period of change which is a phase between childhood and adulthood and is characterized by various physical, social, emotional, and cognitive changes that not only provides privileges but also challenges for families, adolescents, and educators.

The major means through which adolescents communicate nowadays is through Internet which they use it either for official purpose like school works or gathering of information or as a forum to connect with their friend and family globally. Most adolescents communicate with their peers through social media like WhatsApp and Gmail. Furthermore, adolescents also use these SNSs in order to create their public profiles and to traverse their list of connections.

SNSs bring with it both advantages and disadvantages where on the one hand its usage enhances the sociability and networking of the users, on the other hand, obsession with the virtual world also affects their daily physical, academic activities along with face-to-face interaction with their family and peers.

Teenagers in India mostly access and us these major SNSs:

1. WhatsApp;
2. Facebook;
3. Instagram;
4. LinkedIn;
5. Twitter.

Adolescents' nowadays mostly use social media in order to connect with their peers and family, which not only helps to increase their sociability and reputation among their friends, but also helps them to practice and construct their notions of identity among their peers. As a result of these factors, social media is producing a significant impact among the youngsters and has also emerged as a major arena for academic research as well.

There are various issues that are addressed by internet research varying from the construction of gender identity in the virtual world through the usage of social media like experiences shared by women to the ways by which boys and men negotiate their identity. Hence, gender identity is constructed even in the virtual world, followed by how teenagers present themselves on personal homepages over social media.

The period of adolescence is a phase where adolescents, irrespective of their gender, spend their leisure time in frequent usage of SNSs like WhatsApp, Facebook, and Instagram. The virtual world produces an enormous impact on adolescent lifestyles, which also helps in constructing their masculine or feminine identities.

Against this backdrop, the present chapter will explore how adolescent boys develop and construct their notions of masculinity by accessing and engrossing in SNSs like WhatsApp, Facebook, Instagram, and Twitter since there has hardly been any research carried out in Indian academia on the construction of Indian masculinity in social media, especially in North Kolkata.

1.2 LITERATURE REVIEW

From a historical perspective, masculinity studies can be traced back to the inception of boyhood during the nineteenth century. Gender as a category is not only an important component of social relations but also signifies power relationships. The concept of gender can be understood only with the historical interpretation of masculinity.

The history of masculinity can be traced back to a seventeenth-century which was categorized into four phases of man:

1. **Household Patriarch:** This phase which emerged during the seventeenth century, the eldest male member was the patriarch who had sexual control not only over himself but also over women where all other contributing elements of male reputation was meaningless (Harvey, 2005). However, the sexual control of men still extended beyond their own selves.

   Hegemonic masculinity was the major ideal characterizing this phase of patriarch since this phase exemplified patriarchy. Such notion was popularized by Raewyn Connell, which was based on the gender division of labor where the socially constructed belief existed that women's earning in the economy would lend them more power than men, which would be detrimental for the economy. As a result of the gap between patriarchy and social practice, a new model of masculinity came into existence during this period.

2. **Fops and Libertines:** Historically, the emergence of Libertines can be traced back to the eighteenth-century during the time of the Renaissance, where tradition was embodied by figures like Francis Dashwood and John Wilkes. This was followed by the advent of the effeminate sodomite during the year 1720, which helped to define heterosexual men and hetero normative masculinity. This signifies that the attribute which helped to define the heterosexual man was his sexual desire and obsession for the opposite sex. Thereby, the attribute of a fop turned out to be a self-obsessed who failed in his effort to cater to the integrity of a gentleman.

3. **Gentleman Who was Polite and Humble:** This phase was characterized by a polite soft-spoken gentleman with good mannerism during the eighteenth century whose nature sharply contrasted with the Libertines and Fops. A notable figure like Phillip Carter carried out the work on masculinity and politeness where he defied such politeness as a social refinement which linked virtue with balanced sociability and integrity.

   One of the other major attribute and element of politeness was the nature of social interaction with women-it was observed that men mostly reduced their voice tone while communicating with women, which enhanced smooth and proper social interaction between both the genders.

   Such smooth social interaction with women also helped them to attain status and reverence and even motivated them to interact in their domestic sphere. It even taught them to be polite in public places where women were not allowed for any kind of interaction in assemblies and gardens and town walks.

   Another major component of this phase was sensibility which was a major variant of refinement along with politeness. Such sensible nature among men helped to draw a relation between their inner virtue and outside mannerism since it focused both on the physical and emotional portrayal of men's sensitive nature along with their feelings.

4. **Domesticity and Etiquette:** Politeness and sensibility declined with the emergence of the eighteenth century. However, the major developments that took place during this phase mainly comprised of:

   i. **Etiquette:** The shift and change from politeness to etiquette also led to the alteration from soft-spoken nature to rules of courtesy which comprised right and wrongdoings (do's and don'ts) of everyday life of men.

   ii. **Domesticity:** This development was characterized by the advent of domesticity, which not only challenged masculinity by building intimate relationship with women but also helped to prove masculinity by associating only with men.

   This denotes that qualities like tenderness and self-control characterized this phase which was celebrated for both the gender in children's literature. Furthermore, while toughness and violence were major characteristics of boys, the cynosure of children's books were also ripe with feminine attributes of emotional dependency and refinement.

These four phases through which men and their masculinities have evolved historically finally led to the development of middle-class American masculinity who tried to preserve their childhood that remained untouched by their gender socialization. Thus, it was middle-class Americans who emphasized and valorized the difference between children and adults. However, though mothers were responsible for the upbringing of their children, they were also ambivalent about the changes of their male youngsters into boys. '*Boyhood did not properly commence as a stage of life until boys were outfitted in their first set of trousers, a momentous day for parent and child alike, and not always without trauma*[3].'

1.3   CONSTRUCTION OF MASCULINE IDENTITIES IN GLOBAL NORTH (INDIA)

The term *'masculinity'* signifies traits, attitudes, and behavior associated with men[4]. In the Indian context, the socialization of male child occurs in a gendered manner due to their little or lack of contact with their female friends due to which their gender relation gets affected. This kind of discrimination leads to the formation of maladjusted personality among men, the attributes of which are gender inequality, sexual domination of males along with inequality of sexual attitude towards women.

Such gender discrimination initiates during childhood during assignment of toys to boys and girls; boys are socialized to play with toys like cars and guns, which symbolize physical toughness, strength, and aggression, while girls are mostly given dolls to play with since dolls exemplify soft nature, emotional dependence, and nurturance.

In the Indian scenario, gender inequality continues even during adolescence when boys enjoy the opportunities and advantages as they are socialized by the gendered norms-social mobility, independence in terms of dress code, and decision making. On the other hand, girls are socially constructed to bear the restrictions socially imposed on them, which include their mobility, dress code, obedience, and even interaction with their male peers. This kind of gender inequality commences in the family where girls are mostly socialized to look after the domestic sphere by helping their mother in household responsibilities while boys are socialized to be independent from most family obligations.

Gender stereotypes are also prevalent in an Indian family where boys are socialized to abide by the notion of hetero normative hegemonic masculinity-physical toughness, strength, courage, leadership, and violence. Boys are also socially constructed to play games with their peers outside their household, oblivious of family responsibilities and tasks, while girls mostly play games with their group within the domestic sphere due to issues of safety and security and the different forms of risk that they might encounter due to their gender.

As a social construct, the masculinity of youngsters helps to understand the cultural rules which are associated with their actions. Adolescent boys in Indian society who are unable to conform to the norms of heterosexual and dominant form of masculinity of being 'macho' (physically strong, tough, aggressive, courageous with good physique) become victims of bullying and social humiliation by their peers and family members and are even regarded as 'effeminate.' The socially constructed physical traits are highly significant for boys as such attributes provide the mechanism for the Indian boys to use their sexual prowess to seduce the opposite sex.

Research suggests that for the purpose of proving masculinity, young men engaged in illicit activities like unwelcomed sexual gestures and comments, whistling, eve-teasing of women, and bullying both female and effeminate male peers since such activities are also socially constructed to be associated with men and their masculinity.

Henceforth, certain factors determine the social construction of hegemonic masculinity among adolescent boys who are socialized to be daring and physically more active than any female member-the treatment of the family members along with the mixture with the peers and impact of mass media, exposure of boys to pornographic and sexually explicit movies.

Despite the increasing work on the significance of masculinity in the West, hardly any such information exists on the ways by which masculinity is constructed in India and the ways by which such masculine identity have been enforced in the lives of male adolescents.

1.4 HEGEMONIC MASCULINITY AND BOYHOOD

Adolescence has been derived from the Latin word *'adolescere'* meaning growing to be matured. This signifies that adolescence is a stage involving

physiological, emotional, and social changes, which is a phase characterized by transition in the behavior and attitudes and traits of individuals,
which produces a significant impact on the lifestyle of adolescent boys
and girls[5].

One of the major concepts in understanding men and masculinity is
the concept of hyper or hegemonic masculinity. The term 'hegemony'
was coined by sociologist Antonio Gramsci which signifies domination
and superordination by the ruling class of society whose domination is
justified by the lower or subordinate class. The significance of gender
inequality in contemporary society can be understood by a critical and
in-depth understanding of the concept of hetero normative masculinity.

Hegemonic masculinity has been defined by Mike Donaldson as,
*'exclusive, anxiety-provoking, internally, and hierarchically differenti-
ated, brutal, and violent.'* Boys who are hyper-masculine are characterized
by the attributes like physical strength, stoicism, homophobic attitudes,
and racist stance. Hyper masculine men mostly accept the challenges and
opportunities and even incorporated the rival representation of masculinity.
This signifies that heterosexual masculinity relies more on significance
and evolvement of consensus and is less dependent on any kind of force.

Raewyn Connell regarded hegemonic masculinity as one of the central
components of patriarchy, which is located in four major sites-domestic
sphere in the form of unpaid work of women, paid employment, violence
against gender, and state. These sites are dichotomous to the sites of hyper-
masculinity proposed by Sylvia Walby-domestic responsibilities, paid
work, culture, and any form of violence against gender.

The pro-feminist men's organization regarded hyper-masculinity as the
greatest social evil as a result of which atrocities against women continue
to exist. Violence can be noticed in three aspects-violence not only helps
to maintain the predominance of a specific form of masculinity but is
also related to gendered practices, all of which signifies that men are the
conveyers of violence against women.

Hetero normative masculinity involves socially constructed traits like
heterosexuality, strength, physical toughness, aggression, while femininity involves characteristics of emotional dependence, nurturance, and
softness because of which is mostly regarded as subordinate to masculinity. Since the hegemonic form of masculinity is always the dominant
socially constructed masculinity, so it reduces involvement in all kinds of
opportunities.

Patriarchal ideology and cultural practices are the major origins of hetero normative masculinity which though not applicable in all cultures, is often over represented by media in the 21ˢᵗ century. Such an issue of hegemonic masculinity was clearly elaborated by McLean, who examined the impact of hyper-masculinity in turning a boy into a 'macho' which involves all attributes of being a man like physical strength followed by emotional detachment along with detachment from sensitivity and delicacy. Such awareness mostly affects the boys though they might not experience the treatment.

Demetriou regarded that hyper-masculinity has to be reconceptualized in a way that does not subdues any other subordinate forms of masculinity but rather hybridizes them. As a result of this, metrosexual movements have evolved during the 21ˢᵗ century. Most men are described by such metrosexual movement who not only survived on the dominant form of masculinity but even maintained social status. However, men hardly challenge such hegemonic masculinity as it involves the cost which men are unwilling to risk.

Hegemonic masculinity is socially constructed to exert control over most men in such a way such that men mostly conform to its notion of being masculine and physically strong, while men are discouraged to adhere to any kind of feminine behavior like emotional dependence as it stigmatizes boys possessing feminine attributes like 'effeminacy.'

Certain theorists have conceptualized masculinity differently where Raewyn Connell explored the impact of changes on masculinity along with capitalism which has brought about changes in gender identity, Jeff Hearn have also analyzed how men have used power publicly. Hearn also regarded that masculinity's representation in public domain overshadowed private domain as an important aspect of capitalism and modernity. On the other hand, Connell also portrayed how masculinity is represented and reflected in school through co-curricular activities like sports from where boys derive their prowess at the reluctance of those boys who do not develop an interest in the activity.

Masculinity has been defined in different ways by feminists by exaggerating the negative aspect of it. The critical study of men, masculinity, and their attitudes and traits was the cynosure of emerging sociology of masculinity. This was dichotomous to Parson's theory of gender where he assigned different gender roles-instrumental role for men where men would be the bread earner of the family while expressive role for women where women would look after household activities like housework and childcare. Whitehead (2002) regarded that the overemphasis on dominant discourses or lack of ideologies are blurring the notions of masculinity and femininity. In addition to this, Gloria Teinem defined masculinity as, *"a social construct that makes men shorten their own lives, distance themselves from children, punish women in their headlong effort to be not-women, and try to defeat each other"* (Smith, 10).

A significant role was played by feminism in the critical study of men and masculinities (Hearn and Morgan; Michael Kaufman). Different theorists have conceptualized about the changing nature of masculinities where on the one hand Frank Blye (1996) portrayed the changes in masculinity and is subjected to conflict. On the other hand, Robert Connell (1995) regarded that masculinity is socially constructed to cater to the demands of knowledge-based industries by focusing on technical knowledge rationality and capitalism. He recognized three important factors through which negotiation of masculinity takes place[6]:

i.　Position within gender relations;
ii.　The ways and practices by which men and women get involved that place in gender; and
iii.　The impact of these practices on culture and bodily experience.

Current theorists of masculinity like Connell (1996) followed by Jackson and Salisbury (1996) and Wayne Martino (1999) pointed out the fluid nature of masculine identities, which is not fixed but is in a constant state of flux being socially constructed by social institutions like family, sports, and school. There are different activities of everyday life like acting, speaking, listening, thinking, reading, writing, and playing, which is accomplished in manhood (West and Zimmerman, 1987). Boys display and negotiate their gender identities and masculinities within different social contexts, which they sustain by their interaction within social spheres (West and Zimmerman, 1987)[5].

Manhood or masculinity is always tested and justified by the social construction of boyhood, where there is valorization of physical toughness, bodily strength along with over-emphasis on power. It even signifies, *"the entitlement to get your way, to be heard, the often-invisible privileges that come from being a man, the ability to see your reflection (at least if you are also white and heterosexual) in virtually every television show, action-hero comic book and movie, and be seated at every board room in the nation.''* In other words, the social construction of boyhood denotes the exhilaration and exaggeration of power and its relations.

1.5   GENDER AND TECHNOLOGY

As a category, gender is portrayed by the performance of specific acts as per the socially constructed norms of masculinity and femininity.

The inseparable relation between gender and technology is one of the major emphases of feminist technology studies where both gender and technology shape each other mutually. Gender plays a significant role in shaping certain technological artifacts, which also produces an impact in the usage of such technologies in terms of gender.

SNSs or social media has emerged as one of the major spheres of the virtual world, which allows youngsters to explore and express their ideas and also provides a web-based platform to interact with family and friends along with sharing of pictures and information globally.

Shayla Marie Thiel regarded that gender determines how a male or a female perform followed by cultural learning regarding the social construction of gender. Individuals, especially youngsters, can freely choose their identity and change their gender in the virtual space, which is dichotomous to reality because research has shown that men and women in the real world portray the traits which are demanded by the opposite gender (Albright, 2001; Schmitt and Bus, 1996).

According to Anthony Easthrope, heterosexual masculine identity is formed due to the socially constructed norms and expectations as a result of which men who are effeminate find it difficult to conform to his feminine nature. However, one of the predominant traditional attributes associated with masculinity has always been physical toughness and strength, which is highly reflected and portrayed in media where men are mostly projected as active and physically capable while omen are projected as docile who are subjected to sexual objectification and commodification.

Vigorito and Curry (1998), in their research on popular magazines, portrayed that while on the one hand, men's portrayal in magazines confirms the traditional ideal of hegemonic masculinity, on the other hand, women readers have nurturing vision about men. Raewen Connell popularized and propounded the concept of hegemonic masculinity, which justifies the dominant position of a man and subservient position of a woman and involves socially constructed traits of masculinity-physical strength, toughness, violence, capability, emotional detachment. Extensive research on men and masculinities was conducted by Connell, which also became one of the most cited sources to understand the notion of dominant heterosexual masculinity.

The nature of shifting or changing masculinities can be understood by exploring the notion of hegemonic masculinity where socially constructed strategies are used to position men not only against women but also over subordinated forms of masculinity like homosexuality. The idea of 'manhood' is also constructed by hegemonic masculinity which involves symbolic ideal by means of which men are socialized to position themselves. This signifies that multiple masculinities exist since gender identity is fluid; all men are socially positioned in order to conform to the hegemonic ideal.

1.6   SIGNIFICANCE OF SOCIAL MEDIA IN CONTEMPORARY SOCIETY

Social media involves services that help users not only to construct a public profile but also to establish connection with everyone all over the world in order to share information and for a better means of communication. It also enhances users to view their list of connections and those that are created by others within the system.

With the advent of the Internet, various SNSs have also emerged, which helps its users to stay connected with the world, especially with family and friends. Among these forms of social media, WhatsApp, and Facebook have emerged as important means of communication to share information with everyone virtually and also use them as a means of entertainment[7].

An emerging social dimension was added to the web with the onset and explosion of social media. A sudden explosion of social networks like Facebook added a new social dimension to the web. The social content where online social communities can be sustained through the means of connection between users have also been altered due to the advent of online interaction between people through social network like WhatsApp, Facebook, Instagram, and Twitter. Though social media have helped to share information and connect with the world globally, its frequent use and misuse have also produced adverse impact on the lives of people.

Coley has identified certain cyber communities which help youngsters to stay connected with their significant others globally. These communities include:

- Social media like Facebook and MySpace through the means of which users can make new friends not only with their mutual ones but also with strangers by revealing their personal details only to their friends in the virtual world. Such friends have been termed by Coley as 'cyber friends.'
- Chat or instant messaging involves the second form of community recognized by Coley.
- The third type of cyber community involves personal websites and blogs along with commentaries and news.

1.7   USAGE OF SOCIAL NETWORKING SITE AMONG ADOLESCENTS

Since the major aim of SNSs is to connect with the world globally through the means of communication and sharing of information, an important means through which people could communicate with family and friends all over the world came into existence which was known as Facebook. As a social networking site, Facebook became popular not among all age groups but mostly among teenagers. Its creation can be dated back to 2004 as a college networking site where only limited access was allowed to universities in the United States and those individuals who owned university email servers.

Since Facebook as a social media allows for better communication and global connection with significant others like family and friends, its importance has increased among all youngsters, especially among teenagers who use the social networking site frequently. Such frequent usage of social media by teenagers and college goers has adversely affected their face-to-face interaction with their friends and family. Facebook provides a forum not only to connect with everyone globally but also to play different virtual games along with networking[8].

Though Facebook helps in communication with everyone and allows the youngsters to spend time in the virtual space, yet it produces negative impact not only on their physical health, but also hampers them emotionally as any kind of misuse by the teenagers turns them into victims of atrocities like rape, sexual molestation and even murder. All of such atrocities not only affects the teenagers but also adversely affects their family and society as a whole. On the other hand, an adolescent's obsession with social media also affects their time that they spend on their studies and household responsibilities which they have to compensate for the sake of addiction. Addiction of social media is one of the greatest social menaces since some youngsters even compensate on their daily activities of having food and sleeping in order to stay connected over the virtual space.

1.8 PORTRAYAL AND SELF-PRESENTATION OF ADOLESCENTS OVER SOCIAL MEDIA

The traits, tendencies, and attitudes that are associated with men-physical toughness. Strength, courage, aggression, and emotional detachment signify masculinity. When people communicate in virtual space, their major intention is to be aware about each other's personal details. Such notion of creating impression has been related to Erving Goffman's concept of impression management, where individuals involved in such acts which help to convey an impression to others about his/her interests. This signifies that impression management involves the conscious or unconscious attempt in order to impact the perception of others about any concerned person or event by means of controlling the exchange of information in interaction (Lindzey and Arondson, 1985; Dwyer, 2007). When teenagers communicate online, the notion of impression management gets transformed into the need to perform and improve oneself appropriately along with the desire to be evaluated as socially acceptable among all peers (Clark, 2005: p. 217)[9].

In her qualitative study on self-presentation in social media, Monica T. Whitty explored that peoples' self-presentation in social media through the means of their pictures attracts other users to view their profiles for attaining popularity in public forum and to increase self-esteem. This is one of the reasons the online dating sites produces a glamorous shot to accompany their textual profiles.

The fact that adolescents frequently use social media as a means of self-presentation can be justified by Michele Strano's study on Facebook as a social networking site where he explored that people in the virtual world express keen interest in displaying of pictures so that it acne b appealing to their peers in their friend list. Furthermore, Kirsty Young's study also revealed that pictures clicked and posted over SNSs were done in order to increase the popularity of the user among his or her significant others.

1.9 MASCULINITY AND SEXUALITY

The contemporary society is characterized by the dominance of cyberculture which provides a forum for adolescent men to present their bodies erotically, which also question their masculinity along with embracement of self-presentation over social media, which is related with femininity. The ways men sexually portray their bodies in the virtual world provides them an opportunity to explore changes in gender and power in order to flaunt themselves and attain a new self-identity because masculinity is mostly defined as superior to femininity[10].

Research suggests that the ideals of gender roles promote male sexuality as promiscuous and homophobic with the attributes of heterosexual hegemonic form of masculine identity. Such an approach to masculinity, however, suffers from limitations, *"Fixed, a historical characteristic are not conducive to understanding how notions of masculinity shift overtime or the kinds of permutations masculine ideals take on in different contexts and situations"* (Connell and Messerschmidt, 2005).

Most adolescent boys portray and project their multiple masculinities through the means of the Internet, i.e., SNSs. SNSs provide a platform for all adolescent men to publicly flaunt their bodies and sexual identities, all in a bid to attain a new self-identity among their peers and to enhance their self-esteem.

Furthermore, hegemonic masculinity can be constructed through the way adolescent boys project themselves over SNSs. However, it is up to the peer group whose scrutiny and judgment pressurizes the men to prove their manhood to others. Ethnographic research was carried out, which portrayed the ways by which teenage boys regulate each other's behavior in order to conform to the hegemonic ideal of masculinity and negate femininity and homosexuality on a heightened public level. The virtual space, especially social media, has brought with it a new platform which increases any form of cyberbullying or cyber harassment, which has even intensified the pressure to conform to the socially constructed ideal of masculinity.

Despite extensive research being carried out on masculinity in the West, hardly much research has been conducted on masculinity in the global North like India regarding the significant impact of SNSs in the construction of masculine identity. In the light of this context, the present research explores how adolescent boys develop and construct their notions of masculinity by accessing and engrossing in SNSs like WhatsApp, Facebook, Instagram, and Twitter.

1.10   NATURE AND SCOPE

The present chapter mainly explores how adolescent boys develop and construct their notions of masculinity by accessing and engrossing in SNSs (WhatsApp, Facebook, Instagram, Twitter).

1.11   RESEARCH METHODOLOGY

The present chapter mainly studies 20 boys (aged 16–18 years) who study in high schools (Class XI and XII) and reside in Kolkata by using the technique of *'mixed methodology.'*

1.11.1   MIXED METHODOLOGY

The mixed methodology integrates both qualitative and quantitative approaches in order to collect and analyze data, and also to draw inferences in a single program of inquiry[11].

The research is carried out by *non-probability purposive sampling,* which is based on the researcher's judgment followed by *snowball sampling* where and XII) of Kolkata where research begins with few respondents who suggest few other respondents who are known to them and who can meet the criteria of the research. This continues until a chain of respondents is formed who can furnish proper information about the issue and help to carry out the research.

1.12   DATA ANALYSIS

All the male respondents are within the age group of 16–17 years studying in XI and XII standard of an English medium school of North Kolkata.

1.12.1   DEFINITION OF MASCULINITY

The majority of the high school-going boys defined masculinity or boyhood as the ability to portray one's strength, power, heterosexuality, sexual assertiveness followed by the hide of emotions, which is often regarded as a 'feminine' trait and unmanly. The remaining boys regarded that the definition of masculinity or boyhood depends on the way society assigns meaning to it.

1.12.2   BOY'S DEFINITION OF SOCIAL NETWORK

The high school-going boys largely defined SNSs as web-based services that allow and help them to connect with friends, siblings, and also make friendship with strangers whom they meet in these sites. They are highly intrigued by the versatile features of SNSs as they offer them various options to keep in touch with their peers and even to enhance their self-identity by flaunting themselves in these sites.

1.12.3   NUMBER OF SOCIAL NETWORKING SITES USED BY BOYS

Number of Social Networking Sites Used by Boys	Number of Respondents	Percentage (%)
WhatsApp	08	40
Facebook	05	25
Gmail (Google plus)	02	10
All of the above	03	15
Others (Instagram, Twitter)	02	10
Total	20	100

Out of 20 high school boys, 13 (65%) of them have reported of using WhatsApp and Facebook as the major social networking site since they found them to be the easiest medium to connect with friends through texting, sending academic documents, and sharing pictures and videos which allows them to enhance the connectivity along with their self-esteem (by posting different pictures of themselves). The remaining 07 (35%) schoolboys have reported of using other networks like Gmail

(Google plus) along with Instagram and Twitter both for official purpose and to keep track of their favorite celebrities.

1.12.4   FREQUENCIES OF SOCIAL NETWORKING SITES

Frequency of Using Social Networking Sites	Number of Respondents	Percentage (%)
Daily	18	90
Twice a week	02	10
Once a week	00	00
Once a month	00	00
Never	00	00
Total	20	100

Out of 20 schoolboys, 18 (90%) of them use SNSs like WhatsApp, Facebook, and Gmail daily for the purpose of keeping in touch with friends, sharing pictures and videos, which even include exchanging documents (through WhatsApp). The remaining 2 (10%) schoolboys use networks like Gmail for checking notifications or any updates regarding their school curriculum.

1.12.5   TYPES OF SOCIAL NETWORKING SITES USED (ACTIVE USER)

Types of Social Networking Sites Used (Active User)	Number of Respondents	Percentage (%)
WhatsApp	08	40
Facebook	08	40
Gmail (Google Plus)	02	10
Twitter	00	00
All of the above	02	10
Others	00	00
Total	20	100

Out of 20 schoolboys, 16 (80%) of them actively use WhatsApp and Facebook in their *leisure time* in order to communicate with their friends, acquaintances, and even their lovers. They engross or engage most of their leisure time in accessing these two SNSs, which helps them to reduce proximity with their friends made possible through its varied features (video calling) and also to escape from the mundane and hectic schedule of life. On the other hand, the rest of the 04 (20%) boys use all kinds of sites, which helps them to keep a balance between studies (through updates in Gmail and exchange of documents through WhatsApp) and communication with friends (through WhatsApp, Facebook).

1.12.6   SELF-PRESENTATION IN THESE SITES

Self-Presentation in These Sites	Number of Respondents	Percentage (%)
Yes	15	75
No	05	25
Total	20	100

Out of 20 high school boys, 15 (75%) of them affirmed that they like and even enjoy to flaunt themselves along with their bodies in SNSs like Facebook and Instagram all in a bid to increase their reputation among their peers which will not only enhance their self-esteem but also will increase their craze and reputation among female peers resulting in the formation or construction of masculine identity.

1.12.7   DIFFERENT WAYS IN WHICH BOYS PORTRAY THEIR BODIES IN SOCIAL NETWORKING SITES

Different Ways in Which Boys Portray Their Bodies in Social Networking Sites	Number of Respondents	Percentage (%)
Selfie of themselves or their bodies	12	60
Videos (Dance or body-building)	02	10
Body modifications (Tattoo, body piercing)	06	30
Others	00	00
Total	20	100

Out of 20 respondents, 12 (60%) of the boys flaunt themselves and their bodies in SNSs like Facebook by clicking selfies and sharing such pictures on these sites in order to increase their self-esteem o that it helps them to build reputation among his peers by conforming to the notion of socially acceptable hegemonic masculinity. The remaining 08 (40%) boys either share videos of their body-building or pictures of beautification of their bodies through tattoo and body piercing in order to increase their fame among their friend and even female friends involving strangers.

1.12.8 INTERACTION WITH STRANGERS

Most of the respondents disclosed that besides interacting with friends on sites like WhatsApp and Facebook, they also tend to interact with few strangers who are either mutual friends or someone whom they have neither encountered nor have any kind of acquaintance before. They cited that they interact with these strangers who mainly include girls of their age as they like making new friends, which acts as a solace to reduce loneliness or boredom in their lives.

1.12.9 INTIMATE RELATIONSHIP WITH GIRLFRIENDS IN THESE SITES

The majority of schoolboys responded that they have been involved in romantic relationship with their girlfriends who even went to the extent of sharing intimate pictures with their partners in sites of Facebook and Instagram. This also helped the boys to enhance their status or self-identity among their peer group since engaging in intimate relationships with girlfriends is regarded as a socially acceptable norm for adolescent boys, which further helps in the construction of masculinity.

1.13 CONCLUSION

The high school boys largely defined boyhood or masculinity as the ability to portray one's strength, power, heterosexuality, sexual assertiveness followed by the hiding of emotions which is often regarded as a 'feminine' trait and unmanly.

These adolescent boys frequently use SNSs like WhatsApp and Facebook in order to communicate with their friends, acquaintances, and even their lovers. They engross or engage most of their leisure time in accessing these two SNSs, which helps them to reduce proximity with its varied features (video calling) and also acts as a solace to escape from the loneliness, mundane, and hectic schedule of life.

Adolescent boys spend most of their time accessing SNSs mainly in order to create varied forms of social relations and also to project or portray themselves to social media. High school boys also access these sites for the purpose of gaining reputation among their friends by projecting themselves in a different way than what they are in reality. Some adolescent boys also tend to form intimate relations with strangers on such sites in order to escape from their boredom which might turn out to be harmful for their future. Boys construct different forms of gender identity in the social media, which produces a profound impact on their future.

Adolescent boys studying in XIth and XIIth standards construct their self-identity through the means of self-presentation by clicking selfies of their bodies and posting them over Facebook or beautifying their bodies through tattoos, body piercing, and hairstyling. This kind of self-presentation not only helps to enhance the reputation of adolescent boys but also helps to construct their masculine identity among their peers. High school boys engage in self-presentation over SNSs in order to increase their self-esteem since hegemonic masculinity is characterized by portrayal of socially acceptable form of masculinity like strength, physical toughness, muscular body-all of which produces a profound impact and help in the construction of their masculinity.

However, such obsession with social media also turns the adolescent boys into victims of wrong deeds as their obsession with self-presentation of their bodies coerces them to become narcissist, due to which these boys suffer from identity crisis. These teenagers thereby fall in the trap of their peer group all in a bid to increase their reputation among their peers, least realizing about the ill effects of social media on their everyday lifestyle and their masculine identity.

NOTES:

1. Katerina Dadatsi elucidated about the historical background of masculinity in his work *"Doing Boy" in Male Peer Groups: A Discursive Approach into Adolescent Masculinity*.

2. Danah. M. Boyd defined social networking sites in his work "*Social Network Sites: Definition, History, and Scholarship.*"
3. Definition of masculinity.
4. Karen Harvey elaborated about the history of masculinity in the global North in his work "*The History of Masculinity, Circa 1650–1800.*"
5. Definition of adolescence by Elizabeth Hurlock in her book "*Developmental Psychology.*"
6. R. W. Connell enunciated about the concept of hegemonic masculinity in his work "*Hegemonic Masculinity: Rethinking the Concept.*"
7. Kaitlyn Flad pointed out the impact of social media on Student's academic performance across gender lines in her work "*The Influence of Social Networking Participation on Student Academic Performance Across Gender Lines.*"
8. S. M. Al-Jubayer elaborated about the impact of Facebook on adolescents in his work "*The Use of Social Networking Sites Among Teenagers: A Study of Facebook Use in Dhaka City.*"
9. Andra Siibak, in her work "*Constructing Masculinity on a Social Networking Site: The Case-Study of Visual Self-Presentations of Young Men on the Profile Images of SNS Rate,*" portrayed the social construction of masculinity through self-presentation over social media.
10. Adriana Manago explored the relation between masculinity and sexuality in her work "*Negotiating a Sexy Masculinity on Social Networking Sites, Feminism, and Psychology.*"
11. Teddlie and Tashakkori provided a definition of Mixed Methodology in their work "*Foundations of Mixed Methods Research (Integrating Quantitative and Qualitative Approaches in the Social and Behavioral Sciences).*"

KEYWORDS

- **adolescence**
- **global connection**
- **hegemonic masculinity**
- **impression management**
- **masculinity**
- **social networking sites**

REFERENCES

Al-Jubayer, S. M., (2013). The use of social networking sites among teenagers: A study of Facebook use in Dhaka City. *Journal of International Social Issues*. http://www.winona.edu/socialwork/Media/JISI_Al-Jubayer_1.pdf (accessed on 24 February 2021).

Baker, R. K., & White, K. M., (2010). Predicting adolescents' use of social networking sites from an extended theory of planned behavior perspective. *Computers in Human Behavior*, 2, 3. http://eprints.qut.edu.au/34221/1/c34221.pdf accessed on 24 February 2021).

Boyd, D. M., & Ellison. N. B., (2020). *Social Network Sites: Definition, History, and Scholarship* (pp. 1–3). http://www.danah.org/papers/JCMCIntro.pdf (accessed on 24 February 2021).

Connell, R. W., & Messerschmidt, J. W., (2005). *Hegemonic Masculinity: Rethinking the Concept* (Vol. 19, No. 6, p. 833). Sage Publications, Gender and Society.

Dadatsi, K., (2014). "Doing boy" in male peer groups: A discursive approach into adolescent masculinity. *Hellenic Journal of Psychology, 11*, 138, 140–142.

Einarsdóttir, G. A., (2015). *Social Network Site Usage Among Adolescents: Effects on Mental and Physical Well-Being*, 1, 2. http://skemman.is/stream/get/1946/22550/50901/1/BSc_Thesis_Gu%C3%B0r%C3%BAn_Alma.pdf (accessed on 24 February 2021).

Flad, K., (2010). *The Influence of Social Networking Participation on Student Academic Performance Across Gender Lines*, 8, 9. http://digitalcommons.brockport.edu/cgi/viewcontent.cgi?article=1030&context=edc_theses (accessed on 24 February 2021).

Gender Roles, (2001). *International Encyclopedia of the Social and Behavioral Sciences*. Gender Roles: An Overview. Science Direct Topic. https://www.ScienceDirect.com/topics/social-sciences/gender-roles (accessed on 24 February 2021).

Harvey, K., (2005). The history of masculinity, circa 1650–1800. *Journal of British Studies, 44*(2), 298–305. Published by: Cambridge University Press on behalf of The North American Conference on British Studies. http://www.jstor.org/stable/10.1086/427126 (accessed on 24 February 2021).

Hurlock, E. B., (2016). *Developmental Psychology a Life-Span Approach* (pp. 223–225, 250). McGraw Hill Education (India) Pvt. Limited.

Manago, A. M., (2013). Negotiating a sexy masculinity on social networking sites. *Feminism and Psychology*, 3, 4. http://citeseerx.ist.psu.edu/viewdoc/download?doi=10.1.1.823.5048&rep=rep1&type=pdf (accessed on 24 February 2021).

Siibak, A., (2010). Constructing masculinity on a social networking site: The case-study of visual self-presentation of young men on the profile images of SNS rate. *Young Nordic Journal of Youth Research*, 404, 405, 407. Sage publications.

Teddlie, C., & Tashakkori, A., (2009). *Foundations of Mixed Methods Research (Integrating Quantitative and Qualitative Approaches in the Social and Behavioral Sciences)* (p. 7). Sage Publications.

CHAPTER 2

Digital Transformation and Its Impact: An Analytical Study

JAYANTA KUMAR BEHERA

Department of Sociology, I.G.N. Tribal University, Amarkantak, Anuppur, Madhya Pradesh–484886, India,
E-mail: jkbigntu@gmail.com

ABSTRACT

India is becoming a different nation due to the development of digital technology. The advanced technology, i.e., mobile connectivity and the internet is promoting India towards huge growth in the digital world. The digital India program is to improve the information technology (IT) interface for getting the maximum coverage with the help of e-Governance and e-Service in the world. Digital technology is more suitable for the government as well as the public. The main objective of the scheme is to digitally empower every human being. The present research chapter is to provide a better understanding of the concept, service launched, the scope of Digital India, the impact of digital transformation, and its potential benefits in developing technology applications with a fundamental positive contribution to our quality of life. Simultaneously, as with all significant technological advancements and digitization, social problems can result. The chapter outlines reforms in this context aimed at maximizing benefits and preparing for any possible negative consequences associated with those changes.

2.1 INTRODUCTION

India is struggling to congregate the ambitions of its people where the services of the government can reach a door to door for the help of people and also contribute in the direction of a long-lasting positive impact. "India lives in villages," said the Father of the Nation, Mahatma Gandhi. The former Prime Minister of India Shri Atal Bihari Vajpayee said on television on 22 March 1998, "The Government will make every effort solid to make India a global information technology (IT) power-specifically, [we will] make India one of the largest producers and exporters of software in the world within 10 years." The Prime Minister of India also recommended professionals to deal with the three national tasks to enlarge the role of languages in computers, the citizen of government improves its interface by using internet and also the government of India wants to improve the IT-related appliance in rural areas for rural and agricultural development (Nikam et al., 2004).

The main initiative of digital India is to build the system very transparent. The government of India has planed to remodel the Indian economy as a conversant economy and made the society digitally empowered. This is one of the major steps taken by the Government of India to stimulate and connect the world with the Indian economy. The main focus of this program is to develop India for a knowledgeable future by developing central technology for allowing revolution, which covers many departments under one umbrella program. At present, without science and technology, we cannot imagine our life. In this contemporary India, digital technology is considered one of the most important advanced technologies. As a result, the prime minister of India has launched the scheme on 2 July 2015 to ensure that all the government services are electronically available to citizens by improving online infrastructure and by increasing internet connectivity.

India became a globally connected hub due to the large campaigning of digital transformation programs. To make the country as a digital destination, the government of India invited many domestic and foreign companies to invest in India especially manufacturing companies. Digital India campaign specially focuses on generating jobs and skill enhancement the e-governance system, broadband, electronic gadgets and also in mobile connectivity, etc. This could be resolved the problems of connectivity and also help us to connect with each other. This initiative also helps us to increase the better rural connectivity for which most of the rural people are getting the benefit of it on the one hand and incentives provided by the government on the other hand. These initiatives of the government also create a job opportunities and enhance the skill for the youth, which ultimately leads to an increase in the GDP and revenues. The basic aim of this program is to provide learning education in the Indian language which could help the youth in achieving the objectives of education, getting more digital information, leadership structure, and participation in the global industry.

In the present scenario, India became a cusp of digital transformation. There are more than 500 million internet users (The Economic Times, 2018), and 340 million people are smartphone users (2018) (Hindustan Times, 2018). The digital wave is entering into the lives of millions of people in India and occupied distinctive position in their live. Now India became digitally empowered in some certain sectors such as business, industry, education, and other occupational sectors for achieving higher operational efficiency and to provide better facility to the customers. Due to digital transformation program, many traditional industries have been emphasized on use of modern and innovative technology in different aspects of their business. The government of India is also giving more emphasis on the adoption of digital technology to improve the level and pace of public service delivery.

Digital technologies are drastically changed the live of the people in India. It can change the relation between customers, workers, and employers. Most of the works have been done through digitally. They prefer to do everything through the help of mobile apps such as purchasing of items and mode of payment through online. There is dramatically an improvement of computing and communications, which binds the people across the country to participate in the digital economy.

Digitalization refers to the massive transformation of digital technology in different sectors. Due to the process of digitalization, there is a huge transformation of multiple technologies such as media technology, business technology, computer technology, etc. Continuous adoption of advanced technology, there is discontinuity of traditional technology in different sectors, which affects the local, regional, and global communities. Digital technology affects Indian society in different ways. Digital technology enables the mechanization of business, expanding operational efficiencies, creating new business opportunities, impacting employment and entrepreneurship, which resulted in reduction of transaction cost and also impact the production processes. Digital transformation enhances the provision of health and education, while improving the interaction between citizen and the government. Finally, digital transformation has a great effect on human relationship and also change in behavioral pattern. It has also some potential negative impact on disruption at workplace, vanishing of industries, increasing cybercrime and social anomie.

Digital technology is not considered as a one-time event by the policymakers. Contemporary global society is fully required to accelerate the technological progress and diffusion of new innovations (Solow, 1987: p. 36). The existing technological innovations have a considerable social and economic impact. Since independence, India has come to be an agriculturally based economy to a globalized and single-minded economy. Due to the emerging of new agricultural and industrial technology during the 1990's, India became the fastest-growing economies in the world. India has made a remarkable progress in different sectors of global digital metrics such as subscription of mobile, internet facilities digital transactions in last few decades. However, the growth of digital technology has been seen among the youth and particularly in urban areas. As a result, the digital ranking of India is very low in comparison to other countries (India Website, 2018; World Economic Forum Website, 2019; Indian Telecom Services, 2018, 2019).

2.2   REVIEW OF LITERATURE

In order to have a better understanding of the problem under the study, it is very much necessary to review the existing stock of literature related to it. The researcher must be acquainted with all the materials available on the matter. This early preparation will enable to tackle the problem in the correct perspective and identity the gaps of research. The present study is an attempt to review the related literature in the area of holistic thinking of the impact of digital transformation in present contemporary society. To obtain the in-depth knowledge, which forms the sound base of investigating into the research problem, the related literature is reviewed under the following heads:-

James (2004) has conducted a study on ICT in general, and internet usage is measured by the difference between developed, developing, and underdeveloped countries in global scenarios. The problem was found in India, which are the underdeveloped countries that the uneducated/ unskilled people who have lack of knowledge on computer and internet connectivity, how they can take the advantage of it. This problem can be solved with the help of intermediaries who can transfer their basic knowledge on computer and about internet connectivity to the illiterate person. By using this kind of method in India, it is found that at least 30% of people can take benefit from this idea.

Mistry (2005) developed a theoretical framework to represent how the digital divine is formed and how it can be bridged a good framework in under-developed nations. The government is directly or indirectly involved to give details of a variety of ways in which public institutions can make possible in bridging the digital divide. Government plays a vital role in respect to economic development by taking with the help of digital divine.

Kaur and Neena (2014) was investigated the extent of ICT circulation in India and also estimate the inter-state technology divide. As a result, the topmost ICT player are in the southern part of India like Kerala, Tamil Nadu, Karnataka, and in north side countries Punjab, HP. and the bottommost player of digital India are Uttar Pradesh, Bihar, Orissa, and Assam. The study revealed that the transmission of telecom index will affect the size of the digital divide between both the group large groups and small groups as well as in between high groups and medium groups. There is a change in the value of the digital divide for all states of India are negative during the periods of 2001 to 2012.

Khan et al. (2015) has conducted a study on the concept of digitization along with the socio-economic and ecological benefits of digitization of knowledge and information. As a result, digitization is the social transformation started by the enormous adoption of digital technologies to share and manage digital information.

Gulati (2016) has conducted a study on the successful implementation of the digital program can breed a domestic challenges impede and suggest some feasible remedies to deal with it. The study highlighted the opportunities that cover the way for achieving the goal of the digital programs of making India. There is a preferred choice for both the global and domestic investors to start their investment in India and how far this model of Digital Indian can build an attraction for the investors to invest in this sector which are yet to achieve their full potential in India.

Kaul and Mathur (2017) have analyzed the importance of financial literacy. The result of the study recognized the hindrance in the implementation of various programs to make India financially literate and adopted some important approaches to implement these policies more successfully and resourcefully. Digitization impact on a country can be accessed based on its impact on government, economy, and society. Digitalization has created new job opportunities, has led to sector-specific innovation and economic growth. The government has stressed digitization as it provides accountability, better control, and better job opportunities for the country's citizens.

2.3 OBJECTIVES

The present study was undertaken to understand the results of digitization and the impact of technological revolution in different sectors to make India a powerful digital country of the world. Before digitization, India was a country with maximum numbers of population were educated and skilled with very few job opportunities, after digitization, Indians have lots of opportunities due to the revolutionary "Digitization Mission" and "Make in India" mission going on hand in hand. Despite of having a lot of challenges and hurdles, the main objective is to the achievement of digitalization, i.e., how the digital mission helped in approaching the economical ingots which is a pride to our nation.

Now India became a worldwide huge market with the economic revolution happening. Many investors, who want to invest in India because of its rapid economic development, have demanded attention for digitization. This is possible because of the innovative operations using social media, mobilization, digital technologies and allowing other countries to look at India's mission in India and its economic growth is an overview of the traditional and digital approach and the positive effect of digitization on conventional practice.

The digital revolution is now carrying a transformative changes in different areas such as e-payments methods, digital literacy, e-health system, financial inclusion, development in rural areas, programs for social benefits, localization of language, etc. India's government plays a significant role as a facilitator-cum-provider in moving the nation towards a digitally-driven society. The Indian government has put together a number of initiatives through its flagship programs such as 'Digital India,' 'Make in India,' 'startup India,' and 'smart Cities Mission,' which are expected to have an impact on social and economic fronts through digital technology, digital industry, digital people, and digital skills.

2.4 RESEARCH METHODOLOGY

In the research problem, the data collection methods are a vital part. There are various ways of collecting the data. There are primary and secondary methods of data collection. The nature of the study is both exploratory and quantitative. The secondary information is used for problem analysis. Secondary data come from different sources such as previous research, various journals, books, and online magazines, special investigation team study, websites of India's newspaper and reserve bank (RBI).

2.5 IMPACT OF DIGITAL TRANSFORMATION ON PEOPLE, BUSINESS, AND GOVERNMENT

Digital ambitions of the government and private sectors are bound to influence stakeholders of the digital economy directly as well as indirectly. When companies and government are digitally successful and agile, various stakeholders of the economy (people, business, government) tend to have a larger impact on a country's growth.

Rising technological adoption have brought a paradigm shift in consumer behavior and buying pattern. Some of the most evident changes can be observed in the fields of commerce, communication, and media and 200 average times spent per day by mobile internet users on online activities (as of 2017). In the coming years, digital would become an integral part, as people look for more transparent, connected, and personalized digital experience.

Digitization has yielded operational efficiency, cost reduction and productivity improvement across the value chain of various industries. It provides a unique opportunity to businesses to reinvent themselves and grow at a much faster pace. According to KPMG India CEO Outlook (2018), 9 CEOs in India Consider technology disruption as more a chance than a challenge. With the growing competition and rising consumer expectations, organizations have realized the importance of implementing digital strategy to survive in the rapidly changing global business environment.

The government plays a dual role of a facilitator-cum-provider in the digital ecosystem. As a facilitator, it is responsible for providing supportive digital infrastructure, formulating robust regulatory and legal frameworks, and creating a skilled and efficient digital workforce. Furthermore, the government is leveraging various digital services to enhance its service delivery in the fields of healthcare, education, transportation, etc., and improving the way citizens interact with public services. In FY19, the budget allocation for the Digital India program has been doubled to INR 30.73bn (The Times of India, 2017; KPMG India CEO Outlook, 2018).

The result of digitization has been the effectiveness of government. As for the analysis reviewed above, we depended on three parameters: the accountability of governmental activities, the implementation of e-government services, and the provision of key government services to public education. The co-relational analysis shows that increased digitization allows a society to become more transparent, improving public participation and the ability of the government to disseminate information in an accessible way. Digital technology takes government policies closer to the people and functions an insight that contributes to more active political involvement and promotes human rights growth. In a digitized world, e-Government services are more effective. Current research shows that causality is working both ways in this situation. Lower digitization helps to implement e-government services more effectively, while better e-government services enhance the learning process digitization. Lastly, digitization facilitates the efficient delivery of essential government services, such as higher education. The study shows that digitization definitely has a positive impact on economic growth, social well-being, and the effectiveness of government, while this impact varies depending on the degree of digitization of a nation. Digitization has improved economic and quality of life impacts and expanded access to essential services and education in countries which are just started their journey.

2.6   DIGITAL TRANSFORMATION AND ECONOMY

The Digital India plan could boost GDP to $1 trillion by 2025, according to analysts. It can play a key role in macroeconomic factors, including GDP growth, job creation, labor productivity, business growth, and government revenue leakage. According to the World Bank report, a 10% increase in mobile and broadband stimulation in developing countries increases the per capita GDP by 0.81% and 1.38%, respectively. India is the world's second-largest telecoms market with 915 million telecom operators and the world's third-largest Internet market with nearly 259 million network operators. India still has a big economic potential, as rural

India's teledensity is just 45% where more than 65% of the population lives. In terms of the number of subscribers, potential growth of the telecommunications industry is projected to come from rural areas as urban areas are overwhelmed with a teledensity of more than 160%.

Digital connectivity, information access, and advanced manufacturing techniques are reshaping traditional sectors, yielding operational efficiencies, lower transaction costs, and improved productivity (Financial Express, 2017). Digital technologies enable companies to participate in global value chains and to have direct access to foreign market customers. The benefits for consumers are linked to accessing a broader range of goods and services at reasonable rates. The government also plans to bring policies for quicker adoption of digital technologies such as 5G, artificial intelligence, etc. (DoT website, accessed on 24 January 2019). The Government of India, on 1 May 2018, launched the draft version of the new telecommunications policy, named National Digital Communications Policy (2018). It plans to attract INR6, 838 billion (USD100 billion) in foreign investments by 2022 and seeks to ensure that digital communications contributes 8% to India's GDP by 2022. Ongoing technological changes are creating significant impact across many sectors, driving the country's digital economy.

There is growth in software and business process outsourcing (BPO) industry, rise in manufacturing output leading to higher revenues, Supply chain optimization leading to lower cost of production, Improved market access through better communication channels, Evolution of internet economy with emergence of new business models such as e-commerce, and online booking portals, Rise of online B2B and B2C platforms allowing domestic businesses to address international markets, Use of Big Data/analytics for fraud detection, consumer behavior analysis, promotion, and campaign placement, etc., Smart City management solutions for traffic management, utilities, security, waste management, etc., through IoT and AI, Ease of data management, and higher transparency and security through Blockchain technology and reduction in the cost and time of manufacturing through 3D printing and robotics process automation.

2.6.1 ICT-ENABLER OF DIGITAL ECONOMY

IT-BPM industry has played an instrumental role in the growth of the services sector, which is the backbone of the Indian economy. Often referred to as the 'World Talent Powerhouse,' the industry is the biggest private-sector employer, engaging 3.7 million people directly. IT-BPM industry is forecast to reach INR20, 515 billion (USD300 billion) by 2020 from INR10,531 billion (USD154 billion) in 2017, at an impressive CAGR of 24.9% (Ministry of Electronics and Information Technology, 2019). Rapidly growing technologies such as cloud technology will help the fast growth, AI, IoT, cognitive computing, and robotic process automation (RPA), which are helping firms across industries to drive profitability, thereby contributing to the nation's economy.

Indian IT-BPM companies have reorganized their business strategies over the last few years to focus on high-value services, with a key emphasis on digital offerings. Companies across the sector have taken a range of initiatives to develop their digital capabilities including: Creation of dedicated Centre of Excellence and innovation labs to develop digital technology-based platforms and solutions, Reskilling, and upskilling of employees to build the necessary talent pool to meet the rising demand, and investment in strategic partnerships and M and As (Merger and Acquisitions) to acquire niche digital capabilities.

As a result, digital now accounts for 30 to 40% revenues of leading Indian IT companies and has been growing with an annualized CAGR of 20% (The Economic Times, 2018). According to the report published by a leading global technology company in April, 2018, the digital transformation could eventually lead INR10.531 billion to India's GDP by 2021 (USD154 billion). This translates into an extra 1% annual GDP growth rate (Microsoft Website, 2018).

In today's digital era, every sector is under immense pressure to reinvent itself in the wake of changing market dynamics and rising customer expectations. Digital innovation that begins in large and small business communities, in the context of efficiency and product throughput, has a propensity to affect the majority of the economy and segments. Some of the most widely discussed sectors amid digital revolutions are banking and financial services, healthcare, education, manufacturing, retail, and logistics, Agriculture, and Power and utilities.

2.7   SOCIAL IMPACT

It is difficult to measure the effect of digitization on communities, since there are no standardized indicators that serve as a social development barometer. Studies sometimes tend to look at the level of inequality in a society, but a complicated relationship between economic growth and inequality remains in developing economies that are in the process of raising millions from poverty. There are two levels of societal impact on: The standard of quality of life in a country and the fair access to public services provided by the country. However, the study indicates that the influence of digitization is not as pronounced in countries with lower levels of economic development. The distinction appears to be that factors beyond digitization are more important to quality of life in less developed economies: food, home, cloth, water, and energy are of primary importance; health and, eventually, transportation and connectivity are followed. The digitization outcome only affects quality of life when the population has fulfilled their essential necessities. The relation to overall societal well-being is one of the most significant and relevant factors related to digitization. Digitization, as a social process, empowers institutions through digital communications and applications to generate, cooperate, and create greater benefits and advances for society.

According to Mulrenin and Geser (2001), this transformation of all sorts of economic and cultural material into bits and bytes gives rise to a new level of reaching a large audience by making available economic cultural resources in ways that were not possible in the past. Users from around the world are therefore dependent on the ease and speed of digital access to uncover a lot of new and rare resources, of which they never have any information or find in print collections. In addition, digitization promotes understanding, study, and promotion of past and current history, and information also has a direct effect on people 's overall happiness and satisfaction from the technologies and skills associated with digital technology.

2.8 IMPACT ON HEALTH

Healthcare is one of India's fastest-growing markets, and is expected to reach INR25, 439 billion (USD372 billion) by 2022, at a CAGR of 22% (The Economic Times, 2017). Despite its rapid economic growth, the number of healthcare services are limited to an affluent section of society. In terms of quality and accessibility of health care, India ranked 145 among 195 countries (in 2016) (The Economic Times, 2018). The technology could play a crucial role in rationalizing the uneven doctor-patient ratio, improving quality standards as well as providing affordable healthcare services to remote areas of the country. Digital revolution is already gaining prominence in India's healthcare industry, with efforts from both the public and private sectors.

The government has taken many initiatives to strengthen healthcare services in rural India, which includes the following:

- Launched 'DigiGaon' to provide trainings and education on tele-medicine to villagers.
- Announced plans to promote digital payments at hospitals.
- The expansion of the National Optical Fiber Network would further reinforce rural connectivity, aiding in the expansion of e-health (The Economic Times, 2018).
- In the past few years, the women and child development ministry has distributed smartphones at 62,000 'Anganwadi center' in six states. The program helped in identifying 12,000 severely under-weight children (specifically in 0–3-year age group) in these states through real-time tracking of meals and health data (The Economic Times, 2017).

The government could also partner with other private sector to leverage digital technologies in the healthcare industry include the following subsections.

2.8.1   GOVERNANCE SYSTEM IN HEALTH

E-health is a growing field in medical informatics, public health, and business development. It is very effective when it comes to electronically transferring health services and health care. There are three main areas of e-health in which the first one is transferring health information using the internet and telecommunications second is the use of e-commerce to develop public health services, and last but not the least is to use e-commerce and e-business practices in health systems management. The main advantage of e-health is low cost, easily accessible and providing anonymity to the users:

- To manage performance of various health departments at zonal, state, and national level.
- To create reports and dashboard for tracking diseases, patient inflows, patient complaints and feedback, medical officials' attendance, etc. E-Governance: This will transform all manual work into a fully automated system. It will revitalize the system in the following ways:

o   Online access to applications, i.e., the availability in electronic form of all databases and information;
o   Effortless tracking of allocations;
o   Interface between departments for superior productivity growth;
o   React quickly, analyze, and solve ongoing issues and also more (Gupta and Arora, 2015).

2.8.2   ANALYSIS AND INTELLIGENCE

- Using AI and ML on the extensive clinical data to identify people at risk of the disease, and get them on early intervention programs.
- Creating statistical models from the types of diseases, this could be linked to gene history of patient to create/predict the 'Genetic Report Card' for citizens.

From launching mobile apps to setting up innovation centers, private sector is exploring the use of technology to improve accessibility and quality of healthcare service in India. Several private hospitals have already incorporated technology across various functions such as online appointment, electronic medical record (EMR) management, and digital payment. More luxury private hospitals use IT to promote end-to-end control of health care within their organizations. Healthcare institutes are also using advanced analytics and AI to diagnose and predict critical ailments such as cancer. The rising number of digital health start-ups has influenced these innovations.

2.9   IMPACT ON EDUCATION

E-education is also an important concept which is launched under the Digital India. E-education or online education has become one of the most popular ways of gaining access to education. E-education changes the experience of the student's as well as the instructors. In this, class time does not require we can watch the lecture whenever you are free. In the present scenario, e-education has a distinctive capability to carry all the unrestricted by time or place for the learners. The main advantages of e-education are not necessary to go in the classroom for accessing; it reduces travel time and improves internet skills.

More than 260 million students enrolled in more than 1.5 million schools and approximately 39,000 colleges catering to 27.5 million undergraduates and 4 million postgraduate students; India is one of the world's most important educational markets. As of 2016, the education market in India stands at INR6.8 trillion (USD100 billion) and presents lucrative opportunities for digital transformation. The digitalization of education is evident across the entire ecosystem, starting from primary education to corporate trainings. Growing internet accessibility and the development of mobile devices has led to online courses and learning content being adopted. In 2016, India's online education market was estimated at INR16.9 billion (USD247 million) with approximately 1.57 million paying users and is projected to cross INR134 billion (USD1.96 billion) with about 9.6 million paid users by 2021 (Online Education in India, 2021).

Modern digital tools can help schools easily automate internal processes, streamline routine activities and enhance communication between students, teachers, and parents. Going forward, digital technologies could make a fundamental difference by allowing educators to focus on students rather than paperwork.

The traditional education system is here to stay for the long haul, but digitization can help the system to become more dynamic that can be molded as per student's capability and made available to socially disadvantaged students. Students can now get their study materials related to lectures, seminars captured in the form of audios/videos and delivered to them in person.

A number of education technology start-ups have emerged in the last three decades in India that brought a range of online learning platforms for the students. With interactive learning programs and customized approaches, start-ups care for students' unique needs in order to achieve improved learning outcomes. A number of private schools are also experimenting with ways to integrate Information Communication Technology into their education processes through smart classes, online learning management systems, digital content libraries, etc.

2.10   IMPACT ON EMPLOYMENT

The implementation and enhancement of information and communication technology (ICT) has a significant effect on employment as it generates more positions in the IT field that can be associated with software development, outsourcing, hardware manufacturing, and other IT-related businesses. Moreover, the effect of all these technologies has been recognized in other service sectors, such as in commerce, industry, finance, and health services. El-Darwiche, Singh, and Ganediwalla (2012) Presented an econometric Booz and Company that examined a 0.84% decrease in the nation's unemployment rate due to a 10% rise in digital activity. An additional 19 million jobs were added to the global economy from 2009 to 2010, through the advent of digitization-related activities. A rise of more than 5% is seen in approximately 18 million jobs between 2007 and 2008.

In another Booz and Company report, it is observed that in 2011, digitization gave a US$ 193 billion boost to world economic growth and created 6 million new jobs in 2011. Digitization led to an extra $16.5 billion in output and nearly 380,000 new jobs in the same year in the Middle East and North Africa alone (El-Darwiche and Singh, 2013). Over the last few years, this global development of hundreds of millions of jobs has brought a great boom in society that can contribute heavily to the country's economy. Digitization, therefore, speeds up the country's economic development and prosperity by promoting job opportunities for the populations.

Job creation in the service sector (software, BPO, ICT, etc.), as well as in mass manufacturing industries; Financial inclusion on the back of ICT-supported banking system; Ease of access due to doorstep delivery of services; Better access to public services and information; Change in media consumption habits with the increasing use of digital media, Reskilling/mass movement of jobs across sectors, particularly the low-skilled repetitive jobs, Higher risk of online fraud and data leak due to increasing data collection and weak cybersecurity measures, Rise in indirect employment/new jobs due to increase in internet platforms and digital economy and Rise in business opportunities with emergence of local content and data intelligence.

2.11 AGRICULTURE

Agriculture is a primary source of livelihood for nearly half of the country's population; however, the sector struggles to generate sustainable income for most of them (WE Forum Website, 2018). There are plenty of problems plaguing the sector; right from pre-production to storage and distribution. According to the Agriculture Statistics at a Glance report 2016, India's agriculture yields of various crops are lowest among competing major economies such as China, Brazil, and Russia (Hindustan Times, 2017). Approximately INR957 billion of food production in India is also wasted due to weak supply chain. All these inadequacies make agriculture a high-risk sector, with low returns.

In order to revamp the agriculture sector into an economically viable and ecologically sustainable practice, there is an awful need to move away from archaic practices and adopt technology-assisted methods and systems, in line with global economies such as China and the U.S. These countries have demonstrated that an assortment of technologies such as precision farming, big data analytics, AI, satellite monitoring and geo-tagging, and farm management systems can be applied at various stages of agriculture to increase productivity and farm incomes.

Several organizations in India have already started investing in new agricultural technology solutions. During 2014–2018, there have been 41 deals worth INR6.5 billion in the Indian agricultural technology space. Increased use of the internet, increased penetration of smart cell phones and various government initiatives in rural areas also promote the adoption of technologies in the farm sectors (Your Story Website, 2018). Such measures can be analyzed over the different phases of the life cycle of farming.

2.12   PRODUCTION

Most of the farmers in India presently choose their crops based on preceding season trends rather than technical factors such as soil quality and nutritional level. Additionally, most of the farmers with smaller landholdings are overly dependent on monsoon for irrigation. All these factors along with conventional agricultural practices lead to lower farm productivity and higher farm input cost. AI and data analytics-based platforms could assist the farmers in making a suitable selection of crop, fertilizer, pesticide, and method of irrigation by study of many factors, including the level of soil nutrients, moisture content, groundwater levels, weather predictions, etc. This, in turn, would help in producing higher crop yields with lower farm input.

The government has given over 9 million soil health cards to farmers as of March 2019. This card provides crop-wise recommendations of the nutrients and fertilizers required for individual farms, so that farm inputs can be used judiciously (Home, soil health.dac Website, 2019). In October 2018, the India Meteorological Department and a leading Indian engineering institute has jointly developed a country-wide soil moisture prediction model, which helps in better seed selection and irrigation plan (The Indian Express, 2018). A number of start-ups are using Big Data analytics, AI, geo-tagging, and satellite monitoring to provide real-time farm-related insights and recommendations to farmers to help them optimize their farm productivity.

2.12.1 SUPPLY CHAIN AND DISTRIBUTION

In the current agriculture supply chain, middlemen get a significant portion of farmers' income. The advent of e-market platforms has directly connected farmers to buyers, resulting in higher profit realization for the former. It also provides better price transparency to both, buyers, and farmers.

In April 2016, the government launched National Agriculture Market (eNAM), an online trading portal, to connect existing 'mandis' throughout the nation. The eNAM portal not only removes middlemen by directly connecting buyers and farmers but also provides a fair and transparent commodity pricing through a demand-supply based online auction system (Business Today, 2018).

Start-ups have moved a step further and are offering end-to-end digitalized supply chain that helps in reducing wastage in distribution. Apart from providing solutions, the start-ups are also providing trainings to farmers to effectively use these technologies. E-distribution, marketplace, and other supply chain-related start-ups accounted for more than 60% of the agri-tech start-ups during 2013–2017 (Agri-Tech in India, Nasscom, 2018). The companies have introduced solar-powered cold storage and energy storage solutions to provide efficient and reliable cold storage solutions. Rising number of agricultural technology start-ups are opening new avenues of private sector investment in agriculture. Fresh agricultural expenditure could have far-reaching economic and social repercussions on the Indian economy.

Moving forward, the government role in facilitating technology adoption among farmers will be crucial. Adoption of technology would result in higher yields and returns, in turn reducing the debt on farmers as well as the government. Likewise, the government need to create a framework where the benefits from the investments in food processing sector could reach to the bottom of the pyramid, i.e., farmer. Still, the effort is going on but yet to achieve the goal.

2.13   ENVIRONMENTAL IMPACT

However, the major improvements in the room for innovation do not only transfer improvements to the financial system, they will also add to the natural changes. The cutting-edge advances will help to reduce the impression of carbon by decreasing the use of fuel, squandering administration, greener working environments and thus prompting a greener biological system. The ICT component helps to efficiently control and exploit rare and non-inexhaustible properties. Innovation in distributed computing restricts carbon discharges by increasing mobility and adaptability. Vitality usage can be decreased from 201.8-terawatt hour (TWh) in 2010 to 139.8 TWh in 2020 due to higher availability of cloud server farms resulting in a 28% decrease in carbon impression from 2010 rates.

The major technological changes will not only bring changes to the economic system but will also contribute a lot to the changes in the environment. The innovations of the next decade would help to reduce the carbon footprint by reducing fuel consumption, waste management, greener workplaces and thereby contributing to a greener environment. The ICT sector helps to manage and make efficient use of scarce and non-renewable resources. Cloud computing technology enhances mobility and flexibility by minimizing carbon emissions.

Over the past few decades, healthy living has become the company's main concern. More focus has been placed on health-related matters. This has driven more people to work out, sleep well and use fewer items like vehicles and power strips, as well as other strategies to help the community. The initiative led individuals to take a closer look at the environment and examine their part in making the earth more sustainable for years to come. Digitization will help organizations take advantage of emerging technology and allow workers to access documents at any place and helps to make an ecologically healthy society because people do not use cars to go here and there to reduce emissions.

2.14   EMPOWERMENT OF WOMEN THROUGH DIGITALIZATION

Women's empowerment leads a nation to positive growth and development. Digital India promoting rural Indian women plan. Following are some of the measures taken by the Indian government to empower rural women under the Digital India program:

- Arogya Sakhi helps rural women for developing their personality in order to providing health care in the rural area. Mobile application that enables rural women entrepreneurs to deliver rural doorstep preventive healthcare. Women equipped with tablets and mobile healthcare devices such as glucometers, blood pressure checking machine are visiting homes and collecting village women information. Doctors at any location who could provide remote treatment to the patients can access all the information.
- Internet Saathi attempts to go deeper with rural women's internet activity in India. Ratan Tata has joined hands with Google and Intel to help large numbers of rural Indian women connect to the internet. The three-way Internet Saathi project will introduce 1000 specially built bicycles with connected devices to give villagers an entirely new web experience.
- W2E2 (India) Women for Empowerment and Entrepreneurship, in short W2E2 provides women in rural areas with digital resources, e-learning, and internet access. Women continue to use the internet for their own ventures in various areas, such as organic farming and rural health. Some are going to set up their own stalls and shops to provide online resources for the rural community, whereas others have taken up work in their own local areas as digital literacy educators. Conclusion India will have stronger with the implementation of the Digital India Project.

2.15   CHALLENGES

The first challenge is to set common performance metrics to assess to what degree ICT is being successfully assimilated in societies. Throughout most of the sector's growth, ICT stakeholders primarily focused on connectivity, building the networks that link a large part of the world today; metrics were built accordingly. In an access-related world of near-ubiquity, policymakers need a new way of looking at the ICT market. The second problem concerns the lack of instruments to assess the effect on communities and economies of mass adoption of connected emerging technologies and applications. Government could potentially be more ambitious in developing and investing in the ICT sector with practical, reliable methods to evaluate the benefits of digitization. The third challenge is for governments to implement new policy methods to speed up digitization and reap the benefits that follow it. In the past two decades, governments have laid down guidelines to improve access to telecom infrastructure. The present research work focused on the need to achieve a common understanding of the ways in which consumers, companies, and public bodies can promote adoption and enhance the use of digital applications.

Digital innovations are radically changing businesses, with the speed of technological change making the problem even worse. Organizations need a cohesive strategy that involves a worker's skills retrain program. Although prior technological developments (most notably the industrial revolution) took place over a fairly long period of time, the pace of digital change is such that enterprises need to move rapidly.

The task for governments is equally urgent. Potential unemployment and wage stagnation or even social instability necessitates immediate action to train the workers for a digital future. The challenge is even steeper when it comes to building new and emerging digital ecosystems such as flow-based lending, technology-enabled healthcare delivery, and digital platforms to provide new-age skills and match job seekers with work opportunities, since profitable business models for these digital themes have yet to be fully developed and rolled out at scale; also, the policy and regulatory environment for some of these areas is uncertain at this point. To realize this vision, government must work with the private sector and build a collaborative working model to prompt innovation and investment. It is a challenge to generate demand for mobile services in rural areas, which also results in insufficient investment by private-sector telecoms and internet service providers.

Farmers face the problem of getting access to timely and reliable information on essential agricultural inputs such as sowing crops, rainfall, and other weather conditions, while irrigating farm machinery, availability, and costs, how to supervise animal health, crop health and pesticide use, and adopting good agricultural practices in order to make informed decisions. Farmers in India face the challenge of limited access to agricultural markets. Most of the farmers can sell their products only in the nearby closest mandi, or wholesale market, and thus have very little bargaining power, resulting in poor income realization.

Unlocking opportunities will be a difficult task for government, large and small businesses, and individuals across the subcontinent, and the gains will be accompanied by some pain. Yet if India can carry on its digital growth trajectory and move faster, the benefits for millions of companies and hundreds of millions of people will be tangible.

The challenge for India will be to create affordable and effective retraining programs at scale. This may entail concerted efforts from policymakers, corporate leaders, educators, and individuals alike. Industry leaders and educators, with government facilitation and support, may need to consider developing a new national technology curriculum to teach the skills that will be required by emerging digital technologies.

2.16 CONCLUSION

Socio-economic standard of the people have increased due to the development of technology in agricultural as well as in non-agricultural sectors. Apart from, digital transformations can also offer access to education, health care and financial services. It is important to remember, however, that information communication technology alone could not contribute directly to the nation's overall growth. Overall developments can be accomplished through the support and enhancement of elements such as literacy, basic infrastructure services, general market climate, regulatory environment, etc. Overall the Digital Technology has played a vital role in cultural, social, and business development. By empowering entrepreneurs to come up with their emerging business ideas, this digital revolution has changed the Indian market and its exponential growth in jobs and opportunities in IT sectors. Digital technologies have provided an interactive platform that connects us globally in many sectors, services, and organizations, as well as in the lives of individuals. Digitization is emerging in such a way in which institutions are becoming digital are causing various effects on society, the economy, and academics as well. These drastically changes make the information presentation and distribution more open, rapid, and also easily access the global information. Furthermore, modifying material from analog to digital format decreases some of the costs of providing access to print sources included in digitization processes.

KEYWORDS

- **digital India**
- **digitalization**
- **digital technologies**
- **digital transformation**
- **electronic medical record**
- **robotic process automation**

REFERENCES

Agri-Tech in India, (2018). Nasscom.

Business Today, (2018). *Can eNAM flip Indian Farmers' Fate?*

Dac, (2019). *Home, Soil Health.*

DoT, (2019). *National Digital Communications Policy 2018.*

El-Darwiche, B., & Singh, M., (2013). *How to Reap the Economic Rewards of Digitization.* Retrieved from: http://www.forbes.com/sites/boozandcompany/2013/07/19/how-to-reap-theeconomic-rewards-of-digitization/ (accessed on 24 February 2021).

El-Darwiche, B., Singh, M., & Ganediwalla, S., (2012). *Global Perspective: Digitization and Prosperity.* Retrieved from: http://www.strategy-business.com/article-full-preview/00127?pg=0 (accessed on 24 February 2021).

Financial Express, (2017). *Broadband in India: Without the Right Speed, Term is a Misnomer; See How.*

Forbes India, (2018). *India Climbs Three Spots in IMD's 2018 World Digital Competitiveness Rankings.*

Gulati, M., (2016). Digital India: Challenges and opportunities. *International Journal of Management Information, 10*(4), 1–4.

Hindustan Times, (2017). Agricultural Output Rose Five-Fold in 60 Years But Farming Sector is in Distress.

Hindustan Times, (2018). *eMarketer Report, 337 Million Indians to Use Smart Phones in 2018.*

James, J., (2004). Reconstruing the digital divide from the perspective of a large, poor, developing country. *Journal of Information Technology, 19*, 172–177.

Kaul, M., & Mathur, P., (2017). Impact of digitalization on the Indian economy and requirement of financial literacy. *Proceedings of International Conference on Recent Innovations in Engineering and Technology*, 100–105.

Kaur, K., & Neena, (2014). Pattern of inter-state digital divide in India. *Economic Affairs, 59*(3), 379–388.

Khan, S., Khan, S., & Aftab, M., (2015). Digitization and its impact on economy. *International Journal of Digital Library Services, 5*(2), 138–149.

KPMG in India, (2017). *Online Education in India: 2021.*

KPMG, (2019). *KPMG India CEO Outlook 2018, Technology Disruption as More of an Opportunity.*

Microsoft, (2018). *Digital Transformation to Contribute US$154 Billion to India GDP by 2021.*

Ministry of Electronics and Information Technology, (2019). *Fact Sheet of IT & BPM Industry.*

Mistry, J. J., (2005). A conceptual framework for the role of government in bridging the digital divide. *Journal of Global Information Technology Management, 8*(3), 28–46.

Neeru, G., & Arora, K., (2015). Digital India: A roadmap for the development of rural India. *International Journal of Business Management, 2*(2), 2349–3402.

Nikam, K., Ganesh, A. C., & Tamizhchelvan, M., (2004). The changing face of India. Part I: Bridging the digital divide. *Library Review, 53*(4), 213–219.

Solow, R., (1987). *We'd Better Watch Out*, 36. New York Times.

The Economic Times, (2017). *Indian Healthcare Market to Hit $372 Billion by 2022.*

The Economic Times, (2017). *Smart Phones Help Identify 12,000 severely Malnourished Kids at Anganwadis.*

The Economic Times, (2018). *Government to Expand DigiGaon Project to 700 Villages This Year.*

The Economic Times, (2018). *Indian IT Industry is Making Convincing Strides as Their Clients Demand Digital Transformation.*

The Economic Times, (2018). *Internet Users in India Expected to Reach 500 Million by June: IAMAI.*

The Economic Times, (2018). *Is There Accessibility to Affordable and Quality Healthcare in India?*

The Hindu Business Line, (2018). *Government Doubles Digital India Allocation to Rs. 3,073 Crore; Telecom Sector Disappointed.*

The Indian Express, (2018). *How Wet is the Ground After Rain? For First Time, India Gets Soil Moisture.*

The Times of India, (2017). *Indians Spend 70% of Mobile Internet Time on Social Media, Entertainment.*

TRAI, (2019). *The Indian Telecom Services Performance Indicator July-September-2018.*

WE Forum, (2018). *More Than 55% of Indians Make a Living from Farming.* Here's how we can double their income.

World Economic Forum, (2019). *Networked Readiness Index.*

Your Story, (2018). *Agri-Tech-Enabling a New Green Revolution.*

CHAPTER 3

Virtual Connections: Friendship Relationships in the Cyber Age

ANANYA CHATTERJEE

Assistant Professor, Department of Sociology, Haldia Government College, Haldia, Purba Medinipur–721657, West Bengal, India

ABSTRACT

The basic objective of this research was to assess the impact of communication technologies on personal relationships, specifically friendship relationships. In-depth interviews of 17–24 years old boys and girls living in the Kolkata metropolitan area having at least one active social networking site profile were conducted. The interviews were analyzed by using phenomenological research methodology. In recent years function of the internet has changed considerably for adolescents. There are now various online tools available for communication. Among these, social networking sites (SNSs) have emerged as the most important platform for connecting people. The SNSs are changing the nature of social relationships in an unprecedented way. One such networking site, namely, Facebook, emerged as an important site of doing friendship because of its popularity among adolescents in India.

3.1 INTRODUCTION

We are now increasingly using the internet for fulfilling various needs of our lives. The most important aspect of the growth of Internet and communication technologies (ICTs) has been in the sphere of social relationships as virtual platforms are being used increasingly to develop and maintain such relationships (Haythornthwaite and Wellman, 2002).

Surveys conducted by McKenna, Green, and Gleason (2002) and Parks and Floyd (1996) indicate that the internet is now most frequently being used for communication purposes. Such communications serve dual purposes of the maintenance of offline and existing social ties as well as the development of new social relationships. The relations thereby developed are carried on into other settings (online as well as offline). It is not uncommon for people who have met online to organize meetings and other social gatherings in offline locations and settings. Thus, for the majority of people with access to Internet online platforms have become a new avenue to meet and socialize (Hampton and Wellman, 2002; Mesch and Levanon, 2003; Wellman and Gulia, 1998). Adolescents generally adapt to technical changes faster and quicker than adults and the aged. Lenhart, Madden, and Hitlin (2005) argued that the use of social networking sites (SNSs) in order to maintain the existing ties and to develop the new ones are of special interest to them. In this chapter, the researcher has attempted a nuanced understanding of the use and impact of information and communication technologies (ICTs) on the social relationships in general and friendship relationships of the adolescents, in particular. The chapter provides a critical insight to the degree of influence that SNSs exert on the development and maintenance of friendship relationships and how do these alter the quality of such relationships, especially among adolescents and young adults.

3.2   TECHNOLOGY AND EVERYDAY LIFE

Following Venkatesh and Vitalari (1985) technology can be defined as a system of tool-using behavior. Technology, in other words, is a tool that meets specific instrumental goals, technology has become an inseparable part of our daily life. We use different kinds of technology at our household as well as our workplace. According to Plowman et al. (2008), gadgets and equipment operated through the application of technology has become an intricate part of children's and adolescents' life. New media technologies have become an inseparable part of our life in this late-capitalist, post-industrial, and post-modern era. The survey conducted by Plowman et al. in 2008 in the United Kingdom revealed that children aged between 3 and 4 years of age are being introduced to various technologies in their households as those are one of the prime sites of technology-mediated interactions. Ninety-eight percent of children of those who took part in their survey in 2008 had access to mobile phones. Most of these children had access to laptops and leisure technologies such as television with interactive features, gaming consoles, cameras, and MP3 players. India remains the world's second-largest internet market after China. According to a recently published report, India's top eight metros have a maximum internet penetration of 65%. Of India's overall internet users, 433 million are above 12, while 71 million are in the age bracket of 5 to 11. The latter access the internet on devices owned by their parents and other family members. Only 15% of the users are above 40 (IAMAI-Nielson Survey, 2019).

Households are variously affected by technological innovations, e.g., in their time allocation pattern, leisure activity, and most importantly, the behavioral patterns and the nature of social interaction among its members are also heavily affected (Venkatesh and Vitalari, 1983).

The introduction and wide spread use of new information and communication technologies has altered the social structures in several ways. These major societal changes have affected the individuals as well as the families and social groups in such a manner that they have to underwent structural changes in order to adapt to this new technology mediated social order. This has led to many sociologists and social observers to argue that human action is now being increasingly mediated and governed by the presence and availability of specific devices (Church et al., 2010).

3.3 ADOLESCENCE AND INTERNET USE: INSTRUMENTAL AND EXPRESSIVE

Adolescence is the entry point to adulthood. It is marked by developmental changes in physical ability as well as social skills. In this stage of development, adolescents interact less frequently with their family members, especially the parents. Their friends and peers gain in importance and prominence. Friends provide each other with emotional support and guides them in many other aspects of life. They also serve as models of behavior and attitude (Giordano, 2003).

Still, parents continue to influence children's attitudes and behaviors in significant ways (Collins and Russell, 1991). In childhood, parents play a pivotal role in the lives of their wards. They are the vital and main source of social intercourse. But in adolescence their importance declines gradually. They come to represent only one aspect of adolescents' social life and peer groups and friendship relationships signify a major facet of their life (Giordano, 2003). The adolescents and emerging adults have to master various developmental tasks. Establishing close relationships with their friends and peers and nurturing intimate relationships with their romantic partners are two such major developmental tasks for the adolescents (Brown and Larson, 2009). These associations and contacts reflect adolescents' capability to communicate with their peers. Moreover, research has revealed that emerging adults are early adopters of information and communication technologies and they are enthusiastically involved in using the Internet (Kiesler, Zdaniuk, Lundmark, and Kraut, 2000). Their usage pattern shapes the ways in which the technology is remodeled, developed, and enmeshed into our daily lives (Lenhart, Madden, and Hitlin, 2005).

According to Brown and Larson (2009), friends and peers act as the most significant sources of emotional and social support. In this respect friends assume a far greater role and position than their respective families or parents. Subrahmanyam and Smahel suggested in their 2011 study that use of the internet along with communication technologies expand and reinforce the relationships and interaction patterns of adolescents with their friends and peers. Adolescents' frequent use of communication technology is marked by their tendency to interact with their peer groups as well as with strangers within same age (Smahel, 2003; Subrahmanyam and Greenfield, 2008). The data across various countries indicate that the most prominent use of Internet and communication technologies among adolescents are for social purposes whereby they maintain, develop, and nurture their social, friendship, and romantic (Subrahmanyam and Smahel, 2011). In some countries use of chatrooms are more prevalent while in some other region messengers or online networking sites or photo sharing applications have gained into prominence, the common thread is the use of ICTs primarily for social purposes.

Scholars like Kraut et al. (1999); Weiser (2001) have had classified the Internet usage patterns into three extensive categories: commercial, informational, and communicative. Going along with Petric and Zhao (2006); Tufekci (2008) adopted slightly different (though somewhat interconnected with previous categorizations) classifications and groupings: social and non-social uses or the expressive internet and the instrumental internet.[1]

---

[1] These two terms are adopted from Talcott Parsons' classification of pattern variables. These pattern variables provide a way of categorizing the types of choices and forms of orientation for individual social actors, both in contemporary society and historically.

According to Tufecki (2008), expressive Internet usages relate to the use of ICTs for social purposes; for online communications with friends and peers as well as strangers in order to develop and maintain diversified social relationships. As part of such usages, various platforms such as SNSs are used for self-presentation through publicly visible performances. This, in turn, leads to the creation of new types of social capital as well as the management of existing social capital. Petric (2006) argued that expressive Internet "should be recognized as a social ecology involving other people, values, norms, and social contexts." Use of the Internet for amassing information, seeking knowledge as well as for commercial activities such as banking and online transactions, admission to educational institutions, attending to academic conferences and online classes, job interviews are referred to as Instrumental Internet. Studies by Gross, Juvonen, and Gable (2002) and Lenhart, Raine, and Oliver (2001) show that adolescents primarily use the internet for social purposes. The social use of the internet provides an opportunity for adolescents to develop new relationships, exchange information-academic as well as non-academic. It also gives them an opportunity to be able to communicate after regular school hours and provide as well as receive social and emotional support to each other (Gross et al., 2002). A survey conducted by Wolak, Mitchell, and Finkelhor in 2003 in the United States of America revealed that 14% of adolescents have established close and proximate online relationships.

According to Morrison and Krugman (2001), "new media technologies can be regarded as being internal or external" (p. 142). These pattern variables provide a way of categorizing the types of choices and forms of orientation for individual social actors, both in contemporary society and historically. They also contend that the development of ICTs and SNSs are altering the new media technologies are changing the means, methods, and techniques through which we learn and develop various social skills. As Morrison and Krugman (2001) argue, the use of such technologies also enables "privatization of social activities previously conducted outside the home" (p. 136). The computer as well as game consoles and smart mobile phones can increase social interaction amongst individuals within the home. And in this situation of global pandemics, when we are being mostly confined to the four walls of our home, almost all of our social interactions are taking place over these virtual platforms. In his 2003 article, Fromme argued that contrary to our commonsensical beliefs and perceptions, electronic gaming boosts the existing peer relationships rather than leading to social isolation of adolescents.

This researcher also adopted the dichotomous categorization of Internet usage by Tufecki for the purpose of identifying the patterns of internet usages among the adolescents of the Kolkata metropolitan area (aged 17–23 years). The analysis of in-depth interviews conducted by this researcher revealed that the use of the internet among adolescents includes both instrumental as well expressive use. The most popular use of the internet is for keeping in touch with their friends, and the most popular platforms are Facebook, Instagram, and also various applications providing online chat and video calling facilities.

3.4   ADOLESCENT FRIENDSHIP AND SOCIAL NETWORKING SITES (SNSs)

It has been revealed and reiterated by a number of studies that in contemporary society the adolescents are increasingly using ICTs for inter-personal communications (Valkenburg and Soeters, 2001; Gross, 2004; Lenhart, Raine, and Oscar, 2001; Yuen and Lavin, 2004). The SNSs are the most significant tool for connecting and facilitating social interactions and communications on virtual platforms. These sites center on the profile, "which for users is a representation of their sel[ves] (and, often, of their own social networks) to others to peruse, with the intention of contacting or being contacted by others" (Gross, 2004). Boyd (2006) offers the following definition: "A social network site is a category of websites with profiles, semi-persistent public commentary on the profile, and a traversable publicly articulated social network displayed in relation to the profile" (p. 211). These SNSs are often referred to as the building blocks of today's internet (Jalalian, 2008, 2010). These virtual spaces give access to varied and diverse information available online. But the most unique aspect of these sites is that these spaces also serve as a platform to interact with people all around the world in the click of a mouse (Raskin, 2006). Though communication on these platforms are mediated but they provide an opportunity to interact and communicate with a much larger audience than would be possible in a face-to-face scenario.

These virtual spaces are shaping the personal relationships in such a way that it is altering the nature and ways of doing friendships (Boyd and Ellison, 2007). Mitra (1997) holds that the SNSs (such as Facebook and MySpace) give an opportunity to the users to develop and experience collective associations through discursive practices. These platforms also provide an opportunity to their users to overcome physical barriers and geographical distances. Among various SNSs, the sheer online omnipresence of Facebook is surprising. According to a report published in the Times of India in March 2016, Facebook had over 142 million users in India. Among such users, 133 million access the social media platform through their mobile phones. The same news article reports that about 69 million people in India use Facebook on a daily basis. India is the largest market for Facebook outside the USA. Since its inception in 2004, Facebook has become immensely popular. On this platform, heaps of social interactions take place every day. Facebook allows its registered users to create a profile page where they can upload or display their pictures and profile name. They can add people whom they know from previous offline interactions as well as strangers who are listed as their 'friends.' They can provide personal information regarding their age, sex, gender, marital status, religious affinity to favorite foods, drinks, movies, and hobbies. Apart from some basic information, the user can control who has access to all this information. They can write their views on any topic on their wall, which can be viewed and reacted upon and shared by the public in general or people who are listed as the friend of the concerned individual. One can also identify other individuals by 'tagging' them on photographs or posts uploaded by them. The newsfeed section notifies what the connections/ virtual friends of the concerned individual have been doing on the site. Individuals can upload pictures/ videos or write status reports and their friends can comment or react by using emojis. It has been observed that adolescents generally use their real names and pictures on Facebook. They also engage in a high level of self-disclosure on such virtual platforms and especially Facebook (Tufecki, 2008). According to Boyd et al., this is possible because of the high level of offline-online integration on such virtual networks.

One of the inclusion criteria in this research was that the participant must have at least one active social networking profile. Almost all the participants of the current research had an account on Facebook. Instagram was also a very popular networking sites where they frequently engage in online interactions. "Though I had a profile on Google plus, I rarely used it. Facebook is way better than any other SNS platform. But Instagram is also fun," reiterated one of the post-graduate students from the University of Kolkata. The discussions with participants make it clear that Facebook has acquired a very strong base of users on college and university campuses.

The relevance of Facebook for studying social relationships has gained importance due to several reasons. First, this domain presents unique opportunities to study human social behavior in an unobtrusive manner. The activities performed online serve as a treasury of rich, concrete, and observable data even when the actor is not there (Graham, Sandy, and Gosling, 2011; Webb, Campbell, Schwartz, Sechrest, and Grove, 1981). Secondly, Facebook and other SNSs are worth investigating because apart from providing an opportunity to reflect upon existing patterns of social behavior, it is also creating new patterns of social interactions by changing the very way in which individuals connect to each other. Some social observers tend to question the validity and reliability of virtual spaces as actual reflection of social reality. But in the post-industrial and late-capitalist society of the 21st-century majority of the people live in such a technologically enabled society that their online and offline worlds have become entangled with each other, and it is difficult to set them apart (Ellison, Steinfield, and Lampe, 2007). And Facebook being one of the most popular SNSs (Kreutz, 2009), it is logically the best place to start looking for the patterns and varieties of social processes associated with it. Thirdly, the rise of SNSs brings both new benefits and dangers to society, which warrants careful deliberation. Like every other social process, the use of SNSs have their fair share of concerns such as identity theft, cyberbullying, stalking, and breach of privacy) along with the benefits associated with it.

The analysis of data gathered through in-depth interviews of 34 adolescent participants reveals that the single most important reason for using Facebook and other such SNSs is to keep in touch with friends, especially after leaving school or college (Gross, 2004). Most of the female participants are wary of making friends with strangers through these platforms. This trend has also been confirmed by Wolak, Mitchell, and Finkelhor in their 2003 study. The participants in this research also informed that the misuse of this new communication technology also concerns them. In order to prevent online stalking, bullying, and other security and privacy issues, most of the female participants do not accept friend requests from an unknown person. "I don't even accept friend requests from friends of my friends. I don't feel safe because no one can guarantee how one would behave. If I accept a request from a friend of my friend and if that person does something which is not to my liking, the friendship between me and my friend will also get ruined. So, I don't take any chances," revealed a girl who has just passed her Plus Two exam and taken admission into a well-known Central Kolkata college. The male participants were more open to making friends with people whom they have never met offline. "If someone shares same interests I do send friend requests to them and also accept friend requests from persons with similar interests even if I have never known them or do not have any friends in common," informed an engineering student of 22 years of age. "I have a blog and I share what I publish in that blog on my Facebook page. And if any of my readers want to add me to their friend list in Facebook, I do generally accept their invites confessed a student from a management student, though I am aware that there are some fake profiles and people can misuse the information that we share. But being a male gives a little advantage admitted the aspiring management trainee. These adolescents spend a considerable amount of time on such virtual platforms ranging from half an hour to 4 hours daily. Sometimes they actively interact with their online connections; sometimes, they are there because they have got nothing else to do. The participants reported having between as low as 150 enlisted friends to 650 of them.

The majority of the participants in this research reported that the primary use of Facebook was to keep in touch with people whom they know from face-to-face interactions. That person can be a batchmate, an existing friend, a neighbor, a friend of a friend or some other associates. Barring a few exceptions, the participants hold that the primary viewers of their profile are people with whom they share offline relationships. Using these virtual platforms adolescents enhance and give a more permanent shape to otherwise ephemeral, transient acquaintances. The participants reiterated that they generally get online when their friends are also online so that they can communicate with them in real-time. This trend is also supported by earlier research. Lenhart et al., in their 2001 study, found that 83% of adolescents accessed the internet while their friends were also available online. Most of the male participants of studies conducted by Feieraend and Kingler (2001) and Fromme (2003) revealed playing online games with friends at least once a week. Lenhart, Madden, and Hitlin (2005) found that a third of all teens in their study use instant messaging on a daily basis.

One of the salient features of social interactions that take place over the internet consists predominately of on-screen text. Thus, any visual cues typical of offline, face-to-face interactions are obscured during online conversations. Kraut et al. (2002) have argued that using computers and virtual networks with friends, particularly online chatting, has increased social interactions rather than replacing more conventional means of communications such as talking on the phone (Walther, 1992).

3.5 SOCIAL NETWORKING AND FRIENDSHIP QUALITY

Given the pervasive social interaction associated with computer use, another theme that emerged through in-depth interviews with the participants is the issue of friendship quality. Engaging in online communication and computer games has been associated with positive friendship quality (Valkenburg and Peter, 2007), a larger social network (Zhao, 2006), more time with friends (Colwell, Grady, and Rhaiti, 1995), and decreases in loneliness (Shaw and Gant, 2002). Adolescents who communicated online with their existing friends reported enhancement of the quality of offline relationships as well (Valkenburg and Peter, 2007).

According to Knapp and Vangelisti (2000), intimate self-disclosure can be assumed to be an important predictor of the quality of close relationships. Online communication promotes adolescent' intimacy to existing friends. A number of studies have indicated that online communication furthers intimate self-disclosure (Joinson, 2001; Tidwell and Walther, 2002). According to Altman and Taylor (1973), both breadth (refers to the degree to which respondents experienced online communication to be more effective than offline communication) and depth (refers to the degree to which adolescents experienced online communication to be more effective than offline communication in self-disclosing intimate information) are important determinants of relationship maintenance (Knapp and Vangelisti, 2000). Breadth of communication serves an important function by providing interaction partners with an essential tool to uncover common topics and interests and, by so doing, presents opportunities for more intimate communication. Depth, in turn, is vital for the development and maintenance of intimate relationships (Altman and Taylor, 1973).

Analysis of interviews revealed that activities that foster personal disclosure and discussion (and thereby improves the friendship quality) are more valuable for adolescent girls' friendship relationships. Searching the internet with friends (in cybercafé or computer centers of college/school) or searching for information on similar topics on the Internet offer adolescents with issues for dialog. Similarly, online communications provide the opportunity for adolescents to discuss personal information, particularly for adolescent girls.

"There are many things which I cannot discuss face to face situation. Because there are always so many people around in college. And you don't want to reveal your innermost thoughts to everyone. But when I am chatting online with my bestie, there are only two of us. And we discuss a hell lot of things from boyfriend to parents to bitching about teachers. We keep chatting late at night almost every day," confided a girl who is currently pursuing her engineering degree. In fact, investigators have constantly found that online exchanges involve informal and impersonal deliberations, including boy/girlfriend-related issues, upcoming events, school work and gossip (Boneva, Quinn, Kraut, Kiesler, and Shklovski, 2006; Grinter and Palen, 2002; Gross et al., 2002; Schiano et al., 2001). The degree of disclosure of confidential information is related to the depth of social bonds. Findings from a range of studies indicate that females engage in greater disclosure of their innermost thoughts and feelings than males (Buhrmester, 1996). Gender differences are observed both in the topics that friends choose to discuss and in the style of the conversation itself.

"I am a bit emotional and sensitive. But in real-life situations, I have to hide these feelings, you know, since I am a boy. Most of the people don't understand me and they call me all sorts of names, you know what, if I betray my emotions in any situation. I feel so disgusted. But my best friend understands me. Yes, I do have a girlfriend. And sometimes, the three of us chat together online. I can be me while I am talking to them online. This is the story of a 3rd-year student in an undergraduate college.

But he is an exception. An analysis of in-depth interviews with adolescent boys reveals that the central focus of boys' chats typically consists of the shared online activities, such as features of a computer game, a computer programming, or websites. Orleans and Laney (2000) found that discussions among adolescent boys, in particular, focused largely on computer-based activities, such as the configuration of the computer, the contents of the game they were playing, new software and applications, smartphones, and their features and included numerous instances of joking around with one another. Shared activities are acknowledged as important for boosting intimacy among boys (e.g., Berndt, 1982; Maccoby, 1990; McNelles and Connolly, 1999) in case of offline relationships also. Mathur and Berndt (2006) found that as adolescent boys tend to be less anxious about their interpersonal relationships in comparison to girls (Berndt, 1982), they may not take part in conversations that would promote a deeper understanding of one's peers while using computers with friends.

Evidently, in today's world, young adults' friendship practices are enacted within their uses of SNSs that represents material change in social structure that are actively creating social realities through digital discursive practices (social action and interaction, Fairclough, 1993). These practices constrain, enable, and shape people's interaction and involve power relations (Foucault, 1981). The structure and function of SNS technology as affordances (opportunities for action provided by technology, Norman, 1988) to be taken up into friendship practices may constitute friendship in particular ways.

3.6   ONLINE FRIENDSHIP RELATIONSHIPS AND SOCIAL CAPITAL

The researcher here argues that the online friendship networks add to the social capital accumulated by the adolescents through face-to-face interactions and relationships. Social capital can loosely be defined as the resources accumulated through the relationships with people (Coleman, 1988). Social capital is a flexible term with an array of definitions in multiple fields (Adler and Kwon, 2002). Social capital is conceived of as both a cause and an effect of powerful and meaningful social relationships (Resnick, 2001; Williams, 2006). Bourdieu and Wacquant (1992) has defined social capital as "the sum total of the resources, actual or virtual, that is accumulated by an individual or a group by virtue of possessing a durable network of more or less institutionalized relationships of mutual acquaintance and recognition" (p. 14). According to Adler and Kwon (2002), social capital has been associated to a multiplicity of constructive social outcomes, such as better public health, lower crime rates, and more efficient financial markets. Social capital can be seen as a positive outcome of interactions between members in a social network (Helliwell and Putnam, 2004). From the standpoint of an individual social capital allows them to depend and draw on the resources of the members in the group to which they belong to. These resources can assume the forms of useful contact, information, personal relationships or access to other material resources (Paxton, 1999) as well as employment connections, which provide benefits to the individual (Granovetter, 1973). Additionally, researchers have found that different forms of social capital, including ties with friends and neighbors, are related to psychological well-being, which enhances self-esteem and satisfaction with life (Bargh and McKenna, 2004; Helliwell and Putnam, 2004).

Putnam (2000) has distinguished between bridging and bonding social capital. The former one is somewhat related to what network researchers describe as weak ties, i.e., the loose connections between individuals who provide valuable information or new point of view for one another but they do not share close emotional bonds (Granovetter, 1982). On the other hand, bonding social capital is found between individuals who have developed close, intimate, stable, durable, and emotionally meaningful relationships, such as family and close friends. The increasing use of Internet and SNSs has simultaneously been linked both to increases and decreases in social capital. Nie (2001), argued that increasing use of interferes with face-to-face communication with others, which might result in diminishing an individual's social capital. However, Nie's views have been strongly criticized (Bargh and McKenna, 2004). Apart from Nie, Wellman, Haase, Witte, and Hampton (2001), have also alleged that online interactions may strive to complement or restore in-person interactions, alleviating any loss from time spent online.

For the purpose of the present study, Internet-based relationships can be conceptualized as weak ties. These ties serve as the groundwork of bridging social capital. Since online relationships are supported by technologies and practices such as distribution lists, photo directories, and search capabilities (Resnick, 2001), it results in the development of new forms of social capital through the use of online networking sites. Bridging social capital is expanded by use of Facebook. By allowing its users to create and maintain a larger and dispersed network of relationships from which they can draw resources, if necessary, this online platform support loose social ties. This view is also supported by Donath and Boyd (2004); Resnick (2001); Wellman et al. (2001). Donath and Boyd (2004) hypothesized that SNSs could significantly enhance the weak ties one could form and maintain, because the technology is well-suited to maintaining such ties with ease without much investment of resources.

Adolescents in this study confirmed that they do often maintain a relationship with friends of their friends through Facebook. This results in the widening of their social network. At the same time, online activities with their offline friends fortify the ties that they already have established. Connecting with friends of friends cement the relationship with the mutual friend they are attached to. These adolescents also find the social network very useful while they are seeking admission-related or any specific course or job-related information. A Jadavpur University student pointed out to the importance of these ties while campaigning for any social cause or organizing a social movement like 'Hok Kalarob.' "One of my friends was being harassed by a very senior Professor at her college. She was scared to lodge any formal official complaint as she thought it would adversely affect her career. She posted the incident on her Facebook wall without naming anyone, and that post was shared by hundreds of students of this college as well as by the larger public. And after that the harassment stopped. Actually, that Professor was also on our friends' list and he could clearly notice that public opinion is against him. And afraid of being exposed, he stopped harassing this girl. That's the strength you have from Facebook." This incident reported to me by a student of 2nd year also justifies the claim by the researcher that online networks do add to the existing repertoire of social capital.

Another interesting fact is that, the composition and nature of social networks change over time as relationships are formed or abandoned. Some researchers have coined the term 'friend sicknesses to refer to the suffering caused by the loss of connection to old friends when a young person moves away to college (Paul and Brier, 2001) or from college to Universities for further study or to take up jobs after finishing their study. Significant changes in social networks may affect one's social capital, especially when an individual moves or is forced to move from the geographic location in which their network was formed and thereby losing access to those social resources.

3.7 CONCLUSION

Due to the emergence of a network society (Castells, 1996; Knorr-Cetina, 2001), individuals can find similar others across time and place. The distinctive composition of mediated communications enables self-disclosure, trust, and intimacy, which are central to the establishment of strong ties, especially among youth and adolescents (McKenna et al., 2002). The internet and the SNSs thus entails a new form of interaction on virtual platforms that gives a new philip to offline relationships (Wellman et al., 2001: p. 438) by filling up the communication gaps between face-to-face meetings. According to DiMaggio et al. (2001), "the internet is a way of increasing interaction with family members and closeness to friends" (p. 317). But the amount of time spent online can serve as an important predictor of relationship quality. Mesch (2006) found that "adolescents who have low internet usage had better relationships with parents and friends than was high internet use" (p. 122). Latour (2005), explored the social networking site, Facebook, in terms of what he referred to as sources of uncertainty about the social and Introna (2007) suggested the notion of disclosive ethics as that technology mediates (that is, transforms) the meaning of what it carries. The findings of this research indicate the ways in which Facebook and such SNSs has become an integral part of the life of adolescents. The social practices tied to their friendship relationships and the specific processes of sense-making are now increasingly being mediated by such virtual platforms. The increasing use of SNSs to conduct friendship and other intimate relationships limit as well as expand adolescents' friendship experiences. The increasing use of virtual platforms also leads to the creation of collapsed contexts where boundaries are hard to maintain, and there is an elision of virtual and real as well as public and private spheres.

KEYWORDS

- **internet and communication technologies**
- **offline communication**
- **social networking sites**
- **social structures**
- **technological innovations**
- **virtual platforms**

REFERENCES

Adler, P., & Seok-Woo, K., (2002). Social capital: Prospects for a new concept. *The Academy of Management Review, 27*(1), 17–40.

Altman, I., & Taylor, D., (1973). *Social Penetration: The Development of Interpersonal Relationships.* New York: Holt, Rinehart, and Winston.

Bargh, J. A., & McKenna, K. Y. A., (2004). The internet and social life. *Annual. Review of Psychology, 55,* 573–590. doi: 10.1146/annurev.psych.55.090902.141922.

Berndt, T. J., (1982). The features and effects of friendship in early adolescence. *Child Development, 53*, 1447–1460.

Boneva, B. S., Quinn, A., Kraut, R. E., Kiesler, S., & Shklovski, I., (2006). Teenage communication in the instant messaging era. In: Kraut, R., Brynin, M., & Kiesler, S., (eds.), *Computers, Phones, and the Internet: Domesticating Information Technology* (pp. 201–218). Oxford: Oxford University Press.

Bourdieu, P., & Wacquant, L. J. D., (1992). *An Invitation to Reflexive Sociology*. Chicago: The University of Chicago Press.

Boyd, D. M., & Ellison, N. B., (2007). Social network sites: Definition, history, and scholarship. *Journal of Computer-Mediated Communication, 13*, 210–230. doi: 10.1111/j. 1083-6101.2007.00393.x.

Boyd, D., (2006). Friends, Friendster, and myspace top 8: Writing community into being on social network sites. *First Monday, 11*(12).

Brown, B. B., & Larson, J., (2009). Peer relationships in adolescence. In: Richard, M. L., & Laurence, S., (eds.), *Handbook of Adolescent Psychology*. New Jersey: John Wiley & Sons.

Buhrmester, D., (1996). Need fulfillment, interpersonal competence, and the developmental contexts of early adolescent friendship. In: Bukowski, W. M., Newcomb, A. F., & Hartup, W. W., (eds.), *The Company They Keep: Friendship in Childhood and Adolescence* (pp. 158–185). New York: Cambridge University Press.

Castells, M., (1996). *The Rise of the Network Society: The Information Age: Economy, Society, and Culture* (Vol. I). Oxford: Blackwell Publishers.

Church, K., Weight, J., Berry, M., & MacDonald, H., (2010). At home with media technology. *Home Cultures, 7*(3), 263–286.

Coleman, J. S., (1988). Social capital in the creation of human capital. *The American Journal of Sociology, 94*, S95–S120.

Collins, W. A., & Russel, G., (1991). Mother-child and father-child relationships in adolescence: A developmental analysis. *Developmental Review, 11*, 99–136.

Colwell, J., Grady, C., & Rhaiti, S., (1995). Computer games, self-esteem and gratification of needs in adolescents. *Journal of Community and Applied Social Psychology, 5*, 195–206. doi: 10.1002/casp.2450050308.

Donath, J., & Boyd, D., (2004). Public displays of connection. *BT Technology Journal, 22*(4), 71.

Ellison, N. B., Steinfield, C., & Lampe, C., (2007). The benefits of Facebook "friends:" social capital and college students' use of online social network sites. *Journal of Computer-Mediated Communication, 12*, 1143–1168. doi: 10.1111/j.1083-6101.2007.00367.x.

Fromme, J., (2003). Computer games as a part of children's culture. *Game Studies, 3*(1).

Giordano, P., (2003). Relationships in adolescence. *Annual Review of Sociology, 29*, 257–281.

Graham, L. T., Sandy, C. J., & Gosling, S. D., (2011). Manifestations of individual differences in physical and virtual environments. In: Chamorro-Premuzic, T., Von, S. S., & Furnham, A., (eds.), *Handbook of Individual Differences* (pp. 773–800). Oxford: Wiley-Blackwell.

Granovetter, M., (1973). The strength of weak ties. *American Journal of Sociology, 78*(6), 1360–1380.

Granovetter, M., (1982). The strength of weak ties: A network theory revisited. In: Peter, V. M., & Lin, N., (eds.), *Social Structure and Network Analysis*. New York: Sage.

Grinter, R. E., & Palen, L., (2002). Instant messaging in teenage life. In: *Proceedings of ACM Conference on Computer-Supported Cooperative Work (CSCW)* (pp. 21–30). New Orleans.

Gross, E. F., (2004). Adolescent Internet use: What we expect, what teens report. *Journal of Applied Developmental Psychology, 24*, 633–649.

Gross, E. F., Juvonen, J., & Gable, S. L., (2002). Internet use and well-being in adolescence. *Journal of Social Issues, 58*, 75–90.

Hampton, K., & Wellman, B., (2003). Neighboring in Neville: How the Internet supports community and social capital in a wired suburb. *City and Community, 2*, 277–311. doi: 10.1046/j.1535-6841.2003.00057.x.

Haythornthwaite, C., & Wellman, H., (2002). The internet in everyday life: An introduction. In: Wellman, B., & Haythornthwaite, C., (eds.), *The Internet in Everyday Life*. Oxford: Blackwell Publishers.

Helliwell, J. F., & Putnam, R. D., (2004). The social context of well-being. *Philosophical Transactions of the Royal Society B: Biological Sciences, 359*(1449), 1435–1446. http://doi.org/10.1098/rstb.2004.1522.

IAMAI-Nielson, (2019). *Digital in India: 2019 Round 2 Report*.

Intorna, L. D., (2007). Maintaining the reversibility of folding: Making the ethics (politics) of information technology visible. *Ethics and Information Technology, 9*(1), 11–25.

Jalalian, M., Latiff, A. L., Syed, H. S. T., Hanachi, P., & Othman, M., (2008). Application of internet and information technology in recruitment of safe blood donors. *Journal of Applied Sciences, 8*(24), 4684–4688.

Jalalian, M., Latiff, A. L., Syed, H. S. T., Hanachi, P., & Othman, M., (2010). Development of a questionnaire for assessing factors predicting blood donation among university students: A pilot study. *Southeast Asian Journal of Tropical Medicine and Public Health, 41*(3), 660–666.

Joinson, A. N., (2001). Self-disclosure in computer-mediated communication: The role of self-awareness and visual anonymity. *European Journal of Social Psychology, 31*, 177–192.

Kiesler, S., Zdaniuk, B., Lundmark, V., & Kraut, R., (2000). Troubles with the internet: The dynamics of help at home. *Human-Computer Interaction Special Issue, 15*(4), 323–351.

Knapp, M. L., & Vangelisti, A. L., (2000). *Interpersonal Communication and Human Relationships* (4th edn.). Boston: Allyn & Bacon.

Knorr-Cetina, K., (2001). Theorizing sociability in post social environment. In: Ritzer, G., & Smart, B., (eds.), *Handbook of Social Theory* (pp. 520–537). London: Sage.

Kraut, R., Kiesler, S., Boneva, B., Cummings, J., Helgeson, V., & Crawford, A., (2002). Internet paradox revisited. *Journal of Social Issues, 58*, 49–74. doi: 10.1111/1540-4560.00248.

Kraut, R., Patterson, M., Lundmark, V., Kiesler, S., Mukhophadhyay, T., & Scherlis, W., (1998). Internet paradox: A social technology that reduces social involvement and psychological well-being. *American Psychologist, 53*, 1011–1031.

Kreutz, C., (2009). *The Next Billion-the Rise of Social Network Sites in Developing Countries*. Retrieved from: http://www.web2fordev.net/component/content/article/1-latest-news/69-social-networks (accessed on 24 February 2021).

Lampe, C., Ellison, N., & Steinfield, C., (2007). A familiar Face(book): Profile elements as signals in an online social network. *Proceedings of the SIGCHI Conference on Human Factors in Computing Systems* (pp. 435–444). New York: ACM Press.

Latour, B., (2005). *Reassembling the Social: An Introduction to Actor-Network-Theory*. Oxford: Oxford University Press.

Lenhart, A., Madden, M., & Hitlin, P., (2005). *Teens and Technology: You are Leading the Transition to a Fully Wired and Mobile Nation.* Retrieved from: www.immagic.com/ eLibrary/GENERAL/PEW (accessed on 24 February 2021).

Lenhart, A., Raine, L., & Oliver, L., (2001). *Teenage Life Online: The Rise of the Instant-Message Generation and the Internet's Impact on Friendships and Family Relationships.* Pew Internet and American Life Project [online serial]. Available at: https://www. pewresearch.org/internet/2001/06/21/teenage-life-online/ (accessed on 24 February 2021).

Maccoby, E. E., (1990). Gender and relationships. A developmental account. *The American Psychologist, 45*(4), 513–520.

Mathur, R., & Berndt, T. J., (2006). Relations of friends' activities to friendship quality. *The Journal of Early Adolescence, 26*, 365–388.

McKenna, K. Y. A., Green, A. S., & Gleason, M. E. J., (2002). Relationship formation on the internet: What's the big attraction? *Journal of Social Issues, 58*, 9–31. doi: 10.1111/1540-4560.00246.

McNelles, L. R., & Connolly, J. A., (1999). Intimacy between adolescent friends: Age and gender differences in intimate affect and intimate behaviors. *Journal of Research on Adolescence, 9*, 143–159.

Mesch, G. S., & Levanon, Y., (2003). Community networking and locally-based social ties in two suburban localities. *City and Community, 2*(4), 335–351.

Mesch, G. S., (2006). Family relations and the internet: Exploring a family boundaries approach. *Journal of Family Communication, 6*(2).

Mitra, A., (1997). Diasporic web sites: Ingroup and outgroup discourse *Critical Studies in Mass Communication, 14*(2).

Morrison, M., & Dean, M. K., (2001). A look at mass and computer-mediated technologies: Understanding the roles of television and computers in the home. *Journal of Broadcasting and Electronic Media, 45*(1), 135–161.

Nie, N. H., (2001). Sociability, interpersonal relations, and the Internet: Reconciling conflicting findings. *American Behavioral Scientist, 45*(3), 420–435.

Parks, M. R., & Floyd, K., (1996). Making friends in cyberspace. *Journal of Computer-Mediated Communication.* doi: 10.1111/j.1083-6101.1996.tb00176.x.

Paul, E. L., & Brier, S., (2001). Friend sickness in the transition to college: Precollege predictors and college adjustment correlates. *Journal of Counseling and Development, 79*, 77–89. doi: 10.1002/j.1556-6676.2001.tb01946.x.

Paxton, P., (1999). Is social capital declining in the united states? A multiple indicator assessment. *American Journal of Sociology, 105*(1), 88–127.

Petric, G., (2006). Conceptualizing and measuring the social uses of the internet: The case of personal websites. *The Information Society, 22*, 291–301.

Plowman, L., Joanna, M., & Christine, S., (2008). Just picking it up? Young children learning with technology at home. *Cambridge Journal of Education, 38*(3), 303–319.

Putnam, R. D., (2000). *Bowling Alone.* New York: Simon & Schuster.

Raskin, R., (2006). *Facebook Faces its Future* (pp. 56–58). Young consumers (Quarter 1).

Resnick, B., (2001). Testing a model of exercise behavior in older adults. *Research in Nursing and Health, 24*, 83–92. doi: 10.1002/nur.1011.

Shaw, L. H., & Gant, L. M., (2002). In defense of the internet: The relationship between internet communication and depression, loneliness, self-esteem, and perceived social support. *CyberPsychology and Behavior, 5*(2), 157–171.

Subrahmanyam, K., & Greenfield, P. M., (2008). Communicating online: Adolescent relationships and the media. *The Future of Children, 18*, 119–146. doi: 10.1353/foc.0.0006.

Subrahmanyam, K., & Smahel, D., (2011). *Adolescents' Digital Worlds*. New York, NY: Springer.

Subrahmanyam, K., Smahel, D., & Greenfield, P. M., (2006). Connecting developmental constructions to the Internet: Identity presentation and sexual exploration in online teen chat rooms. *Developmental Psychology, 42*, 395–406. doi: 10.1037/0012-1649.42.3.395.

Tidwell, L. C., & Walther, J. B., (2002). Computer-mediated communication effects on disclosure, impressions, and interpersonal evaluations: Getting to know one another a bit at a time. *Human Communication Research, 28*, 317–348. doi: 10.1111/j.1468-2958.2002.tb00811.x.

Tufekci, Z., (2008). Can you see me now? Audience and disclosure regulation in online social network sites. *Bulletin of Science, Technology and Society, 28*(1), 20–36.

Valkenburg, P. M., & Peter, J., (2007). Preadolescents' and adolescents' online communication and their closeness to friends. *Developmental Psychology, 43*(2).

Valkenburg, P. M., & Soeters, K. E., (2001). Children's positive and negative experiences with the Internet: An exploratory survey. *Communication Research, 28*(5), 652–675.

Venkatesh, A., & Vitalari, N., (1985). *Households and Technology: The Case of Home Computers-Some Conceptual and Theoretical Issues* (pp. 187–203). Marketing to the Changing Household.

Webb, E. J., Campbell, D. T., Schwartz, R. D., Sechrest, L., & Grove, J. B., (1981). *Nonreactive Measures in the Social Sciences*. Dallas, TX: Houghton Mifflin. (Unobtrusive Measures revised, updated, and retitled.)

Weiser, E. B., (2001). The functions of internet use and their social and psychological consequences. *CyberPsychology and Behavior, 4*, 723–743.

Wellman, B., & Gulia, M., (1998). Net surfers don't ride alone: Virtual communities as communities. In: Kollok, P., & Smith, M., (eds.), *Communities in Cyberspace*. London: Routledge.

Wellman, B., Haase, A. Q., Witte, J., & Hampton, K., (2001). Does the Internet increase, decrease, or supplement social capital? Social networks, participation, and community commitment. *American Behavioral Scientist, 45*(3), 436.

Williams, D., (2006). On and off the 'net: Scales for social capital in an online era. *Journal of Computer-Mediated Communication, 11*, 593–628. doi: 10.1111/j.1083-6101.2006.00029.x.

Wolak, J., Mitchell, K. J., & Finkelhor, D., (2003). Escaping or connecting? Characteristics of youth who form close online relationships. *Journal of Adolescence, 26*, 105–119.

Yuen, C. N., & Lavin, M. J., (2004). Internet dependence in the collegiate population: The role of shyness. *Cyber Psychological Behavior, 7*, 379–383. doi: 10.1089/cpb.2004.7.379.

Zhao, S., (2006). Do internet users have more social ties? A call for differentiated analyses of internet use. *Journal of Computer-Mediated Communication, 11*, 844–862. doi: 10.1111/j.1083-6101.2006.00038.x.

CHAPTER 4

Digital Self: Men and Women Motorcyclists 'Doing Gender' Through Social Networking Sites

SUKANYA PAL

PhD Research Scholar, Department of Sociology, Jadavpur University, West Bengal, India

ABSTRACT

In this digital world with the rise of social networking sites (SNS) in a rapid pace has also allowed for new opportunities for both men and women to examine personality and gender differences in online behavior. This chapter mainly incorporates the theory of 'doing gender' to understand the perception of 'passionate' male and female motorcyclists' pictures/videos that they usually upload in their timeline. This chapter mainly focuses on how the individuals perform gender via these digital sites. Since machine and masculine traits run too deep, women find it difficult to induce themselves into this male-dominated field. The first half of the analysis part would show how men in motorcycling are doing gender and the next half would depict how women in motorcycling are forced not to do gender at least while on a ride. Motorcyclists not performing the same are often ridiculed, emasculated, and are isolated.

4.1 INTRODUCTION

Without a doubt, it can be very well seen that billions of individuals bank on the social networking sites (SNS)[1] for many different purpose or also for leisure activities. In this digital age, individual are concerned about constructing their impression on a daily basis and perhaps somehow dependent on modern communication technologies. These technologies can include simple form as mobile phones to any form of virtual world of communications which is mainly computer-mediated communication (CMC)[2]. We could very well see the SNS are increasing at dramatic rates with significantly developing individuals to invest time and energy in those sites. It has become significantly a global alarming phenomenon and eventually a natural extension of an individual's life. Due to the widespread prevalence of SNS s as Facebook, Twitter, MySpace, Instagram, it has well integrated into the young population, and with ease, it has now become a way to develop social relationships and also maintaining relationships with various people in which the communication can easily enhanced. Research has also suggested the relatively easy access of Facebook has led the various individual to keep in touch with one another and also helps in maintaining the respective relationships otherwise not possible (Young, 2000). They duly report that investing time on these distant relationships (not on the basis of geographical location) was not feasible without Facebook. Online networking has increased significantly to the extent that it allows an individual to keep himself/herself updated by exchanging a great amount of information largely about them. It is highly inaccurate to say, those information are the real truth. The accessibility and the convenience of using the mobile or wireless devices have also allowed individual to keep updated on the status information of the Facebook friends with ease. Research also suggests that this actually promotes face-to-face socialization (Alpizar et al., 2012). The heightened ability to build process and maintain any social relationship has also affected the intensity of these established relationships through online. Hence self-presentation is largely important and also has significant implications in performing genders.

Motorcycle riders in contemporary society rely on motorcycles for their daily transportation for mundane activities from buying groceries to going to colleges/universities and/or to earn a living. There is an immense increase of motorcyclists on roads. This is mainly because the sense of freedom they achieve via riding a motorcycle is never less than flying to work when stuck in traffic for hours in a car or bus. Moreover, the motorcycle save a lot more time as well as is a cost-effective transportation. Apart from mere transportation, motorcycles are also used for recreational activities as well as professionally. There is an influx in such activities where individuals ride their motorcycles to distant places occasionally, and also they participate in many motorcycle-related sports professionally. There is distinctive culture found all over India, mainly in south metropolitans. Details regarding this distinctive motorcycling activity[3] can be found easily all-over SNSs. SNS is filled up with their blogs and videos, uploaded while they keep traveling or attending such sports. SNS helps them to maintain the network with other participates of such sports all over the country, even outside the country. Therefore, it is largely necessary for these participants of motorcycling sports to maintain a distinctive identity over SNS. Here the notion of digital marketing/strategies comes into place where it is important to maintain a particular image in front of the SNS users. But these specific images are never constructed without 'doing gender'[4]. It is easier to perform gender in SNS than in real life. Doing gender is important to maintain the social image that an individual craves for. Doing gender is so embedded in an individual's life that it itself forms a pattern without getting noticed. SNS is a virtual platform where it can be easily created. This study focuses on such notions of constructing gender by passionate[5] motorcyclists in the virtual world of SNS.

4.2   EXISTING LITERATURE ON DOING GENDER

In this study, the researcher would like to situate the framework of doing gender to understand the role of male and female motorcycle riders performing gender through SNS. To understand 'doing gender,' it is important to know what exactly the difference between sex and gender is. According to West and Zimmerman (1987), the notion of "gender is not a trait, a social role or as societal representation, but rather as an accomplishment." Or in other words, gender is always performed, it is mainly accomplished but not considered as a role, and this trait doesn't represent society. 'Doing gender' theorist conceive of gender as "an active, behaviorally based, and demonstrate accomplishment, a situational accountable feature of sexually categorized human being" (Frenstermaker, 1985: p. 190). The 'doing gender' largely legitimizes the social structure hence eventually validate the men and women dichotomy as natural. The notion of gender role is constructed largely by complex form social guided perpetual, micro-political and interactional activities. These activities are structured and well processed since birth and are embedded into any individual. In their article 'Doing Gender' (1987), West, and Zimmerman focused on the process of how individuals "do gender" as a "routine, methodical, and recurring accomplishment" (p. 126). Hence doing gender is a routine accomplishment with is largely embedded into mundane interaction.

Generally, gender is more than an individual has (that is femininity/masculinity). It is something that basically an individual does in each instances or situations because the situation constantly presents different approaches or opportunities for doing gender. The reason any individual do gender in different situations because of different societal norms related to prescribed gendered societal norms. These gendered behaviors or norms are learnt by series of patterned interactions through which individuals learn the appropriate expected masculine or feminine behaviors. According to West and Zimmerman (1987), individuals are held accountable, which is largely based on interactions since birth, for maintaining the expected behavioral norms largely through socialization that features men and women to be distinctively and naturally different. As for example *trying on*[7] process, when a girl child is discussing about a trip to a beach with her friends are imagining things that they would play beach volleyball wearing a bikini. At the same time, these girl children are encouraging themselves to experiment with what they perceive as women's ways of doing gender. It was as if they were looking into some mere future mirror but usually often with unease. This is largely a process of experimenting, anticipating, resisting, retreating what is referred to as *trying on* gender. According to Susan Williams (2002), "the trying-on process is related to, but distinct from, doing gender. Doing gender is an apt metaphor in general but fails to capture gendering as developmental and contextual" (p.30). So, in other words, doing gender is developed via the pattern of mannerism/ behaviorism that are tried on by an individual since birth or even before it.

Generally, gender theorist claims that gender largely evolves after birth itself. But evidences prove it that it starts before birth itself. As the gender reveal in western societies during pregnancies happens to be with color segregation that is, blue for identifying boys and pink for girls is very common. But on the contrary, we hardly talk about babies doing gender. Hence Williams (2003) claims, "doing gender implies action and outcome; actors accomplish doing gender" (p. 31). It can be easily stated that even if doing gender may begin at a very early stage soon after birth but a new born infant does not initiate the process. Hence though the development involves transitions and *trying on* gender includes the process of gendering but the tentativeness and experimentation helps in the ultimate process from a girl child to a woman. Need not say the factors of class and race and other contingencies shape gendered experiences. Similarly, masculinity like femininity is also shaped with series of patterned behavioral norms that are been entrusted to a boy by interaction since childhood in order to fulfil the expectations of the patriarchal culture.

The notion of manhood which is related to masculinities has now resulted in a form of alienation. Ignorance of emotions, needs, feelings results in men's alienation. This alienation results from the societal constructed social distance from women and other men. In the book *Masculinities* Connell (1995) states "It follows that adult masculinity, as an organization of character around sexual desire, must be a complex, in some ways precarious development construction it is not given a priori in nature of men as European culture generally assumed"(p.13). So the construction of masculinities is created to the process of one's socialization and the most significant in creating such construction is the societal norms and underpinnings. There is a huge imbalance in bodily efficacy between men and women, which is being carried from generation after generation through social practices, which is highly misguided to prioritize these differences. The small physical differences such as strength, size or reproductive functions is developed in such a way into relative physical advantage to men, which is also hugely multiplied by the technological access. Manhood or being an ideal man is definitely not the exhibition of the inner essence rather it is socially constructed. The definitions of ideal man are constantly changing. It does not occur to an individual's consciousness from the biological self rather it created through an individual's culture. Through culture, a man comes to understand what exactly is being a 'man' by othering the minorities, sexual minorities, and mainly women. Masculinities are basically based on the power relation that includes relation with children, young people, women, and less able-bodied men.

There are few core principals or components of 'doing gender.' They are firstly, doing gender is an activity which is *accomplished* instead of just role and status. Secondly, doing gender framework is the idea of gender *accountability*. Thirdly doing gender is *situational* or contextual. Finally, the last component of doing gender involves both structure and social practice of agency. With this framework of the theory 'doing gender' the next sub-head would show how men and women motorcyclists constructs their gender through SNS. It would also show how doing gender helps them to maintain the 'biker image' and of course the oomph factor in them.

4.2.1 IMPORTANCE OF DOING GENDER THROUGH SNS

The importance of doing gender in SNS is simply popularity. Without getting noticed or being followed, it is not possible to be a trendsetter. And without be a trendsetter, it is difficult to be followed by many individuals. So it goes vice-versa. It is important for these participants in such sport to maintain identity through SNS because the concept of '*seeding*' only happens when an individual has many followers in Facebook and Instagram. This method that has been identified by MacGabhann (2005) is called seeding, where cool and popular kids are given free clothing or beauty products to wear and promote them to their friends. Similarly, in motorcycling culture, it is seen that motorcycle companies conduct motorcycle shows or promotional rides. In this promotional ride prominent riders are invited to ride the particular motorcycle for few days to different parts of Kolkata. The sole reason for such an investment for a company is only to promote. The rider who promote the products, mainly new motorcycles or its accessories (helmets, riding jackets and pants, riding boots) has many followers in SNS. That is the first criterion a company would notice before asking that motorcyclists to promote their product.

As of example: Raneet (26, HR) a prominent RE rider in Kolkata, states "*I was called for the promotional ride of RE Café Racer, when it was just launched in Kolkata. They even gave me the motorcycle for almost a week to ride.*"

Boral (47, Business) "*we got the sponsor from TVS Apache 200, where they gave us four brand new motorcycles (which was launched in India but did not hit the Kolkata TVS showroom then), apparels, and gears just to ride till Changser Khangri (Ladakh) to make a new Guinness Book of World Record.*"

In motorcycle shows, they invite renowned motorcyclists and other newbies for a test ride of new motorcycles that are newly launched. Initially, they start with inviting prominent motorcyclists to launch events, which are held at five- or seven-star restaurants or party halls, for example, ITC Sonar, JW Marriott, etc. Not to mention these shows and launch events or parties does not go un-uploaded in SNSs. Such practice will eventually lead the other motorcyclists (SNS followers) and might influence them to buy the product. This is a tactic used to attract more consumers as much as humanly possible. Gradually the motorcyclists will emulate their more popular peers through their series of posts and YouTube videos.

Therefore, when such dominance of a brand is so prominent in a person, it sends a message to all other newbies after MacGabhann (2005) states, "possess, consume, spend, own." He also states, "Youth has been re-branded to make it profitable, and society has adopted a value system that relates individual self-worth directly to material possessions" (p.135). So it is highly important to do gender while posting pictures as without portraying certain dominant traits an individual with never has the desired amount of followers. And without followers, the concept of seeding won't work. Hence companies only look for motorcyclists who has a huge amount of followers. A motorcyclist who portrays feminine traits is unacceptable as a hard-core tough rider. So men motorcyclist has to portray masculine dominant traits to be noticed by the other SNS users.

4.3   OBJECTIVES

In this empirical study, the researcher would observe whether the male and female motorcycle riders are performing gender through these sites. Secondly, it would also explore if they perform gender, then how they are 'doing' their gender through SNS. Lastly, the researcher would like to find out how performing gender are helping these above SNS users to gain more popularity among their network builders.

4.4   METHOD

This empirical study is largely based on qualitative research and the author also followed the analysis part of the same method. Here in this study, it is very important to mention that the sample comes from a sector of people who rides motorcycle not only for mere transportation but also out of passion for motorcycles. Passion for motorcycles, the researcher would define that individuals going for motorcycle tours or trips to different places or professionally participate in many motor games. These respondents all come from a particular class (middle and upper) but are not from the working or lower class. As to participate in this category of sports, motorcycle riders riding motorcycle out of passion, going for trip on a motorcycle or participating in moto-rallies professionally requires a huge amount of monetary investment. It is evident that all the motorcyclists in this research use SNSs. They access their profile mainly by their costly smartphones and laptops.

The sample size of the study is 30. Out of 30, 20 of them are male respondents while 10 were female respondents. Initially, the aim was of collecting equal numbers of both male and female respondents riding motorcycles and vivid SNS users. But surprisingly hardly women motorcy- clists in Kolkata were found, therefore with the help of purposive snowball sampling, only 10 respondents was found, and it was a quite difficult task too. 'Purposive' because the first three of them were known to the author and others were the snow all effect, whereas for male respondents, it was easily found without any difficulties. Initially, since the study is on SNSs, they were chosen by viewing their profile in Facebook and Instagram after getting their links via known respondents. All of the respondents have accounts in both the networking sites. Out of them, 7 men respondents have their own YouTube channels 3 men are bloggers. Out of ten female respondents, only 2 of them are bloggers and none had their own YouTube channels. The age group that the male respondents belong to was 25 years to 45 years, while for female respondents, it was 25 years to 35 years of age. They were observed keenly for few months in those networking sites then the author texted them for their phone numbers. So they would be contacted over the phone to schedule the in-depth interview. Definitely, they were clearly explained about the interview and its objectives. It was also added that their interview would be recorded with the help of a phone recorder, but for anonymity, their photographs would not be used, and would definitely assign a pseudonym to each of them. The researcher went for the interview with a semi-structured interview schedule. After commencing the interview, the data/recording was transcribed into notes. After reading these notes, the researcher tried to analyze it quantitatively, the data that was collected. Also, the notion of thematic approach according to Gibbs (2007) was followed and then coded.

4.5 FINDINGS

Ann Oakley (1972) had given a proper differentiation between the biologically given sex which is not unambiguous and the perception of gender constituted through culture. Though it has correlated with sex but our society dramatically distinguishes sex hierarchically. Nevertheless, the power relation generates such gender gap, which is also carried forward to motorcycling. Eventually, because of the conventional, already established relation between machine and masculinities, the gender divide runs too deep and are structurally prominent. Ideals of masculinities are mainly constructed through specific social situations. Through interactions motorcyclists demonstrate the know-how which establishes a group identity which is intensely connected to motorcycling, which is predominantly a masculine culture. Group identity and masculinities connects largely in motorcycling as still men dominate technical know-how. This also helps men to group closer to motorcycles.

As Wacjman (1991) also states that men dominate this technological field in times in-memorial. She also states, "men had to be visible in their physicality if patriarchal gender relations were to be seen clearly 'working' both at work and in the domestic space" (p.37). Since motorcycle represents heavy machines and machines are predominantly masculine, it proves the gender difference in the sample where 20 of them were men and only 10 were female. This difference also states that the motorcycling is mainly a male-dominated area. Even the same can also be found in abundance in SNS. In Facebook, Instagram male dominance can be easily found in this field. One would hardly find a woman on Facebook who is a vivid rider and post pictures now and them with her motorcycle and about her trips. There is a huge gender divide which can be easily found in any SNSs. But for those 10 women motorcyclists, it is important to know how women motorcyclists negotiate the gender order and also eventually it forms a pattern in their lives. These women motorcyclists do post pictures and upload status in their SNS account, which at times results in downplay of the femininity. Unlike women, men motorcyclists do perform gender via these networking sites.

4.5.1 MEN MOTORCYCLISTS

The first core belief that doing gender theorist held is that doing gender is an activity which is largely accomplished instead of just a role or status. According to many sociologists, gender is not based on biological differences, but it is socially and culturally constructed. Doing gender theorists claim that the mundane behavior that we perform is never biological rather is largely constructed through the series of pattern of interactions that an individual encounter on a daily basis. Since an individual do not move out on the streets exposing their genitalia therefore the judgement is not based on whether someone is male or female-only on genitalia alone. Instead, it is merely based on the appearances (clothing, make-up, hairdo, shoes, etc.), and/or through their behavior/mannerism such as being feminine/masculine. These above traits are mainly learned from socialization (Connell, 1995). Individuals are socialized in various distinctive ways as per the norms of the respective society an individual is brought up. As for example, a girl child is always asked to sit with closed legs while a boy is exempted from anything like that (West and Zimmerman, 1987). Eventually, this forms a pattern, and women continue to perform that life-long. Many respondents reports that they 'do gender' without giving much of a thought or even realizing it. After noticing certain activities or *distinctive attitudes* even just in posing, following their networking sites that they have uploaded (pictures wearing riding jackets, pants, and helmet while standing with legs wide apart or what is known as manspreading), the researcher asked showing them, why they engage in such performance that is standing with legs wide apart. Many of the respondents causally say they do it because every other motorcyclist does the same.

> Rupam (30, Doctor) *"I post pictures standing legs wide apart because everyone does the same."*
> Biplob (43, Senior Manager) *"That is how it needs to be done."*
> Rahul (32, Painter) *"Don't you think it looks cool and that is how it's supposed to be. It just happens, I never really thought about it."*

As the specific features comes from the socialization itself individuals usually does this without thinking or knowing why.' Many gender theorists would condemn such practices as it is a representative of a misogynistic patriarchy that is, a man takes up as much space as possible especially in public places in order to assert his authority which largely undermines a women's right to space. These specific practices are so embedded since childhood it becomes difficult for them to distinguish between the meanings of their behaviors. This also portrays their authoritative behaviors that generally a man does, which is also a part of doing gender for a man. There is another explanation for this specific situation is making one portray being masculine in Facebook or Instagram, or in YouTube videos. This practice is not only limited in motorcycling but in also other field too. This practice largely is legitimized as 'inherently gendered.' It is important for a rider to portray his masculine traits than the less abled motorcyclists just to be the 'one' in SNS. Even if a rider is not manly enough in the physical world, but if that individual takes up certain measures such as manspreading while clicking a photograph then he would be considered macho and masculine in SNS.

Another way of accomplishing gender in motorcycling is *using/riding of heavy motorcycles or superbikes* and posing with them in front of the camera, which eventually meant for the virtual world. It is largely seen in the SNS that men usually tend to buy heavier motorcycle if not superbikes, which costs a fortune. Royal Enfield (RE) motorcycles are quite common among the respondents. Out of 20, 14 ride RE[8] motorcycles. Five of them are quite famous among their networks with more than 5k friends on Facebook and with 12.1 k followers on Instagram, while 6 of them ride Superbikes[9] with 5k friends in Facebook and 15.1k followers in Instagram. Motorcyclists with such huge fan followers are silently competing with each other socially via the SNS or social media. To create a strong network, it is definitely important to portray the masculinity over the weaker sex or less-abled riders. Choosing a heavy motorcycle is definitely significant to a motorcyclist as it is largely seen that by riding a heavy motorcycle, an individual emasculate the less heavy motorcycles in terms of the rider's strength and capabilities. By riding a heavy motorcycle or costly motorcycle, a rider portrays masculinities which create hegemony over the other riders using lesser-abled motorcycles.

> - Sayak (32, Business) *"obviously metals bikes are obviously superior if you consider the durability. I am out and out an Enfield person."*
> - Puskar (31, Service) *"there is somewhere a little bit of macho feeling. Because there comes a feeling since I am riding a heavy bike and managing it quite well, compared to the other bike which is not that heavy so my bike is superior."*
> - Srikant (40, teacher) *"I would always go for Enfield, it has a different status and respect."*

Differentiation in mentalities and behaviors are found in people where they engage themselves into virtual fight on heavy and less heavy motorcycles and are clearly seen in the SNS. They even reported that they have blocked the users who engaged with them in an argument about the metal, heavy bikes (RE) with the non-metal comparatively less heavy. This is mainly because an individual who rides a heavy or metal motorcycles tend to be stronger and more masculine than the other non-metal riders. This notion is well understood if their timeline in SNS are followed carefully. Metal/heavy motorcycle owners keep on sharing news or links which will help them prove that metal motorcycles are better than others and vice versa. In revenge of that the non-metal riders mainly uploaded the adverse news of breakdown in sarcasm, of RE Himalayan[10] as there were severe mechanical and electrical faults that the RE owner suffered. In all over the country, lots of RE Himalayan were called off from the showroom itself, to repair that mechanical fault. Whereas, motorcyclists riding a superbike is always considered to be more superior and are hierarchically above the other riders. To buy and maintain a superbike is worth a fortune. People riding superbikes have followers more than RE riders. Three of my respondents rides a super-bike and also own a YouTube channel.

> ➢ Sathis (27, Lawyer) *"Moreover if (superbike owners) they own YouTube channel, riders follow them like crazy."*
> ➢ Rupam (30, Doctors) *"superbike owner are treated as the VVIP person when they attend any motorcycle gatherings."*

Posing with a superbike is even considered to be more fashionable and also 'macho.' Lots of riders only attend motorcycle gathering just to click a picture with the motorcycle as stated by Anbee, a superbike owner. Even in the timeline of Anbee's Facebook and Instagram, it can be easily verified as those individuals has tagged Anbee in bike courtesy. When those individuals' profile are opened, it can be very well found that they may have never ridden a superbike or not even a RE. Hence it can be very well derived that men motorcyclists 'do gender' by clicking pictures with those socially constructed macho motorcycles so that they would secure more *likes* in their Facebook and Instagram accounts. It is also found that superbike owner have a huge amount of virtual followers, which the RE owner does not have. The networking that they create is unquestionable and other riders look at them with awe. Here according to Wajcman (1991), as machines are masculine and technical know-how is largely taken for granted; therefore, men clicking pictures with either heavy machines or costly machines portray the masculine traits which are largely restricted for women. Out of 10 women, none of the women rides a superbike proving the above statement that 'machines are masculine,' true. And to add only one of them ride RE Himalayan and another woman ride a

RE classic[11]. Other eight respondents ride Bajaj Avenger[12] or other brands which are non-metal fewer heavy motorcycles.

Lastly another possible that they 'do gender' is by their distinctive *tattoos* that they usually portray. Being noticed like any other field is quite common and also an important aspect in the motorcycling as well as in virtual media. Showing their tattoos is one more way to be more popular or being noticed, which make them unique. Tattoos are also one of the easiest ways to portray masculinity. Motorcyclists do gender by tattooing hard core 'macho' images. Doing tattoos are itself painful, which also makes them manly as they undergo such pain. Tattoos are usually made to identity a community and to mark their members and were also somewhat known as anti-social (noting the tattooed criminal population). It was also considered to be a resistance towards the stereotypical order that society has. But in contemporary societies, tattoos are an emerging trend and also are making a difference towards the stereotypical thought. Grumet (1983) examines tattooed men and claims that they usually go for tattoos generally to ease their sense of inadequacy and also isolation. But his significant observation was the stereotypical masculine attitude of strength (physical), hyper-sexuality, and of course aggressiveness. His research also signifies that the addiction of tattooing are equated with a man's need to make himself complete. As for example Anbee, a superbike rider's SNS profile almost got increased by 1k followers soon after he made video of tattooing at the tattoo parlor with the concept of *Iron Man*[13]. He states:

- ➤ Anbee (32, teacher) *"I always wanted to do a tattoo, but never thought will get so many. I feel it makes me more complete."*
- ➤ Subrata (37, Service) *"I love to do tattoos. My tattoos are my important features of my identity."*
- ➤ Rohit (37, Business) *"don't you think tattoos look cool with my motorcycle? I also feel more powerful"* showing me the Goddess Shiva[14] tattoo holding the chillum, the smoking pot of marijuana.
- ➤ When asked what is power, he meant by the tattoos, he answered, *"powerful to be man is important in life otherwise it is difficult to sustain in the society."*

Powerful here can be analyzed in two distinctive ways one having Goddess Shiva (a symbol of power) as a tattoo or/and he meant more masculine. To add he also has the same tattoo (Shiva holding the smoking pot) painted on his motorcycle. Rohit is a RE rider and a vivid SNS user with many followers. Out of 20 male respondents, 12 of them have tattoos which are quite visible while clicking a picture or riding a motorcycle. Doing gender also involves attracting the opposite gender by their masculinity which sometimes is hegemonic too. Galbarczyk and Ziomkiewicz's (2017) study also states that women are likely to find men with tattoos to be more macho and masculine. Tattooed men are also aggressive and dominant in nature, and this is largely associated with good health and elevated levels of testosterone. The amount of pain that an individual usually undergoes during the process is a sign of a healthy heart and a strong mind. So tattoo is also an important part of doing gender and they portray them in the digital world to get more followers in YouTube, Facebook, and Instagram.

The second principle of doing gender framework is the idea of gender accountability. In this framework, an individual is accountable for their gender accomplishment at both structural level and through social practice or agency. They are very much accountable to the brotherhood[15] or to motorcycle fraternity for performing masculinity. So whatever the riders uploads in their SNSs, they have to answer if anything goes wrong or wrongly posted to the fraternity or largely called brotherhood. Riders having a great number of followers in their SNS and if they do not go for rides have to even answer to the criticism of the followers or the brotherhood. They often get into fights to prove that they are the best one out of the whole.

> ➢ Pritam (31, Business) *"going to a grocery or to the market riding a motorcycle, is definitely not a rider even if he rides since 20 years."* Pritam commented this on a senior rider's post where the senior rider tries to prove he is a better rider as he is riding for the past two decades.

Another example is of Veer 28, who is a bisexual and wear shots with complete waxed legs and chest and upload pictures with fancy goggles in SNS is also criticized and laughed at by the other members of his motorcycling group.

In sarcasm, Subrata (37 Service) comment in the Facebook post with two laughing smiley *"Bhai I am having a boner."*

Another example is of Rana 25, who is straight but might have some feminine traits. He uploads pictures holding fairy lights close to his face giving a smile unlike a man. Sarcastically,

> ➤ Kaustab (27, Content Writer) comments *"are you sure of your 'P' (penis), are you thinking of joining the 'T' (transgender) team."*

Here Rana and Veer are often emasculated or termed effeminate by the so-called able-bodied riders. There are series of expectations from motorcyclists to be masculine and manly. If they resist being one, they are confronted with criticisms, sarcasm, and jokes which finally make them more isolated and depressed. These expectations are largely presented in the motorcycle fraternity through the agencies of re-socialization, which demands the men motorcyclists to be real motorcyclists and portray the traits of masculinity often which creates hegemony over the other riders. These agencies of re-socialization are referred to as brotherhood or motorcycling fraternity that also includes motorcycling clubs. One more agency is media. Media keep posting advertisements like '*boys rides toys and men rides Enfield*' or '*this children day go and purchase toys for kids or wait for next day and purchase the legend Jawa*[16].' By such advertisement it instigates the riders in buying these machines to be the 'real motorcyclists' as expected by the brotherhood. According to West and Zimmerman (1987), individuals become accountable for engaging in these above expectations for being masculine through social practices in which they learn through interaction and consequences of doing gender in appropriate and inappropriate ways.

Another core principle is that doing gender framework is situational or contextual. It is clear from the above derivation that performing masculinity is important in motorcycling, if not in real life but at least in SNSs. Riders need to portray being strong, aggressive, risk taking attitude in front of the camera. Every motorcyclist is constantly rating himself and is obsessed with restless competition of manhood. Respondents tend to maintain a 'macho' front cover of everything that they do.

> ➤ Deep (46, Advocate) *"people ride to Ladakh nowadays and it so overrated. It is like you can't be a rider if you haven't visited Ladakh."*
> ➤ Anbee (32, teacher) *"Ladakh has to be any rider's 1ˢᵗ choice of place to ride, then only brotherhood consider them as a rider."*
> ➤ Srikant da (40, teacher) *"I know people who went to Ladakh but could not complete the whole ride due to some bad road terrain and fell many times. But he took his bike on a camper (jeep with a luggage carrier) just to click photos with the bike at the high mountain passes (laughs)."*

From the above narration, it can be observed that those riders who cannot complete the motorcycling trip for whatever reasons, but only to upload a picture in SNSs they had to click a picture with the bike at the passes just to show people that they have really done it. As failure is something a man is largely scared of as it might term them as non-masculine. These ideologies start from the birth itself, and media has easily constructed such notions from generations through movies and advertisements. Statements like 'boys don't cry' or '*mardh banno*' (be a man) has affected men in such a way that they are scared to fail. In order to win, they might take some unjust measures too. So it is clear that what they would wear, where they would go, with whom they tend to accompany everything contains a gender codded language. Even what beer they would drink also strictly contains codded languages which are socially constructed but are well maintained by every other individual.

➢ Kaustab (27, Content Writer) "*I would never wear a pink shirt or a shirt with frills (laughing). Even I don't have one. Maximum t-shirts that I have are black. I hardly wear any girly colors.*"

➢ Rahul (32, Painter) "*I would prefer drinking a strong beer with my friends not a breezer that's so sissy.*"

But these performances vary from place to place. They would never follow the same routine nor won't perform the same while they are in a family holiday. They would post pictures with their family too but not the same way they would do while they are out with their friends.

➢ Rahul (32, Painter) "*I would definitely not drink like a fish when I am with my family.*"

➢ Puskar (31, Service) "*Honestly speaking my mannerism would be different in front of my wife and children and with my biker friends.*"

So doing gender is also largely situational to the respondents where they are largely accountable for their performance. What they post to their timeline is important because it draws attention eventually increases in number of followers.

Thus machines, here motorcycle and performing masculinities goes hand in hand, it also creates isolation for few less abled bodied motorcyclists or who are not that much active SNS users. Men always expected to show a certain degree of masculine strength in times of despair. Motorcyclists not being able to perform or portray in SNSs the same are often ridiculed or emasculated.

4.5.2 *WOMEN MOTORCYCLISTS*

Women here in motorcycling are rejecting the traditionally prescribed roles of being weak, expressive, and emotionally fragile. Women, unlike the men motorcyclists does not 'do gender' at least in motorcycling. Or at least when they upload pictures of them in SNSs with motorcycles. They are basically downplaying the femininity, unlike men does. Or they try hard not to be feminine in their attitudes, at least when they ride. It does not mean they restrict themselves from wearing kajal or a lipstick on a ride, but all of them do not engage in it. While men are trying to be hegemonic in their attitudes but women are not engaging in emphasized femininity[17]. This is simply because women are not easily accepted in the field of motorcycling. Women motorcyclists have to prove their worth to get selected in any kind of trips or to secure a membership in motorcycling clubs which men did never have to face even at initially days of his motorcycling. As for example:

> ➤ Aaheli (31, teacher) *"initially in the year 2008 I wanted to ride with a group from my locality but they never selected me because they were not confident in taking me. But the next year 2009 I got selected for a Ladakh motorcycling expedition with YHAI, New Delhi. After completing my trip when I came back to Kolkata, I was in the newspapers. That group from my locality saw the newspaper called me and checked my Orkut (only SNS available) and asked me to come down for that year trip to Visakhapatnam."*
> ➤ Raima (24, Homemaker) is founder of one and only lady biker club in Kolkata states *"Initially I really didn't even think about forming a group with only female riders. It was about 10 years back when women are not easily accepted in motorcycling groups, rather hardly accepted. I went to many, but was not encouraged. There was only one lady rider group at Pune which was hardly accessible. Thus I finally formed Bengal Lady Biker, my own group. We are few members and are very compatible."*
> ➤ Mouha (29, Business) *"initially I was never accepted in any motorcycling groups that is, 5–6 years ago. I requested them, once they have allowed me for a very short ride, but they limited my movement even after reaching the spot. Finally, Bengal Lady Biker group of Raima came to my rescue."*

> ➤ Soma (25, Student) *"I looked for a motorcycling club after I got permission from my home to ride but sadly, I found none who would easily accept me. They want me to prove that I can ride. I doubt whether a boy had to prove when he wanted to be a member of that club."*

They have to be 'one of the boys' or 'social men' (Kavande, 1999) to be accepted in such field, like wearing complete black skull prints, lifting up heavy motorcycles after a fall or carry own heavy saddlebags and other luggage while checking into a hotel like a muscular man. It becomes quite difficult for them sometimes, but that is how girls negotiate the gender order in order to be at par with men. They perform such activities willingly and sometimes unwilling too. They portray what Connell (1995) calls masculine sexual character traits as being aggressive, risk taking, fighting over silly tussles. It is also equally important for the women motorcyclists to upload pictures and have a quite good fan base otherwise it might be difficult for their acceptance in the brotherhood. Since women are less in numbers in this field therefore women who ride and post easily gets noticed. Women who ride solo have a huge number of followers and are respected similarly as men motorcyclists. But they have to prove their worth, unlike men has to. However, even if women are at par with the men riders but still they faces humiliation and taunting related with makeup and tidiness and directions sense.

> ➤ Biyas (31, Service) states *"I can't deny of them loving me as I am. But I hear at times they even joke about me, but that's not harmful."*
> ➤ Nabanita (30, Yoga Instructor) *"it's true that they respect me as a woman but never misses a chance of mocking me something which is quite humiliating; but all doesn't do the same."*
> ➤ Himadri (29, teacher) *"When I was riding with a Delhi motorcycling group though they never have given me different facilities because of my gender, that's true but they use to joke, saying I should put Lakme stickers in my bike instead of other different stickers of my ride."*

Still, women do not take on a pre-determined set of behavior rules in motorcycling rather they construct and reconstruct the notions of gender roles; they are basically a part of the construction process. Even if downplay femininity they are taunted for several reason of their femininity.

Machines do not go well with femininity, especially motorcycling. But women who rides RE are breaking the stereotype where scooty is consider to be the feminine version of machines. Even the term scooter is considered as scooty in order to be feminine. So it is important for women to not 'do gender' at least in front of the virtual media or the brotherhood. But it does not mean that they restrict themselves from wearing sarees or feminine attire or go traditional. They are also appreciated in those dress and with loud makeup but not while they are in a ride. Hence it is also important to them to portray some specific masculine traits via SNSs to maintain their position as a motorcyclist. If they are unable to engage in non-feminine traits they are laughed that and often ridiculed. Women respondents also claims to get much more attention only when they limit themselves in posting most picture with their ride rather than wearing sarees.

4.6   CONCLUSION

Involving in voluntary risk-taking activities such as riding a motorcycle for distant tours or professionally participating in any motorcycling activities, makes themselves more vulnerable than daily commuters is significantly 'doing gender' for men. This is because the portrayal of aggressive, risk taking attitudes only defines masculinities and is largely called masculine sexual character (Connell, 1995). 'Doing gender' for men involves engaging in such activities. It also becomes hegemonic for the daily commuters and less hegemonic for the experienced senior RE/superbike riders if compared to the newbie's motorcyclists. It quite difficult for the contemporary generations to be without mobile phones hence they tend to create a network among their groups via SNSs. It would be difficult for them to create a network without hegemonic performance of gender, which often leads to what Connell (1987) calls *hegemonic masculinity*[18]. Therefore, they have to take part in the socially constructed notions of the brotherhood or the society which demands men motorcyclists to be *real* motorcyclists. 'Real' largely means aggressive, risk-taking, rational, un-expressive, and non-fragile overall unlike woman.

Among other advantages of SNSs, we cannot overlook the disadvantages. Bloggers, u YouTubers, and addictive SNSs users are so busy in making videos, clicking, uploading, and editing; they usually forget to look beyond the conventional arena. Indeed they work pretty hard when others/

team mates are busy drinking or gossiping after the day's ride talking about the unexpected that they had overcame. Even during the day's ride, these YouTubes are busy taking footages for their videos, and vivid SNSs users are 'doing gender' while clicking pictures to upload. They miss most of the time when other people are enjoying the quiet nature of the place. Hence they pay the price by being alienated from these events. Even at home/hotel, they are also alienated from their family/friends as they have to edit those content and have to put up in the SNSs. They need to have a proper content otherwise they might lose their followers.

Another significant disadvantage is not being his/her true self. Without a doubt, many individuals fake or exaggerate their experiences with motorcycling in virtual media in order to get more followers in SNSs. Regarding women motorcyclists, just to be accepted in this field they might sometimes even fake or exaggerate an incident to be on the limelight. Similarly, men motorcyclists too participate in the similar fashion of exaggerating an incident, which we can derive from the above analysis part. Hence motorcyclists, both men and women, are silently participating in the rat race of creating a strong network and being more followed by the SNSs users.

NOTES

1. SNS means social networking sites. For example, Facebook, Twitter, Instagram, MySpace, etc.
2. The concept of CMC is borrowed from the chapter "comparing impression management strategies across social media platforms" by Jeffrey H. Kuznekoff.
3. SNS designed for news update for this distinctive motorcycling world are missing years, raw adventures (renowned YouTube channel for Kolkata motorcyclists) www.powerdrift.com (world-renowned site for motorcycle and car reviews), etc.
4. The concept of doing gender is taken for West and Zimmerman theory of doing gender where he states how individual, both male and female does gender in everyday lives.
5. By passionate motorcyclists, I mean individuals riding a motorcycle not only for mere transportation but also goes out for trips and tours in a motorcycle or also professionally attend moto-rallies.
6. Qualitative research "is defined as an inquiry process of understanding a social or human problem, based on building a complex, holistic picture, formed with words, reporting detailed views of informants and conducted in a natural setting" (Cresswell, 1994).
7. The concept on 'trying on' gender process is taken from the article 'Trying on Gender, Gender Regimes, and the Process of Becoming Women' by Susan Williams (2002).

8. Royal Enfield: First produced in 190, RE is the oldest motorcycle brand in the world still in production. The parent company is Eicher Motors. All most all the parts of this motorcycle is made up of metal parts, unlike any other motorcycle companies, making it heavier than the other motorcycles. Though it has a lot of electrical and technical manufacturing faults but still it is the most bought bikes in India. Consumers simply buy RE because it holds a specific status and hype. It has many models available in all over the country as well as abroad.

9. Superbikes: Any motorcycle above the cubic capacity of 800 is considered to be a superbike. It is quite costly and is hardly affordable by the majority.

10. RE Himalayan: A model owned by Royal Enfield. The genre of this motorcycle is for off-roading. The advertisement for this model itself 'says build for no-roads.' The height of his motorcycle is pretty high compared to the other models of RE.

11. RE Classic: A model of a bike owned by Royal Enfield. The design of this model is largely cruiser. It is also owned by many RE riders. It has also useful for people of this country for commuting purpose too. The Indian standard of height has increased the consumers of his particular brand.

12. Bajaj Avenger: Avenger is a model of the brand-named Bajaj. The styling of this motorcycle is cruiser and the height is quite low of 140 mm compared to the other motorcycles available in the Indian market. As the Indian standard of women's height, for many women, only this bike fit them well.

13. Iron Man: it is a famous movie character from Marvels production, produced series of movie under the same. And has a huge fan base all over the world.

14. Goddess Shiva: Shiva is a symbol of power and are considered to be immensely masculine than the other Goddess that Hindus worship. Shiva is also depicted as a marijuana addict.

15. Brotherhood: it's camaraderie where it involves both brothers and sisters who ride a motorcycle. It is a socially constructed special bond between the riders.

16. JAWA an old reputed motorcycle company since 1929. Jawa motorcycles were not in production for years. JAWA was a renowned brand in the motorcycling world.

17. Emphasized femininity: Connell (1987) had theorized that in dominant patriarchal culture, femininity is 'emphasized femininity,' which he argued is an ideal of conduct and a set of related practices by which women comply with men's power, compliance being central to femininity. Connell claimed emphasized femininity is "Sought after an attainable goal for women to achieve." It is "The global subordination of women to men...(in which women comply) with this subordination...(and accommodate) the interests and desires of men" (Connell, 1987: p. 183). Connell labels a sort of mainstream femininity as "emphasized femininity" that focuses on compliance, nurturance, and empathy as womanly virtues.

18. Hegemonic masculinity is defined as "the pattern of practice (i.e., doing things and not just a set of role expectations or an identity) that allowed men's dominance over women to continue." (Connell, 1987). It forms a social ideal for masculinity and is a way of being masculine which not only marginalizes and subordinates' women's activities but also alternative forms of masculinity such as effeminate masculinity. It is normative, embodies the most honored way of being a man and requires men to position themselves in relation to it.

KEYWORDS

- **computer-mediated communication**
- **global alarming**
- **hegemonic masculinity**
- **modern communication**
- **Royal Enfield**
- **social networking sites**

REFERENCES

Alpizar, K., Islas-Alvarado, R., Warren, C., & Fiebert, M., (2012). Gender, sexuality and impression management on Facebook. *International Review of Social Sciences and Humanities*, *4*(1), 121–125.

Connell, R. W., (1987). *Gender and Power*. Oxford: Polity Press.

Connell, R. W., (1995). *Masculinities*. Berkeley: University of California Press.

Cresswell, J. W., (1994). *Research Design: Qualitative and Quantitative Approaches*. Sage Publications.

Fenstermaker, B. S., (1985). *The Gender Factory: The Appointment of Work in American Households.* New York: Plenum Press.

Galbarczyk, A., & Ziomkiewicz, A., (2017). Tattooed men: Healthy bad boys and good-looking competitors. *Personality and Individual Difference, 106*, 122–125.

Gibbs, G., (2007). *Analyzing Qualitative Data.* Los Angeles: Sage Publications.

Grumet, G., (1983). Psychodynamic implications of tattoos. *American Orthopsychiatric Journal, 52*(3), 482–492.

Kavande, E., (1999). In the belly of the beast: Constructing femininities in engineering organizations. *The European Journal of Women Studies, 6*, 305–328.

MacGabhann, B., (2005). Marketing youth culture. *An Irish Quarterly Review*, *94*(374), 133–139.

Oakley, A., (1972). *Sex, Gender and Society*. London: Temple Smith.

Wacjman, J., (1991). *Feminism Confronts Technology*. Cambridge: Polity Press.

West, C., & Zimmerman, D. H., (1987). Doing gender. *Gender and Society*, *1*(2), 125–151. doi: 10.2307/189945.

William, S., (2002). Trying on gender, gender regimes, and the process of becoming women. *Gender and Society, 16*(29), 29–52. Sage Publications. doi: 10.1177/0891243202016001003.

Young, K., (2001). Social ties, social networks and the Facebook experience. *International Journal of Emerging Technologies and Society, 9*(1), 20–34.

CHAPTER 5

E-Governance: Impact on Society

CHAITALI GUHA SINHA

Assistant Professor, Amity Institute of Social Sciences, Amity University Kolkata, West Bengal, India

ABSTRACT

The study deals with the utilization of information technology (IT) in transforming the society into a Digital Society. It highlights the revolution brought by communication technology which managed to introduce flexibility in government work. As globalization is defined as social, political, and economic interconnection between different countries, technologies are used to maintain this interconnectivity. Technology, specifically Information and communication technologies have been used to reduce the differences and inequalities from different corners and transform the society into an integrated whole which is often referred to as "global village." Encouraging new communication technologies in government services is known as electronic governance. The traditional notion of public administration seems to become obsolete as the government at various levels is having the demand of more modern and improved quality of governance. E-governance has acceptability all over the world for its transparency and accountability. E-Governance is considered as an indispensable strength to a revolutionary development in the efficacy of government. The chapter analyzes the impact of e-governance in the public administration of India. The focus of the study is on the role of e-governance and the main obstacles in the universal implementation of the program. In India, with a huge population, low level of literacy, and increasing level of diversity, it is difficult to run the administration by the government in the traditional way. So, it is needed to have modern centralized initiatives which can bring transparency and accountability in the system. In the digitized era, it is obvious that the progress of any government depends on the utilization of information and communication technology (ICT) in the form of E-Governance. In fact, the efficiency and the success of a government can be understood by the reach of electronic governance to its citizens. The study is based on secondary data, specifically published data. All the data utilized in the research are collected from various publications of the central, state are local governments; books, magazines, and newspapers; government reports and publications of various associations connected with the system, and other sources of published information. Based on secondary data, this study tries to find out the obstacles the Indian government has to overcome to implement and utilize the new system, find out the opportunities available and examine the challenges encountered by it. In this digitized society, e-governance is no doubt a better method of governance, but due to the socio-economic condition of the country, it needs some supportive program to make it successful.

5.1   INTRODUCTION

Digitization is a modern process. It has become a trend in modern societies. India is also in the process of digitalization. Indian society is experiencing the process by initiating different programs-Digital India is one of them. The expectation and aim of this program is to transform the society into digitally equip one. The aim of this program is also to introduce knowledge economy. The new system assures fast and induce Government services for the population. Now, most of the government-related services are available electronically to the population. This program would try to maintain accountability and transparency in government services. Digital India Program is a long-awaited project for the citizen and Industries in India; it tried to connect different past and current projects to bring India in the global arena. This project connects the rural and urban areas and all the government facilities are now available throughout the country without any hassle. The project maintains its efficiency and quality through ICT. E-government is the delivery of government's services through electronic media. For instance, a Unique Disability ID and E-Pramaan are the initiatives to establish transparency and accountability in government services for everyone. These initiatives helped to maintain authentic and standard-based integrated government applications and databases. It can help to introduce digital innovation and create positive vibes for the people living in rural and urban areas. This program will also attract investors to invest in product manufacturing industries. The first state opted for this initiative in Andhra Pradesh. The Digital India project took the target to transform India into a digital economy. It encouraged digital economy with maximum participation of citizens from the various areas. The program assures that services and information are always available to the citizens in any place and anytime. Digital India Project ensures to reduce the gap between the rural and urban areas by initiating standardized service. The world is in the process of digitization of society, India is in transition period. One instance of digitization of society is reflected in the notion of introducing the program of Digital India. E-Governance is one pillar of it. The e-stands for electronic in e-governance. Thus, e-governance is mainly for carrying out government responsibilities and services with the new communication technologies. The main aim of E-governance is to establish more transparency and accountability in government affairs. This digitalize government is also ensuring equal and easy access to the public. The aim of this new system is to ensure good governance in society.

Governance means a manner of governing the state. It highlights more efficiency, effectiveness, and productivity by any government and semi-government institutions that are performing public service delivery. The government is considered as the head of a Nation-State, but the term governance is the experience of the government. The term governance increasingly came into the picture in the 1990s. Governance means better control or rule. In this context, the term is used as a pattern of activities of the state, non-state, quasi-state, and market entities, i.e., civil society organizations, other organizations such as World Bank and IMF; and market entities are corporate sectors. The term governance has become similar with government and privatization by increasing the use of civil society in service delivery, in public sector and social sector. The major outcome of these changes is that the service by government changed to cross-cultural and plural in nature. The technological revolution in the past decades encourages changes in different areas of society. Particularly, the forcible overthrow of the government in IT and computer technologies, along with the explanation of governance as effectiveness, transparency, and accountability have resulted in increasing computerization and digitization of governance functions. This process enhances the decentralization process. E-governance is empowerment to citizens. It provides them the right to be informed, and also allow them to take part in government affairs. The concept of e-governance is popularizing another concept, that is, good governance. Good governance is better governance which enhances effectivity, efficiency, accountability of government system. The aim of the system is to maintain transparency to reduce corruption in government affairs. The growth of digital technologies, information technology (IT) and telecommunications has made the state to change the ways they perform their functions. Technology is also driven by capitalism. This encourages a particular type of work environment and employee. This technology has high potentiality to alter the functions of government, procedure of governance in recent future. E-Governance brings change in society. This has many applications in governance and society.

5.1.1 METHODOLOGY

In modern societies where ICT is playing a vital role in connecting people from varied areas, the efficiency of a government can be determined by the reach of governance to its citizens. The study is based on secondary data, specifically published data. The data used in the research are gathered from different publications of the central, state, and local governments; different books, journals, magazines, and newspapers; government reports and publications of various organizations associated with the system and public records and statistics. The data has been collected from the case studies of different countries and many other sources of published information. Based on secondary sources of data, this study tries to find out the advantage and disadvantage of implementing the new system, restrain challenges to implement it properly, to find out the opportunities available, and to identify the obstacles for implementing this new program. In this advanced society, e-governance is no doubt a better method of governance, but due to the socio-economic condition of the country, it needs some supportive program to make it successful.

5.1.2 OBJECTIVE

This chapter is illustrating the concept of the program Digital India with special reference to E-governance. The focus of this qualitative study is to explain the function of e-governance, its positive impact on society and to examine the challenges faced by the country in implicating the system in various levels of government. The chapter is also discussing about the impact of digitization of government in cities, towns, and villages.

5.2 DIGITAL INDIA AND E-GOVERNANCE

The aim of the project is to make India digitally empowered. Digital India actually took the initiative to include various measures under one program. The programs are introduced to prepare our country as a knowledge economy and for introducing good governance for the citizens through a coordinated involvement of the entire government. Digital India aims at maintaining interconnection in society. It has taken different initiatives to transform the traditional society into a well-connected digital India.

These initiatives include:

1. **Availability of Internet Connections and Broad Bands in the Highways:** The program was implemented to provide high speed internet on the highways which will connect the remote areas. These broadways connect all the different villages, government sectors, research areas and universities. It is also required to initiate web portals for desktops or tablets and also develop mobile applications to access online information anywhere and everywhere. The project Bharat Net, aimed to connect all 25,000 village Panchayats of the country. This is the biggest broadband project.

2. **Easy Access to Mobile Connectivity:** There are many villages in India that do not have proper electricity, so it is obvious that many parts of India are not under the mobile coverage area. By considering this situation, the development project initiated a plan to provide mobile coverage to interior villages for North East India. BSNL launched Next Generation Network, and this will replace 30 years old legacy telephone exchanges in order to take care of every type of communication services like voice, data, multimedia, and others. The aim of India is to connect the villages by 2020 through mobile technology. The objective of this initiative is to prepare the nation for smart governance. The motive of the government is to establish a well-connected State.

3. **IT Knowledge Sharing:** The objective of digitalized India is to provide technical training to the youth of the society to enrich them with the required knowledge for applying in IT sector jobs.

Different steps have been taken to raise the employability of citizens. In partnership with NASSCOM and ERNET in Bangalore, the government providing infrastructure to educate the youth in the IT sector. BPO sector is creating many job opportunities for the young population in IT-enabled service industry. They offer online services 24/7 in every field, which creates more job opportunities.

4. **Electronics Manufacturing:** This is another strong step taken by the program to reduce the import of the products. This strategy aims at promoting electronics manufacturing in the country. Target NET ZERO Imports is the main dream of the project. The success of this initiative requires coordination actions of different fronts.

5. **Internet Access for Public:** Post offices and Common Service Centers are two elements of Public Internet Access Program. There are two sub-components of Public Internet Access Program. Technologies having high moral standards that support cost-effectiveness, coordination, security, fast service, social-connectivity, and essential intelligence that helps to access information from anywhere. This evolution in public administration is creating a new horizon of e-services to every citizen. The government aims to provide accountable and fast internet services to almost all villages by March 2020. These post offices are considered as multi-service centers of India.

6. **E-Governance:** This type of electronic governance is transforming every manual activity into a completely automatic system. It can transform the system in the following ways:

    i.   All government-related forms will be available online. Also the databases and other information will also be found in electronic format;

    ii. Tracking and monitoring of assignments will be more effective;

    iii. Different departments will interact with each other electronically, which in turn will result in superior production of work between departments;

    iv. Persistent problems will be more quickly responsive and analysis and resolve of persistent problems will be faster.

7. **E-Kranti:** The main components of e-Kranti have been sanctioned by Union Cabinet on March 15. The vision of the project is to initiate e-governance for transforming governance. This program will focus on knowledge of education, health, farming, financial,

and other services electronically. Digital knowledge is the focus of this project. Territory will not be a concern for these digitized societies. Everyone can avail any information and data faster than before.

8. **Global Information:** To know is the right of the citizens in any democratic society. Information, statistic, report, data all are available in government portal in today's world. Availability of statistics and data is maintaining the transparency of government and help to reduce corruption.

MyGov.in is established to maintain reciprocal communication between citizens and government. People now can send in their ideas, suggestions, and comment on different issues and affairs of government, like net neutrality.

9. **Early Harvest Programs:** This type of project will create short timeline initiatives where every manual service is changed by e-service. E-services like:

i. People will use digital media for different purposes like amusement, weather forecast and up to date information;

ii. All universities will be under Wi-Fi;

iii. Online information can be accessed from Public Wi-Fi spots;

iv. Study materials will be available online. E-books will be accessible to the students;

v. All manual attendance will be converted to biometric procedure.

5.3 E-GOVERNANCE-MEANING AND NATURE

Osborne and Gaebler (1992) defined e-Government as; The government's use of technology, in particular, web-based Internet applications to increase accessibility and delivery of government services to citizens, trading partners, employees, and other government entities. It is a way to utilize the new information and communication technologies to improve the quality of services. E-governance ensure accountability and transparency in the system. It allows citizens to take part in governance which is the essence of democracy.

Application of E-governance encourage better governance for its citizens. By introducing this new system, the government tries to improve the quality of information. E-governance tends to focus on establishing accountable and transparent service towards the population. The purpose of E-governance is to enhance information and service delivery. This system makes governance citizen-friendly, responsible, accountable, transparent, efficient, and fast. So, e-governance is the application of information and communication technology (ICT) in government functioning to bring in SMART governance. S-M-A-R-T indicates S-simple, M-moral, A-accountable, R-responsive, and T-transparent governance. This S-M-A-R-T governance actually means:

- **Simple:** ICT is used in government services to make the system easy or simple. E-Government is trying to make the process better by simplifying rules and regulation. It is simple in providing services, and the user-friendliness of the system is making it popular in the society. It is also trying to make information accessible to the citizen in a more simple way.
- **Moral:** e-governance establish dedicated service to the citizens. The system tries to establish transparency in governance. The new modern system also aims at establishing ethical values in governance. This SMART governance establishes a system that can combat against corruption and interpret the actual meaning of democracy by allowing participation of the citizens in the process.
- **Accountable:** Good government needs to be accountable in nature. Accountability is the main criterion of good governance. Accountability means answerability and enforcement. Answerability means; they need to justify their decisions; they are answerable to the citizens for their actions. Civil society tries to enforce standard of good performance of the officials. Through E-Government the government tries to maintain accountability.
- **Responsive:** E-governance is much more accessible, approachable, and sensitive towards the society's interest so e-governance is responsive form of government.
- **Transparent:** E-governance encourages reciprocal communication between citizens and governments. It aims at open communication, which supposed to be the aim of democracy. Thus e-governance uses ICT and the internet for promoting public information.

E-governance is simple, moral, accountable, responsible, and transparent. This smart government plays a very important role in modern government. Contribution of e-governance can be understood by explaining the functions of e-governance.

The functions of this SMART governance:

- The most important function of SMART government is to maintain interconnectedness. This system is Emphasizing open communication within the organization and with the different sections of the government.
- It provides better information and more efficient service delivery.
- The rate of corruption can be reduced by ensuring the use of ICT in government affairs. This system highlights accountability and transparency in the service. Thus, the important function of smart governance is to stop corruption by ensuring accountability and transparency.
- The role of this governing device is to enforce political reliability and accountability.
- This system promotes democratic values through public participation in various ways.

This chapter is mainly analyzing the impact of e-governance in society. Adaptation of e-governance is leading to multiple advantages. This initiative is changing the structure of government services. It is not only simplifying the process of information accumulation but it allows the individual to gather information of the government as an active participant of the government regarding any department.

This process is helping them to take active part in the decision-making processes. The target of E-Governance is to promote the essence of democracy by the people of the people for the people by ensuring participation from every section. E-Governance ensures the availability of information about any activities of government on public welfare in the website which can reduce the rate of corruption. E-Governance revolutionizes the functioning of the government by making it transparent. This assurance of transparency significantly contributes to the elimination of corruption. Government officials are also aware of the fact that their actions are closely scrutinized by the population, which in turn will make the process more efficient.

The proper implementation of the system will make it hassle-free for the citizens. The people now can get their job done without facing unnecessary delays. It can make the system citizen-friendly and break the inflexibility of government services.

Proper and successful implementation of e-governance can lead to good governance. This system offers better service delivery to the citizens it also empowers them with proper information about government decisions. The system focus on better inter-organizational and intra organizational interaction. It is much more effective to manage the governmental services. Not only that, it is much more convenient for the busy population. E-Governance also helps in revenue growth and cost reduction.

E-governance encourage reciprocal communication which helps to nourish good relation between government and citizens and brings citizens closer to the government. For instance, the initiative taken by West Bengal government, Didi K Bolo, which is trying to establish good relation with the people, to understand the condition of the citizens. This initiative is much more convenient for the citizen as well as for the government to keep the track of the present political and social situation.

Furthermore, the government is trying their level best to make the initiative successful by making these facilities accessible to the population. Service centers are located near to the citizens.

E-governance is also helping different business and research organizations by making the data and information accessible easily.

E-governance is a simple method of governance. It simplifies the process of service delivery and receiving. E-Governance provide important information and services to citizens and empowers them, which is considered as the basis of a democratic welfare state. It improves efficiency in the service delivery. This system makes the process accountable and transparent to combat the social problem like corruption. The other important aspect of e-governance is it makes the services standardize. All kind of government services as well as information are accessible to the population and organizations because of this initiative. It is inclusive in nature as the voice of minorities and the most vulnerable sections are also taken in to account. The use of technology in the governing process is making the system effective for most of the sections in the society. E-Governance is responsible to the needs of the society and can keep pace with the changing society.

5.3.1   E-GOVERNMENT AND E-GOVERNANCE

E-Governance and E-government though we use the term simultaneously but the meaning and role of these terms are different. Government and governance are about getting cooperation of the governed by Thomas B. Risley. Government is one of the basic elements and is the most important element of a State. It is the head of a nation. Governance is the effect or result as experienced by the citizens. E-government, if properly implemented and managed, can be a very productive and effective version of governance. E-Governance is encouraging participation of the population in government activities. Through this type of governance a state can initiate participatory democracy. E-governance can establish participatory democracy if it is supported by proper principles, objectives, and infrastructure. E-government is thus an up-gradation process and services of government by using the modern communication techniques. It uses the modern technologies to establish standardize services towards the population, thus this system is trying to maintain better relation with the individuals of the society. It enhances the accessibility of government services to benefit the society. E-government and e-governance are not same. E-governance is not only initiated for service delivery, but it is something more than that. It can be seen as a decisional process as well. This use of Information and Communication technologies in government process is making governance open and accountable. E-Government is for Good Governance.

Reform of public administration and government issues introduced and popularized the concept of good governance. Governance is the ability to structure or form and implement policies and functions. Good governance is not only efficient public administration but also a citizen-friendly servicing technique. Good governance is like a bridge between the state and society through effective people-oriented administration. The concept of good governance was mentioned first in 1989 in a World Bank Report on Sub-Saharan Africa. Good governance is citizen-friendly and responsive administration. Good governance ideally and in practice will follow proper separation of power between legislatures, executive, and judiciary. Its purpose is to improve the quality of life of the people. E-governance is for establishing good governance by utilizing the modern techniques.

E-governance is a process of applying modern techniques to the process of government. The role of e-governance is to confirm efficient and effective governance. This system has full capability to reduce corruption and increase transparency in governmental affairs. The Department of Electronics established in 1970, that indicated the increasing dependence on electronics. National Informatics Centre was established in 1977, which brought ICT into the limelight. The establishment of the National Informatic center is the first step towards e-governance in India. In the early 1980s, very few organizations use computers for word processing. Gradually, with the introduction of better software and up-gradation of the old one, computers were put to other uses like keeping records and processing information. Advances in communication technology improve the reach of computers in different government departments. Many government departments started using this technology to track the movement of files, monitoring of development programs, keeping records, etc. The launching of NICNET and the District Information System of the National Informatics Centre set the background of e-governance in India. This program introduced computers in all district offices. In future, e-governance initiatives were brought in the state and union level with ongoing computerization, mobile connectivity and all. A National Task Force on Information Technology and Software Development was formed in May 20, 1998. This program focused on utilizing it for assimilating and processing knowledge. It suggested the launching of an Operation Knowledge' targeted at spreading computer literacy and making people aware of its use. The Union Ministry of IT was created in 1999, and by 2000; the government of India identified a 12-point minimum agenda for e-Governance for implementation in all the Union Government Ministries/ Departments. Furthermore, this path of integrating government services through technology increased in rapid way. Almost all departments and every Ministry now can be accessed faster than before. This process of transformation from governance to e-governance has surely improved the quality of government role with proper accountability, accessibility, accurate storage and transparency in governance. E-Government is empowering citizens in various ways. Globalization has impact on e-governance. Globalization encourages the growth of technology in the government services, it makes people active in different procedures. This new initiative also empowers the minorities of the society. E-government optimistically believes that this system can bring change in the government procedure and structure of the government services.

5.4   IMPORTANCE OF E-GOVERNMENT FOR THE SOCIETY

Since e-governance has a huge impact on the society, the Indian government has introduced the implementation of e-governance projects in multiple states of India. The government has started introducing awards in the following categories like:

- Digital transformation through the excellence of re-engineering in the Government Process. The main purpose of this category is to identify the projects which provide re-design of a workflow and involves efficiency in terms of performance, cost, quality, or a combination of these.
- A government can have an outstanding performance only if e-governance is applied in citizen-centric approach of Service Delivery. The motive of this category is to recognize the projects which help to enhance the value to its beneficiaries in terms of quality and quantity or both, through effective and proper use of ICT.
- Outstanding performance in district-level initiative in citizen-oriented service delivery. These categories of awards are given to the district level projects which benefits through delivery of enhanced value to citizens.
- Exemplary re-use of ICT-based solution: This category of awards recognizes the e-governance projects which use the existing technology and enhance the efficiency and effectiveness of the process, cost, quality, etc.
- Innovative technology in e-governance: This category of awards recognizes the e-governance projects which demonstrate the use of path-breaking ICT or innovative use of technology and enhance the efficiency and effectiveness of the process, cost, quality, etc.
- Innovative use of ICT by State or Central Government PSUs or cooperatives or federations or societies for Customer's Benefits in terms of quality, cost, effectiveness.
- Best government portal that use ICT effectively to enhance the quality and cost of individuals through e-governance.
- Specific sector award-focus sector local government: This award recognizes achievements in the focus sector for the year for innovative use of ICT for customer benefit.

Gujarat Government has furnished with 69 awards in state-level for the introduction of e-governance project which other states can also follow.

E-governance project can benefit the society from different perspectives. It could an important measure for country like India. Though India is not well prepared for universal and uniform application of this new form of government, but it is continuously developing its infrastructure for utilizing the benefit of e-governance.

E-Governance helps society in different ways. Followings are a few positive impact of E-Governance on society.

5.4.1 MAINTAINING STRONG INFORMATION CHAIN

E-Governance provides up-to-date information to the population. It empowers individuals with the information of government activities. Citizens can take benefit of this service to get information effectively and fast. It helps to maintain strong information chain. Most of the information, statistical records, records of individuals, cases, and the data related to any issue and statistics of any city are now available and accessible to the population. Everything is now available on the internet. By browsing over the Internet/website and filing appropriate forms, anyone can access those data, government can also respond on the basis of their interest. The government provides data to the citizens on the basis of their needs. Citizens can take advantage of e-governance in this way.

5.4.2 QUICK SERVICE TO CITIZENS

E-government makes the government procedure faster and efficient. It provides information faster than before. Now citizens can apply through electronic services and gather data via mail or government notification through respective websites. Now citizens can download required information in softcopy or print it to convert it to hardcopy as per the requirements. Now they don't have to wait in a long queue and can apply online from their places. In other words, online services are making life easier than before. Digital signature has also enhanced the power of e-governance. Through this, we don't have to present in person to submit different application forms but they can be done through online.

5.4.3 PROPER RESOURCE UTILIZATION

E-governance helps to use the resources wisely. In this context, counter-trained resources and digital platforms can be used. These computers, trained employees, internet, etc., can be used for better governance, which is not possible through manual system. These resources are used to maintain records and information which can help in various ways.

5.4.4 INTEGRATING THE PLURAL SOCIETY

Diversity is the essence of Indian society. India is a plural and democratic society, but there should be proper representation of every section. E-governance initiates integration in plural society. E-governance considers the voice of minorities in society and tries to ensure standard service for everyone. However, by utilizing the benefit of e-governance, every community can be included and integrated into the larger system. Integration between several communities is important for the larger system. E-governance also helps to maintain communication within the government departments which in turn increase interdependence and solidarity in the organization.

5.4.5 CONTROL DELAYS, RED TAPISM AND CORRUPTION

E-governance restructured the government procedures and services to break off the rigid bureaucratic form of the service delivery. The bureaucratic structure of the government often delays the services and increases the rate of corruption. The strict bureaucratic structure often invites rigidity, inflexibility, and red-tapism in the system. On the other hand, the flexible nature of e-governance allows controlling delays. Availability of information empowers the citizens, which in turn reduce the rate of corruption in government offices. This restructurization of services offers an opportunity for improving the public service delivery and strong and efficient administration. E-governance targets to transform the work culture and service delivery. It lowers the transaction cost and promotes transparency and accountability. E-governance thus can be considered as effective measure against corruption. It effectively reduces delays and increases the pace of the services.

5.5 IMPACT OF E-GOVERNMENT IN INDIA

Impact of E-Government is immense in society as through this process, the government tried to introduce good governance. It is important to discuss the situation of e-governance in India as it is a challenge to introduce the digitization process to the large section of uneducated and technologically not so equipped society. The newly implemented processes are also need to be reexamined and scrutinized properly to understand its acceptability in society. Impact of this new system required to be analyzed in three situations.

First is the electronic environment; the next is about examining the affectability of an e-governance project; and the last one is the effect of e-governance on government processes, economic growth and service delivery. Accordingly, three types of approaches are needed to evaluate. They are as follows:

- The condition of states or regions to accept or implement e-governance, that is, e-governance readiness in states and regions;
- Different types of steps implemented by e-governance project; and
- Impact of e-governance as a whole.

India improved its position in the global E-governance index 2018. India secured 96th position in United Nation's E-governance index 2018 whereas it was in 118th rank in 2014. This leap indicates how the society is moving towards digitalization. This change also indicates how ITC is influencing public sector. There are different success stories in the state levels also which clearly indicate the positive impact of the project in society. It is becoming an essential part of the digital transformation effort. To encourage the states and to motivate the ministries, the Department of Administrative Reforms and Public Grievances and Pensions hosted the National E-governance Award, on February 2019. Example of successful e-governance projects are: TDS Reconciliation Analysis and Correction Enabling System, Stamps, and Registration Automation with Technology and Information. Passport Seva Project is another project which was rewarded in the category of Outstanding Performance in Citizen-Centric Services. Kanyashree Prakalpa of the Department of Women Development and Social Welfare Government of West Bengal is another important project which managed to secure award in this category. In the category of using technology in a more innovative way in E-governance Suraksha Setu-Safe City Surat organized by the office of the Commissioner of Police, Surat, Gujarat also secured an award. Other important Projects are Effective Vehicles Database Management to trace the owners of Unclaimed Vehicles Lying in Police Stations organized by district police,

Home Department, Karnataka, which is also known as SARTHI project under the government to introduce communication model in the state of Rajasthan. There are many projects which clearly indicate the positive impact of the project in society.

5.6   E-GOVERNANCE ACCEPTABILITY IN INDIA

In societies like India, where the majority of the population is suffering from poverty, illiteracy, and other infrastructural problems, it is difficult to expect complete acceptability of e-governance. Under this condition also e-governance is getting prominence in India. The process of using computers in governance in twenty-first century has popularize the concept of e-governance. The concept of e-governance emerged, in parallel with the liberalization of country's economy. It is to promote better governance. The government of India approved the National e-Governance Plan with the main idea to make government services available to the mass population at affordable rates at the time to ensure efficiency and reliability of the service.

E-governance can be treated as a path to solve social and economic problems. E-governance can be justified by its adoption and expansion of e-governance as cost-effective, reduces waste, citizen-friendly, account-able system. It can be the solution of many problems pertaining to gover-nance in India. Government has taken many initiatives to make the process successful. Now, different programs and policies are introduced to support the e-government for better governance. One of the important initiatives is the IT act 2000, which defines the issues related to regulating cyberspace. Ministry of IT plays an important role in supporting e-governance. The National Institute of Smart government is also facilitating e-governance in various ways. The NeGP consists of some of mission mode projects (MMPs) and Support Components which are being implemented at the Central, State, and Local Government levels. These include Projects such as Income Tax, Customs, and Excise and Passports at the Central Level, Land Records, Agriculture, and e-District at the State Level and Panchayats and Municipalities at the Local Level. There are also many integrated MMPs like e-Procurement, Service Delivery Gateway, etc., where delivery of services envisaged in the project entail coordinated implementation across multiple departments of the government.

E-governance is able to provide government services in a cost-effective manner. The programs like BHOOMI, CARD, GYANDOOT, VAHAN, and SARATHI are accepted by the common people. BHOOMI is the automation of land records implemented by the Government of Karnataka. It provides computerized records of Rights Tenancy and Crops. It is easy and fast access to land records which makes the initiative acceptable to the poor farmers. CARD is a Computer-Aided Administration of Registration Department implemented by the Government of Andhra Pradesh. GYANDOOT is Intranet in the Tribal District of Dhar by Madhya Pradesh. Farmers are facilitated by this initiative. GYANDOOT provides the appropriate price for their crop without any mediators. They can easily access the land records. It also helped farmers to show their grievance for poor quality seeds, fertilizers, non-functioning of schools of Panchayats. VAHAN and SARATHI are vehicle registration and permit driving license project by the State Government of Tamil Nadu. Online accessibility of vehicle information, monitoring the selling and purchase of vehicle make the program beneficial for the population. Collection of taxes and fees of registration, license permit are faster and much more efficiently done by using this project. These projects are also helping to reduce corruption in various levels and control the growth of middlemen. Acceptability of e-governance is also reflected in the initiative taken by the State governments of West Bengal to utilize the essence of modern technology for better public service. For instance, the initiatives taken by West Bengal Government named Didi K Bolo, Mayor K Bolo to reach the population directly. These initiates are trying to reduce the gap between public representatives and the public. E-Governance is enhancing participatory democracy by making the population active recipient of the governance.

5.7   PRESENT CONDITION OF E-GOVERNANCE

The present condition of E-governance is reflected in E-Governance Survey report by the United Nations Department on Economic and Social Affairs in every 2 years. This survey looks at literature and data and ranks countries' performance through an e-government development index. This includes indicators on infrastructure, skills, and content and also focuses on other aspects like employment, education, economy, health, social welfare and environment. The latest survey, published in 2018 presents the current scenario of digitalized society. Some countries like Denmark, Australia, and the Republic of Korea showed their excellence on E-government. This was the first time, the study and ranking also focused on local e-government development in 40 countries, including America, Asia, Africa, Europe, and Oceania. Majority of United Nations Members States are experiencing rapid growth of e-governance globally. According to the latest survey the Americans and Asians share almost equal standing with European countries.

The points can be discussed here:

1. First, every country today has online presence. The rate and scope of online presence is increasing every day. E-governance is not only for providing better governance to the public but to make it more interactive and transactional. E-governance Apps in mobile are also more popular now a day than they were few years back. The Internet of Things and geographic information system are likely to influence the system.

2. Second, E-government is growing rapidly in countries but not in equal pace. E-government is growing more extensive in some societies than others. The rich countries getting more benefit from e-governance than poorer countries because the latter are lacking infrastructural support.

3. Third, E-government enhances efficiency in government services by maintaining integration and coordination among the departments. E-government makes the service more accessible to the majority. This system makes life simple for the digitally literate population though it also increases the risk from hacking.

The United Nations Department of Economic and Social Affairs (DESA)'s survey indicates the great potential of e-governance to improve efficiency in government service. E-governance is not only using technology in government affairs but also the way of using it by the government. Three vectors can be identified for that good government, impact, and inclusiveness, which are discussed in subsections.

5.7.1 GOOD GOVERNMENT AND E-GOVERNMENT

Firstly, E-government is digitalization of government service. E-governance does not ensure good government. Governments that have no commitments towards the well-being of its citizens is not good government, and e-governance will not be an efficient means of governance in those societies. On the other hand, when government is keen towards improving the lives of citizen the quality of e-governance will also improve. The reluctant government can misuse the benefits of digitalization. Digitalization of government service can prevent corruption if the government intends to do so. Thus, e-government can confirm good governance if the government is committed to its citizen.

5.7.2   UNDERSTANDING THE IMPACT

Secondly, a broader evidence base is required to understand the impact of e-governance as a whole. Both supply-side data (DESA's Survey) and demand-side data (Heek's design) is important in this context. Supply-side data could be related to the condition of the infrastructure, available platforms and websites, transaction data, etc. Whereas to judge the reality gap of e-governance, various demand-side data is also important like: usage of e-governance by the people and the purpose of using them, the effectiveness and impact of e-governance on people of all class, the actual cost benefits, etc.

5.7.3   INCLUSIVENESS

Next come the principle of Sustainable Development Agenda, which clearly mentions everyone should be benefitted from the initiative. In societies where there are many inequalities on the accessibility of government services, it is evident only better-offs will be progressed with the blessings of the benefits of e-governance. Access to government services require availability of basic connectivity, skilled personnel, and digital literacy, which lacks on the poor and rural areas. Hence it is difficult to progress together with the benefits of e-governance.

So the main challenge of government is to find an effective way to provide the e-services by taking various measures like spreading computer education in rural areas, improving internet connectivity, proper power and resource backup and necessary service maintenance staff to help the people who are not accustomed in online affairs. This way e-governance services can make life easier for people at a large. E-government services and benefits should be implemented and introduced to meet the need of common people in affordable price.

A similar point applies to e-participation. Interested participants in consultations, petitions, online voting, on radio phone-ins or social media platforms are those having strong opinions and time, but not the participants whose voices are hardly noticed by governments. Participants never get influenced by new ways of offering and that encourage participants. There should be a long-term initiative to make people understand its benefits.

5.7.4   E-GOVERNMENT FOR THE PEOPLE, NOT OF THE PEOPLE

E-governance influences the quality of Government service and public administration. This system is for the people, to make the people aware of the state affairs. But this digitalized government is not an answer in itself. If the majority is gained from it, then it is for them. The task of e-governance in plural society is also to make sure that they don't exclude any group.

5.8   RESERVATION OF E-GOVERNMENT

Richard Heeks and colleagues found out the high rate of failure in E-Government projects in the year 2001. They developed Design-Reality Gap model to identify the causes of failure and success of e-government. The basis of Heeks's Design: Reality Gap model is the idea that there are two main points in any e-government project, one the reality, that is, where we are now, and the goal of the project, that is, where the e-government project wants to get us. The larger gap between the points indicates difficulty in successfully completion of the project, and the smaller the gap higher will be the chances of success.

The e-government projects usually fail because often proponents fail to understand the citizen's intension and capabilities E-government fails when the low-income population does not get support from the government. To make the system successful, the duty of the government is to make resources available and accessible to the majority of the population. E-governance is not only about introducing digitalized system but making it a success considering long term goal.

5.8.1   ISSUES FACED DURING E-GOVERNANCE IMPLEMENTATION IN INDIA

E-governance is a very effective and efficient means of public admin-istration. E-government project implementation can be beneficial to every individual, company, and institution to get useful government documents, to collect data and can help to bring up the living standard of the people. However, government offices of our country still prefer offline documentation and paper filling is done for official purpose, so it is little problematic to bring in electronic media and addition the following factors are also main obstacles for the government. There are a number of challenges in the implementation of e-governance in India. Some barriers are like, cybersecurity, variation in access equality in the technology field of the citizen, setting up the e-government solution is costly, etc.

5.8.2   TRUST

Individuals of the country need to believe in each other for implementing public administration service via e-government. Trust means the user, that is, the citizens must be confident, comfortable, and must have faith on the tool and technology with whom they will interact. The other important factor of trust is that they must have trust for the government. Recently, confidential information regarding the security of the country was compromised when the source containing confidential information was lost. This type of incidents leads to distrust or break the confidence of the users.

5.8.3   LOW EDUCATION LEVEL

Literacy means people of the country will be able to interact with each other in any language like Bengali, Hindi or English both verbally and through written and also they should understand the language. An educated person is the one who can both read as well as write in any language which is understandable by others. Illiteracy is still a social problem in India. In this condition, it is really a challenge to promote e-governance. Most of the populations are totally unaware of techno-logical advancement they have to depend on others for filling up form, checking records, etc. The government is trying to alter the situation by providing infrastructural support.

5.8.4   LOW AVERAGE INCOME

Per capita income measures the numerical quotient of national production by per person in a given area, in monetary terms. In India, where per capita income is average most of the people can't afford to have computer education or internet facilities, so implementing universal application of e-governance is difficult.

5.8.5   LIMITED FINANCIAL RESOURCE

Financial resource is the money available for spending in introducing and implanting e-government project in the country. The government needs to have enough financial resources to promote success and maximize the health of the country's economy. India has limited resource, which is an obstacle in the rapid growth of the new system.

5.8.6   LACK OF SKILLED RESOURCE

A country that lacks human resource finds it difficult to implement e-governance projects and make it a success. Government offices have very few resource having proper skill, and for this reason, it is difficult to incorporate e-Government project in our country. Proper training and understanding of information and technology is essential for the implementation of electronic governance. So man power is an important aspect for the government to roll out e-governance projects within the country. Hence first thing government should do is to prepare sufficient trained and knowledgeable resources.

5.8.7   LACK OF AWARENESS/TRAINING

Proper awareness and training is another obstacle for implementing E-governance. Before government implement any e-government project successfully, they must introduce proper training for every staff of the project for all departments, so that the staffs are well known to understand the project and the project ends up successfully. Also, awareness should be provided to people, to citizens of the country, who will be benefitted from the initiative. Different types of awareness programs must be in various parts of the country so that people get to know about how to use the system and the importance of having e-governance in the country. Training and knowledge transfer will lead to the successful implementation of e-government.

5.8.8 OTHER

Some other challenges for the implementations are infrastructural problems, skills of citizen and awareness, various legal issues, tendency not to accept modified but improved work culture. Aged people usually prefer to depend on the conventional method of doing things.

5.9 CONCLUSION

At the end of the chapter, we can conclude that in changing society, it's not easy to maintain pace with the old traditional form of governance. E-Governance is always a better option for the modernized digitized society. E-Governance empowers all the sections of the society which supposed to be the main essence of society. It empowers women in different ways by initiating schemes related to health, poverty alleviation. Mexico practices The Cash Transfer system to support women of the society. E-governance is an inclusive policy. But to make the process a success story, it has to be implemented properly. Society should have digital preparedness to utilize the new system. India took the challenge to depend on e-governance which is praiseworthy but also need to work on the challenges. At last, we can conclude that e-government is a modern technique for better governance, but its impact is depending on the individuals, society, and organizations who are applying it. In spite of poor infrastructure, language dominance, illiteracy, and technological unawareness India has some award-winning e-government projects like Passport Seva Project and Kanyashree Prakalpa Portal, etc. The Indian government has also facilitated e-governance by initiating different infrastructural support. In the end, we can conclude that e-governance is a promising initiative for developing countries like India to implement good governance in society and to combat the problems like corruption.

KEYWORDS

- **department of economic and social affairs**
- **digital innovation**
- **digitization**
- **e-government**
- **information and communication technology**
- **mission mode projects**

REFERENCES

Bhatnagar, S., (2004). *E-Government from Vision to Implementation*. Sage Publication New Delhi.

Bhattacharya, J., (2008). *Critical Thinking In E-Governance*. Gift Publications.

Brautigm, D., (1991). *Governance and Economy: A Review.*

Heeks, R., (2017). *Information and Communication Technology for Development (ICT4D)*. Routledge Publication, UK.

Jain, N., (2011). *Cyber Crime: Prevention, Detection and Prosecution*. Career Motivation Centre Sagar.

Khanna, S. R., & Singh, P., (2018). *Digital Drive, E-Governance and Internet Services in India*. New Century Publication, New Delhi.

Osborne, E. D., & Ted, G., (2000). *Reinventing Government: How the Entrepreneurial Spirit is Transforming the Public Sector*. Prentice-Hall Publication, United States.

Prabhu, C. S. R., (2012). *E-Governance: Concepts and Case Studies*. PHI Publication, New Delhi.

Riley, B. T., (2000). *Electronic Governance*. Commonwealth Secretariat Publications, London, UK.

PART II
Digital Marketing and the Service Industry

CHAPTER 6

Digital Marketing in Today's Privacy-Conscious World

RAHUL SINGH

Assistant Professor, St. Xavier's College, Burdwan, and PhD Research Scholar, Adamas University, Kolkata, West Bengal, India

ABSTRACT

In this modern era, different sectors of marketing are moving towards the digital field to promote their computerized space. However, these marketing efforts are being shaped as well as restricted by consumer privacy concerns with security tied in with controlling the progression of individual data. The computerized disturbance that has reformed the manner in which individuals convey and work together has changed its course lately even in many organizations, advertisers are entrusted with acquiring new clients and thus speaking to their voice.

While customers are careful about their online security, advertisers ought to be significantly increasing concerned on the grounds that protection matters the most. The main concern which is been raised is that a worthy utilization of private data in a single setting might be an unsatisfactory attack of security in another. On the other hand, the administrations offered by trust are planned for furnishing Internet customers with a believed brand of protection. The issue of customer security is changing the showcasing scene and putting weight on advertisers from three edges of security regulations, data breaches and purchase fear. The internet is rapidly turning into the world's biggest open electronic commercial center. It is assessing to contact 50 million individuals around the world with development evaluations averaging roughly 10% every month. This chapter was tried to understand consumer privacy concern about Internet marketing as well as we have tried to present a clearer view on how to adopt digital marketing strategy without affecting online privacy. Results found that an appropriate advanced promoting effort requires significant speculations of their time and exertion. Building up a decent system is critical for achievement in computerized promoting whereas dismissing their viewpoint can include dangers for both the businessman and clients.

6.1   INTRODUCTION

With the steady decay of TV and print media, promoting procedure is moving to the computerized space. This has likewise observed expanded challenge in the new medium, compelling advertisers to search for approaches to customize substance to get through the commotion and get to singular purchasers. While this methodology may improve the client experience, there is consistently the danger of organizations having a lot of data about our own undertakings. It is considerably increasingly risky when we are inadequately educated about the particular kinds of information gathered about us or how these organizations utilize the information. As long as customer experience initiatives are subjects of discussion, data driven marketing is considered as the key. However, these marketing efforts are being shaped as well as restricted by consumer privacy concerns (Stephen, 2016). With the advancement of social media coverage of data breaches and wrong utilization of data, privacy regulations all over the world seems a big deal in this contemporary world. Nevertheless, it is still in the hand of an individual who can keep their privacy secured provided they are following guidelines apply.

While information protection and security are firmly related (and frequently conflated) there are significant contrasts. Security is tied in with controlling the progression of individual data. What's more, the privilege to control how ones' data is imparted to others by means of advanced channels. Information security takes the idea of protection above and beyond by concentrating on the wellbeing of that data. Once more, for purchasers, these are regularly one and the equivalent: Information must be remained careful and secure as methods for controlling its stream (Martin and Murphy, 2017). Security is important to look after protection, however for organizations, information security is a lot more extensive: It is tied in with guarding client information, but on the other hand, it's tied in with keeping organization licensed innovation, representative data and numerous other informational collections secure.

How do protection and security relate to digital marketing? While purchaser desires might overarch, taking care of information protection and security are regularly two particular errands for organizations. The previous is normally an increasingly front-end process and includes the purchaser consenting to sharing their data. The last is a back-end process that requires noteworthy coordination between frameworks, innovation, and foundation to respect that assent and keep the information secure from outside gatherings getting to it illicitly. While enactment, for example, general data protection regulation (GDPR)[1] expects organizations to oversee information protection and security, a significant part of the advanced showcasing exchange today centers around information security, explicitly overseeing what purchasers agree to share and for what purposes.

Individual data falls into two primary classifications: a client willfully sharing individual information and ignorant accumulation by invested individuals. Any of these choices represent a genuine danger to online security. In any case, once more, clients can likewise profit by the gathering or sharing of individual data. This slight line is our focal point of dialog today. Normally, we as a whole have things we need to mind our own business on the grounds that, as people, we are especially delicate to social weight. In any case, when the things we need to secure are put away or happen on the web, at that point we stay defenseless (Aguirre et al., 2016). In this way, we need some type of online security to ensure our touchy data and, all the more significantly, keep undertakings from utilizing what they think about us for showcasing control. Today, security is a top worry for online clients, with a larger part (86%) of them finding a way to protect their wellbeing on the web. Similarly, governments, businesses, and private ventures over the world are placing vigorously information security guidelines and approaches, further showing the significance of buyer protection. Accordingly, digital privacy is considered as the essential focal point of this report.

6.1.1 PROBLEM AREA OF THE STUDY

The computerized disturbance that has reformed the manner in which individuals convey and work together has changed its course lately. Where shoppers had turned out to be acquainted with sharing their own data in return for advantages and administrations from organizations, many are presently feeling a growing concern for the protection and security of this data and are less ready to share. They've understood the disadvantages of putting their lives on the web, principally that opening up their data to brands can welcome marketing practices that are, even from a pessimistic standpoint, profoundly intrusive. Brands that utilize customer's information to target and contact their audiences are presently faced with the challenge of tending to purchasers' hesitance to share while as yet meeting their business objectives. They have to utilize successful marketing practices to get new clients, yet additionally be careful about not exceeding the limits these clients have set up.

A key factor in the situation marketers are facing is the waiting purchaser desire for exceptionally important, customized content. Customers would prefer not to share the personal subtleties of their lives; however, they additionally would prefer not to get offers that have no pertinence to them. Sadly, without data about their clients, marketers have no real way to create and convey content that is customized to their needs. Sadly, there is a distinction between how individuals talk about the significance of online protection and how they manage it. From one viewpoint, buyers are increasingly educated about the hazard that accompanies sharing individual information. Then again, despite everything, they share this data uninhibitedly on the web and consent to security approaches they haven't read. This issue carries us to the truth of security conundrum, which entangles the circumstance for advertisers.

About 18 months prior, a group from the Stanford Institute for Economic Policy Research and MIT analyzed more than 3,000 understudies to comprehend their security inclinations. Shockingly, a dominant part of these college understudies were happy to surrender their private information if there was a motivator to do as such. The examination group discovered that understudies were prepared to share their companions' email addresses in return for a free pizza. The purpose of referencing this investigation is to comprehend the job marketer plays in this blend. Like understudies, normal customers are vocal about the need to regard their protection. Be that as it may, when advertisers attempt to dissect their exercises, clients regularly show they ache for comfort.

In many organizations, advertisers are entrusted with acquiring new clients and, thusly, speaking to their voice. Yet, the inquiry is: do they advocate for buyers' protection or comfort? As we consider on that, here is a similarly significant inquiry: by what method would marketers be able to exceed expectations in their activity without client insight?

6.2 AIM AND OBJECTIVES

The major aim of this study was to analyze online privacy vs. digital marketing which matters more. Accordingly, the objective of this study was:

- To understand consumer privacy concern about internet marketing;
- To present a clearer view on how to adopt digital marketing strategy without affecting online privacy;

6.2.1 RATIONALE OF THE STUDY

An examination led by Accenture uncovered that 80% of customers in the UK and the US, matured somewhere in the range of 20 and 40, consider protection to be a relic of times gone by. To them, shields aren't sufficient to secure individual information. Shockingly, about a portion of them wouldn't fret organizations following their online practices, on the off chance that it brought about progressively significant, customized proposals. It shows up as though the buyers are all the more sympathetic if there is a trade-off (Krafft, Arden, and Verhoef, 2017). We completely comprehend that for advertisers to focus on their shoppers successfully and offer an increasingly customized understanding, they should follow their online conduct. As a matter of fact, brands would prefer not to burn through their cash and time promoting to prospects who won't change over. In this way, from a business viewpoint, it bodes well. Besides, data putting away may likewise profit shoppers. It encourages them direct online exchanges all the more rapidly.

Be that as it may, once more, we are conscious of the risks of giving a lot of data to associations. Not by any means the purported 'trustworthy' organizations are safe from abusing purchaser information. The two models underneath reveal to everything. The Cambridge Analytica outrage alone has revealed insight into the degree to which customer data winds up in surprising spots. In the event that that was insufficient to crack you out, possibly the Equifax rupture[2] will effectively express the idea. The Equifax break probably won't have been greater than other startling information ruptures that went before it, however it traded off the character of just about 146 million Americans. Significantly progressively troubling is that the very rupture undulated through the monetary framework to influence purchasers who have never collaborated with the firm (Chaffey and Ellis-Chadwick,

2019). These two cases give obvious motivations to make a move to shield shoppers. Lamentably, security laws still fall behind.

While customers are careful about their online security, advertisers ought to be significantly increasingly concerned on the grounds that protection matters the most. Presently like never before, advertisers have the chance to address the security worries of their clients, and conceivably affect online protection. They should:

- Make information utilize progressively straightforward;
- Use innovation that is security cognizant as a matter of course;
- Claim and control clients' information.

Up until this point, finding a parity is as yet a subject of extensive discussion, so there is a requirement for more grounded enactment to ensure buyers. It has neither rhyme nor reason that guarding individual data depends altogether on the gathering who holds it.

The Internet is rapidly turning into the world's biggest open electronic commercial center. It is assessed to contact 50 million individuals around the world, with development evaluations averaging roughly 10% every month. Creative business experts have found that the Internet can be misused to offer various administrations both for their clients and for their vital accomplices. The Internet has likewise upset retail and direct promoting. Shoppers can shop from their homes for a wide assortment of items from makers and retailers everywhere throughout the world. They can see these items on their PCs or TVs, get to data about the items, and envision the manner in which the items may fit together, and after that request and pay for their decisions (Dimofte, Haugtvedt, and Yalch, 2015). The Internet has changed current business and displayed another worldview of business connections and exchanges. Notwithstanding the much-proclaimed late accomplishments in using the Internet-commercial center, one of the significant obstacles against full-scale mix of the Internet-commercial center with present-day business is the absence of certainty Internet purchasers have in the recently created showcasing apparatus[3]. The most vital issue that Internet shoppers have distinguished is dread and doubt in regards to loss of individual protection related with the rising electronic business commercial center. One ongoing review embraced by Equifax and Harris Associates discovered that more than 66% of Internet customers considered the protection worry to be significant[4].

In spite of its significance, the accessible writing on Internet advertising and security is frequently specially appointed, scrappy, and on occasion opposing. There is an unmistakable requirement for precise research to incorporate thoughts from different sources so as to land at an extensive image of the applicable issues. This chapter displays such an exhaustive picture from the purchaser's security point of view. For organizations taking part in Internet promoting, this chapter empowers them to turn out to be better mindful of purchaser protection issues and better prepared for the usage of security codes for reasonable data rehearses (Kannan, 2017). For purchasers, this chapter gives an extensive image of the issues in question and information of the applicable security upgrading advancements and instruments that they can use to ensure themselves.

6.3 WHAT IS CONSUMER PRIVACY?

The individuals, who drew the many-sided and perfect pictures of creatures in caverns, for example, those in Lascaux in France, did as such in profound and dull environment. Their specialty was intended for the chose few and they frequently "marked" their compositions by blowing shade over their hand to leave their imprint—a sort of early biometric. People have constantly comprehended the idea of protection and utilized it to uncover, or not, different parts of themselves. Protection is about decision, the decision to uncover or not to uncover, insights regarding yourself and your life. These early individuals uncovered a piece of what their identity was and this ethos of what security is, stays with us today[5].

We each need to feel as though we have authority over what data we show to the outside world. Regular, we wind up in circumstances where we unveil to people and associations, different snippets of data about what our identity is, our main event, and how we do it. When we enter our work environment, we may "check-in" indicating what time we arrived. When we hand over our bank card to the café at noon to purchase our lunch, the bank presently realizes that we were at that shop and burned through $10 at 12 early afternoon on Tuesday (Martin, 2015). On our way home, we make a call to our accomplice to tell them our entry time, the telephone organization at that point knows our area and which number was called.

Security as an idea has not changed in a long time since Homo sapiens appeared, yet protection as an activity has changed, and the computerized age has acquainted layers of intricacy with the basic idea of protection that we need, as advanced residents, to disentangle and get it. As we head into a period where we are characteristically associated to our gadgets and each other through the Internet of Things, security will turn into a much increasingly divergent and complex scene. We have to go ahead into this new period with a more profound comprehension of how to ensure security rights are kept up and regarded (Confos and Davis, 2016).

From one perspective, individual data that isn't relied upon to change drastically after some time can be alluded to as static private data, for example, referential data, authentic money-related data, wellbeing data, individual affiliations and convictions, and individual records. Other private data incorporates data that changes drastically after some time, however all things considered can be gathered and broke down so that a well-educated individual profile might be produced. This data is alluded to as unique individual data, for example, movement history, and action content.

6.4   A TAXONOMY FOR PRIVACY CONCERNS

There exists a wide scope of Internet advertising exercises that have adverse effect on the Internet purchaser's individual security[6]. The security concerns are not restricted to the more notable instances of garbage mailing[7], or unlawful Web treat conveyance, however, have extended to specific practices that have moved toward becoming foundations of Internet dealers' income streams, for instance, the selling of purchaser databases for direct showcasing purposes (Athey, Catalini, and Tucker, 2017). In the course of recent years, we have seen proof of an expanding number of security-related cases, as identified with the development of internet showcasing exercises:

- Privacy concerns identified with the exercises of garbage email showcasing associations, for example, cyber promotions and net. net.
- The exercises of web-based promotions that track the client's utilization history and inclinations through treats, for example, those from DoubleClick.net, Preferences.com, and numerous others.
- Protection worries over malevolent projects that can be built through security openings in numerous Internet devices, for

example, Java, ActiveX, JavaScript, and numerous others. Surely understood vindictive procedures incorporate ActiveX controls that can acquire an individual's credit data and JavaScript that gets to individual records.

- privacy concerns with respect to the utilization and move of private data, represented by the cases including: MSN (Microsoft Network) and their routine with regards to following all exercises of their endorsers; Microsoft SideWalk watchers and their survey action examples to be utilized for Microsoft showcasing purposes. Decisions to quit such practices are regularly non-existent or amazingly hard to work out (Michaelidou, Keeling, and Siamagka, 2019).
- Concerns over dissemination, frequently for monetary profits, of private data, regularly for purposes other than the reason for which it was gathered: a prominent case is the ongoing case of America online selling its supporter contact data, money related data, and internet exercises.

Here are some additional privacy concern terms designated below:

1. **Improper Access:** To penetrate an Internet customer's private PC without notice to or affirmation from the shopper. This sort of security encroachment brings about the introduction of private data to unapproved watchers, regularly bringing about the accumulation of such data for promoting purposes (Armstrong et al., 2018).

2. **Improper Collection:** To gather a purchaser's private data from the Internet without notice to or affirmation from the customer. Such private data incorporates a customer's email address, kinds of programming the purchaser utilizes, the buyer's Web get to history, private records or databases, and so forth. Generally, inappropriate accumulation will prompt ill-advised examination and ill-advised exchange.

3. **Improper Monitoring:** To screen (lead reconnaissance on) a buyer's Internet exercises without notice to or affirmation from the purchaser. By utilizing treats, Internet showcasing organizations can watch where and when the shopper visits Web destinations, to what extent the buyer stays, and what sort of exchanges the purchaser conducts. By and large, inappropriate checking will bring about ill-advised examination.

4. **Improper Analysis:** To break down a purchaser's private data without appropriate notice, and to get ends from such an investigation. Such determinations may incorporate a purchaser's shopping and spending designs, shopping practices and inclinations. The accumulation of private data by an Internet dealer at first for one specific reason, yet its ensuing use for different purposes without assent from the purchaser, not exclusively could be depicted as ill-advised examination yet in addition could bring about ill-advised exchange (Chester and Montgomery, 2017).

5. **Improper Transfer:** To move a customer's private data to different organizations without notice to or affirmation from the purchaser. For example, different Internet organizations sell, distribute, circulate, and share their client databases, which contain client private data, for example, postal, and email addresses (Ryan, 2016).

6. **Undesirable Solicitation:** To transmit data to potential Internet shoppers without their affirmation or authorization. Such security attacks incorporate garbage mail, mass direct email, and garbage Internet push channels (Ridley-Siegert, 2015).

7. **Improper Storage:** To keep private data in a non-secure way bringing about an absence of reliability of the put away data, or absence of confirmation control for data get to. For example, empowering individual record-holders to see private data concerning different records, changing data without appropriate approval would establish such protection concerns. Ill-advised capacity is normally identified with the worries of data secrecy and information honesty (Kucuk, 2016).

6.5   HOW THE INTERNET CHANGED PRIVACY FOREVER?

The Internet changed how protection is taken care of in light of mass introduction. The Internet opened up correspondence channels that we had never utilized and moved data at speed, crosswise over a large number of outlets. There was no layer incorporated with the Internet for security or individual personality. Without this layer, settling on a decision about when, to whom, and for what reason to uncover certain information, was never going to be direct[8].

In any case, the Internet was convincing, so these apparently little issues were overlooked, and we as a whole, as people and organizations, grasped the power that the Internet gave us. Before long, nearly everybody had a site, business associations digitized their procedures and brought them online for all to get to. It was this digitization of procedures and assignments that expected us to uncover individual data, which carried security into the spotlight.[9]. We should view an ordinary procedure, that was completed pre- and post-the internet.

Prior to the internet, on the off chance that you shared some close to home subtleties, for example, your place of residence, it was for the most part in paper design, for example, a structure. This would then be turned in or presented on the bank; a couple of individuals who utilized it to set up your financial balance would then observe the structure. You'd presumably need to demonstrate who you were utilizing a service bill, or driver's permit, which you'd show to the bank employee legitimately, or present in duplicates on the bank. All paper subtleties would then be recorded in some dusty bureau, until it was destroyed a few years after the fact. The quantity of individuals associating with your subtleties was negligible[10]. Security breaks happened, yet it was on a lot littler scale as a result of the numbers associated with the procedure.

In the online financial balance arrangement, your information is presently put away carefully and open by numerous people. It can conceivably be gotten to in the accompanying situations if security isn't all around actualized:

During stockpiling by directors of the database (at the bank and the credit document organization). By cybercriminals who can hack into the database, perform assaults during exchange, or phish login qualifications from either the individual or the framework director. The subsequent situation is the most concerning and we will really expound on that later. The Internet has changed protection perpetually and the genie is out of the sack. Except if you have had no online communications over the most recent 20 years, regardless of where you live, your own information will be on numerous large numbers of databases, on numerous data enters over the world[11].

6.6 ADMINISTRATIVE PROTECTION FOR PRIVACY

Security is a mind-boggling idea. A worthy utilization of private data in a single setting might be an unsatisfactory attack of security in another. Nonetheless, numerous security issues are in the supposed "dim" territory.

Numerous businesses in the private segment are currently presenting significant, customer agreeable, self-administrative security systems in their tasks. These incorporate instruments for encouraging mindfulness and the activity of decision web-based, assessing private area selection of, and adherence to reasonable data practices, and question goals (Beck, 2015). The direct market association (DMA)[12] has, for instance, set up various codes and rules for self-administrative activities for its individuals. For example, the mail preference service (MPS)[13] and the telephone preference service (TPS)[14] handle spontaneous garbage mail and telemarketing. Organizations in the Internet markets are giving more consideration to the requirement for purchaser security. A developing number of willful organizations, from banking and protection to coordinate Internet advertising and media communications, have composed their own security codes with an end goal to battle off enactment and support a genuinely necessary level of certainty among their shoppers (Belk, 2016).

6.7   PROTECTION ENHANCING TECHNOLOGIES

While administrative methodologies planned for tending to protection issues in Internet showcasing have gotten impressive consideration, the effective coordination and across the board acknowledgment of security guidelines are as yet not a reality. Then again, a self-started private industry planned for giving innovative answers for down to earth Internet advertising protection concerns has been developing at a sensational rate. Rising gauges just as the horde of items encapsulating security improving innovations are giving an abundance of individualistic mechanical decisions that one can make to upgrade the assurance of one's protection with regards to internet business (see Table 6.1).

6.7.1   P3 AND OPS

One of the main endeavors by the innovation business planned for institutionalizing security inclination articulation has been attempted by the world-wide-web consortium (W3C), a non-benefit gathering gaining practical experience in proposing and implementing gauges on the Web. The platform for privacy preference (P3) standard will empower Internet buyers to be educated and to settle on decisions about the gathering, use, and divulgence of their private data on the Web. Under P3 every Internet trader will profile and enlist their very own protection practice. In an occasion wherein an Internet purchaser's security inclination matches with the protection practice profile of the Internet dealer, at that point no move will be made. Something else, the Internet customer will be educated regarding the inconsistencies, and the person in question will have the option to settle on decisions in regards to whether to acknowledge or dismiss every disparity. The P3 standard depends to a great extent on the OPS (open profiling standard[15]) put together by Internet innovation merchants: Netscape (which has effectively declared designs to help P3 in program and server conditions), Firefly (utilizing a restrictive innovation in which customers can submit inclination profiles), and VeriSign (which will issue the believed personality for every one of the gatherings associated with the Internet showcase). Microsoft has likewise demonstrated that it means to help the P3 standard in its future items.

The Internet customer network has, to a great extent, bolstered the institutionalization endeavors, for example, P3 and OPS, however by the by is worried about the absence of review and implementation procedures managing inconsistencies between the protection profile and genuine security rehearses. Profiling methods can just halfway manage the worry of absence of customer protection in the Internet-commercial center (Stephen, 2016).

6.7.2 TRUST FRAMEWORK

Various firms offer mechanical administrations to handle the focal issue of general trust framework. Such an administration gives non-disavowal of personality, practices, and benefit for both Internet buyers and Internet vendors. The administration offered by VeriSign (www.verisign.com) manages the issue of building up a confided in character through the accreditation of the open key, creating what is normally known as a computerized authentication. Confirmation of way of life as set up by VeriSign is done through a procedure called Digital Signature, in which the endorsement is checked for VeriSign's validation signature. From a security point of view, both the Internet shopper and Internet vendor should be confirmed to be confided all together for an electronic exchange to happen. By managing an Internet vendor that is viewed as believed, Internet purchasers won't need

TABLE 6.1 Relationships between Seclusion Technologies and Seclusion Concerns

| | Recognition Principle | | Authorize Principle | | | | Remedy |
	Merchant Profiling	Trust Framework	Access Control	Use of Preference	Unknown Object	Encoding	Index
Irregular access	–	S	S	P	–	–	–
Irregular collection	P	P	–	P	–	S	–
Irregular monitoring	P	P	–	P	S	P	–
Irregular use	P	P	–	–	–	–	–
Irregular transfer	P	P	–	P	–	–	–
Undesirable request	–	–	–	P	P	–	S
Irregular storage	P	P	–	P	–	S	–

Note: S = Successful; P = Predictable.

to be worried about ill-advised access to their private information. Moreover, issues of inappropriate data accumulation, ill-advised checking, and classification can likewise be managed along these lines through confided in characters (Martin and Murphy, 2017).

On the other hand, the administrations offered by Trust (www.truste. org) are planned for furnishing Internet customers with a believed brand of protection rehearses. Trust can survey and review locales to guarantee they accurately reveal their data rehearses. This methodology looks like an administrative methodology in their endeavors to manage inappropriate accumulation, use, and move in a design that is restricted by the degree of the all-inclusiveness of TRU.

6.7.3   STE'S ADMINISTRATION

6.7.3.1   SECRECY AND ENCRYPTION

At present, the best and broadly utilized innovation that has significantly affected the security worries of Internet customers has been cryptography. Classification of correspondence between the two conveying gatherings is managed, as any watching outsider cannot see the substance of a message. Moreover, encryption can likewise be used to secure one's own information, since unwanted gatherings can't gather helpful data in regards to the Internet customer (Kannan, 2017). Encryption protection improving innovation is frequently packaged with computerized signature innovation as the innovation fundamental a worldwide secure framework, giving powerful validated, secret, and unquestionable methods for Internet trade between Internet vendors and buyers.

Another method for securing the Internet shopper's protection is to empower Internet customers to complete their exercises in a mysterious way. Various current endeavors are planned for empowering Internet shoppers to do mysterious exercises, such endeavors incorporate Cyber-Cash (www.cybercash.com), which empowers unknown money use in Internet business; different unknown remailers that empower unknown email interchanges; Anonymiser.com, which grants customers to peruse the Web secretly; and wise Web operators, for example, Jango (www. marimba.com).

6.7.3.2   NEARBY CONTROL AND FILTERING

As far as ensuring one's own security, a wide assortment of protection upgrading advances have been created, allowing an individual Internet purchaser to pick the level and extent of individual data to be made accessible to Internet dealers. The principal class of individual security improving innovation manages the issue of access control, as in data is given to Internet dealers just when the required authorization is conceded. Such an innovation has been broadly utilized in the region of controlling access of Internet dealer applications, for example, Java, ActiveX, JavaScript, and numerous others. Singular Internet shoppers can empower or debilitate gets to (e.g., record framework gets to, or speaking with the Internet dealer) in light of the showcasing reason for the trader application (Martin, 2015). As of late, Internet shipper applications have embraced the declaration and trust structure to furnish the shopper with a superior feeling of comprehension as to the inception of such applications, bringing about confided in Java and ActiveX innovations. Partnerships have since a long time ago applied different access control advances, for example, firewalls, and intermediary servers, not exclusively to ensure the security of individual corporate clients, yet in addition to secure the privacy of the association all in all.

An individual Internet buyer additionally may choose to use the different protection improving innovations that play out the capacity of sifting singular Internet advertising messages dependent on their substance. In the zone of electronic message separating, items, for example, Intermitted, and Junk Mail channel have empowered the shopper to oppose direct Internet mail promoting endeavors and consequently address the protection worry of undesirable sales. Moreover, guardians have for some time been securing the protection of their youngsters by utilizing well known Internet sifting programming, for example, Net Nanny and Cyber Sitter, which channel out the improper substance that might be available.

6.8   ADVERTISERS ARE SURROUNDED BY PRIVACY CHALLENGES

The issue of customer security is changing the showcasing scene and putting weight on advertisers from three edges:

1. **Security Regulations:** Worries over buyer security assurance are driving stricter government guidelines. The EU GDPR expects advertisers to proactively request assent before gathering or following a client under any character, even an IP address. It additionally gives clear direction on how a business must speak with their clients once a rupture has happened[16].

   To put it plainly, any organization working with the EU must demonstrate they have sufficient information insurance and have the option to erase individual information if a client asks them to. Resistance can be exorbitant: $20 million or 4% of yearly income, whichever is higher. Notwithstanding a lot of media consideration, the GDPR still found numerous organizations napping: as indicated by CompTIA, just 13% of firms said they were completely consistent with GDPR one month before guidelines became effective (Athey, Catalini, and Tucker, 2017). In the US, the territory of California passed a comparable law this year. What's more, with the continuous worry over online security getting expanding media investigation, more enactment could be end route.

   This puts more weight on advertisers who need to make exceptionally important, directed battles, however, now need as far as possible on their past wellsprings of client information and the genuine danger of violating new and entangled laws.

2. **Danger of Data Breaches:** Programmers are persistent, and the dangers (and dangers) of information ruptures are high. The Identity Theft Resource Centre detailed the quantity of information ruptures hopped 29% in the primary portion of 2017, up from an unequalled high of 1,093 out of 2016. They're additionally costly. As indicated by IBM's 2018 Cost of a Data Breach Study, the expense of an information rupture rose 6.4% to $3.86 million that is $148 per lost or taken record. Advertisers' absence of power over corporate information security just adds to the weight they feel and the duties they face (Chester and Montgomery, 2017).

3. **Purchaser Fear:** An ongoing overview directed by Kelton Global, main worldwide bits of knowledge firm, revealed purchasers' most recent mentalities and assumptions regarding how they need brands to treat their information and speak with them, especially in light of the much-promoted Facebook information rupture. The review of 1,000 customers indicated they:

   i. **Are Suspicious of Organizations:** 73% accept brands utilize their own data without their insight.

  ii. **Care About Their PII:** Eighty-three percent have worries with the sort of information brands gather.

 iii. **Don't Care for Being Shriveled:** Just 17% need brands utilizing web following, and just 8% need brands utilizing web-based social networking following.

Shoppers are more protected than any other time in recent memory, and that is simply one more obstacle advertisers need to survive. Every one of the three protection concerns dissolves purchaser trust and make purchasers less inclined to buy. Furthermore, they represent an extraordinary test in light of the fact that at their center is the issue of how brands handle client information—the backbone of each promoting effort[17].

6.9　IS THIS THE END OF PERSONALIZATION?

Each computerized advertiser realizes that personalization drives results. Research demonstrates that 78% of web clients state by and by important substance from brands builds their buy purpose. What's more, the outcomes confirm: 88% of U.S. advertisers detailed seeing quantifiable enhancements because of personalization. Truth be told, personalization can drive 5–8x ROI on promoting spend. Purchasers need advertisers to make them feel exceptional without advertisers finding out about them clandestinely or sharing knowledge behind their backs. Furthermore, organizations stress over putting away outsider information that new laws have made considerably harder to gather[18].

Digital Marketing holds a gigantic potential for organizations and purchasers; however, it might likewise cause security infringement. The adjusting of useful employments of these information sources with the protection privileges of people is really one of the most testing open strategy issues of the data age. Customers in the Internet commercial center need to control what individual data is unveiled about them, to whom, and how that data will be utilized and further circulated. In this chapter, we have plotted a scientific categorization that portrays, sort, and dissect customer security concerns. We have additionally audited the present cutting-edge innovation, and brought up the up-and-coming coordination of business self-guideline, directed law implementation, and the customer's capacity to upgrade singular security assurance using innovation. In any case, what's to come isn't all blushing. There is much that should be done so as to make the Internet a generally worthy commercial center for the trading of merchandise and ventures among dealers and shoppers.

6.10   ANALYSIS AND DISCUSSION

With regards to our aggregate feeling of web security, 2018 is unquestionably the time of mindfulness. It's amusing that it took Facebook's unholy association with a little-known information mining counseling firm named Cambridge Analytica to raise the alert. All things considered, there were at that point inexhaustible instances of how our data was being utilized by unidentified powers on the web. It truly took just composition the words "Cabo San Lucas" as a major aspect of a disposable line in some close to home email to a companion to start a huge number of Cabo resort advertisements and Sammy Hagar's face putting the edges of our web-based social networking encourages.

6.10.1   *INTERNET USERS WORRY ABOUT ONLINE PRIVACY*

In 2018, it's never been clearer that when we grasp innovative advancements, all of which make our lives simpler, we are genuinely grabbing hold of a twofold-edged sword. Be that as it may, has our enlivening come excessively late? As a general public, would we say we are as of now so snared on the comforts web empowered innovations give us that we're hard-squeezed making the case that we need the control of our own information back?

It's an intriguing inquiry[19]. Our computerized showcasing firm as of late directed an overview to all the more likely see how individuals feel about web protection issues and the new development to restore authority over what application suppliers and interpersonal organizations do with our own data.

Given the present media condition and terrifying features with respect to online security ruptures, the survey results, at any rate superficially, were genuinely unsurprising. As per our investigation, web clients overwhelmingly article to how our data is being imparted to and utilized by outsider merchants. Nothing unexpected here, an astounding 90% of those surveyed were very worried about web protection. In a great case of "Goodness, how the compelling have fallen," Facebook and Google have all of a sudden arrived in the positions of the organizations we confide at all, with just 3% and 4% of us, individually, professing to have any confidence by the way they dealt with our data.

Notwithstanding customers' obvious worry about online security, the review results additionally uncovered members do next to no to shield their data on the web, particularly if doing so comes at the expense of comfort and time. Truth be told, 60% of them download applications without perusing terms and conditions, and near one of every five (17%) report that they'll keep an application they like, regardless of whether it breaches their security by following their whereabouts.

6.11   DO UNITED STATES VS WORLDWIDE MOBILE USERS UNDERSTAND HOW COMPANIES USE THEIR DATA?

While the overview uncovers just 18% state they are "extremely certain" with regards to believing retails locales with their own data, the segment is still on track to surpass a $410 billion web-based business go through this year. This, in spite of the greater part (54%) revealing they have a sense of safety acquiring from online retailers in the wake of finding out about online break after online rupture.

What's turned out to be evident from our review is that while individuals are unmistakably disappointed with the condition of web security, they feel deadened or essentially not well prepared to take care of business. It seems many are snared on the accommodation's internet living manages them and surrendered to the loss of protection if that is the thing that it expenses to play. The discoveries are not novel to our study. In an ongoing Harvard Business School study, individuals who were told the promotions showing up in their online life courses of events had been chosen explicitly dependent on their web search narratives appeared far less commitment with the advertisements, contrasted with a control bunch who didn't have an inkling how they'd been focused on. The examination uncovered that the genuine demonstration of organization straightforwardness, confessing about the showcasing strategies utilized, prevented client reaction at last.

Similar to the case with blameless schoolchildren, the world is a much better place when we accept there is an omniscient Santa Claus who mystically knows our mystery wants, rather than it being a sly present trade fixed by the guardians who obviously know the substance of our list of things to get. We state we need protections and security. We state we need straightforwardness. However, with regards to a worldwide web (WWW), where every one of the treats have been erased and our online life timetable thinks nothing about us, the client experience turns out to be less liquid.

The incongruity is, right around 66% (63%) of those surveyed in our review don't accept that organizations approaching our own data prompts a superior, progressively customized, online involvement with all, which is the main explanation organizations like Facebook state for needing our own data in any case. But, when an application we've introduced doesn't give us a chance to label our area to a post or advise us when a companion has labeled us in a photograph or alarmed us that the gadget we were looking for is on special this week, we feel insulted by our courageous modern lifestyle.

With the presentation of GDPR guidelines this late spring, the European Union has taken, by and large, the significant initial moves toward recapturing a portion of the online protection that we, as people, have been not able to take. GDPR throws the principal stone at the Goliath that is had free rein utilizing our own data against us. By doling out cruel punishments and fines for the individuals who misuse our private details-or if nothing else the individuals who aren't bounteously straightforward regarding how they expect to utilize those details-the EU, and by augmentation, those nations leading on the web business with them, has at last started a development to diminish the until-now free enterprise practices of business web endeavors. For this the internet Wild West, there's at long last another sheriff around the local area.

6.11.1 PERCEPTIONS OF ONLINE DATA PROTECTION AND INDIVIDUAL PRIVACY IN INDIA

With the development of web access driven by less expensive availability crosswise over geologies and moderate yet ground-breaking cell phones, the # of web clients in India are ascending by the millions every month. Mainstream exercises online incorporate messages, visits, and internet-based life connections and online buys from web-based business stores.

These require sharing of individual data-email IDs, passwords, age, sexual orientation, city, individual interests, IP address, and individual data partook in messages and visit sessions, and so on. While the web clients in India comprehend security issues at an abnormal state, particularly with the ongoing exposures on NSA's worldwide information snooping, numerous clients are as yet uninformed of how their information is caught and not certain that these will remain carefully private.

It is basic that we comprehend the common-sense issues associated with teaching clients about information security, while hoping to implement stricter protection controls by means of lawful methods. A late investigation (directed August 2013) by EMC Privacy Index uncovered that Indians positioned first among 15 nations for their readiness to exchange security for online accommodation.

The netizens of India felt security is a zone of enormous worry for them today and hope to be so throughout the following 5 years. While there is ability to share private data for accommodation and a continuous worry about assurance of protection, a critical percentage are not acting even at an individual level.

The netizens of India felt security is a zone of enormous worry for them today and hope to be so throughout the following 5 years. While there is ability to share private data for accommodation and a continuous worry about assurance of protection, a critical percentage are not acting even at an individual level.

To summarize, Indians are eager to exchange online security for comfort, while simultaneously incredibly worried about their own information. However, critical percentages are not acting to take individual protections, notwithstanding when it is simple and viable. Indian online clients anticipate that the administration should administer laws securing their online individual information. They likewise expect online shippers/associations to deal with the individual information gathered, under severe security contemplations. At the same time, they don't have overpowering trust in the capacities of the legislature/online associations-on the two aptitudes and morals fronts. India's web base is developing and is relied upon to contact 500 million web information endorsers in the following 4 years. In the above setting, it is anything but difficult to see a tremendous and enlarging hole in online security assurance of individual information.

Today no particular enactment exists in India (rather than the EU or Brazil), unmistakably commanding on the web protection strategies. It is basic to address the accompanying, to quicken online business development in the nation.

6.12 THE RIGHT TO BE FORGOTTEN

A most stressing aspect regarding the Internet is its life span and reach. In the event that you put an image of themselves on Facebook following a night out, looking somewhat wornout' in 2010, odds are in 2020 despite everything, it'll be there for the entire world to see. That situation is awful enough.

Internet-based life has been one of the best utilization of computerized innovation. People love to prattle, and stages like Facebook have taken this human impulse and made a fruitful plan of action around it. The model they have utilized depends on free get to. In any case, this includes some major disadvantages to our protection. Social stages hold colossal measures of our own information. We pursue a record, entering different subtleties, for example, name, address, date of birth, etc. When we start utilizing the stage, we enter information about our day-by-day lives, our inclinations, and preferences and whom we know—we even let the stage know our private connections to other people. The majority of this structures the social diagram, which can be utilized by engineers to remove and use different social information.

6.13 CONCLUSION AND RECOMMENDATIONS

In summary, programmers are continually delivering progressively refined programming to slither the web, take data, or simply unleash destruction. All the web stages, instalment frameworks, and online life locales you use should have every single imaginable shield set up. Checking your site for interruption or suspicious conduct is likewise an absolute necessity. You ought to incorporate safety efforts for your computerized showcasing efforts similarly as you would with any online action.

An appropriate advanced promoting effort requires a significant speculation of their time and exertion. To acquire achievement, you have to lead statistical surveying, distinguish their group of spectators, create content, plan client maintenance versus prospect transformation, and consider how everything fits into their business channel.

Building up a decent system is critical for achievement in computerized promoting. Notwithstanding, you likewise need to consider web security. Dismissing this viewpoint can include dangers for both you and their clients. Here are some normal types of digital assaults and ways marketers can make them and their clients safe.

6.13.1 MALWARE OF ALL SORTS

When carrying out any responsibilities on their PC, an essential concern is guarding their data. When they are taking care of organization and client information, they have to give security considerably more noteworthy idea. The web has made our lives more straightforward, additionally fascinating, and the greater part of us cherish it. Nonetheless, it is additionally loaded up with potential risks. In the event that a site is noxious, at times it's sufficient just to open it to get tainted, without tapping on anything. Mal-advertising is another way programmers can get into their framework. They introduce malware in promotions that show up on confided in sites. On the off chance that they click on them, they could accidentally download and introduce malware on their PC.

There are various sorts of malware that can jeopardize their framework. Infections can spread through their system, tainting information and framework records. Spyware can be introduced on their PC to record keystrokes, messages, passwords, and other information that can be sent back to programmers. Ransomware can assume responsibility for their framework and the digital hoodlums request cash before they'll discharge the seized assets back to them. Messages can likewise contain hurtful connections or connections. They don't need to tap on the connection, now, and then it's sufficient just to open an email and get contaminated. Programers could introduce malevolent programming on their server too. This implies they could likewise contaminate the PCs of their clients who snap on advertisements on their site or connections in their bulletins. On the off chance that this occurs, their clients aren't probably going to return. The majority of this sounds terrifying-and it very well may be-yet it isn't that hard to remain safe. It is imperative to know how our frameworks get tainted and how to stay away from unsafe circumstances.

The primary line of safeguard is to get the best firewall and hostile to malware programming conceivable. At any value, it will probably spare them from unquestionably progressively exorbitant digital assaults. Update it consistently and be cautious. Try not to tap on anything in messages from obscure senders and if their companions send them something sudden, get in touch with them before opening it. Be cautious when perusing the web; don't open locales that appear to be suspicious. Introducing an antivirus program module or augmentation can enable them to choose whether to click or not.

6.13.2 WORDPRESS SECURITY

WordPress is the most prominent substance the executive's framework utilized today-so programmers realize it well. This stage is a most loved objective since in excess of 70% of WordPress destinations are not advanced for security. In the event that they use WordPress, it's a smart thought to get acquainted with its security highlights and introduce refreshes as they become accessible. Most of the programmers aren't keen on taking their information or erasing documents; however, assuming control over their email accounts. Deceitful spammers need to utilize their server to send spam emails. Spamming is a typical practice, and most ISPs and programming channels will obstruct an IP address recognized as a wellspring of spam. By utilizing their email servers, programmers maintain a strategic distance from this, yet their very own email crusades can be seriously restricted on the off chance that they start getting boycotted.

More up-to-date forms of WordPress and security modules explicitly address framework fixes and new security dangers. WordPress has a wide help network where they can discover help on the correct designs and best modules for their security. Be certain their site is facilitated by an organization that spotlights on client security, including framework separation and day-by-day record reinforcements. Normal reinforcements guarantee they can supplant any data that might be lost. On the off chance that their site is focused by programers, the best reaction is to remain quiet, reset their passwords, and run an output to recognize any malware. They ought to likewise contact their web have on the off chance that they need assistance with any issues.

6.13.3   NON-HUMAN TRAFFIC

In excess of a portion of web traffic is non-human. This incorporates bots submitting click extortion, scrubbers that record joins and other data from each page on a site, spambots, and that's just the beginning. The computerized idea of web-based publicizing is an ideal chasing ground for these bots. Impersonators are bits of programming that can catch and reproduce client accreditations. These can open the best approach to spy bots, DDoS (distributed denial of service) specialists, or deceitful programs. Publicizing that gets minimal human consideration might be slithered over and again by these impersonators, making false traffic tallies. Botnet location devices check the PC's attributes against a rundown of dangers and screen correspondences for practices that can be utilized by bots. Organizations need additional assurance in light of the fact that their systems can progress toward becoming wellsprings of botnet-based assault. That is the reason they ought to likewise consider executing a honey pot, a bogus invasion opportunity. In the event that it progresses toward becoming penetrated, they may have the option to get botnet acknowledgment marks for it.

Another approach to battle these dangers is to impart the data to parties who can follow the starting IP locations, or uncover false area records. Sites can battle bots with CAPTCHA tests which guarantee the client is human.

6.13.4   INDIVIDUAL AND PAYMENT DETAILS

So as to pay for publicizing, they'll need to give a strategy for installment. Tragically, there will be programmers hoping to catch their record and secret word data. On the off chance that they don't take the suggested wellbeing safety measures, their PC could at one point wind up being tainted with keylogging spyware. This kind of spyware monitors each keystroke. Thus, when they are signing into their email or installment accounts, programmers could without much of a stretch log their username and secret key. This implies they could rapidly get tightly to the majority of their own data which could even prompt fraud. It is critical to realize how to avoid this by introducing the essential programming and utilizing two-factor validation.

They additionally need to play it safe that will give their very own clients a protected installment technique, which means their clients' card and bank subtleties can't be taken. On the off chance that one of their customers experiences misrepresentation through their site, they could lose business from the hit to their image notoriety and the loss of customer certainty. The clients need to believe their business with their data so as to return. Pick PayPal, as perhaps the most secure technique for installment on the web. Ensure they execute secure sockets layer (SSL) innovation on their site. This will guarantee that all information that is transmitted between their site and their clients is scrambled with the goal that programmers can't catch delicate data.

6.13.5 WEB-BASED SOCIAL NETWORKING

Programers know about the real social locales. They aren't constantly after record data; some simply need to make tumult for themselves and their clients. They can make changes to their profile, including hostile photographs or false proclamations, which will insult their devotees. They may send spam or unseemly messages from their record to their clients, make perilous connections, and that's only the tip of the iceberg. So as to avoid this, they should utilize solid passwords and change them routinely. Solid passwords have at any rate 12 characters: lower-case and capital letters, numbers, and images. Try not to utilize word reference phrases or evident substitutions, such as supplanting the letter "O" for zero. Take a stab at utilizing irregular expressions: stir up words that don't normally go together, and make passphrases. Stop to consider the potential dangers and outcomes of anything they post on social destinations. Maintain a strategic distance from individual data, and never click on anything suspicious.

In the event that they effectively work in web-based life, they ought to know about brandjacking. It's hacking the entrance to their web-based social networking record and posting content that can hurt their image picture. Here's the notorious instance of Nokia New Zealand.

6.13.6 FORESTALL SOCIAL MEDIA CRISES AND BRAND JACKING

What may come valuable here is a web-based social networking checking device. It permits gathering continuously online notices of predefined watchwords, for instance, a brand name. Truth be told, here's a whole article associated with dealing with their online nearness. With a web-based social networking observing device set up, they're ready to follow ongoing notices about their image and promptly detect any suspicious conduct around their social channels.

6.13.7   CLIENTS AS THREATS

They need to manufacture great associations with their clients, however, there's constantly an opportunity a client may attempt to swindle them. Extortion can occur with numerous sorts of promoting efforts. This is the reason they ought to have programming that can recognize deceitful movement and conflicting client data. The initial phase in extortion avoidance is its location. The most straightforward approach to recognize it is through their site. Investigate the client's telephone number, postal division, and their detailed living arrangement. Do they coordinate? On the off chance that they don't, they realize something isn't right. So as to avoid this, their site ought to have an intricate lead approval content.

They ought to likewise audit login action, for example, the IP address traffic is originating from. Numerous leads originating from a similar IP address could demonstrate misrepresentation. They could likewise catch up on leads that appear to be suspicious, for example, conveying "client overviews" mentioning extra data. At last, if a lead or retail deal bomb the approval procedure and they disclose to them why, they simply help them submit extortion. They will effectively change the data that they found suspicious. Rather, simply acknowledge the lead, yet don't give deals kudos for it. Square the IP address where the lead originated from and don't do business with them.

NOTES

1. The EU General Data Protection Regulation (GDPR) is the most important change in data privacy regulation in 20 years. The regulation will fundamentally reshape the way in which data is handled across every sector, from healthcare to banking and beyond.

2. Equifax's Security team observed suspicious network traffic associated with its U.S. online dispute portal web application. In response, the Security team investigated and blocked the suspicious traffic that was identified.

3. Stephen, A. T., (2016). The role of digital and social media marketing in consumer behavior. *Current Opinion in Psychology, 10*, 17–21.

4. Aguirre, E., Roggeveen, A. L., Grewal, D., & Wetzels, M., (2016). The personalization-privacy paradox: Implications for new media. *Journal of Consumer Marketing, 33*(2), 98–110.

5. Martin, K. D., & Murphy, P. E., (2017). The role of data privacy in marketing. *Journal of the Academy of Marketing Science, 45*(2), 135–155.

6. Hartemo, M., (2016). Email marketing in the era of the empowered consumer. *Journal of Research in Interactive Marketing, 10*(3), 212–230.

7. Krafft, M., Arden, C. M., & Verhoef, P. C., (2017). Permission marketing and privacy concerns: Why do customers (not) grant permissions? *Journal of Interactive Marketing, 39*, 39–54.

8. Kerber, W., (2016). Digital markets, data, and privacy: competition law, consumer law and data protection. *Journal of Intellectual Property Law and Practice, 11*(11), 856–866.

9. Chaffey, D., & Ellis-Chadwick, F., (2019). *Digital Marketing*. Pearson UK.

10. Kamleitner, B., Mitchell, V., Stephen, A., & Kolah, A., (2018). Customers could be the weak link in consumer data management systems. *Journal of Data Protection and Privacy, 2*(2), 171–176.

11. Taylor, J. F., Ferguson, J., & Ellen, P. S., (2015). From trait to state: Understanding privacy concerns. *Journal of Consumer Marketing, 32*(2), 99–112.

12. The Data and *Marketing Association* (DMA), formerly the Direct Marketing Association, advances, and protects responsible data-driven marketing.

13. The MPS is here to make your choice known-so you get the mail you want and. a bereavement or just want to stop unsolicited mail register with the MPS.

14. The Telephone Preference Service (TPS) is a free service. It is the official central opt-out register on which you can record your preference not to receive unsolicited sales or marketing calls.

15. Open Profiling Standard (OPS) is a proposed standard for how web users can control the personal information they share with websites.

16. Voigt, P., & Von Dem Bussche, A., (2017). The EU general data protection regulation (GDPR). *A Practical Guide* (1st edn.). Cham: Springer International Publishing.

17. Goddard, M., (2017). The EU general data protection regulation (GDPR): European regulation that has a global impact. *International Journal of Market Research, 59*(6), 703–705.

18. Kucuk, S. U., (2016). Consumerism in the digital age. *Journal of Consumer Affairs, 50*(3), 515–538.

19. Lamberton, C., & Stephen, A. T., (2016). A thematic exploration of digital, social media, and mobile marketing: Research evolution from 2000 to 2015 and an agenda for future inquiry. *Journal of Marketing, 80*(6), 146–172.

KEYWORDS

- **direct market association**
- **distributed denial of service**
- **general data protection regulation**
- **mail preference service**
- **Microsoft network**
- **open profiling standard**

REFERENCES

Aguirre, E., Roggeveen, A. L., Grewal, D., & Wetzels, M., (2016). The personalization-privacy paradox: Implications for new media. *Journal of Consumer Marketing, 33*(2), 98–110.

Armstrong, G. M., Kotler, P., Harker, M. J., & Brennan, R., (2018). *Marketing: An Introduction.* Pearson UK.

Athey, S., Catalini, C., & Tucker, C., (2017). *The Digital Privacy Paradox: Small Money, Small Costs, Small Talk* (No. w23488). National Bureau of Economic Research.

Baker, M. J., & Saren, M., (2016). *Marketing Theory: A Student Text.* Sage.

Beck, E. N., (2015). The invisible digital identity: Assemblages in digital networks. *Computers and Composition, 35*, 125–140.

Belk, R., (2016). Extended self and the digital world. *Current Opinion in Psychology, 10*, 50–54.

Chaffey, D., & Ellis-Chadwick, F., (2019). *Digital Marketing.* Pearson UK.

Chester, J., & Montgomery, K. C., (2017). The role of digital marketing in political campaigns. *Internet Policy Review, 6*(4).

Confos, N., & Davis, T., (2016). Young consumer-brand relationship building potential using digital marketing. *European Journal of Marketing, 50*(11), 1993–2017.

Dimofte, C. V., Haugtvedt, C. P., & Yalch, R. F., (2015). *Consumer Psychology in a Social Media World.* Routledge.

Hollebeek, L. D., & Macky, K., (2019). Digital content marketing's role in fostering consumer engagement, trust, and value: Framework, fundamental propositions, and implications. *Journal of Interactive Marketing, 45*, 27–41.

Kannan, P. K., (2017). Digital marketing: A framework, review and research agenda. *International Journal of Research in Marketing, 34*(1), 22–45.

Karimi, S., Stoev, Y., & Zander, O., (2017). *Ethical Issues in E-Permission Marketing: A Study of How Consumer Behavior is Affected by Unethical Practices Involving E-Permission Marketing.*

Krafft, M., Arden, C. M., & Verhoef, P. C., (2017). Permission marketing and privacy concerns: Why do customers (not) grant permissions? *Journal of Interactive Marketing, 39*, 39–54.

Kucuk, S. U., (2016). Consumerism in the digital age. *Journal of Consumer Affairs, 50*(3), 515–538.

Martin, K. D., & Murphy, P. E., (2017). The role of data privacy in marketing. *Journal of the Academy of Marketing Science, 45*(2), 135–155.

Martin, K., (2015). Privacy notices as tabula rasa: An empirical investigation into how complying with a privacy notice is related to meeting privacy expectations online. *Journal of Public Policy and Marketing, 34*(2), 210–227.

Michaelidou, N., Keeling, D., & Siamagka, N. T., (2019). Consumer psychology and cross-cultural research SIG. In: *International Symposium on Consumer Personality in Contemporary Contexts* (Vol. 13, p. 14).

Ridley-Siegert, T., (2015). Data privacy: What the consumer really thinks. *Journal of Direct, Data and Digital Marketing Practice, 17*(1), 30–35.

Ryan, D., (2016). *Understanding Digital Marketing: Marketing Strategies for Engaging the Digital Generation*. Kogan Page Publishers.

Stephen, A. T., (2016). The role of digital and social media marketing in consumer behavior. *Current Opinion in Psychology, 10*, 17–21.

Verhoef, P. C., Stephen, A. T., Kannan, P. K., Luo, X., Abhishek, V., Andrews, M., & Hu, M. M., (2017). Consumer connectivity in a complex, technology-enabled, and mobile-oriented world with smart products. *Journal of Interactive Marketing, 40*, 1–8.

Vladeck, D. C., (2015). *Consumer Protection in an Era of Big Data Analytics* (Vol. 42, p. 493). Ohio NUL Rev.

CHAPTER 7

A Strategic Analysis of the Rise and Fall of Uber in the Private Urban Transport Business in the Metropolitan Area of Guadalajara

JOSSÉ G. VARGAS-HERNÁNDEZ

Research Professor, Department of Administration,
University Center for Economic and Managerial Sciences,
University of Guadalajara, México, E-mails: Jvargas2006@gmail.com;
jgvh0811@yahoo.com; josevargas@cucea.udg.mx

ABSTRACT

The objective of this study is to analyze the strategies for entering the private urban transport services market managed by the multinational company Uber in the Guadalajara Metropolitan Area, the growth conditions in coverage, its influence on urban mobility movements, and the decline due to competition and finally to the 2020 pandemic. The objective of this chapter is to reveal information about the Uber company in Guadalajara, Jal, and its foray into the Mexican private transport market. The entry of Uber into the local metropolitan area of the Guadalajara market has experimented an impressive rise despite the conflicts with the traditional taxi systems of private transportation of passengers. However, the pandemic has suddenly turned down the increasing growth into a falling and decreasing phase. In the same way, the present document deepens in Uber from a strategic and economic point of view, where an approach is made to the service that this firm provides through its platform, could conceivably be a part of the same important market of different types of transport private in the Metropolitan Area of Guadalajara. As a result, the analysis of this work shows the determining factors that have placed Uber as one of the leading companies within its area of influence and ends with some recommendations on the conflicts that the firm presents when entering a new market in the location.

7.1 INTRODUCTION

Uber is currently an international firm that offers its customers a private transport service through its platform, an application for smartphones, which associates travelers with drivers of vehicles registered in the system to offer a service of private transportation through vehicles to people. The organization classifies travel in many urban communities around the world, and its headquarters are located in California. Initially, drivers had vehicles that the company certified as appropriate. After 2012, Uber includes a broader determination of cars for the market. The cars are assigned with the portable application. With this application, customers can track the area of accessible cars and the qualities of both the car and the driver.

The big data solutions of the Uber Movement platform analyzed as a set of resources that allow the management and analysis of massive amounts of data, as Montealegre Gallocod (2017) concludes, have an important role in companies that need the information to plan or organize market strategies that impact society by generating positive value for their clients.

The company's operations begin in July 2014 in Mexico and Guadalajara, according to its official website. The qualities of this organization are the association between the driver of the automobile and the traveler who requires the benefit of the vehicle. Operating simultaneously, and also a stage of virtual private connection and not as a taxi organization. His method of connecting the customer and the supplier has been a progressive path for the market and has changed the big point of view of transport to a creative method of world rivalry. The entry of the firm in Latin America has caused an extraordinary confusion in the organization of the relationship of the taxi drivers with the commercial risk implied by the prominence that Uber obtains step by step. Therefore, there is a solid resistance.

The objective of this work is to reveal information about the Uber mobile application and its foray into the Mexican open transport market, in particular from Guadalajara. The objective of this study is to analyze the strategies for entering the private urban transport services market managed by the multinational company Uber in the Guadalajara Metropolitan Area, the growth conditions in coverage, its influence on urban mobility movements and the decline due to competition and finally to the 2020 pandemic.

To begin with, the document presents a general description of the strategic aspects of Uber and the service it provides. At this point, a description is made of how it has entered the Mexican market and has entered into direct competition with the conventional taxi service and other firms with a platform model similar to Uber. The chapter shows a general outline of the idea of Uber and the administration it provides and a brief synopsis of how it has entered the global transportation showcase.

In addition, the document delves into Uber from a strategic and competitive point of view (especially the taxi service), where an attempt is made to discover if the administration that provides this service, with its particularities and its competitive advantages, could possibly be considered as a component of the same important market of different types of public and private transport. It is intended to raise the advantages and disadvantages of this company in the market and what measures should be taken to solve the latter, as well as raise some competitive advantages that could be beneficial for the firm.

7.2 BACKGROUND OF THE PROBLEM

7.2.1 MARKET STUDIED

Guadalajara is one of the three most important cities in Mexico, accompanied by the CDMX (México City) and Monterrey, which receives thousands of national and foreign visitors daily who require transportation to visit its squares, colonial monuments, museums, religious buildings, etc. In addition to its mariachis, its great tequila fame, and the cordial treatment of its people that make Guadalajara a very attractive city for the general public. As for the subject of private auto transport Guadalajara in a great location that receives thousands of visitors daily.

According to González Pérez (2018) the technocity-system, has configured a motorized urban transport service with peculiar characteristics in the Guadalajara Metropolitan Area. In the land of tequila, the combination of use as a driver of the car should have been regulated after having had a wheelie or other types of intoxicating drinks. For this reason, on November

15, 2013, the Operation Saving Lives began, which can be summarized in street and avenue fliers where alcohol tests are performed on drivers; If it is positive, you are credited with an economic fine or an administrative closure in the Urban Center of Alcohol Retention for Alcoholmetry (CURVE) (González, 2017).

From that, many Tapatíos and visitors were scared; the first weekends, the bars and clubs looked half empty. However, the habits of city dwellers began to change, looking for mobility alternatives because people were not willing to stop drinking alcohol. Months passed, and the 2014 World Cup in Brazil arrived, and on those days where fans watched games from noon, and the party dragged on, a new mobility alternative to the city appeared: Uber. A "shared travel" app to travel quickly and reliably in just minutes, day or night. Without having to park or wait for a taxi or bus. With Uber, you request trips with a simple touch, and it is very easy to pay by credit card, or cash in some cities (González, 2017).

Complementary to the above, the market area and its geographical coverage are clarified, for this case. In July 2014, Uber arrives in Guadalajara and later in other states of the Republic, where people can enjoy the benefits provided by the Uber application, registering on the Uber website. It is worth mentioning that the service is currently present in more than 38 cities in Latin America (Ferrer, 2016). The authorization to Uber to operate in private urban transport contributes to increasing the urban mobility chaos experienced by the Guadalajara metropolitan area, whose horizontal expansive infrastructure congested by a vehicle overload (Hernández and Galindo, 2016).

Initially, the Uber service had accessibility restrictions through the mobile application that required payment by the user's credit card in exchange for delivering quality service with friendly service, offering music, bottled water, etc.

Uber's arrival in the city was not to everyone's liking, much less the taxi drivers, who responded with attacks on the drivers-partners of the North American company. Taxi drivers assaulted partner-drivers. Some of the places where attacks were registered were the New Central Trucking in Tlaquepaque, the vicinity of the Expo and other areas (González, 2017).

In the beginning, the sector to which this company is directed should be established. The transport services platform through mobile devices, Uber, launched a new modality in our city that had already been implemented in other cities in the world, it is the XL service. This modality that is already reflected in the application for Guadalajara users, allows you to have an Uber SUV-type service, but at a cheaper price due to the type of vehicles that can provide this service, such as Toyota Highlanders, Ford Explorers or Nissan Pathfinders, just to mention a few. These Van-type vehicles will accept to move up to a total of 6 passengers at a much more accessible price than an Uber SUV, which has a similar space, but is considered a Premium service (Trafficzmg, 2016).

Uber, in the country, has three modes of service: UberX, UberPool, and UberBlack; the two initial benefits are accessible or, rather, are typically taken by individuals who tend to use typical services, large space or shared use; UberX: it is Uber's most well-known and recurring alternative, it incorporates vehicles with a maximum 10-year model, although this depends on the Uber criteria for each city, it recognizes a maximum of four passengers and, alternatively, it allows the distribution of load between the traveler, Uber Pool: it was a simultaneous launch of UberX, delivering the door open to 3 customers from several areas to request an exit to a typical target that is close to all the customers who share the trip, thus saving a considerable sum of monetary resources.

On the other hand, UberBlack is a Premium administration, it was for clients with greater resources, it is part of the latest model of luxury cars, with a limit of four passengers, it is frequently used by associations and organizations for the transport of personnel (Uber, 2016).

At Uber, the user calculates the benefits to the portfolio with the launch of a calculator called #EnUberATodo, which compares the cost of your car with that of using this platform to move. One of the characteristics of this system is that it also helps you define if you want to use #UberX or #UberPool, the latter modality shares your journeys with other people and also the fare (González, 2017). To give an idea of the costs, this service costs approximately 112 pesos on a trip from Plaza del Sol to the Omnilife Stadium, with the ease of being able to transport up to 6 passengers.

The same Uber SUV trip would cost between 225 and 290 pesos (Trafficzmg, 2016). The uberfication generated a boom a few years ago in Guadalajara.

Since arriving in Guadalajara, Uber has caused problems with conventional taxi systems due to the way it operates and its working conditions. When the taxi drivers demonstrated in the city center and tried to paralyze the city with their demonstrations in the main vehicular arteries of the metropolis, some of them were injured and some of their cars were hit by stones and other objects that fell from the roof of the technology plaza located on Av. September 16 (González, 2017).

The regulation of the service has become one of the main issues to be addressed to solve the differences that drivers of this company face in relation to conventional taxi drivers (Pérez, 2016). In the city of Guadalajara, in the plenary session of the Jalisco Congress, the so-called "Uber Law" was tested. This law regulates Transport Network Companies, it applies to all private transport companies that work in the state, among which is Uber and Cabify. Changes in the law were foreseeable. What forced the Jalisco Congress to approve the so-called #LeyUber, on March 18, 2016, a legislation that regulates the transportation network companies (TNCs) that forces them to pay 35 thousand pesos for the operation permit and 1,600 pesos a year for each of the vehicles. In addition, they must allocate 1.5% of their income to allocate it to a green fund (González, 2017).

In theory, this regulation balances the working conditions between this company and that of regular taxi drivers. However, with regulation in place, some characteristics of the private taxi service have to be approved. So some recognized characteristics of the Uber service were modified (Pérez, 2016). The initial conditions of the Uber service leaned towards a relaxation accentuated by pluricausal social acceptance due to an increase in demand subsequently subject to regulations on citizen mobility (González, 2017a).

While in the course of the third month of the year 2017, several of the companies that provide the transport service through digital platforms had already registered with the Ministry of Mobility (Semov), Uber resisted doing so, and there was a reason. They were processing an injunction not to do so. Drivers and companies had until April 28 to register. However, they filed two injunctions. The first by Uber México Technology and Software S.A de C.V; and another by a group of company drivers. In May 2017, a federal judge granted the company a definitive suspension regarding some provisions of the Mobility and Transportation Law of the state of Jalisco, so that drivers will be able to continue operating without fear of being arrested for not registering with the state authorities (González, 2017).

When Uber completed 3 years of operating in the Guadalajara Metropolitan Area, they reported that they had created 33,000 jobs with their so-called "partners," who are the drivers of the cars. But what else did Uber bring? What "moved" in the city? Are they still the "best" option? (González, 2017).

Uber is the fastest-growing urban private transport company in the Guadalajara Metropolitan Area that has generated the greatest number of expressions, giving rise to regulatory changes in the field of motorized urban mobility (González, 2017b, 2018). Uber currently has 1.4 million users in the city. However, the prospect of the uberfication phenomenon in the Guadalajara Metropolitan Area is a deduction of González (2018) under the assumption that the traditional way to access the transport service exceeds the conditions of a reality subject to irreversibility is highly questionable. The entry of the multinational company Uber into the private urban transport market of the Guadalajara Metropolitan Area has led to the incorporation of cyber services from local companies such as Siggo and Sitio 40 Taxis Las Águilas, among others. Siggo offers as an innovation the Pink service intended for the exclusive transport of women and carried out by women (El Informador, 2016).

In May 2020, Dara Khosrowshahi, CEO of the multinational company UBER announced that as part of its economic readjustment process due to COVID-19, the firm decided to close its offices located in Guadalajara. According to the company's new reorganization in Mexico, some of the employees who worked in these offices are relocated, but operations continue to operate normally. Due to the dramatic impact of the pandemic and the unpredictable nature of any eventual recovery, the technology company eliminated 6,700 jobs worldwide, due to the reduction in travel through this platform, since most people are confined to their homes (SUN, 2020; Martínez, 2020). Although it was anticipated that Uber could resist the crisis thanks to its delivery services, the reality is that the firm is positioned as one of the platforms most affected by the pandemic, which has forced it to radically modify its business (Gonzalez, 2020).

At a global corporate level, Uber reported revenue of $ 3.553 billion between January and March 2020, which exceeded the expectations of specialists. Although the number is not bad, the reality is that the company also registered a loss of 2,940 million dollars, an item that it had managed to contain in its past reports. With the intention of minimizing these losses, the firm announced cuts in its workforce equivalent to 14%, with which nearly 3,700 employees were notified of their departure from the company. In accordance with this new reorganization of the company in Guadalajara, some of the employees who worked in these offices will be relocated, and operations will continue to operate normally (Gonzalez, 2020).

In search of a possible recovery Uber focuses its efforts on its main mobility and home delivery platforms, resizes the company by stopping non-essential investments and reducing the size of the workforce to match with the new realities of the market (SUN, 2020; Martínez, 2020; Gonzalez, 2020). In a scenario that González (2018) characterizes as entropic, mobility that extends into a perceived horizon that falls into vices such as the obsolescence of means of transport and the hostile attitudes of service providers towards users, Uber has a lot to offer.

7.3   THEORETICAL-CONCEPTUAL REVIEW: COMPETITIVE ADVANTAGE

7.3.1   *ACTORS STUDIED*

The characteristics of current and potential consumers are defined by the fact that Uber, all over the world, is a company that functions as a link between the driver and the customer. Whoever requests it has a need: to be transported. But not only a few individuals must be transported, as a whole. This type of service is required by society sooner or later, on a day-to-day basis. It is at that point, while there are alternatives to how to do it, for which numerous factors intervene, among which is the measure of cash that we can pay for the service, the speed of travel, comfort, and security (Ávalos, 2015).

The above-described consumers are around 18 to 40 years of age, since they are the closest to effectively manage the application that interacts with the driver. These customers are willing to pay for a trip at a reasonable price, as well as ready to share the road. In Mexico, more than half of the population agrees to travel with another person. No doubt, Uber came to achieve the Mexican market will pay through debit cards, understood that not all customers could access a loan, so, in its progress, has begun to cash in real money. At the end of the day, the buyers of this service are and have a habitual monetary position (Pallares, 2016).

It is worth mentioning that more than half of current customers, instead of using Uber, would use their own car. All consumers have a smartphone, less than half have a credit or debit card, however, they all have cash available. On the other hand, a relevant fact is that more than half would drive in a drunken state if it were not for Uber, implies that through this benefit accidents and conceivable deaths that happen every day are reduced. In the United States, Uber has coverage of 75% of the population, of which 22% of active drivers are women. In Mexico, more than 500,000 clients have joined the service (Pallares, 2016).

The company has recently implemented the issuance of invoices, that is, it still has this benefit unlike the competition, which different organizations need to produce charge credit, so current customers may require this voucher, be they moral persons, as well as to individuals, and thereby achieve a superior position in the market (Bustamante and Vargas-Hernández, 2018).

7.3.2 CONFLICTS STUDIED

Urban private land transport has been affected due to the emergence in the market of the transnational company UBER considered by García (2018) as based on the application of collaborative economy in the service sector. This condition has questioned the legality of activities in the private urban transport services market that conflict with the interests of traditional transport systems known as taxis. These conflicts have generated legal debates that take into account at one extreme, whether it is a service that can be provided in a free market or whether it should be subject to regulations, such as obtaining a government authorization.

The taxi-based urban private transportation systems are facing the incursion in the market of collaborative model of leasing the vehicle with driver supported by person-to-person (P2P) platforms like the case of Uber that compete in a monopolized market by the traditional taxi systems. Guillén (2018) concludes that the debate on the benefits are associated with the freedom for the provision of these services focusing on the legal regimes to regulate the struggle and conflicts between the traditional taxi sector and the advancement of these P2P service to be solved.

An investigation carried out by Navarro and Ortiz (2016) in order to determine the advantages and disadvantages of the Uber service compared to the individual Taxi public transport service, they conclude, among other matters, that in order for the multinational urban passenger transport company to have the proper operation, it must be legalized as a provider company of the public transport service, to be governed by the rules and competent institutions, providing both users and drivers with the benefits required by law, as well as paying the taxes corresponding to their income.

A detailed analysis of the conflicts originated on the basis of the legality of urban passenger transport in cars with platform support, as in the case of Uber, is considered by Guillén (2018) as the transition from a collaborative transport model to Regulated vehicle leasing with a driver has led to disputes and disputes with the traditional taxi transport sector.

The dangers that threaten this company as an organizational entity that provides a private transport service, in the first place, is the professionalism with which it is handled, there is no guarantee that the driver can complete an expert driving, as is hypothetically guaranteed by the certification and in contrast to taxi drivers. The problem of the driving test and the basic requirements to acquire a driver's license in the corresponding modality shown to offer the service of taxis and other permits that are essential to deal with this specific car, which evidences legal shortcomings that decrease the safety of the traveler (Hernández, Galindo, and Vicente, 2015).

Another conflict is the certified identification of the driver, even though the driver must be a member of the firm and be registered as such in the application and the system, sometimes abusing the stipulated conditions, some drivers subcontract to others, to generate a business model in which the cars work on behalf of someone else and generate greater profits to the owner. On the other hand, another problem is the insurance coverage, since as the service provides a private car that is granted private transport benefits, the company's protection covers the accidents of the driver and not of the passengers in some cases (Hernández, Galindo, and Vicente, 2015).

According to Ávalos (2015), another inconvenience is the lack of loyalty that some leading partners can have towards the company. Some taxi drivers claim that there is an unjustifiable lack and disadvantage, since Uber would not be obliged to accept all the needs that are expected from the other organizations that report to the SAT (tax administration service).

7.4 REVIEW OF THE EMPIRICAL LITERATURE

7.4.1 STRATEGIC REASONS

Some of the competitive advantages that belong to Uber have to do with the fact of the price that the customer is willing to pay, and the methods of payment. In addition, requesting a taxi in Mexico, includes numerous circumstances. The first is the fare, in many parts of Mexico, including Guadalajara is common to be familiar with the idea that taxis have an excessive rate, since drivers not only take advantage of the lack of time that the traveler has, also of the region and the time for which the trip is made. A taxi does not charge the same in case it is requested it in different areas of the city.

The Mexican, therefore, pays a taxi of about 40 pesos when talking about a reasonable trip. In any case, normally, the benefit is not what is really worth, since travelers run the risk of being robbed or arriving unpunctually at the established place. This is a serious disadvantage with respect to services such as Uber, because due to this circumstance of stress and uncertainty, it achieves its objective in the quality, speed, and convenience of transport (Barranco and González, 2016).

Regarding the issue of the terms in which the payment is made, it must be emphasized that Uber (whose number of members increases at a rate of 20% each week in Mexico) only allowed payments with debit or credit cards and for that, the card should be linked with the application. But recently, Uber also cashes in cash, this is due to the way in which Mexico generally cannot get a payment by card or by fees and that the money used for transportation is a part of their daily spending plan (Uber, 2017).

Another important point that has been a strategic feature of Uber is the growth trend in the market. The development of Uber around the world has been exponential. It is available in more than four hundred cities, in seventy nations and makes more than 5 million departures per day. In Mexico, the company is available since 2014, and from then on its development is no less amazing. Each week the number of downloads of its application increases between 10% and 15%. It is also taken as a competitive advantage of the company's performance that around 30% of the drivers complement their common salary working with Uber (Ávalos, 2015).

For the case of the components that allow their development in the market, emphasis should be placed on the use of innovation. All consumers of the service in Mexico have a cell phone and know how to use it. From that point of view, where are the cars that work as Uber, it can be chosen a traditional car or a larger one, as mentioned above. In addition, the application allows to see the brand of the vehicle, the color and the image of the driver. It can also be seen the progress before and during the trip on the map of the application. The foregoing is how, progressively, Uber has taken this strategy to reach the client (Barranco and González, 2016).

Another factor that is additionally significant is the dynamism, transparency, and accessibility of the rates, and these cannot change once the trip is accepted, these are not established through the channel. The cost of the trip is estimated not by meter, but by the GPS of the app, and the course is recorded in the application. When the consumer pays, as a client of Uber, when the company entered the Mexican market, it was important to enter a bank card number and at the end of the service, the application charged the agreed amount at the beginning, with the objective that the clients do not should deal with cash or stress over the fee or if the driver has enough change.

Likewise, in Mexico, Uber saw that a large part of the clients could not access a credit, so the payment method has been updated to make it in cash. If the trip is shared, the application also allows to separate the passage. This clearly draws attention on the basis that the fees never exceed the desire to pay for a typical taxi (Barranco and González, 2016).

The results found by González (2017a) in an investigation focused on content analysis and ethnographic exercises in the Guadalajara Metropolitan area, suggest that there are variations in the exercise of motoring, through complex hybridizations of the modus normalis and this new transport management option, which does little to discourage the practice of motorized urban mobility.

In the daily life of the consumer, when it is transported and the service provided causes some dissatisfaction, the company gives the option of accessing a driver rating system, an innovative and really useful aspect, which is that, upon completion of the travel, the app asks the consumer to value, through stars, how was the provision of transport service. With which, the company system records and evaluates the conditions and opinions of the consumer, in addition to checking if there is a conflict, taking some measures to receive the full satisfaction of the user, and can even reimburse the payment if it is the case. It is noted that these features are in no way presented in the taxi service.

Another factor that impacts its performance in the market is the advertising coverage it has. Uber manages the promotion through social networks, and with a recommendation method, and much of the Internet. The models and conditions of the cars also impact on the way to reach Mexican consumers, in contrast to taxis. Uber offers distinctive car models, regularly ventilated and substantially more current than regular taxis (Ferrer, 2015).

The competitive advantages that Uber has play an extremely important role, since derived from them this company is positioned as a leader in the market. The drivers enjoy that there are no established hours to work, also that the commission charged for the use of the platform is about one fifth of the ticket and a part is involved in the promotion costs with the objective that the system keep working.

The assignment of orders for trips is done automatically as the system will request the service depending on the vehicle that is closest to the customer. There are no fees for opening or registration fees. The collection of services is typically week after week and with automatic deposit. Finally, it provides a reliable environment for the driver, because the trip is recorded in the system and who is the passenger.

The consumer also has several strategic advantages that the company has established, for example, through the app that is user friendly and easy to use, the cost for the service is specified and does not change before requesting it, in addition the application is accessible to change the route. The client can also evaluate and provide feedback to the service. On the other hand, Uber intends that the user is in a reliable and comfortable environment, because whoever takes it knows that his order, the trip and the driver are registered in the system. It also allows to monitor the trip. And finally, a vehicle is available quickly.

On the contrary, to the above, it is relevant to establish what competitive disadvantages Uber has and analyze later what it can do to solve them. The driver may appreciate that, for example, he has no labor protection, unlike taxi drivers. The type of coverage provided by insurers in a lawsuit may be uncertain. One aspect that usually occurs when Uber enters a new city is that the company has to negotiate with the corresponding authorities, since they do not have the proper regulations for this type of service at present. Another disadvantage is that it is necessary to have data to connect with the platform.

7.5   RESEARCH METHOD

7.5.1   *ANALYSIS OF COMPETITIVENESS IN THE PRIVATE TRANSPORT BUSINESS*

For the projection of demand of the company to study, it is proposed to take as a reference the city of Guadalajara, which has a population of approximately 3 million citizens. It is in this sense that the projection of interest is expected to increase by 1 year around 35% in terms of the people who need and use the Uber in Guadalajara, as well as in different urban areas where the benefit of Uber is accessible (Uber, 2016).

Regarding the competence analysis, it is established that Uber works in a similar way to that of traditional taxis, causing direct rivalry with this type of transport; Be that as it may, it is not your most important rival. New applications that offer a feature such as Uber, for example, EasyTaxi or Cabify that have a place with a similar rank, qualify as immediate rivalry; It can also be said that car manufacturers could be displaced by this service, so they run the risk of reducing consumer demand.

Normally, in the market of public and private transport, the offeror chooses the places where the traveler is picked up and left, while, on account of the taxi, the client decides them. In other words, there are some significant differences between the types of public transport, for example, the train, the trolleybus, the ecobici or the buses, the taxis differ by choosing the stops. The variables that impact when choosing the service type of any option, for example, Uber, lie in the season, the amount of traffic and the speed of the service.

EasyTaxi or Cabify are not transport companies; they are organizations that grant the delivery of private vehicles (which can be registered as taxis) and, from time to time, process this modality. Be that as it may, a similar passenger transport benefit is given by an alternative legal person to these organizations, that is, the driver of the vehicle.

7.6 ANALYSIS OF RESULTS

For the analysis of Uber's competence from a global point of view, it can be understood that Easytaxi is broad in 420 urban areas and in 30 countries, close to where Cabify has a reach only in Latin America, Spain, and Portugal. Uber is on the five continents since 2011 and is developing as one of the most revolutionary organizations in the world sector. This firm registers a growth of 10% around the downloads that are made of the application.

In the case of allude to the classification of requested cars, it can be reasoned that there are two groups of consumers, the principal obtains the car by necessity and the second simply requests the car to acquire social status. The customer of need looks for a car for safety, comfort, quality, space, and a lower price, so when choosing a car depends on the costs. However, the customer who only needs to have the car by status does not focus on the cost alone in the comfort and image of a luxurious year-round car.

On the side of the prices of the use of taxis in Guadalajara depend on many variables such as the price of gasoline, distance, time, supply, demand, traffic expectation, the area, the state of the car, insurance, etc. On a general average, the price per kilometer should be around 7.25 pesos, with an increase of approximately one-fifth at night. The tariffs in the different platforms are based on five variables mainly: time, distance, efficient route, traffic, and demand.

According to Uber's behavior as a company, it is within an oligopolistic market structure. An oligopoly is a market governed by few organizations specialized in the sector. As a result of having two members in this type of market, each oligopolist knows the activities of its rivals. Since the choices of an organization influence or cause effects on the choices of others, a circumstance of equilibrium is established by the companies, with which the rivalry will not be exhibited. It is worth noting that, in an oligopoly of this type, there is no evident rivalry for the fact that organizations can collude to leave no space for another firm to position itself as a contender and to have communication between the companies involved in the oligopoly process can get the best benefits, or on the contrary if they compete with each other, what the leading company does will impact and cause a specific response from the rival.

According to what the game theory establishes, if an organization is a pioneer or leader (Uber) instead of waiting for an equilibrium in which all competitors simultaneously reach an equilibrium (Nash, for example), the advantage of the leader company over the followers, that is, having a dominant business advantage over the other firms, which results in first making a decision to which they respond, that is, they take it later, the followers. A clear example in this model is the decision Uber made when agreeing to an alliance with cell phone companies (Telcel and Movistar) to offer their free wireless Wi-Fi service with customers who hire a rate plan.

This leads the leader to consider, for each election, that the followers will react according to their decision, so they correct their method of positioning themselves in the market, taking into account what the others' choices will be, as if in some way I could control them and result in their own advantage.

One strategy of the oligopolies, in recent times, is to reduce the cost below costs in order that the other companies cannot compete, and once they are built, they raise their prices indiscriminately. By establishing the oligopoly as a conceivable case, there would also be the possibility of collusion. This happens when the firms in the oligopoly agree to act in a planned manner when they offer their products or services and increase costs, in this sense, they achieve a greater advantage more important for each of them than when they act independently.

If Uber or other platforms were prohibited, the oligopoly of the taxis would be maintained since they would impose their prices according to their criteria. In case they were allowed to enter these platforms without restrictions, either fiscal or monetary, these would include the new oligopoly that would replace the conventional taxi service. In this sense, it is understood that, in some way, no measure is reasonable for the current financial situation.

In spite of the above, it is not the only answer that could be shown by a competitor, it should be considered the scenario where Uber develops exponentially and becomes an imposing business model, that is, a Monopoly.

Limited to the above, it would be normal that, once the taxi service and the different contenders were eliminated, Uber will raise its rates and the commission it charges drivers. Most likely, as has happened with the taxi, the absence of rivalry will have an opposite effect on the nature of the company's initial. From the perspective of travelers and drivers, the situation of a private tax business model may not be entirely different from what was previously established with taxis.

Beyond Uber building its market control as a monopolist, it is currently smaller and should be considered. Particularly in the possibility that the firm has strategies to evade rivalry. For example, the imposition of Uber-Pool (accessible in Mexico City) represents a significant disadvantage for rivals with smaller market scales.

A relevant aspect related to the analysis of prices; the rates are different in each city. In Guadalajara, the rates vary due to the types of trips, these are estimated by base rate, distance, and time. The standard fare is 7.25 pesos per km and 3.50 pesos per minute, where Uber charges by commission between 20% to 25% of the final fare of all trips. The cost of the fare also depends on the type of car chosen, of which the most relevant ones were already mentioned.

This type of services uses the dynamic rate, which applies when there are numerous trips requested in a specific area of the city and there are not enough drivers. For example, if there are a couple of cars and numerous requests, the service estimate will be doubled by the estimation of the dynamic rate. The dynamic rate is calculated by increasing the base rate of the service by estimating the current dynamic rate.

The provision of this type of service works according to the law of supply and demand. The more consumers there are, the higher the cost to achieve a balance in the offer, or there would be an unstable demand. For example, if the cost is the same, but there are limited-service providers. The waiting time would increase considerably, to the point where it will be unreasonably expensive, and customers would not wait much longer. This is solved by increasing the cost, so that customers who travel value the service even more. The above is shown in Figure 7.1.

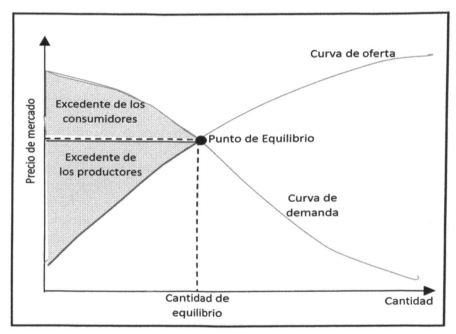

FIGURE 7.1   Balance point regarding supply and demand.

Source: Own elaboration with data from the MTJ (2011).

The company has reasons to increase costs, and that means it can put more cars available for use, since drivers would get more cash on each trip, and they will be encouraged to activate the app and provide the service. That would suggest an expansion in the offer, so more users could travel, and therefore, Uber will have more benefits. Prices can go up well in times of high activity of people, big events. There are several cases of people who have paid four times more than normal for not risking public transportation in Guadalajara.

7.7 CONCLUSIONS AND RECOMMENDATIONS

After the analysis conducted on the entry of Uber, a multinational firm of private passenger urban transportation to the market of the Metropolitan Area of Guadalajara, and the successful increase in the segment, despite the legal conflicts due to competitive activities with the main sector of public and private passenger transportation based on the traditional taxi systems. However, the turning point of this increasing and sustainable growth has been the pandemics. Now the operations of Uber in the Metropolitan Area of Guadalajara is falling down and decreasing posing new strategic challenges to the firm.

A Smart City, or smart city, is that city that applies information and communication technologies (ICT) with the aim of providing it with an infrastructure that guarantees sustainable development. The netizen who has used applications that provide the private transport service, offered by organizations that work with pairing between the user and the driver, has clearly changed the act of its urban versatility. Therefore, these organizations are also designing another method to offer the benefit of transportation, even though, first of all, the service was considered elitist and selective for a part of the population in its beginnings, for example, because of having credit cards. From now on, with the modifications and changes according to the collection system, the market opens up for a more prominent number of people.

Taking into account the previous analysis, it can be affirmed that Uber in the Mexican market has placed itself as an oligopoly that, little by little, has managed to control its competitors (followers) that provide a similar service. Without a doubt, the market that Uber covers to provide this service maintains the specific attributes identified with the simplicity of its platform, through the app, the low cost, the comfort it offers, its service monitoring interface, and its attention to the client. The latter is what differentiates it mainly from the taxi service. The above added to the effectiveness of the service have allowed users to start adopting this service from casual to usual.

Apart from the fact that Uber has its own market, it is not the only solution to satisfy the demand for transport, an example of this is its direct competitors. The economic theory of the producer, states that these options are called substitute goods and are one of the components that affect the demand for the service. For this situation, the demand for Uber could have been met with these substitute goods, for example, taxis, trains, trucks, or ecobici.

However, in the event that the client considers that the cost, ratio, and quality of service are insufficient to choose another option, he chooses to pay the increase in the cost created by an increase in Uber's demand. The theory of the producer mentions that, instead of establishing a maximum tariff for the benefit of the consumer, the entry of competitors should be encouraged and the conditions of the alternatives improved. It is concluded that a maximum rate does not solve the problem of excess demand, competition does.

KEYWORDS

- **competitive advantage**
- **information and communication technologies**
- **person-to-person**
- **platform**
- **private transportation**
- **tax administration service**
- **uber**

REFERENCES

Ávalos, M. (2015), Baby, you can't drive my car. The case of Uber in Mexico, in *Economy Informs*, no. 390, February 2015, 104–112.

Barranco, M. C., & González, M. G., (2016). Intracondominal transport in the daily mobility of periurbanization: the community link of the Guadalajara Metropolitan Area.

Transport and Territory Magazine, 14, 167–188. Obtenido de: http://revistascientificas. filo.uba.ar/index.php/rtt/article/view/2434/2092 (accessed on 24 February 2021)

Bravo, M. (2015). *Expensive and bad, public transportation in Mexico.* (May 26, 2018). Retrieved from https://meganoticias.mx/tu-ciudad/guadalajara/especiales-meganoticias/ item/85874-caro-ymalo-el-Transporte-publico-en-mexico.html (accessed on 24 February 2021).

Bustamante, C., & Vargas-Hernández J. G. (2018). Uber's competitive advantages over its direct competition in the private transportation business in Guadalajara, Jal, *Economic Sciences, Faculty of Economic Sciences UNL, 15*(2), 107–116. UNL.

El Informador, (2016). *New executive taxi platforms arrive.* https://www.informador.mx/ Jalisco/Llegan-nuevas-plataformas-de-taxi-ejecutivo-20160526-0207.html (accessed on 24 February 2021).

Ferrer, A., (2016). *Taxi drivers against Uber: the fight for passengers in Mexico City.* Obtenido de: http://www.milenio.com/df/conflicto_uber_taxis_df-pelea_uber_taxis_ciudad_mexico-apps_debate_taxis_df_0_647335583.html (accessed on 24 February 2021).

García, S. M., (2018). *The case of UBER from a public view of Law.* Final Master's Thesis in the practice of law. International University of La Rioja. Madrid June 11, 2018.

Gonzalez, F., (2020). Uber says goodbye to its Monterrey and Guadalajara offices: What will happen to the employees? *Merca2.0* https://www.merca20.com/uber-dice-adio-a-sus-oficinas-de-monterrey-y-guadalajara-que-pasara-con-los-empleados/ (accessed on 24 February 2021).

González, J., (2017). In three years, how has Uber moved to Guadalajara? *Okupo+.* http:// okupo.mx/tres-anos-ha-movido-uber-guadalajara (accessed on 24 February 2021).

González, P. M. A., (2018). Uberification and urban mobility in the Metropolitan Area of Guadalajara: entropy in the new access configurations to motorized transport. *Science ergo-sum, 25*(2). Available at http://cienciaergosum.uaemex.mx/article/view/9500 (accessed on 24 February 2021).

González, P. M. G., (2017a). Uber and urban mobility in the Guadalajara metropolitan geography: Rise and decline. *Geographing, 13*(1), e020. https://doi.org/10.24215/2346898Xe020.

González, P. M. G., (2017b). Motorized mobility and transport infrastructures in Culiacán: an entropic situation, in I. J. Jasso (coord.), *Power, Culture and Development* (pp. 60–77). Mexico: University of Guanajuato.

Guillén, N. N., (2018). The leasing of vehicles with a driver (VTC) and its legal framework: the advance of Uber, Cabify and the collaborative economy. *Journal of Local and Autonomous Administration Studies, 9*, 128–147. https://doi.org/10.24965/reala.v0i9.10470.

Hernández, R. Y., & Galindo, S. R. V., (2016). UBER transport service management model. Who loses and who wins? *Public Spaces, 19*(47), 157–175.

Hernández, Y., Galindo, S., & Vicente, R., (2015). Conflict due to the operation of public passenger transport (taxi mode) in urban areas of Tecámac, State of Mexico, *Review Public Spaces, UAEM, 18*(42), 135–156.

La, P., (2016). *Uber Will Receive Payment in Cash. In Press.* (March 29, 2018). Obtained from http://www.prensa.com/economia/Uber-recibira-pago-efectivo_0_4543795641.html (accessed on 24 February 2021).

Martínez, C., (2020). Uber closes offices in Guadalajara, Monterrey and relocates employees. The universal. https://www.eluniversal.com.mx/cartera/uber-cierra-oficinas-de-guadalajara-monterrey-y-reubica-empleados (accessed on 24 February 2021).

Montealegre, G. A. C., (2017). *Importance of the big data solution in the mobility application Uber movement* Monograph Diploma Big. Universidad Libre Faculty of Engineering. Systems engineering program. Bogotá D.C. September 2017.

MTJ, (2015). Study of supply and demand of taxi transport services and the new transport network companies UBER and CityDrive in the Guadalajara Metropolitan Area. *The Informant* (March 18, 2018). Retrieved from https://issuu.com/el_informador/docs/estudio_taxis_uber (accessed on 24 February 2021).

Navarro, P. K. L., & Ortiz, A. A. F., (2016). *Evaluation of advantages and disadvantages of Uber compared to the taxi transport service between streets* 53 to 45 and av. Caracas and Seventh. Degree work. Catholic University of Colombia. Faculty of Engineering. Civil Engineering Program. Bogota Colombia.

Olivares, E. M., (2014). *Economic systems and models of modern economy.* Bogotá: Autonomous University of Colombia.

Pallares, M. A., (2016). Uber has 1.2 million users in Mexico. *The Universal* newspaper. (April 19, 2018). Obtained from http://www.eluniversal.com.mx/articulo/cartera/negocios/2016/03/8/uber-suma-12-millones-de-usuarios-en-mexico (accessed on 24 February 2021).

Peng, M. W., (2012). *Global STRATEGY.* Cincinnati: Thomson South-Western.

Pérez, D., (2016). 7 points of the Uber service that will change with its regulation in Guadalajara. *Attraction 360.* https://www.atraccion360.com/que-es-ley-uber-en-guadalajara (accessed on 24 February 2021).

SUN, (2020). Uber announces the closure of its offices in Guadalajara The company adjusts its business model in the midst of the crisis caused by COVID-19. *The reporter.* https://www.informador.mx/economia/Uber-anuncia-el-cierre-de-sus-oficinas-en-Guadalajara-20200522-0129.html (accessed on 24 February 2021).

Tiongson, J., (2015). Mobile App Marketing Insights: How Consumers Really Find and Use Your Apps. *Think with Google.* (May 28, 2018). Retrieved from https://www.thinkwithgoogle.com/articles/mobile-app-marketing-insights.html (accessed on 24 February 2021).

Tráficozmg, (2016). *Uber launches the XL version for Guadalajara* https://traficozmg.com/2016/01/uber-lanza-la-version-xl-para-guadalajara/ (accessed on 24 February 2021).

Uber, (2016). *Uber moves Guadalajara.* (April 19, 2018). Obtained from https://www.uber.com/es-US/cities/guadalajara/ (accessed on 24 February 2021).

Uber, (2017). *Newsroom.* (May 8, 2018). Obtenido de: https://newsroom.uber.com/locations/#na-region14 (accessed on 24 February 2021).

Yeung, E., (2012). *How to Launch Your App in an International Market.* Mashable. Obtenido de: http://mashable.com/2012/02/13/mobile-apps-international/#aeYWOgIPIOq8 (accessed on 24 February 2021).

PART III

**Societal Consequences of
Technologies and Solutions**

CHAPTER 8

Impact of Digitalization on Pedagogical Innovation and Changing Work Life of a University Teaching Professional in West Bengal

PUJASREE CHATTERJEE

Assistant Professor, Department of Sociology, Vidyasagar University, Midnapore, and PhD Research Scholar, Department of Sociology, University of Calcutta, West Bengal, India, Phone: 9432928107/ 8240343902, E-mail: pujasree.chatterjee@gmail.com

ABSTRACT

The impact of digital technology can be seen across different sectors, including the education sector. Since the last decade, the higher education landscape in India has been undergoing a transformation by creating widespread access to affordable, high-quality university education and reaching out to students in different locations from diverse backgrounds. The economic development of a nation is linked with its higher education and research opportunities that can meet the requirements of a skilled workforce for the economy. Digital technology can be used for curriculum innovation as well as for updating teaching-learning methods, which can lead to better learning outcomes and would match the global requirements. In this setting, the teaching professionals along with the students play a significant role. This study has been done on the basis of face to face interview with 90 University teaching professionals (Professor, Associate Professor, and Assistant Professor) across different universities in West Bengal and it seeks to understand the changing work-life of a teaching professional by focusing on issues as diverse as innovation in pedagogy, changes in teaching-learning techniques and application of Information and Communications Technology (ICT) and the simultaneous changes brought about in the role of a teacher from being a teacher to becoming a mentor as well as the perception of the faculties regarding the nature of teaching job.

8.1   INTRODUCTION

Digital technologies have made inroads across all spheres of society, including education sector. In the last 10 years, the Higher education sector in India has made enormous expansion in terms of opening of several new academic institutions in different locations and providing affordable and quality education to a large segment of young population in the age group of 18 years to 23 years and above. In 2012–2013, India had 712 universities and today there are 920 Universities throughout the country (UGC, 2019). These universities offer a diverse variety of courses to cater to a heterogeneous student population who has diverse needs and demands and provide holistic education to the mass of the Indian population. Many universities which are located in remote regions have student population with dialectal and regional diversity as well as a balanced gender profile. These universities are providing access to various direct as well as digital and online techniques of teaching and learning. This has resulted in increasing the enrolment numbers as well as improving the learning outcomes. Digitization in the higher education has enabled it to resolve the dichotomy between access and equity, improve faculty student ratio to some extent and making teaching an attractive career option. Lakshmi and Rao (2016) in their research highlighted the significance of the digital era. It is at the center of innovation and is altering every sector including healthcare, finance, education, banking, insurance, and more and this will help India be at the fore front of innovation and job creation and this digitalization is the sign of smart India. In order to enhance the economic development of a nation, it should be linked with transformation in the education sector especially there should be an assimilation of higher education along with research. The introduction of educational technology and its use in teaching-learning process have changed the nature and quality of education in India. This further requires a curriculum which will be updated and match with global competitive requirement and can fulfil the needs of the economy and society. In this scenario, not only the students but also the teaching professionals are at the forefront to take the advantages of digitalization in the education sector. The main goal is to foster innovation and choice in the curriculum, changes in the delivery of teaching and learning, and Information and Communications Technology (ICT) based learning that will enhance access as well as quality. Digitalization also creates an impact on savings in the resources by blurring physical distance as well as by introducing scientific ways to impart knowledge (Marathe, 2018). Teachers today are professionals who are entering the teaching profession with their knowledge, skill, aspirations, passion, commitment as well as to take the benefits of increased and revised pay structure of the government. To match up with the changing needs, demands, and outlooks of the learners and to assist them to gain new, advanced, and relevant knowledge, the higher education teaching professionals today are experiencing a change in their work life. Teaching is a field of professional endeavor and the profession of teaching rests its claim for consideration on the fact that it deals with the making of life (Williams, 1921). Teaching as a profession is centered on a specialized area of knowledge, possessing skills which are necessary for teaching, knowledge about science of teaching (didactic) and also certain individual abilities which are required to be a teacher and which is essential for being in the teaching profession. Individuals who choose teaching as a profession needs to possess the subject matter knowledge, skills to teach as well as a personality which is suitable and essential for the success of the educational objectives (Hotaman, 2010). The profession of teaching possesses some characteristics of an ideal type of profession but may possess a lesser degree of many others. Hence, teaching will be a quasi-profession (Strike, 1990). In these days, teaching is considered to be a profession which is one of the most challenging and stressful one as the pedagogues are confronting difficulties in professional and personal life both nationally and globally (Punia and Kamboj, 2013). Teachers in university are not just engaged in teaching as was their primary mission once (Prince et al., 2007). The teachers are required also to devote proportional time on publication from research projects and fulfill various administrative responsibilities. Bils (2019), in a study on FernUniversität in Hagen, Germany, observed that there are different ways by which learning and teaching using digital technology takes place, and its implementation brings about a huge change in a large number of lecturers. The sociological investigation of work stresses on how social structure as well as economic structures impacts individual experiences towards work and life. Edgell (2012) viewed the significance of globalization and its implication for both paid and unpaid work. According to Edgell, Marx, and Engels referred to the global character of industrial capitalism and capitalism as the spur to establish connections to every corner of the world with wide-reaching interconnectedness in all aspects of social life. The author in this text, mentioned of two concepts, globality, and globalism. Globality refers to the extent to which individuals are aware of living in the world as one place and globalism as the neo liberal ideology of world market domination. The author has also highlighted technology as one of the four main interrelated factors (rationalism, capitalism, regulation) that caused expansion of globalization. From the perspective of sociology of work, technology denotes the application of scientific knowledge mainly to solve real-life issues. Technological innovations in information and communication were particularly important during the late modern phase of globalization which enables individuals and companies to develop global connections, which has been illustrated by the author in the research explorations on call centers. The author of this book also focused on economic globalization as this dimension is the most relevant to the impact of globalization on paid and unpaid work. In this sociological analysis of work it has been shown that, all forms of work need to be explained with reference to the increasing globalization of economic life and that each type of work impacts every other type of work and no one type of paid or unpaid work can be understood in isolation. Therefore, in this research, the researcher seeks to highlight the contemporary requirements of higher education in India to be diverse and significant, ranging from shifting student's expectations and changing teacher's roles to the impact of technology as well as the impact of globalization on higher education. Any of these factors can create an impact and it will be transformative in nature. In the phase of one's entire career, every teacher faces the competition that creates uncertainty and anxiety. The researcher, through this chapter, attempts to comprehend the impact of digitalization on teaching and outlining the increasing complexity and the changing role of a teaching professional in the present social situation. It focuses on issues ranging from innovation in pedagogy to changes in teaching-learning methods and introduction and application of ICT in the teaching-learning process and the changes brought about simultaneously in the role and responsibilities of a teacher as well as their perception towards changing nature of their work life.

8.2 RATIONALE

This empirical study is done on teaching professionals at the higher education sector to observe the changes that the teaching faculties are undergoing since the last decade with a global change in the higher education setting with an emphasis on digital technology, enlargement, and a focus on research and strategies of pedagogical innovation. A study on perceptual understanding of teaching faculties at different levels such as Professors, Associate Professors and Assistant Professors is likely to differ regarding impact of digitalization and their changing work life. Earlier existing researches focuses on issues of innovation and teacher's quality of work-life, but not much theorizing has been done on changing the work-life of a teaching professional.

8.3 REVIEW OF RELEVANT LITERATURE

Sociology of work has been addressing the changing nature of work since Post World War to developments in the field in recent times (Edwards, 2013). People in every society are engaged in some kind of work that determines the economic system of that society, and they vary across cultures and societies. The sociological exploration of work constitutes a significant part of sociology because the economic functioning of a society influences all other aspects of society and work is related with wider structures of society as well as social processes and also issues of social inequality.

In the sociology of work, classical sociological theorists like Marx, Durkheim, and also Weber, were interested to understand the origins of industrial capitalist societies. Today study of work is considered to be essential to the study of sociology. Marxist tradition examined the situation of workers in the factories that originated in England during the industrial revolution, and he was interested in capitalism as a forceful, exploitative system and also analyzed how the factory system of production led to deskilling and alienation among the workers. Durkheim was concerned with the division of labor in society and how work and industry transformed through the industrial revolution and stability was achieved in society. In traditional society, there exist mechanical solidarity, which was based on homogeneous norms and customs that revolved around feudal obligations and familial ties, which began to disintegrate during the industrial revolution, and a new type of social order based on organic solidarity emerged in society. Durkheimian sociologists were interested to study the development of professions and their associations (Vidal, 2011). Weberian approach concentrated on the emergence of different types of authorities in modern organizations by distinguishing traditional form of authority to a rational-legal form of authority.

Glenn (2008), in their study, examined how technology is impelling the future prospect of higher education. According to the study, technology will continue to have its influence on higher education. As online mode of learning is expanding; partnership between corporate sector and academia will enhance contribution of universities in the coming times.

Casares et al. Rochester Institute of Technology (RIT, 2011) in their report on future of teaching and learning in higher education, highlighted that the factors affecting changes in higher education are wide-ranging and substantial extending from technology and globalization to ever-changing student and employer expectations and any of these factors can be significant. Considering students and technology, economy, and employers as the main agents of transformation in higher education, there has been an enhancement in the number of online courses that are designed by higher education institutions, and some universities are making their course content available online and free access to everyone. RIT highlights that, it is vital to address three interrelated aspects, people, process, and technology.

Brennan et al. (2014), in their report on innovation in higher education, particularly aims to contribute to understand how recent advances affect higher education and shows how during times of change, innovation can support higher education. To highlight processes of innovation in the higher education sector, desk research and seven case studies methodology has been used, that fall within three themes which are connected to one another (the changing setting of teaching and learning in higher education, technology, and the student performance in higher education, globalization, and multi-campus universities) which has got system-wide significance and effects for all stakeholders in higher education. It stressed the significance of education and particularly higher education as a key facilitator of smart, sustainable, and inclusive growth.

Walder (2014) in a qualitative research explored how thirty-two professors at Université de Montréal defined their conception of pedagogical innovation. Researcher defined pedagogical innovation to be any method of teaching that is delivered other than the traditional form of lecture. After analysis of the data, the researcher proposed to group the sub-themes into seven formal categories, and also proposed a restructured definition of pedagogical innovation to be different for that which is commonly used and it involves teaching in a new way, which is modified and which amazes the students.

Gonzalez (2017) shared his feelings about how the faculty roles are changing and how it is influencing the achievement of students and the institution and those who are frontrunners in the universities need to be aware of changes in expectations of students from their prior classroom and school experiences. Faculties role are changing in response to educational priorities, forces which comes from top to down, changing student requirements, and the faculties are expected to completely assimilate technology in support of education and they also need to explore innovative ways to replicate the advantages of teaching face-to-face instruction and on-campus involvements for students who are becoming increasingly dependent on digital technology-based communications.

From the above review of relevant literatures, the researcher in this chapter wants to explore the following objectives:

- To assess the socio-demographic profile of teaching faculties considered in the study across West Bengal;
- To explore the approaches undertaken by the teaching professionals towards innovation of pedagogy and curriculum with the use of digital technology;
- To analyze the perception of teaching faculties towards pedagogical innovation and their understanding of change in work life.

8.4 METHOD

Variables:

1. **Digitalization:** It is the approach by which many aspects of social life are reoriented around digital communication and media structures and digitization is the process of adapting analog streams of information into digital bits (Brennen and Kreiss, 2016). digitalization involves using technology within organization and considering the role of the individuals. In the context of the education sector, it can be referred to technology-assisted

teaching-learning process and use of ICT. Jurgielewickz (2019) reviewed the existing definitions of digital transformation and presented the common points, which are technology, organization, and people, which are essential in building a digital strategy while initiating a transformation in the digital sphere. Digitalization means implementation of digital technology and using digitized material to generate and produce newer values (Gobble, 2018).

2. **Pedagogical Innovation:** It is an important aspect of higher education today, and digital technology has influenced it to a large extent. Pedagogical innovation can be conceptualized as newer ways in which teaching can be delivered and which is different from the traditional practice of lecture (Walder, 2014). Universities can introduce new products and services such as new syllabus, textbooks, educational resources, new processes for delivering their services and new ways of organizing their activities through digital technologies, new marketing techniques which are regarded as "improvements" and which aims at improving the delivery of education services (Guerriero, 2017).

3. **Work-Life:** It is a term which means the allocation of an individual's time to work roles and other aspects of life, which can include one's own interest, family roles and responsibilities, and social relations. It is a state of equilibrium in which all the roles of an individual's life such as one's personal, professional, and family roles are equally balanced. Changes that have been occurring in the work role and responsibilities of a faculty are also changing their nature of work life. Faculty members constitute a fundamental part of university; therefore, it is essential to pay more attention to their work life and their work conditions (Mirkamali and Thani, 2011).

4. **Area:** Eighteen universities (including Central, State, Private, and Deemed) from Five administrative subdivisions in West Bengal.

5. **Sample:** Ninety respondents (30 professors, 30 Associate Professors and 30 Assistant Professors) on the basis of purposive sampling have been selected for the study.

6. **Criteria for Selection of Respondents:**

   i. Experience of the respondent: At least 1 year of teaching experience at University level;

   ii. Respondents should have at least 5 years of total teaching experience;

iii. Sex: Male, female, and others;

iv. Teaching as either full time substantive faculty or contractual faculty.

7. **Data Collection:** Data were collected through face-to-face, in-depth interviews by visiting the respondents in their respective universities. General information schedule (containing both open and close-ended questions has been used) for conducting the interview. Participants were asked open-ended questions regarding their opinion of regular pedagogical innovation and perception of change in their work life. After collection of data, it has been coded, tabulated, and analyzed using descriptive statistical techniques.

8.5 ANALYSIS AND DISCUSSION

8.5.1 SOCIO-DEMOGRAPHIC PROFILE OF THE RESPONDENTS

Socio-demographic profile indicates the particular characteristics of a population, which comprises a combination of social factors as well as demographic factors. The study of respondents' socio demographic profile has its significance as it assists us to understand the various factors that affect the perception of the respondents.

Table 8.1 shows the socio-demographic profile of the faculties. In this study, 43.33% of Assistant Professors are in the age group 24.5 to 34.5 years, 50% of Associate professors and 56.66% of Assistant Professors are in the age group of 34.5 to 44.5 years, 43.33% of Professors and 46.66% of Associate Professors are in the age group 44.5 years to 54.5 years, 56.66% of professors and 3.33% of Associate Professors are in the age group 54.5 years to 64.5 years. Most of the faculties belong to the age group 34.5 years to 44.5 years. In this study, 63.33% of the respondents are males and 36.66% of the respondents are females. Ninety percent of the respondents in the study are married, and 10% are unmarried. Sixty percent of the respondents have a nuclear family setting, 17.77% have joint or extended family, 16.67% are staying single and 5.56% are in other types of family. Around 47.79% of the faculties have Post Graduate, NET/SET, PhD educational qualification. Around 37.78% of the faculties have more than 10 years up to 20 years of teaching experience. Around 63.33% of the professors have more than 30 years of work experience.

TABLE 8.1 Distribution of Faculties on the Basis of Their Socio-Demographic Profile

	Professor (N = 30) No. (%)	Associate Professor (N = 30) No. (%)	Assistant Professor (N = 30) No. (%)	Total (N = 90) No. (%)
Age				
24.5–34.5	–	–	13 (43.33)	13 (14.44)
34.5–44.5	–	15 (50)	17 (56.66)	32 (35.56)
44.5–54.5	13 (43.33)	14 (46.66)	–	27 (30)
54.5–64.5	17 (56.66)	1 (3.33)	–	18 (20)
Gender				
Male	17 (56.66)	21 (70)	19 (63.33)	57 (63.33)
Female	13 (43.33)	9 (30)	11 (36.66)	33 (36.66)
Other	–	–	–	–
Marital Status				
Married	27 (90)	29 (96.67)	25 (83.33)	81 (90)
Unmarried	3 (10)	1 (3.33)	5 (16.67)	9 (10)
Widow/Widower	–	–	–	–
Divorced/Separated	–	–	–	–
Family Type				
Staying Single	5 (16.67)	1 (3.33)	9 (30)	15 (16.67)
Nuclear Family	16 (53.33)	23 (76.67)	15 (50)	54 (60)
Joint Or Extended Family	7 (23.33)	4 (13.33)	5 (16.67)	16 (17.77)
Others	2 (6.67)	2 (6.67)	1 (3.33)	5 (5.56)

TABLE 8.1 *(Continued)*

	Professor (N = 30) No. (%)	Associate Professor (N = 30) No. (%)	Assistant Professor (N = 30) No. (%)	Total (N = 90) No. (%)
Educational Status				
Post Graduate	—	—	1 (3.33)	1 (1.11)
Post Graduate, NET/SET	—	—	9 (30)	9 (10)
Post Graduate, MPhil, NET/SET	—	—	2 (6.67)	2 (2.22)
Post Graduate, MPhil, NET/SET, PhD	—	1 (3.33)	3 (10)	4 (4.44)
Post Graduate, NET/SET, PhD	11 (36.67)	17 (56.67)	15 (50)	43 (47.79)
Post Graduate, PhD	19 (63.33)	12 (40)	—	31 (34.44)
Total Teaching Experience				
0–10 Years	—	—	19 (63.34)	19 (21.11)
More than 10 Years to 20 Years	—	25 (83.33)	9 (30)	34 (37.78)
More than 20 Years to 30 Years	11 (36.67)	5 (16.67)	1 (3.33)	17 (18.89)
More than 30 Years	19 (63.33)	—	1 (3.33)	20 (22.22)

8.5.2   STRATEGIES TOWARDS PEDAGOGICAL INNOVATION

For enhancing student's learning and outcome, some faculties undergo pedagogical innovation and transformation of teaching practices in order to be excellent teachers (Boden, 2019). Regular innovation is essential to keep up with the advances in digital technology, the need for speed of response, constant availability of different types of knowledge, rapid change. Strategies for pedagogical innovation involves constant update of curriculum, teaching-learning methodologies, Information, and communication technology-based classes, shifting role of a teacher to a mentor who is involved in guidance and counseling of the students beyond classes, and an absence of strict demarcation of work and personal life, all of which are changing the nature of work and life of faculties.

Data highlighted that syllabus of the different courses are updated regularly by the faculties of the departments of the universities. In most of the institutions, semester system has been introduced to match with international pattern of education, which indicate a shift or change in the teaching-learning pattern. The focus of our present education system today is to develop youth who have the ability to compete locally, regionally, nationally as well as globally. It necessitates innovation in curriculum and new methods of teaching along with the need for the teachers to develop a "learner-centric approach." The flexibility in the education system today allows students to choose inter-disciplinary courses depending upon their interests. This has been further made possible with the introduction of a choice-based credit system (CBCS), an internationally recognized system at the undergraduate and postgraduate levels. The CBCS provides chances to learn core subjects and also explore additional channels of learning outside the core subjects for the overall development of an individual. The introduction of the semester pattern of education, as well as, CBCS facilitates enhancing the standard and quality of our higher education system. Updating the syllabus on a regular basis is an important part of pedagogical innovation. It is done mostly to keep up with the recent developments. In most of the Indian universities, there has been an update of syllabus with the introduction of choice-based credit system (CBCS). Maximum a syllabus is followed at a stretch for 3 to 5 years. From Table 8.2, it could be seen that 75.55% of the faculties responded that, syllabus revision is undertaken every alternate years. Faculties are themselves involved in syllabus update and sometimes external experts are also involved in the task of updating of syllabus. Participants in a study reported that, the process of innovation necessitates continuous attention on students, curriculum, and potential innovative ideas (Boden, 2019). Walder (2014) defined pedagogical innovation to be any new technique of teaching or presenting lecture which is different from what has been traditionally practiced, and the researcher proposed to group each of the sub-themes into one of the seven formal categories, which the researcher calls the Distinctive Notions. Each of the concepts of pedagogical innovation emphasized by the author is different and unique. The first communicates to Novelty which implies originality, while the second highlights the idea of change which can be understood as transformation. The third implies Reflection, which can be understood as thinking, while the fourth invokes the application idea. The fifth concerns with improvement. The sixth explores the relationship between technology and pedagogy, while the seventh maintains Human Relations.

TABLE 8.2 Distribution of Faculties on the Basis of Their Designation and Syllabus Update Frequency for Regular Pedagogical Innovation

	Professor (N = 30) No. (%)	Associate Professor (N = 30) No. (%)	Assistant Professor (N = 30) No. (%)	Total (N = 90) No. (%)
	Syllabus of the Different Courses Updated			
Annual Basis	4 (13.33)	–	3 (10)	7 (7.78)
Alternate Year	22 (73.33)	23 (76.67)	23 (76.67)	68 (75.55)
Every 3–5 Years	4 (13.33)	7 (23.33)	4 (13.33)	15 (16.67)

According to a Professor at a State University, Female, 51 years, "*All faculties were indirectly involved, the areas taught by the faculties are discussed jointly to upgrade, to remove the tough portions, the areas which can be modified, changes according to need of the students are done every 3 years. This is a mutual or joint exercise by all faculties.*"

8.5.3 TEACHING-LEARNING METHODS

An important component of pedagogical innovation is the application of new and different teaching-learning methods and using innovative method of teaching to make the learning better. Usually, 95.56% of the faculties responded that they use lecture and interaction session with the students as the most preferred method of teaching. It gives the advantage of face-to-face interaction and the students also get an opportunity to respond actively within the classroom structure (Table 8.3).

TABLE 8.3   Distribution of Faculties on the Basis of Their Designation and Teaching Learning Methods Adopted Towards Pedagogical Innovation

Teaching Learning Methods	Professor	Associate Professor	Assistant Professor	Total (N = 90) No. (%)
Lecture and interaction session with the students	30 (100)	29 (96.67)	27 (90)	86 (95.56)
Lecturing via ICT assisted technology, smart class	14 (46.67)	28 (93.33)	30 (100)	72 (80)
Practical based classes, using demonstration, field visits	16 (53.33)	14 (46.67)	13 (43.33)	43 (47.78)

Eighty percent of the faculties lecture via ICT-assisted technology by preparing the content and making it accessible to the students in online mode and using Google classroom or teaching in smart classrooms. Lectures are recorded and are made available to the students later and using the flip classroom method, hybrid classes are also becoming popular among the faculties. Around 47.78% of the faculties take practical based classes, demonstration or field visits. In Science departments, practical classes are frequent, but field visits are also gaining importance in various arts and social science departments as it gives a direct exposure to the students and helps in developing their understanding. Faculties mostly prefer the Lecture and interaction method. PowerPoint is less preferred among social science faculties as most of the social science and humanities subjects involve conceptual understanding, and digital technology is used in the form of developing case study approach to problem solving, providing materials or video content through online platform. Faculties belonging to the Mathematics department mostly prefer board work, either traditional boards or smart boards. Smartboards give the advantage of saving the work once it is done on the board and refer to it later. From the data, it could also be seen that, Professors mostly prefer lecture interaction method (100%) and Associate and Assistant Professors prefer Lecturing via ICT-assisted technology and smart class. Gonzalez (2017) stressed that many faculties identify student dispositions towards interactions through digital technology and are applying innovative instructional approaches to assimilate technology and student community. Faculties need to be alert of factors that are shaping their forthcoming roles and need to maintain their opinion on their changing roles and ensure that any changes support professional standards for scholarship, teaching, and service.

8.5.4   INNOVATIVE METHOD FOLLOWED

Apart from the methods usually followed in the classroom by the faculties, 98.89% of the faculties use other innovative techniques in the teaching-learning process.

Table 8.4 indicates that 50% of the respondents (including professors, associate professors and assistant professors) indulge in interactive discussion and debates, encouraging original ideas, generating awareness, sharing, and experiencing field, 12.22% participates in outreach programs, live projects, practical orientation-based learning and field industry interface, 8.89% encourages research and publications, 11.11% uses technology-based e-learning and visual aids method and professor's responses reflected a comparatively less preference of using technology-based teaching-learning compared to associate professors and assistant professors. Around 17.78% of the respondents use more than one innovative approach. Thus, data reveals that faculties variously seek to update the pedagogy to make it interesting to the students as well as to capture their attention. This requires a lot of effort by the faculties, and mostly, the thought process involved in doing this innovation cannot be strictly demarcated into the work sphere only.

According to an Assistant Professor at a Private University, Female, 29 years, "*Live projects based on fieldwork is undertaken to gather experience; also we encourage classroom presentation by the students, feedback is taken from the students about methods most appropriate for them. The case study method is also followed, and sometimes we take project presentation from students.*"

8.6   INFORMATION AND COMMUNICATION TECHNOLOGY (ICT)

According to UNESCO (2006), information and communication technology (ICT) is defined as diverse tools and resources such as the computers, internet, technologies which can be used for live broadcasting, recorded

TABLE 8.4 Distribution of Faculties on the Basis of Their Designation and Innovative Teaching Learning Methods Followed for Better Learning

Innovative Teaching Learning Methods	Professor (N = 30) No. (%)	Associate Professor (N = 30) No. (%)	Assistant Professor (N = 30) No. (%)	Total (N = 90) No. (%)
Interactive discussion and debates, encouraging new ideas, generating awareness, sharing, and experiencing field	16 (53.33)	14 (46.67)	15 (50)	45 (50)
Participation in outreach programs, live projects, practical orientation-based learning, and field industry interface	5 (16.67)	3 (10)	3 (10)	11 (12.22)
Encouraging research and publications	3 (10)	3 (10)	2 (6.67)	8 (8.89)
Technology-based e-learning and visual aids	2 (6.67)	4 (13.33)	4 (13.33)	10 (11.11)
More than one approach followed	4 (13.33)	6 (20)	6 (20)	16 (17.78)

broadcasting technologies, and telephone which are used to communicate, store, create, share or exchange information. Faculties use ICT regularly such as internet, audiovisual, PowerPoint presentation for classroom teaching. The extent of use varies from one teacher to another, some may use it for all the class lectures throughout the week, and some others may use it only for 1–2 lectures/ week. Once the structure is prepared, then it is updated regularly. Preparation of the initial structure takes a lot of time. Sometimes, the faculties are able to give time while in the department or it gets carried over to home. Around 95.5% of the respondents regularly use ICT in teaching-learning process. According to 80% of the faculties interviewed, 1–4 hours are required per day to prepare the resources, 11.11% gives more than 4 hours up to 8 hours per day, and 8.89% stated that it depends on the content. According to Brennan et al. (2014), a higher education innovation system involves a set of functions, components, and relationships. It allows disaggregating the numerous levels of interactions among the elements of the system and analyzing the unfolding of innovation in higher education. So, higher education basically involves teamwork and involvement of all levels, including faculties, administrative support as well as student's involvement. Walder (2014) also proposed an updated explanation of pedagogical innovation to be a way of teaching, which is new; it is modified and surprises the students and it brings a change driven by a transient adaptation to pedagogical objectives. Innovative pedagogy should be knowledgeable, innovative, psychological, and unrelenting, and it progresses through various levels and diverse impact process linking receivers and the technology and that intends to improve quality which can make the subject understandable and bring about success. Pedagogical innovation involves thinking about academics and education, unlike technological innovation and it involves human relations, the determination of the devoted professor. In a study by Glenn (2008), university respondents highlighted the positive impact of technology on campus and higher education is becoming responsive to globalization. Respondents expect an interesting range of potentials about how technology is most expected to influence future academic offerings, along with pioneering faculty research, student commitment and the pursuit of academic partnership. Also, technology as an agent of change has given rise to a generation of students who are adapted to technology. These changes will have a significant impact on higher education, and in the current time and in the coming days; advanced technologies will put education within the range of many more individuals globally by making it affordable and allowing greater specialization in curriculum and teaching methodologies than was available earlier. With these comes the task of confirming that university infrastructure and processes are in place to support the implementation of technology within the campus.

8.6.1 PERCEPTION OF TEACHING FACULTIES TOWARDS PEDAGOGICAL INNOVATION AND THEIR CHANGING WORK LIFE

8.6.1.1 ENGAGEMENT WITH THE STUDENTS BEYOND CLASSROOM HOURS

All the faculties responded that they work with the students beyond the structure of the classroom for various purposes. That can be student's academic queries, non-academic doubts, or any other counseling or mentoring assistance. Eighty percent of the faculties, prepare the teaching resources or prepare themselves for classes or engage in innovative thinking for better outcome of the students both during working hours at the university and mostly at home. So, practically it is a continuous flow between work and life, and this extension is presented by the use of the term work-life. Time is frequently considered to be a limitation suggesting online delivery methods, such as videos, may be utilized to provide access to faculty. Application of these pedagogical methods implies an experience which necessitates continuous improvement of current teaching practices, especially as an accumulating process (Boden, 2019).

According to an Associate Professor at a State University, Male, 40 years, *"there is no fixed timing or method for thinking academically. Apart from being a teacher, I am an individual too and consider that I need time for myself. So what I do, I prepare a time schedule for the students 2 hours in the morning and in the evening during which I can talk to the students or give time over phone. Other than that, I can't. And the students know that. Apart from that during weekends or usually, yes checking copies, question paper setting huge module for semester takes time especially bilingual paper setting. So, we need some time, outside department too. Throughout the week, other than university timing, 6–8 hours is required to be devoted for self-study and other academic activities."*

8.6.1.2   PERCEPTION REGARDING NATURE OF ACADEMIC JOB

Since academics is around the clock, 24×7 job, the work often continues at home. Sometimes official work and academic work mostly is required to be done at home. Table 8.5 indicates that, 76.67% of the faculties undertake official works during the weekend, 97.78% of the faculties continue academic work during the weekend. The amount of time devoted for work depends and varies as per the situation, since academics is a continuous process 24×7, exact hours cannot be specified. Moreover, students have continuous access to their teachers beyond working hours at the university and even during the weekends. Their needs and requirements are also kept in mind by the teachers as their role today as their role is evolving from just being a teacher within the classroom to become a mentor, guide, and in counseling them as well. This study revealed that the teaching faculties at a university are required to be engaged in not just teaching but also divide their time between other works related to the academic profession. It is often truly a 24 x 7 job without any fixed boundary between work and life. Moreover, the faculties who are working at private universities have a fixed entry and exit time which makes the structure even rigid. All these have been a recent change in the work-life of the faculties since the last decade.

TABLE 8.5   Distribution of Faculties on the Basis of Their Designation and Time Given for Academic or Official Work During Weekend

Time Given for Work During Weekend	Professor	Associate Professor	Assistant Professor	Total (N = 90) No. (%)
Official work conducted during weekend	23 (76.67)	26 (86.67)	20 (66.67)	69 (76.67)
Academic work done during weekend	30 (100)	29 (96.67)	29 (96.67)	88 (97.78)

8.6.1.3   INTERFERENCE WITH OWN TIME OR FAMILY TIME

According to 74.44% of the respondents, work interferes with family time and 25.56% of the respondents do not feel so and that both can be compartmentalized. Clark (2000) highlighted that work and family are two different domains that people associate themselves with and individuals frequently crosses the borders of the two domains depending on the nature and flexibility of the domains and that influences work/family balance (Table 8.6).

TABLE 8.6 Distribution of Faculties on the Basis of Their Designation and Interference of Work with Own Time or Family Time

Time Given for Work During Weekend	Professor (N = 30) No. (%)	Associate Professor (N = 30) No. (%)	Assistant Professor (N = 30) No. (%)	Total (N = 90) No. (%)
Work interferes with family time	14 (46.67)	26 (86.67)	27 (90)	67 (74.44)
Work does not interfere with family time	16 (53.33)	4 (13.33)	3 (10)	23 (25.56)

8.7 THEORETICAL DISCUSSION AND CONCLUSION

The idea of work or labor as explored in the sociological analysis of work takes into account work in its social settings, conditions, and the different dimensions of work and also by investigating the relationship between workers and all other agents who are involved in the work process. Work is also discussed in relation to non-work aspects of society which can include leisure, family life as well as social life and responsibilities. Work is undoubtedly a significant activity and it gives an identity to an individual, but the nature of work changes over time and that also creates an effect on physical and psychological well-being of an individual. From a social structural perspective, an individual's experiences in particular jobs are influenced by opportunities for employment in certain kinds of jobs as well as an individual's situation in the occupational arrangement and the joining of work roles and various other roles such as marital roles and parental roles. Many aspects of our working life are shaped by the structure of a society, its age composition, racial, ethnic, gender, and class divisions and distributions of power and authority (Volti, 2012). Work when done in exchange of a regular pay or salary is called an occupation, or job. The kind of occupations individuals are involved are also influenced by the degree of technological advancement. Technology is relevant to social structure as because society enables the creation of new and advanced technology as well as in technological growth. Life and work in 21st century post-industrial society is very much different from work in earlier times. It is a reflection of current social arrangements and structure. Technological change is one of the major forces propelling the economic, social, and cultural changes coupled with the influence of various forces, which results in those changes and have produced a world that is more interdependent and integrated. This process can be subsumed under the term globalization (Volti, 2012). After the agricultural and industrial revolution, currently we are experiencing a huge transformation in terms of technological change, which has led to the emergence of post-industrial society and economy. The intensification of the service sector as the principal source of employment signifies one of the most important transformations of life and work in human history (Volti, 2012). The service sector is the third sector in the three-tier economy and a large number of individuals are currently employed in the tertiary or service sector. Education and teaching are included within this sector. Hüfner (2010) in the Encyclopedia of Higher Education mentioned that the tertiary sector embraces higher education institutions which include universities and equivalent higher learning institutions. Research, scientific knowledge, advancement of technology has been continually bringing about change in this tertiary sector. The main deliberations, amongst the more present-day theorists, are how to contextualize these fast-paced changes in technology and patterns of consumption. There are some who sees an end to a meta-narrative entitled 'modernity' and that we are in a new phase, i.e., postmodernity and the emergence of the decentered subject. Many contemporary theorists do not necessarily see an end to what is termed as 'modernity.' There may be shifts within the patterns of 'modernity,' but the main characteristics as such have not changed. Giddens, for example, calls this 'late modernity.' More importantly 'modernity' is a dynamic process, in which the macro characteristics identified, continuously emerge in different forms. The dynamic processes that make such institutions possible are constantly being restructured. This fits in with Giddens' own structuration theory. In such a conception, structures of practice do not exist in a set form, rather they are constantly being re-shaped and reformed through the actions of human agency. Giddens identifies these processes through three main features-Distanciation that involves, time, and space separation; distanciation then leads to disembedding which is 'lifting out' of social relations from local contexts of interactions and their restructuring across indefinite spans of time-space" (Giddens, 1990: p. 21) and modernity is characterized by greater reflexivity, where "social practices are constantly examined and reformed in the light of incoming information about those very practices, thus constitutively altering their character" (Giddens, 1990: p. 38).

In the higher education sector, there has been a huge impact of globalization as well as impact of advancement of technology. Time and space distanciation is no longer creating a barrier to gain knowledge. Advanced facilities like e-learning materials, easy accessibility to online content, remote access facilities of library has bridged the time and space separation. The students as well as the faculties in higher education today are constantly accessible and disembedding occurs where interaction is not just restricted to classroom structure and it acts like both a boon and a bane for both.

According to Longhofer and Winchester (2016), Bauman was a prominent theorist of postmodernity between 1980s and 1990s. In contrast to other theorists, Bauman contended that postmodernity and modernity do not reflect a major disruption rather he considered modernity by an ambivalent, "dual" nature. According to Bauman, from one aspect modern society is considered as a need for order but, again, is it regarded by radical change, by continuously rejecting tradition and traditional forms of economy, culture, and relationship whereby solid transforms into air as this aspect of modern society has been characterized by Marx. Afterward, Bauman considered the term "postmodern" to be problematic and referred to the term liquid modernity to define the situation of relentless movement or mobility and the change. Bauman indicates a transition from solid modernity to a more liquid (fluid) form of social life. According to Bauman, the result of this move can be seen in current approaches to self-identity. It becomes difficult to construct an identity in liquid modernity which will be resilient that fit together over time and space; they do not hold their shape for long like all fluids. Since the last decade, there has been a remarkable change in the higher education pedagogy where the role of a student is not just a passive recipient but an active partaker in the education process and the role of a teacher has shifted from that of an instructor providing one-way monolog lecture to that of an enabler and facilitator. Liquid modernity can justifiably be used by Bauman to indicate the constant mobility and change as experienced by the faculties and students. Regular update of curriculum is done to match with the requirements of the students and economic sector and also in engaging the students in developing passion for learning. Also, there has been a change in the teaching-learning methodology which now involves various kinds of digital technology and interactive and innovative learning methods above and beyond only the lecture-discussion method. New pedagogical techniques like flipped classroom (online content as well as face-to-face delivery), blended learning, case study method of teaching, etc., have been adopted by faculties today to develop problem-solving and critical thinking skills. In the 'Flipped classroom' model, learning is flipped and students can finish before the class, cognitive tasks which are in lower order by taking support from MOOC or some other resources which are available digitally and they can involve in learning of the higher cognitive levels through interaction among students and teachers when they are in class (Bakhshi, 2020).

Presently, the widespread on-going coronavirus pandemic in 2020 and consequent closing of various institutions, including educational institutions, have brought various digital mode of education on the fore front. Curriculum is covered using digital form of technologies, whereby faculties and students are keeping themselves updated by using remote access facilities to access various academic resources as well as institutes are developing Learning Management systems which are enabling e-learning of the students. Updated multidisciplinary, industry-oriented course content will enable students to get broad exposure and holistic worldview. Faculties are required to develop content/ pedagogy in accordance with the requirements of the market/ learners. As of now, we are in the phase of Education 4.0, which denotes changes, relevant to the emerging fourth industrial revolution. In this version of the industrial revolution, the main focus is on smart technology, artificial intelligence, and robotics. These things broadly impact various aspects of our everyday lives. Hence, universities today need to make the students ready for entering this new phase of the industrial revolution by making students aware of these new technologies. These technologies will have to be made a part of the core curriculum, and the approach to learning altogether can be changed by making the students use them in order to better improve the university experience (James, 2019).

In the current scenario, growing importance has been placed on digital education, where the role of a teacher in higher education is undergoing remarkable changes. This pandemic and the global crisis, in a way, has increased the importance of digital learning, and institutions and faculties are falling back on online teaching-learning method as an option to face the crisis and continue the teaching-learning process. However, the objective of education has not changed, that is, empowerment of individuals towards successful life and contributes for their own self, family, society (Srivastava, 2019). Education helps a student to explore their true potential and teachers have a significant role in mentoring them. Like all methods, the digital method of teaching-learning has its own benefits as well as disadvantages. It is never a replacement to conventional teaching rather it acts as a supplement to the conventional method. Presently, with the advancement of the 'knowledge economy' there is an emphasis on the constant learning and self-upgradation which makes an individual a lifelong learner. A teacher and a learner both have to be active and adaptive to the changing requirements and time and be dynamic in the face of constant challenges and changes. There is a concern that by implementing various digital technologies in teaching-learning, there will be an extra workload added on teachers. There are several elements of digital technologies that must be assimilated judiciously to permit the class to attain the chosen objectives. These challenges, including the digital divide needs to be addressed to apply the various models of online education successfully. Teachers are needed to be trained professionally at all levels to adopt a new methodology of teaching and learning which emphasizes on interaction so that it facilitates learners to attain higher-order learning skills (Bakhshi, 2020).

Today, there has been an enormous change in the role of higher education as well as that of teaching professionals. The focus presently has shifted towards a learner-centered approach where the students are at the center stage of the learning process, and to meet the diverse requirements of students, new and innovative ways has to be devised continuously by the institutions and teachers. New roles of a teacher in higher education necessitate one to be tech-savvy with ICT skills, and the teacher must also be able to manage virtual classrooms. A teacher also has to be proficient in developing e-content and online education. In the 21st century, a teacher is anticipated to outshine in these constantly changing newer roles, and among the various factors, digitalization certainly acts as one, which is bringing about a change in the nature of the work-life of a faculty.

KEYWORDS

- **choice-based credit system**
- **digital technologies**
- **digitalization**
- **pedagogical innovation**
- **perception**
- **teaching professionals**

REFERENCES

Bakhshi, A. K., (2020). *Flipped Classroom for 21ˢᵗ-Century Learning Needs.* Retrieved from: https://www.educationtimes.com/article/editors-pick/76728031/flipped-classroom-for-21st-century-learning-needs.html#gsc.tab=0 (accessed on 24 February 2021).

Bils, A., (2019). Digitizing teaching and learning. Examples from fern Universität in Hagen. In: Theo, B. J., (ed.), *Proceedings of EdMedia + Innovate Learning* (pp. 531–535). Amsterdam, Netherlands: Association for the Advancement of Computing in Education (AACE). Retrieved from: https://www.learntechlib.org/p/210047 (accessed on 24 February 2021).

Boden, K. E., (2019). *Pedagogical Innovation among University Faculty* (Vol. 10, No. 5, pp. 848–861). Scientific Research an Academic Publisher. Retrieved from: doi: 10.4236/ce.2019.105063.

Brennen, J. S., & Kreiss, D., (2016). Digitalization. In: Jensen, K. B., Rothenbuhler, E. W., Pooley, J. D., & Craig, R. T., (eds.), *The International Encyclopedia of Communication Theory and Philosophy.* doi: 10.1002/9781118766804.wbiect111.

Casares, J., et al., (2011). *R.I.T. The Future of Teaching and Learning in Higher Education.* Retrieved from: https://www.rit.edu/academicaffairs/sites/rit.edu.academicaffairs/files/docs/future_of_teaching_and_learning_reportv13.pdf (accessed on 24 February 2021).

Clark, S. C., (2000). Work/family border theory: A new theory of work/family balance. *Human Relations, 53*(6), 747–770.

Edgell, S., (2012). *The Sociology of Work. Continuity and Change in Paid and Unpaid Work* (2ⁿᵈ edn.). Sage Publications.

Edwards, P., (2013). *The Sociology of Work: From Industrial Sociology to Work, Employment and the Economy.* Discussion Paper 2013–01. The University of Birmingham. Discussion Paper Series. Retrieved from: http://epapers.bham.ac.uk/1715/ (accessed on 24 February 2021).

Giddens, A., (1990). *The Consequences of Modernity.* Originating Publisher, Stanford University Press, CA.

Glenn, M., (2008). In: D'Agostino, D., (ed.), *The Future of Higher Education: How Technology Will Shape Learning.* The Economist Intelligence Unit.

Gobble, M. M., (2018). Digitalization, digitization, and innovation. *Research-Technology Management, 61*(4), 56–59, doi: 10.1080/08956308.2018.1471280.

Gonzalez, G., (2019). *Changing with the Times: Faculty's Role in Delivering a Great Student Experience.* The evolution. Retrieved from: https://evolllution.com/programming/teaching-and-learning/changing-with-the-times-facultys-role-in-delivering-a-great-student-experience/ (accessed on 24 February 2021).

Guerriero, S., (2017). *Pedagogical Knowledge and the Changing Nature of the Teaching Profession.* OECD Publishing, Paris. Retrieved from: doi: https://dx.doi.org/10.1787/9789264270695-en.

Hotaman, D., (2010). The teaching profession: Knowledge of subject matter, teaching skills and personality traits. *Procedia-Social and Behavioral Sciences, 2*(2), 1416–1420. Retrieved from: doi: Https://doi.org/10.1016/j.sbspro.2010.03.211.

Hüfner, A., & Hüfner, K., (2010). *International Encyclopedia of Education* (3ʳᵈ edn., pp. 582–589). Germany. https://doi.org/10.1016/B978-0-08-044894-7.01406-8.

James, F., (2019). *Everything You Need to Know About Education 4.0*. Retrieved from: https://www.qs.com/everything-you-need-to-know-education-40/ (accessed on 24 February 2021).

Lakshmi, V. S. M., & Rao, K. S. S., (2016). A sign of smart India: The rise of digitalization. *International Journal of Innovative Research in Advanced Engineering (IJIRAE), 12*(3), 40–42. Retrieved from: https://www.academia.edu/30797213/A_SIGN_OF_SMART_INDIA_THE_RISE_OF_DIGITALIZATION (accessed on 24 February 2021).

Longhofer, & Winchester, (2016). *Social Theory Re-Wired: New Connections to Classical and Contemporary Perspectives*. (2nd edn.) Routledge, member of the Taylor & Francis Group. Retrieved from: http://routledgesoc.com/category/profile-tags/liquid-modernity (accessed on 24 February 2021).

Marathe, S., (2018). Digitalization in education sector. *International Journal of Trend in Scientific Research and Development (IJTSRD)*, 51–56. doi: https://www.ijtsrd.com/papers/ijtsrd18670.pdf (accessed on 24 February 2021).

Mirakamalia, S. M., & Thanib, F. N., (2011). A study on the quality of work-life (QWL) among faculty members of the University of Tehran (UT) and sharif university of technology (SUT). *Procedia-Social and Behavioral Sciences, 29*, 179–187. Retrieved from: https://core.ac.uk/download/pdf/82397245.pdf (accessed on 24 February 2021).

Prince, M. J., Felder, R. M., & Brent, R., (2007). Does faculty research improve undergraduate teaching? An analysis of existing and potential synergies. *Journal of Engineering Education, 96*(4), 283–294.

Punia, V., & Kamboj, M., (2013). Quality of work-life balance among teachers in higher education institutions. *Learning Community, 4*(3), 197–208.

Srivastava, A. K., (2019). *Is Education 4.0 the Future of Learning?* Retrieved from: https://www.indiatoday.in/education-today/featurephilia/story/is-education-4-0-the-future-of-learning-1557292-2019-06-27 (accessed on 24 February 2021).

Strike, K. A., (1991). Is teaching a profession: How would we know? *Journal of Personnel Evaluation in Education, 4*, 91–117. Retrieved from: https://link.springer.com/chapter/10.1007/978-94-011-3884-0_7 (accessed on 24 February 2021).

Tratkowska, K. (2019). Digital Transformation: Theoretical Backgrounds of Digital Change. *Management Sciences, 24*(4), 32–37. DOI: 10.15611/ms.2019.4.05.

UNESCO Office Bangkok and Regional Bureau for Education in Asia and the Pacific, (2006). *Using ICT to Develop Literacy*, 14. Retrieved from: https://unesdoc.unesco.org/ark:/48223/pf0000146426 (accessed on 24 February 2021).

University Grants Commission, (2019). Retrieved from: http://www.ugc.ac.in (accessed on 24 February 2021).

Vidal, M., (2011). *The Sociology of Work*. Accessed at: http://www.everydaysociologyblog.com/2011/11/the-sociology-of-work.html (accessed on 24 February 2021).

Volti, R., (2011). *An Introduction to the Sociology of Work and Occupation*. Pine Forge Press.

Walder, A. M., (2014). The concept of pedagogical innovation in higher education. *Education Journal, 3*(3), 195–202. doi: 10.11648/j.edu.20140303.22 Retrieved from: https://www.researchgate.net/publication/301687758_The_concept_of_pedagogical_innovation_in_higher_education (accessed on 24 February 2021).

Williams, L., (1921). Teaching as a profession. *The High School Journal, 4*(2), 31–33. Retrieved from: www.jstor.org/stable/40359201 (accessed on 24 February 2021).

CHAPTER 9

Career Choice: A Critical Study in the Age of Digitalization

SANCHARI DE

Assistant Professor of Sociology (W.B.E.S.), Government General Degree College Mangalkote, Burdwan, West Bengal, India

ABSTRACT

In the 21st century contemporary society, digitalization is penetrating in every sphere of our life including the education sector. The gradual usage of technology in delivering education, knowledge, and skills is taking place in innovative ways to enable education to attain the globalized character. But this digital penetration is coupled with changes in the mode and pattern of work and learning new skill needs for efficient functioning in the current economic uncertainty and political shifts. Thus the use of these technologies have contributed to transforming learning and skill development into a lifelong process where we have to refresh our knowledge and skills to keep updated with the constant developments in the digital world to maintain our relevance in society (Grand-Clement, 2017).

Thus the objective of my study is, how digital India with its global vision on education and technology-based e-learning curriculum, affecting urban secondary and higher secondary school students (both male and female) while making career choices both positively and negatively.

A review of secondary literature and theoretical perspectives have been used for the qualitative analysis of my study.

Choosing an appropriate career in accordance to one's interest is an important decision in life for shaping one's identity so that he/she can contribute efficiently as a human resource according to the changing labor market scenario leading to the development of the national economy.

9.1   INTRODUCTION

With the liberalization and globalization of the Indian economy, rapid changes have taken place in the scientific and technological world, initiating the need of reducing poverty and thereby improving the quality of life of the people in the nation. In this context, education has become intrinsic in assessing inequalities of opportunity and acts as a significant contributing factor to individual's income status, health issues, and the ability to interact and communicate with others because inequality in education contributes to inequality in other important dimensions of wellbeing (World Bank, 2006). In this digital information era, knowledge has become the key factor for social and economic development (see, https://ecsn.ru/files/pdf/201407eng.pdf; European Commission, 2010) and in the context of globalization, education as a system and process with its innovative trends is not only trying to establish 'knowledge as the pillar of wealth and power of nations' but also treating it as a mere commodity subject to market laws and private appropriation (Rifkin, 2000). In today's contemporary society, the digitalization process with its various opportunities and threats have spread in every sphere of our lives from day-to-day activities to even the education sector, making us more vulnerable and dependent on it (Grand-Clement, 2017).

For the society, Information Communication and Technology (ICT) has been viewed as a "major tool for building knowledge societies" and as a mechanism at schools for improving the quality of education for all by rethinking and redesigning the education systems and processes (UNESCO, 2003: p. 1). School as a formal educational institution helps in providing the necessary information, the required skills, and the much-needed specialized knowledge. It is a measure of one's level of education, a deciding factor in the selection and rejection of people for professional roles…, trains the mind to adapt to a 'modern, technologically advanced civilization' (Pathak, 2002: p. 21). 'The Department of School Education and Literacy,' Government of India, highlights secondary education as crucial in the educational hierarchy for the world of work, meant for transforming the economy. Education deals with empowering students with appropriate culturally relevant information and developing skills necessary to face real life situations in positive and responsible ways (https://www.education.gov.in/sites/upload_files/mhrd/files/upload_document/Framework_Final_RMSA_3.pdf). Side by side, the economy also becomes more productive, innovative, and competitive with the existence of more skilled and talented human potential. Thus we see that the societal changes due to globalization and technology gives rise to many challenges as well as tremendous opportunities for the national economy to expand by creating various jobs in the labor market (Okolie and Yasin, 2017). So it becomes important for school students to learn and acquire necessary digital knowledge and skills which will help them to contribute to the development of the economy of the nation efficiently (Agrawal and Ramesh, 2013).

India has 1,39,539 Secondary and 1,12,637 Higher Secondary schools serving 3,91,45,000 secondary and 2,47,35,000 higher secondary students with an average teacher-student ratio of 1:27 in secondary schools and 1:37 in higher secondary schools (https://www.mhrd.gov.in/sites/upload_files/mhrd/files/statistics-new/ESAG-2018.pdf) and significant difference in the curriculum offered correlating to the various examination boards whether Central or state (http://cbseacademic.in/curriculum.html). The National curriculum framework (NCF) for All 2012 pointed out the need for plurality and flexibility within education driven by globalization, ICT development, competition, shift of traditional values and new paradigms while maintaining the standards of education (http://curriculum.gov.mt/en/Resources/The-NCF/Documents/NCF.pdf). Secondary level students' school experiences often do not prepare them adequately for higher studies and for the world of work with proper employability skills. There is a serious lacuna visible, where integration of strong academic content into career-focused classes and proper collaboration of post-secondary institutions, economic development agencies, and employers are missing to help out students for smoother transitions to college and workforce (Bangser, 2008: pp. 4, 5). After the implementation of the right to education (RTE) Act (2009), it became furthermore necessary for the students to generate and actively engage with intentions regarding future life and make appropriate educational choices by formulating and committing to a particular career goal. Career choice, planning, therefore, becomes unavoidable in the selection of disciplines and courses so that India becomes a youthful engine of economic growth (Cheney et al., 2006) matching the challenges of competitive market opportunities.

9.2 OBJECTIVE AND METHODOLOGY

Thus the main objective of my study is in this contemporary phase of digital education and the constant urge to apply ICT in education for improving quality to achieve the global character, how, and in what way urban secondary and higher secondary school students (both boys and girls) are getting affected while making their career choice.

A review of secondary literature and theoretical perspectives have been used for the qualitative analysis of my study.

9.3   REVIEW OF LITERATURE

Prior to the digital era, it was difficult for the majority of people to get access to information and current updates so easily and instantly because traditional education depended on educational institutions such as schools, colleges, universities, libraries, and print media like newspapers, journals, and magazines. But the modern society wants to attain real-time global information instantly as it is transforming into a knowledge society. Thus education holds the highest priority even more, and brainpower is becoming the most valuable asset of any organization. Development in digital technology have opened up many avenues of learning, transmitting information anywhere and everywhere, making education reach most parts of the world with ICT becoming an integral part of human life (Wikramanayake, 2014).

Globalization as an important phenomenon tends to initiate the various socio-cultural, economic, and political processes around the world by bringing in new concepts, values, perspectives, and information to the society thus contributing towards a world which is much more interactive, where people can involve in many kinds of communication without even physically meeting them (Stromquist, 2005). Learners can now easily access, assess, adapt, and apply knowledge to think independently, exercise their appropriate judgment to do teamwork in collaborative ways to deal with new situations. With the use of advanced information and communication technologies, it breaks the boundaries of space and time, enabling new systems of knowledge in teaching and learning that helps both the teacher as well as the student. Globalization encourages new explorations and experimentation everyday so that ICTs can be upgraded to newer versions, thereby making learning more effective (Cogburn, 2000) and supporting policymakers and practitioners to rethink education by exchanging ideas and experiences in line with new trends.

Due to globalization, schools in India are trying to prepare a curriculum with an international appeal that is acceptable worldwide. Thus there is a growing demand to learn the English language and focus on the overall development of personality. Instead of rote learning and providing bookish knowledge, teachers are applying newer means of teaching-learning pedagogy. Schools with proper infrastructure and facilities are also being highlighted so that students get the opportunity of quality education, preparing them for the global world since, in the contemporary context, students are seen as customers as well as partners in the process of learning (Anand, 2015).

The European Commission through its e-Learning Action Plan is also promoting the use of ICT in various learning processes whose main aim being "to improve the quality of learning by facilitating access to resources and services as well as remote exchange and collaboration" (Commission of the European Communities, 2001: p. 2). The report suggested that broadband facilities should be more widely spread across remote areas, teachers should get support regarding professional development policies, more training should be provided to teachers for using ICT and high-quality online content should be developed so that schools can make use of ICT easily (UNESCO, 2008). Governments and administrations have been putting the effort to provide schools with good equipment but still analysis shows that educational usage of ICT in the classroom has been lacking, so there is a need to develop appropriate strategies to face this new teaching role and the students' role when integrating ICT in the teaching and learning processes. In this context, the role and the perspective of teachers become crucial and highly relevant on how they should use technology in their classrooms and in relation to their work and specific to their needs (Sangra and Gonzalez-Sanmamed, 2010).

In Sweden, too adoption and use of digital technologies in school education has been given prime importance and acknowledged by scholars and researchers on regional, national, and European authority levels (Salavati, 2013). According to the Swedish Digital Commission (2015), every sphere of our lives have become predominantly digital in nature influencing growth, sustainability, welfare, equality, safety, economy, and democracy. So it becomes obvious that this digitalization has a massive transformative impact on the society, constituting on how education is to be carried out and what is expected from the future generation (Salavati, 2013). According to the reports of Swedish IT policy, "school children must, and teachers should, have access to modern learning tools that are required for contemporary education." The latest national curriculum report also stated that it is the responsibility of the school to ensure that every student should be made ready to use modern technology as a tool in their studies for searching appropriate information, for global communication, for becoming creative individuals, and learning essential upgraded knowledge (Salavati, 2016). The European Commission also states that Information and Communication Technologies (ICT) help us in overall development of individuals by learning more efficiently and creatively to innovate oneself constantly to deal with complex problems in flexible manner both indoors and outdoors (Dillenbourg, Järvelä, and Fischer, 2009; Pachler, Bachmair, and Cook, 2010; Scardamalia et al., 2010; European Commission's Digital Agenda for Europe, 2015).

There are diverse actors, factors, relationships, and perspectives attached with education and school practices, which are highly influential and challenging in nature (Salavati, 2013). It is found that in Swedish classrooms within a span of 4 years (2008–2012), interactive whiteboards in compulsory schools tripled from 11% to 33% and the use of tablet devices in schools increased 10% between 2008 and 2012 but by 2015, the number of tablet-devices increased to 40%. It was also seen that children were allowed to bring their own private devices for education and learning purposes in schools. Even all teachers at the high school level and compulsory school level possessed their own individual computers or laptops. So it is observed that even though the use of digital technologies in classrooms has increased from before but still various reports from Swedish authorities have stated that utilization of digital technologies for education has been limited and highly dispersed in nature and are normally used for regular administrative work rather than as supporting tools for pedagogical tasks. Nevertheless, according to the latest report from the Swedish National Agency of Education, the use of digital technology has indeed increased during the last few years (Salavati, 2016). Despite the challenges of utilizing digital technologies, Scardamalia et al. (2010); and Milrad et al. (2013) argued that technology enables more opportunities for in-depth learning experiences across various settings. According to teachers participating in Salavati's (2013) research, the use of digital technologies, tries to shift teaching-learning from the four walls of the classroom to the outside world, hence providing realistic exposure to students at large and even enhancing them to collaborate with each other to perform teamwork. Due to political decisions, digital technologies have been pushed into schools without paying heed to the fact that infrastructural modifications and pedagogical practices need to be made only by people working in these specific institutions and organizations (Salavati, 2016). Tallvid (2014) states that the school and Swedish authorities has imposed on the teachers the use of information and communication technology (ICT) tools to teach in smart classrooms which traditionally, teachers had the authority to organize and design their own teaching without direct influence or involvement from school leaders or governmental authorities. Thus, teachers within their normal mundane work activities had to train and conduct how to adapt to digitalized schools (Tallvid, 2014). The merging of schools, municipalities, and industries are highly recommended for better adoption of digital technologies in regular everyday educational practices (Salavati, 2016). Therefore, as Tallvid (2014) asserts that in spite of the fact that technology does affect the daily life of a school organization, Swedish schools has not yet changed the traditional teaching-learning processes. Worldwide initiatives are being carried out, including Sweden, that every enrolled student should attend school with their own laptop or tablet, in order to access digital learning materials, digital textbooks, and internet easily. But since buying technological devices for students as well as teachers involved high costs, the initial support by the municipalities were later carried forward by the schools through loans.

In the present day, globalization has made education as an internationally traded commodity which is purchased by a consumer to build a set of skills that can be utilized by Multi-National Corporations in the labor market, rather than emphasizing on attitudes and values to participate effectively as citizens contributing in modern society (Agrawal, 2005). But to maintain the quality of this commodity, there is a lot of cost involved, which governments are not being able to bear, thus leading to the gradual process of privatization (Shah, 2006a). So in the current global climate since private returns on education is growing, the market with its effective and efficient provision of goods and services which can benefit all are given utmost importance in the predominance of a knowledge economy. On the basis of this ideology, policies are being formed in India, but it is highly debatable whether giving too much significance to market needs can surely ensure the perfect result for education (Agrawal and Ramesh, 2013).

Papert (1980), in his study, 'children, computer, and powerful idea' stated the significance of how by using digital media, children can learn better within a proper teaching-learning ambiance helping them to assemble and modify their imaginations which were inadequate with traditional tools like pencils, copies, and textbooks. Computers were considered as the appropriate tool to facilitate learners to take control of the whole learning process because there is a harmonizing relationship between technology and constructivism, so educators need to integrate technology in the classroom to create a constructivist approach (www.shodhganga.inflibnet.ac.in).

Laird (1985) states in 'Approaches to training and development' that effective learning occurs when the senses are stimulated and online instructions initiate learners to use their sensory systems to register the information in the form of sensations due to audio-visual impact. His study report suggests that the majority of the adults around 75% grasp knowledge visually by seeing, next most effective way of grasping knowledge is by hearing approximately 13%, and the other senses like touch, smell, and taste account for 12%. Therefore, it can be claimed that when students use the internet for doing research or project work and tries to publish it on various websites, their 29 organization skills gets enhanced by connecting with real audiences all over the world with a better understanding of the world wide web (www.shodhganga.inflibnet.ac.in).

Many plans and policies in India on education have modified pedagogical structure according to the digital global need creating vast opportunities and global exposure to enable school students to make appropriate career choice for their future.

According to the Twelfth Five Year Plan by the Government of India (2012–2017), quality of education depends on many factors such as proper infrastructure, text materials, classroom teaching processes, assessment, and evaluation procedures and even what kind of academic support provided to the faculty members. It focuses on improving the quality of schools on regular basis so that comprehensive system of education is maintained by strengthening academic support with efficient leadership and management system, measuring, and improving learning outcomes in a continuous manner and finally effective participation of parents and community at large. There should also be provision for child-friendly schools with proper hygiene, water, sanitation, toilets, and mid-day meal facilities available for the wellbeing of the students (Planning Commission, 2013). The NCF 2005 also gave prime importance to meaningful classroom experiences between students and teacher, well-planned physical/ sports activities for the overall physical development, other co-curricular activities for students should be conceptualized also with proper resources like debates, quiz, creative art and craft exhibitions, taking into account the health and nutrition of each and every students for improving the quality of school ethos and creating inclusive school ambiance by making appropriate reforms (NCERT, 2006).

The National Policy on Education (1986), as modified in 1992, also stressed that technology in the education sector needs to be employed to improve the quality of education. The significant role ICT can play in school education has also been highlighted in the NCF 2005, highlighting on the necessary need for variety and flexibility within education while maintaining the quality and standard. The use of ICT for quality improvement also figures in the Government of India's flagship program on education, Sarva Shiksha Abhiyan (SSA). Again, we observe that ICT has figured widely in the school norms recommended by the Central Advisory Board of Education (CABE), in its report on Universal Secondary Education, in 2005. As various technologies are merging with each other, it is important to highlight and choose specific ICTs which will fulfill holistic approach of education by initiating sound policies in school education so that it aims at preparing youth to participate creatively in the establishment, sustenance, and growth of a knowledge society leading to all-round socio-economic development of the nation and dealing global competitiveness (National Policy on ICT in School Education, Department of School Education and Literacy, MHRD, GOI, 2012).

Repeated experiments in pedagogy have revealed that instructional aides not only help in better learning and retention but lend vividness to learning while catering to individual differences among pupils. India was one of the earliest countries in the world to institutionalize the use of effective teaching aids. The Secondary Education Commission (1952) under the chairmanship of Dr. Lakshmanaswami Mudaliar, commented on the significance of the role of audio-visual aids, where the students get not only theoretical instruction but also a graphic presentation of the subject. The Kothari Commission 1964–1966 recommended a training paradigm for teachers in preparing them to evolve new methods of teaching. After the institutionalization of the program 'ICT @ Schools' in 2004 by the Department of School Education and Literacy, important issues of creating an ICT-enabled school education paradigm and sharing of ICT-based education resources across the country gained prominence. It had wide influence across state education boards, with schools opting for the use of computers and technology-enabled teaching aids, leading to better curriculum management by teachers and improved conceptual progress, ease of learning, and retention by students (The Statesman, 2016).

With the upcoming of digitalization, many educational tech apps have come up offering live streaming programs and lectures to help simplify complex subjects for career aspirants. The increasing stress of exams and parental pressure and worry leads to rampant use of EdTech apps in their smartphones in a productive way. Some are providing online courses in various fields; some are providing career advice, while some are merging education with virtual reality to change how education is perceived in the country. The current top five learning app used by students are:

- Gradeup is India's largest exam preparation platform for students to participate in competitive exams and score better. It has been leveraging the latest technologies to fill the gaps in the current education system. Their virtual classroom learning experience includes interactive live classes, mind maps, mock tests with live analysis as well as 1-to-1 mentorship.

- Unacademy is India's largest free online learning platform and access to quality education where knowledge is shared incomprehensible form by all educators creating courses on various subjects for every single student irrespective of their socio-economic background. Technology has made it possible to connect the best educators to every single aspirant aiming to make a career. This popular learning app strives to create a conducive learning and teaching environment by facilitating the flow of knowledge and exchange of ideas (www.unacademy.com).

- Toppr is India's leading after-school learning app with a mission to make learning personalized by catering to individual learning styles of candidates and provides the widest K12 syllabus coverage with 1 million course combinations. Currently, it has 8 million students preparing for various school board and competitive exams. Along with free online classes, it also offers live classes so that students can learn new concepts or clear any doubts in real-time.

- Adda247 is the second-largest Ed-tech app in terms of paid users. It also focuses on quality education and training to become capable of cracking intensive competitive examinations by leveraging an integrated cross-channel approach.

- Vedantu is also an online tutoring company with its USP of quality teachers who can give personalized teaching using two-way audio, video, and whiteboard tools so that both teacher and student can see, hear, write, and interact in real-time (India Today, 2019; indiatoday.in).

Deaney et al. (2003) in their study 'Pupil Perspectives on the Contribution of ICT to Teaching and Learning in Secondary Schools' found that students viewed ICT resources as helpful in tasks, presentations, and analyzing project reports. ICT has changed the study environment into smart classrooms, and online teaching has changed the relations between teacher and students where we see a lack of physical touch and face-to-face interaction, but the application of ICT has indeed increased the students' interest level and motivation while studying. The students while dealing with the various challenges associated with ICT, are very much concerned that by giving too much value to independent study and reshaping of learning we might be displacing valuable in-depth teaching (www.shodhganga.inflibnet.ac.in).

But several studies also highlighted the threats of digital education and the associated problems which school students face while making career decisions in developing countries, especially India.

Progress in ICT-based education showed signs of stress with unplanned and reckless use of computer-based technology in lieu of time-tested pedagogical practices, and it is becoming an end in itself rather than means to an end. An assessment of the use of ICT-enabled materials in India in the last decade is already showing usual cycles of marketing hype, investment, poor integration, and inadequate educational outcome, e.g., rampant use of smart board at the expense of usual blackboard. But not only does it take away teacher's freedom of creatively using a blackboard, it also renders much of the board student interface mechanical and superficial. There has been no study conducted to date that establishes that the use of such electronic devices has favorable and lasting learning outcomes. The other pitfall in a resource-starved country like ours is that educational technological gadgets have a limited shelf life, thereby making continuous use of updated devices costly and unproductive. There are schools that have made internet-based tablet devices mandatory at the expense of paper-pen-blackboard-based education. Thus typing has replaced handwriting and turning the pages of a book has degraded into a cursory flick of a finger. Though it adds novelty but in the long term, it is harmful in the development of vital cognitive skills and tactile intelligence. The key challenge in Indian education is to keep learners constantly motivated. The use of ICT-based technology can aid the process of motivation, but it can hardly supplant the role of a teacher, his creativity and flexibility in handling the curriculum. Indiscriminate use of these devices in school education based on market considerations and commercial hype not only robs a teacher of his prime asset of flexibility and innovative classroom management but takes away from students the privilege of observing the interface of classroom precepts and real-life practices which traditional teaching aids can ensure easily (The Statesman, 2016).

A statewide study of school children under the school health program has revealed shocking details about how the innocence of children are apparently getting destroyed in the world of cut-throat competition where the child is constantly being fed with the mantra to win and attain top rank irrespective of whatever barriers he/she faces, leading to children now being seen suffering from severe mental disorders and other illnesses. In the state capital, around 133 adolescents, including 63 females, have been found to be affected with attention deficiency and behavior disorders. The program has so far covered 75% of the 558 Higher Secondary schools and 1000 primary schools in Kolkata. The government has tied-up with the Department of Applied Psychology at Rajabazar Science College and has been offering free counseling to students. Mr. Abhishek Hansa, the psychologist, who has been counseling the students, commented that most adolescents were depressed or had suicidal tendencies. Excessive pressure by parents and their failure to live up to those expectations make them frustrated, which are depicted in their behavior (The Statesman, 22.01.14).

"Making an informed career choice is not easy in our overheated system," states former Director of NCERT Dr. Krishna Kumar when speaking about the central issues affecting higher education in India (The Hindu, 2015). Director of Aakash Educational Services, Akash Chaudhry also stated that in this era of cut-throat competition, getting a job for the students is not a cakewalk anymore. He focuses on how engineering has become an extremely challenging course among all curriculum with many divisions, where students enjoy the freedom to take up a desired stream, but this freedom has led to confusion among parents and students, as most parents take a call for their children going by market trends without proper research and consulting with the people in the industry, thus affecting their child's career in the long run. Thus getting a job appropriate to the academic course selected in this competitive economy is indeed a challenge faced by students in this contemporary society (The Statesman, 24.01.14).

Shah and Shah (2014) states that the usage of new educational technology might also fail because: (a) it calls for knowledge, understanding, abilities, and qualities which most teachers do not possess; (b) the students find difficulty in responding due to lack of skills and the qualities that the new technology requires them to possess; (c) the necessary materials and equipment it requires are not available or its costs are too high to meet in developing countries.

Hawkins (2002) states that even though teachers are trying very hard to adapt enthusiastically in the effective use of ICT in classrooms with team projects and soft pedagogy, school administrators do not offer any kind of structural support and incentives to teachers for their performance. So mostly teachers who are receiving adequate ICT support from the administrators are using ICTs in their teaching practice, and those who are not receiving ICT support from the higher authorities in school are not bothered to use computer or any kind of technology while teaching at all. The school principal as an administrator has the prime responsibility to act as a mediator to integrate ICT into the education system by encouraging, supporting, and helping the teachers to use computers in their teaching-learning process. This is extremely necessary and essential to encourage the willingness of the teachers to use the computer as a medium to deliver instruction. Thus, the role of the school administrator is crucial in providing the vigor, backing, and suitable conditions to enhance the use of computer in the teaching profession smoothly (www.shodhganga.inflibnet.ac.in).

Pathak (2013) opines that ever-expanding technology…causes serious ethical and pedagogical problems…we tend to lose critical consciousness or the freedom to see beyond its paradigm. Technology seduces us through its well-advertised narratives of speed, efficiency, and comfort…creating techno-illusion. But education requires the cultivation of a critical/reflexive/imaginative mind, not just a technically efficient consciousness. Pathak emphasizes on Lyotard's identification of the emerging trend that obsessive use of technology is transforming the very character of the learner…becoming consumer of information and the process of consumption must be fast, efficient, and technologically sleek.

There are processes that contribute to the reproduction of gender inequality at the macro-micro and interactional levels. In this way, the gender system is over-determined and represents a powerfully conservative system. The persistence of sex segregation in paid job starts from the time when individuals influenced by cultural beliefs, act on gender-differentiated perceptions while making career decisions (Correll, 2001). There are certain chief factors which affect students' career choice like: (a) when students start enjoying to specializations they are exposed; they are more likely to pursue that career. (b) Role models are another influence on students' career decisions, especially guidance of school teachers. (c)

Social and cultural processes influence career decisions to a great extent (Hill and Giles, 2014). These cultural beliefs about gender tend to bias individuals' perception of their competence at various career-relevant task directions. Gender stereotypes contain specific expectations of competence that create problems for gender equality. Like men are thought to be more competent than women except when performing "feminine tasks." Any kind of mathematical and quantitative task are considered "masculine." These gender beliefs bias judgment of mathematical competencies and influence career-relevant choices (Correll, 2001). (d) Parental education, profession, and income; (e) influence of peers; (f) exposure to media also plays an important determinant because it highlights social travels, global issues, current trends and fashion, portrays the glamour of a culture and glitter of the consumer world. Watching talk shows, documentaries, movies, and dramas portray careers such as law, media, and advertising as very glamourous and appealing thus drawing students towards them. It is important to examine whether students opt for their chosen field forcefully, make compromises or make decisions which are independent without any external pressure (Kazi and Akhlaq, 2017).

Masculinity discourses include male characteristics such as physical strength, decision-making power, liberation, and independence as significant traits within men, while feminine qualities include understanding and caring, interactive, and expressive, and work in a coordinated manner in teams and associations. Stereotypical gendered career choice is very commonly seen in India. According to Poststructuralist feminist critics thinks that gender is not biological, but as performative in nature, i.e., they are learned behaviors and beliefs that have become embodied; 'girls' from the very beginning are made to learn and embody discourses considered feminine, and 'men' masculine, because they are socialized to 'do gender.' But we also do see that men and women embody discourses other than their own if they want to according to their personal choice. But it is visible that in a domain where masculine discourses predominate, feminine qualities have less cultural worth and are therefore more marginalized and considered weaker sections in the hierarchical structure of society. The socio-cultural factor holds that even today, gender, class, ethnicity, and sexuality operate in our society very strongly to restrict available options or choices regarding choosing one's career. And it can also be said that possibilities or opportunities that are available to individuals are mainly determined by an individual's background and the context in which it is operating (Hill and Giles, 2014).

9.4 MAIN FINDINGS

We observe that the process of globalization creates complex trends in all spheres of society, whether economic, social, political or cultural. Today we live in a 'global village' (McLuhan, 1962), where various cultural and historical experiences are intertwined with each other through instant communication through the emergence of developed digitization. ICT has led to the establishment of e-commerce, e-banking, e-learning, medicine, and e-governance. So, nowadays, even in the education sector, change is visible where education is used as a commodity for international trade. It is not limited within the boundaries of domestic scale publicly anymore rather shifting towards global scale through privatization. But it is seen that it is becoming extremely difficult for the government to continuously cope up with the latest technological activities in every sphere of society (Anand, 2015).

We need to pay heed to certain important issues which are related to the youth as well as education like firstly, whether the government and other sectors can clarify that there is adequate funds for schools to maintain the quality and simultaneously make it accessible for all; and secondly, whether globalization is increasing the digital-divide gap between the privileged and disadvantaged isolated groups in the society (OXFAM, 2004). Studies show that children who are fortunate enough to be born in educated families or get the opportunity of having loving, caring, and well-experienced teachers tend to perform very well and are able to find jobs appropriate to the demanding labor market scenario but the average is very low. Sadly, there are students who, even after completing school or college education remain unemployed due to low productivity and poor skills. It is also seen that children who come from deprived backgrounds and do not get proper learning environment in their home to study feel alienated in schools, and it becomes difficult for the government school teachers to deal with their special needs (Aruna, 1998).

Various literature studies state that ICTs facilitates the acquisition and absorption of knowledge, which provides developing countries unprecedented opportunities to enhance...revolutionize the way people work today and transforming education systems (Tinio, 2002; Watson, 2001).

But many studies (Mikre, 2011; Noeth and Volkov, 2004; Daggett, 2010) also reveal that though ICTs played equalization strategy for developing countries, but the reality of the digital divide, i.e., the gap between those who have access to and tries to control technology and those who do not, still exist. Thus to integrate ICTs in different levels of society is an extremely challenging task, failure to which will only increase the deepening of existing social and economic inequalities due to the knowledge gap among developed and developing countries.

Studies show that infrastructural change in the entire school is needed with proper teaching and expensive technological resources for teachers to perform competently and skillfully with ICT medium so that it can give actual effective results (Salavati, 2016). Multiple and diverse actors, relationships, and perspectives should also be kept in mind when carrying out these transformations in effective ways. Some teachers grasp and adapt themselves fast keeping in pace with the latest digital technologies to upgrade their classroom teachings continuously like incorporating new study materials, new techniques for instructions and innovative ways of group work through global exposure, while others seem to ignore the use of it completely (Cuban, 2001). The Organization of Economic Co-operation Development (OECD) (2010) authorities believe that structural changes will automatically alter and change the dominant traditional teaching practices, causing teachers to integrate "these better ways" of teaching (Cuban, 2013: p. 113), leaving the teachers voiceless in the process with no say of their own. Therefore, a clear difference and ideological clash exist between the worldview of the practitioners (i.e., teachers) and authorities (Cuban, 2013; Salavati, 2016), and so the reality of digital technology use in everyday practices is not only complex and challenging but also messy which needs to be investigated from a real-life practice (Salavati, 2016).

Online mode of teaching in schools, colleges and universities is being frequently carried out by teachers, by providing/uploading study materials and lectures on official institute website so that students can get access to anywhere and at any time; and also by teaching the whole class with huge number of students in real-time via various online classroom apps like Zoom, Google Meet, Microsoft Teams, where students simultaneously get to view PowerPoint presentations as well as hear the lecture of the teacher very easily. Webinars are also organized by the institutes so that students' scholars and even faculty members can attend and participate to learn and explore their knowledge sitting at home. Even students are being evaluated by home assignments and online project submissions rather than depending solely on the traditional method of written examinations only.

In today's contemporary society, where everything is always under the realm of uncertainty and crisis, when face to face classroom teaching is not possible, then it is very important to depend and make use of online teaching and learning facilities available to the students so that their precious time doesn't get wasted and every minute can be spent wisely in gaining knowledge. Though online teaching method creates pressure on teachers to regularly innovate their study materials to make students attentive in attending online classes but it helps in covering a huge syllabus in a short span of time. Another crucial problem in developing countries with online teaching-learning mode is having free access to internet facilities and proper network connection speed, otherwise it becomes difficult for students as well as teachers to communicate with each other smoothly without any interruptions and technical lag, making participants lose concentration and irritable with the whole process. Furthermore, every student of various caste class and creed should possess digital gadgets of upgraded versions, and then only can they get the opportunity of attending online classes otherwise equal access to education will be hampered (Tuzun, 2002; Nguyen, 2015).

Studies also reveal that improper usage of ICT in classrooms or at home by students increases their dilemma of making appropriate career choice for their future since the disadvantage of ICT overweighs the advantage in many ways than one like limiting students' imagination; quandaries regarding which information is valid and reliable among the many widely available while making choice; it limits students' critical thinking and analytical skills; students tend to have superficial understanding of the various information they download because they copy everything from the internet; students get distracted easily and tend to visit unwanted sites; students neglect other learning resources due to computer and internet; students have less opportunity to use oral skills and handwriting; ICT usage is difficult for weak students because they may face problems working independently and so might need the support of the teacher; lack of proficiency in English resulting language barrier among students with English medium background and other regional language background; and one major negative physical side effect of computer-based learning is vision.

Though technology advertises as speed, efficiency, and comfort but it creates techno-illusion, ethical, and pedagogical problems. It is changing the learner's character, making them more technically conscious consumer of information and less critical, and reflexive, imaginative persons. The board-student interface becomes mechanical n superficial due to the usage of smart classroom and as typing replaces handwriting, it creates a harmful impact on the development of vital cognitive skills and tactile intelligence.

It is suggested by many that the school examination system should not be abolished since examinations and evaluations will help the children to assess their strength and weakness in a subject. Mahatma Gandhi's Buniadi education, Swami Vivekananda's overall development of the concept of humanity, educational epistemology as perceived by Tagore, should all be blended together while executing the new scheme in education (The Statesman, 26.01.14).

Thus the influence of career choice has a lasting impact on an individual as it serves to be an analyst as well as a factor for their prospective level of income, nature of work and personality. So one wrong decision can change the fate of an individual and can create an impact on a larger scale in the economic prosperity of the nation as individuals who are misfit in their workplace tend to be less productive and efficient and unable to achieve their goals. More career conventions, as an instrument of career information should be conducted: (a) to create awareness regarding areas of interest and prospective career fields; (b) to help shortlisting preferable jobs; (c) provides opportunities in which parents, employees, and career counselors can exchange views (Kazi and Akhlaq, 2017).

9.5 CONCLUSION

With the advancement of digital technology in the globalization's era, we have seen progress in spheres of trading, traveling, migration, spread of diverse cultural influences, and dissemination of knowledge. These global interrelations have been very productive in the development of different countries. Education not only plays a significant role for the comprehensive development of one's personality, but also helps for the sustained growth of the nation, so it has become an important investment in building human capital, which can initiate technological innovation and economic growth. Therefore, it is only through improving the educational status of a society that the multifaceted development of people can be ensured. Today, in the age of liberalization and privatization, India being exposed to the world, has to deal with the three main challenges of its education system, i.e., expansion, excellence, and inclusion, so that it can cope up and keep pace with other developed countries in this competitive global market. Thus the age-old system of education has to be reformed by giving practical knowledge more priority than theoretical knowledge (Anand, 2015).

In any students' life, choosing a proper career is an extremely crucial decision to make, especially when constantly new emerging career options are turning up every day with the already existing prestigious ones, posing a challenge for students to make a decisive choice in this contemporary society. Moreover, there is constant mental and societal pressure as to whose advice and guidance should be given priority, whether one's own independent decision, parents' advice or valuable guidance from teachers. But exerting too much pressure, control, and dominating attitude on students may demotivate and lower their performance. So the types of professions relevant to their interests, skills, or aspirations should be discussed in a friendly way to avoid problems between parents and students. Thus it is very important that students should choose the career which is according to their capabilities and of their interest. The schools should also help the students by making counseling centers so that students can easily understand which career is best for them, keeping in mind their interest in choosing a career path (Kazi and Akhlaq, 2017).

Thus in this context, a comprehensive empirical study needs to be done on how secondary school students in India make their appropriate career choice because then only they can effectively contribute as potential human resources to the economy of the nation.

KEYWORDS

- career choice
- digitalization
- higher secondary school students
- information communication and technology
- National curriculum framework
- Sarva Shiksha Abhiyan

REFERENCES

Agrawal, S., & Ramesh, D., (2013). 'Globalization and school education in India: Some data gaps. *International Journal of Scientific and Technology Research*, *2*(8), 180–183.

Agrawal, S., (2005). Globalization and Academic Performance of the University: A Case study of The M.S. University of Baroda. In: *Paper presented at National Seminar on Issues in Higher Education at Department of Sociology*. Bharatidasan University, Thiruchirapalli.

Anand, M., (2015). 'Globalization and Indian school education: Impact and challenges. *European Scientific Journal*, (special edition), 235–249.

Aruna, R., (1998). Learn thoroughly primary schooling in Tamil Nadu. *Economic and Political Weekly*.

Bangser, M., (2008). *Preparing High School Students for Successful Transition to Postsecondary Education and Employment*. National High School Center.

Cheney, et al., (2006). *A Profile of the Indian Education System*. National Center on Education and the Economy.

Cogburn, D. L., (2000). *Globalization, Knowledge, Education and Training in the Information Age*. https://auislandora.wrlc.org/islandora/object/auislandora%3A73488/datastream/PDF/view (accessed on 25 March 2021).

Commission of the European Communities, (2001). *The E-Learning Action Plan: Designing Tomorrow's Education*. Brussels: Directorate-General for Education and Culture.

Correll, S. J., (2001). Gender and the career choice process: The role of biased self-assessments. In: *American Journal of Sociology* (Vol. 106, No. 6, pp. 1691–1730). The University of Chicago Press.

Cuban, L., (2001). *Oversold and Underused: Computers in the Classroom*. Cambridge, MA: Harvard University Press.

Cuban, L., (2013). Why so many structural changes in schools and so little reform in teaching practice? *Journal of Educational Administration, 51*(2), 109–125.

Daggett, W. R., (2010). *Preparing Students for Their Technological Future* (pp. 1–15). International Center for Leadership in Education.

Deaney, R., et al., (2003). Pupil perspectives on the contribution of information and communication technology to teaching and learning in the secondary school. *Research Papers in Education, 18*(2), 141–165.

Dillenbourg, P., Järvelä, S., & Fischer, F., (2009). The evolution of research on computer-supported collaborative learning: From design to orchestration. In Balacheff, N., Ludvigsen, S., De Jong, T., Lazonder, T. A., & Barnes, S., (eds.), *Technology-Enhanced Learning: Principles and Products* (pp. 3–19). Netherlands: Springer.

European Commission, (2010). *Europe 2020: A Strategy for Smart, Sustainable and Inclusive Growth*. https://ec.europa.eu/eu2020/pdf/COMPLET%20EN%20BARROSO%20%20%20 007%20-%20Europe%202020%20-%20EN%20version.pdf (accessed on 24 February 2021)

Grand-Clement, S., (2017). *Digital Learning: Education and Skills in the Digital Age*. Rand Corporation.

Hawkins, R. J., (2002). Ten lessons for ICT and education in the developing world. In: Kirkman, G., Sachs, J., et al., (eds.), *The Global Information Technology Report 2001– 2002: Readiness for the Networked World* (pp. 38–43). UK: Oxford University Press.

Hill, E. J. R., & Giles, J. A., (2014). Career decisions and gender: The illusion of choice? In: *Perspect Med. Educ.* (Vol. 3, pp. 151–154). Springerlink.com.

India Today, (2019). www.indiatoday.in (accessed on 24 February 2021).

Kazi, A. S., & Akhlaq, A., (2017). Factors affecting students' career choice. *Journal of Research and Reflections in Education, 11*(2), 187–196. https://www.researchgate.net/publication/325987918 (accessed on 24 February 2021).

Laird, D., (1985). *Approaches to Training and Development.* Basic Books.

McLuhan, M., (1962). *The Gutenberg Galaxy: The Making of Typographic Man.* University of Toronto Press.

Mikre, F., (2011). *The Roles of Information Communication Technology in Education, 6*(2), 1–16.

Milrad, M., Wong, L. H., Sharples, M., Hwang, G. J., Looi, C., & Ogata, H., (2013). Seamless learning: An international perspective on next-generation technology-enhanced learning. In: Berge, Z. L., & Muilenburg, L. Y., (eds.), *Handbook of Mobile Learning* (pp. 95–108). New York: Routledge.

GOI, (2012). National Policy on Information and Communication Technology in School Education, Department of School Education and Literacy. *MHRD.*

Nguyen, T., (2015). The effectiveness of online learning: beyond no significant difference and future horizons. *MERLOT Journal of Online Learning and Teaching, II*(2), 309–318.

Noeth, R. J., & Volkov, B. B., (2004). *Evaluating the Effectiveness of Technology in Our Schools.* ACT Policy Report.

Okolie, U. C., & Yasin, A. M., (2017). *Technical Education and Vocational Training in Developing Nations.* USA: IGI Global book series Advances in Higher Education and Professional Development.

Organization for Economic Co-Operation and Development (OECD), (2010). *Inspired by Technology, Driven by Pedagogy: A Systemic Approach to Technology-Based School Innovations.* Paris: OECD Publishing.

OXFAM, (2004). *Highly Affected, Rarely Considered: Access to and Privatization of Education, Partner Organization: Global Campaign for Education.* By Leah Ashley & Kirsten, Mackay, OXFAM, CAA.

Pachler, N., Bachmair, B., & Cook, J., (2010). *Mobile Learning; Structures, Agency, Practices.* New York, Dordrecht, Heidelberg, London: Springer.

Papert, S., (1980). *Mindstorms: Children Computer and Powerful Ideas.* UK: Harvester Press.

Pathak, A., (2002). *Social Implications of Schooling: Knowledge, Pedagogy and Consciousness.* Delhi: Aakar Books.

Pathak, A., (2013). *Recalling the Forgotten: Education and Moral Quest.* Delhi: Aakar Books.

Rifkin, J., (2000). *The Age of Access: The New Culture of Hyper Capitalism.* Where all of life is a paid-for experience. Canada: J.P. Tarcher/Putnam.

Salavati, S., (2013). *Novel Use of Mobile and Ubiquitous Technologies in Everyday Teaching and Learning Practices: A Complex Picture.* Licentiate. Linnaeus University, Sweden. Växjö: Linnaeus University Press.

Salavati, S., (2016). *Use of Digital Technology in Education: The Complexity of Teachers' Everyday Practice.* Linnaeus University Press.

Sangrà, A., & González, S. M., (2010). The role of information and communication technologies in improving teaching and learning processes in primary and secondary schools. *ALT-J Research in Learning Technology, 18*(3), 207–220. Routledge.

Scardamalia, M., Bransford, J., Kozma, B., & Quellmalz, E., (2010). *New Assessments and Environments for Knowledge Builders.* The University of Melbourne.

Shah, B. V., & Shah, K. B., (2014). *Sociology of Education.* New Delhi: Rawat Publications.

Shah, K. R., (2006a). Spending 6% of GDP on education. *Manpower Journal, XLI*(3).

Stromquist, N. P., (2005). The impact of globalization on education and gender: An emergent cross-national balance. *Journal of Education, 37.*

Tallvid, M., (2014). Understanding teachers' reluctance to the pedagogical use of ICT in the 1:1 classroom. *Education and Information Technologies* (pp. 1–17). New York: Springer.

The Statesman, January 4, 2016.

Tinio, V. L., (2002). *ICT in Education.* NY: United Nations Development Program. https://wikieducator.org/images/f/ff/Eprimer-edu_ICT_in_Education.pdf

Tuzun, H., (2002). *Methodology of Online Teaching and Learning.* www.researchgate.net/publication/220058956 (accessed on 24 February 2021).

12th Five Year Plan. https://www.niti.gov.in/planningcommission.gov.in/docs/plans/planrel/fiveyr/welcome.html (accessed on 24 February 2021).

UNESCO, (2003). *Communiqué of the Ministerial Roundtable on 'Towards Knowledge Societies.'* Paris: UNESCO.

UNESCO, (2008). *ICT Competency Standards for Teachers: Competency Standards Modules.* Paris: UNESCO.

Watson, D. M., (2001). Pedagogy before technology: Re-thinking the relationship between ICT and teaching. *Education and Information Technologies, 6*(4), 251–266.

Wikramanayake, G. N., (2014). *Impact of Digital Technology on Education.* www.researchgate.net (accessed on 24 February 2021).

World Bank, (2006). *Equity and Development: World Development Report.* New York, Oxford University Press.

CHAPTER 10

Analyzing Digital Media Public Service Advertisements on Health and Hygiene: A Rural Indian Scenario

SHARMILA KAYAL,[1] RUMA SAHA,[2] and SAYAK PAL[3]

[1]Associate Professor, Department of Communication Management. Adamas University, Kolkata, West Bengal, India, E-mail: sharmilakayal@gmail.com (S. Kayal),

[2]PhD Research Scholar, Manipal University Jaipur, Rajasthan, India, E-mail: ruma.saha.kolkata@gmail.com (R. Saha)

[3]Assistant Professor, Department of Communication Management. Adamas University, Kolkata and PhD Research Scholar, Symbiosis International (Deemed) University, Pune, India, E-mail: palsayak01@gmail.com

ABSTRACT

Advertisement is as old as civilization itself, and the need for public service advertisements are always at a high demand which has acted as a bridge between the government and public. While being educational and persuasive, most of the PSAs are focused on specific issues as well as often hosts multiple subliminal issues of the related fields. Many PSAs are made in the form of short narratives concerned on the growing issues needed foremost care and attention for eradicating them from the societies. Most of these PSA are stressed on bringing positive and favorable behavioral changes through proper awareness campaigns that include health issues like smoking, menstrual hygiene, family planning, AIDS, sanitization, and so on. These advertisements are carefully crafted for a larger group of audiences and involve a lot of research from the subject areas. The purpose of the current study is to analyze the contents of these public service advertisements in the Indian scenario on the digital platform to understand the motive of message creation while being focused on mass health benefits.

The study involves qualitative research methodology as a means of content analysis of ten different public service advertisements made on different social issues concerning rural and urban societies. The measuring parameters include primary health issues, direct, and indirect objectives, target audience, role, and gender of the spokesperson, message appeal, subliminal themes, and for some cases, the involvement of the celebrity. The primary objective of PSAs is to raise awareness among the people by educating them in their comforts while showcasing a familiar atmosphere in which they can relate their association with the commercials. The study is aimed to analyze and discuss the content of the PSAs in detail, making it beneficial for government and non-government advertising professionals to improvise their future offerings for improved results.

10.1   INTRODUCTION

The intention of motivating the public to engage them into action for the good of the society is as old as the establishment of the government itself. Numerous techniques like church bells, town cries, ram's horns, and even word of mouth were used to propagate the message among the mass. In recent times, the media has acted as a vehicle for gathering the attention of the mass and urging them to act in favor of society (O'Barr, 2006).

The definition shows that public service advertisements are non-commercial information produced and aired towards a specific group of people addressing specific problems called "social problems" (Gerhard, 1973). A large quantity of public service advertisements from different counties are focused on issues on multiple social problems, and many of them are educational in nature, directed towards selected mass with focused short-term and long-term aims. Sometimes the advertisers are taken to the route of promoting 'instructive short films' as an effective mode of communication that are made with the drive of growing aware-ness of the society, which on the other hand helpful in creating behavioral changes among the viewers. At the same time, they are primarily consid-ered as communication tools used within the context of both in social advertising and social marketing. One of the main themes of public service announcements which may have a substantial impact on the masses is the "health theme."

10.1.1　PUBLIC SERVICE ADVERTISEMENT IN INDIAN SCENARIO

India, being the second most populated country in the world, has given the freedom to the old and new, traditional, and modern as well as local and international to coexist in self-harmony. This is the reason while in managing brand along with targeting consumers; the advertisers must consider the vast social and cultural diversity of the country (O'Barr, 2008). In India, the advertising tradition can be traced back to 19th century when the 1st published newspaper started carrying advertisements. The first advertising agency B. Datram and Company started its journey in 1905 followed by Indian Advertising Company in 1907, numerous ventures in the same line of business-like Kolkata Advertising Agency in 1909, Bensen in 1928; Hindustan Thomson Associates (1929), Lever International Advertising Service in 1939 started pushing advertisements to the mass market. While early 1980s saw a number of alliances with multiple foreign investors, the recession came at early 1990s forced to bring down a massive chunk on advertising budget ignited a massive competitions among multinationals. In the same era of the 1990s, the market also witnessed an increased level of government advertisements promoting government tourism, army recruitment as well as spreading awareness mostly through the joint ventures with international agencies (Ciochetto, 2004).

India witnessed its first Public Service Advertisement in 1976 with the generation of slogan *"Hum Do Hamaare Do"* for the purpose of population control. Similar other slogans like *"Chhota Parivaar Sukhi Parivaar"* also became popular, targeting citizens through television broadcasting. The campaign was a successful program and it awakened the government about the importance of PSA. Henceforth, the government of India used Public service advertisement to reach out to people for various awareness program.

10.1.2　PSA ON WOMEN'S HEALTH AND HYGIENE IN INDIA

In a recent survey data published in the Times of India e-version (2018), it shows that 18% of women have access to sanitary hygiene in India. The report also talked about how improper hygiene condition in rural India leads to serious health hazard like removal of reproductive organ at tender age. One such case happened in a village near Madhya Pradesh. Victim was a 12-year-old girl. The case has sparked an awareness campaign of menstruating woman hygiene by social entrepreneur *Amar Tulsiyan*. The campaign is named NIINE. This has further sparked more public service advertisement for woman hygiene during menstruation. *Tulsiyan* focused in this campaign to educate rural women and men about this topic. The Government of India has recently taken steps to make people aware, especially in rural India, about the hygiene during menstruation (E-TIMES, n.d.).

10.2 REVIEW OF THE RELATED LITERATURE

Recent research is done on "Using a smokeless tobacco control mass media campaign and other synergistic elements to address social inequalities in India" by Turk et al. in 2012. According to the researchers, the burden of tobacco causing mortality rate in India is ever increasing in the past few years. Researchers have identified that smokeless tobacco is creating havoc in causing this situation and its' consumption is traced by them due to various socio-economic and cultural background. Apart from these gender, regional disparity and income level also matters in the consumption of such products. Looking at the scale of the problem, researchers has adopted a national social marketing campaign where testimonials of doctors and patients from Tata Memorial hospital at Mumbai were used. The researchers have studied the impact of such message on the general public and their subsequent change in behavior. The result shows that effective impact of imagery, testimonial, and graphics for tobacco control on socially challenged groups (Turk et al., 2012).

Research is done on "Effects of Persuasive Appeals in Public Service Advertising" by Lynn in 1974. The researcher talks about the effect of a particular channel on the PSA message they broadcast. The researcher in his paper has investigated various sources that may influence the message evolved in PSA. The study is done on USA during the 1970s (Lynn, 1974).

Research has been done on "*Gutkha* Advertisement and Smokeless Tobacco Use by Adolescents in Sikkim, India" by Sinha in 2005. Researcher tried to investigate the impact of *Gutkha* advertisement on the usage of smokeless tobacco. Survey method was applied and two-step probability sampling method was adopted by the researcher to collect data. Quantitative methodology was used to do statistical analysis. Result shows a strong correlation between exposure to *Gutkha* advertisement and usage of smokeless tobacco by the respondents (Sinha, 2005).

Recent research is done on "Advertisement Claims Grow Taller! A Study of Ethics in Advertising by FMCG Companies in India" by Nagendra et al. in 2011. The researcher focuses on unethical side of any advertisement. Researchers have done data collection through analysis of FMCG advertisement in India and interviewed consumers regarding their reaction to certain specific ads. Qualitative analysis is adopted by the researchers in this research. In the conclusion, researchers pointed out that the advertisers should remove the socially harmful content from the advertisement for the benefit of society, and they should learn to take responsibility towards it. Researchers have recommended maintaining high ethical standard, human dignity, truthfulness, and social responsibility. They also recommend to advertisers to give compensation to injured, issue corrective notice, etc., also encourage more public service advertisements (Nagendra et al., 2011).

Recent research is done on "Public Service Advertising in India: An Evaluation through Literature" by Krishna et al. in 2017. The researcher tried to analyze previous research work on public service advertisement in India. Researcher tried to investigate by doing content analysis of previous research work on PSA in various issue broadcasted in India. The study reveals the impact such advertisement have on mass and the issue handled by them. Moreover, the researcher also took note of various recommendations given in previous research work and how it could enhance the performance of PSA in India (Krishna et al., 2017).

A recent research is done by Ashok J. Tamhankar et al. on "Characteristics of nationwide voluntary antibiotics resistance campaign in India; Future paths and pointers for resource-limited settings / Low- and middle-income countries" in 2019. Researchers were trying to find whether campaign for antibiotics resistance in India can be voluntarily organized. Also, they studied the characteristics of voluntarily organized campaign. The researchers have used community radio to reach out to people in rural India. They run the campaign in 11 different languages. The campaign with the title message "Take antibiotics as prescribed by doctors" was run for ten times in a day, and this continued for four consecutive days to reach up to 5 million audiences. All the researchers and coordinators in this research came to the conclusion that this campaign has created some effect on the audience who will think before buying and consuming random antibiotics (Ashok et al., 2019).

Andres Hueso et al. in his research on "An untold story of policy failure: the Total Sanitation Campaign in India" in 2013 ha showed how Nirmal Bharat Abhiyan failed in its implementation level due to several flaw in its' policy of implementation level. Researchers have showed there was a gap between theory and practice in policy implementation of total sanitation campaign. The researchers could come to the conclusion that there were several flaws in the policy of campaign implementation like flawed monitoring, low political priorities of the issue, distorting accountability, career incentives, corruption, etc. The campaign failed to address key issue hampering the area and creation of demand for it (Andres et al., 2013).

Research is done on "Cigarette advertising in Mumbai, India: targeting different socioeconomic groups, women, and youth" by Bansal et al. in 2005. Researchers tried to find Cigarette Company's marketing strategy in Mumbai. Even though they have to show statutory warning, they are advertised in magazine, newspapers but not in women's magazine. The researchers found that the cigarette companies cannot do direct advertisement of product but doing brand extension and brand stretching. Cigarette advertising is ban in India but despite having law there is loopholes through which easy path is received by tobacco company to reach out to public. These brands try to advertise their product as a symbol of class. Women are not directly used in this advertisement but are shown as charmed by the men who use this tobacco product. The purpose of the researchers was to understand this loophole area of the legislative system so as to minimize the exploitation of such loopholes of tobacco control law (Bansal et al., 2005).

Recent research is done by Prof. Thomas Clasen et al. on "Effectiveness of a rural sanitation program on diarrhea, soil-transmitted helminth infection, and child malnutrition in Odisha, India: a cluster-randomized trial" in 2014. The researcher wants to assess how effective was "Total Sanitation Campaign" of the government in preventing helminth infection and diarrhea. The result showed that increased coverage of the promotion of latrine usage and building of toilets creates a reduction in open fecal. This, in turn, improved health issues (Thomas et al., 2014).

10.3   RESEARCH GAP

Research is done on the area of the persuasive effect of public service advertisement. There is also research done on the area of impact study of smokeless tobacco *"Gutkha"* advertisement is affecting adolescent health in the state of Sikkim, India.

Research is done on the evaluation of public service advertisement through literature review. Their research was done on campaign effectiveness of antibiotics resistance in India through radio broadcasting of campaign for a particular time period to know the effectiveness of the campaign in reception among the target audience. There are several researches done on policy failure of the total sanitation campaign.

After doing literature review of so many literature it can be seen that there is gap in literature and hardly any research has taken place in analyzing public service advertisement on woman's wellbeing and hygiene during digital era in India. This research is to bridge this gap.

10.4   CONCEPTUAL FRAMEWORK

The health belief model (HBM) has two core components:

i.   The desire to avoid illness, or on the contrary get well if already ill; and
ii. The belief that an exact health action will avoid, or cure, illness.

In due course, an individual course of action frequently depends on the individual's perceptions of the benefits and barriers related to health behavior. There are six constructs of the HBM:

1. **Perceived Susceptibility:** This is in reference to a person's prejudiced perception of the risk of obtaining an illness or poor health. There is an extensive disparity in a person's feelings of personal susceptibility to an illness or ailment.
2. **Perceived Severity:** This is in reference to a person's belief on the gravity of constricting an illness or ailment (or leaving the sickness or ailment unprocessed).
3. **Perceived Benefits:** This is in reference to an individual's perception of the effectiveness of different actions accessible to reduce the threat of illness or ailment (or to heal illness or ailment).

4. **Perceived Barriers:** This is in reference to an individual's opinion on the obstacles to performing a suggested health act. There is a huge disparity in an individual's belief of barriers or obstructions.
5. **Cue to Action:** This is in reference to stimulus requirement to generate the decision-making process to admit an optional health action.
6. **Self-Efficacy:** This is in reference to the point of an individual's self-belief in his or her capability to effectively execute behavior.

10.5 RESEARCH QUESTIONS

On the basis of thorough literature of various aspects related to health and hygiene, the following are the research questions that have been framed:

RQ1. What are the different types of PSA prevalent in India?
RQ2. How many of which are dedicated to woman's health and hygiene?
RQ3. Who are the potential target group for this category of PSA?
RQ4. Is there any specific focused age group as target audience of PSA?
RQ5. Does the message of PSA help in improving the health and hygiene condition of target audience in rural and illiterate section of the society?

10.6 RESEARCH OBJECTIVES

Based on the research questions, the broad objectives of the study are:

*   To understand how PSA are catering to fulfilling the need of health and hygiene.
*   To explore different area of health information disseminated through PSA to target audience.
*   To know what are the major domain or programs and area are meant for catering the need for PSA.

10.7 RESEARCH METHODOLOGY

The present research is explanatory in nature. It explains the role of public service advertisements which is specially meant for health and hygiene in rural Indian scenario. For in depth understanding and analysis, it has adopted various tools to decipher the content in digital media for the present study.

10.8   QUALITATIVE METHODOLOGY

Qualitative research is a detailed understanding of the subject through the responses rather than relying merely on the numbers and statistics (Nouria, 2020). For this research study, the qualitative research method has been used where content analysis was adopted as the main parameter to analyze the content of the public service advertisements.

10.9   CONTENT ANALYSIS

For this research purpose, ten different public service advertisements were chosen, which are based on public health and hygiene produced and manufactured by the Ministry of Health. These public service advertisements will be analyzed according to ten important categories that include primary health issue, primary goal, and target audience, role of the message source/spokesperson, gender representation of the message source/spokesperson, estimated age of the message source/spokesperson, message appeal, message frame, and type of the PSA.

10.10   TOOLS OF DATA COLLECTION

The present study has adopted secondary tools of data collection. The various websites, YouTube program content has been taken into considerations for analyzing the different parameters in order to health, hygiene, and sanitation as a whole.

10.11   RESULT AND ANALYSIS

The Bollywood movie "Padman" of Comedy-drama category released on 9 February, 2018 which was based on a villager who got disappointed to see his wife using unhygienic cloth during her menstrual cycles and decided to manufacture a machine to produce affordable sanitary pads and also started spreading awareness of using sanitary napkins instead of unhygienic cloths among women. This public service broadcasting advertisement was also made in the light of the movie "Padman" where the actor "Akshay Kumar" tries to educate the mass on spending on women's health and hygiene by encouraging the usage of sanitary napkin during menstrual cycle instead of spending on tobacco consumption. This advertisement serves not only one but two health benefits through one advertisement.

The association of the celebrity actor "Akshay Kumar" for this PSA was a clever choice not only because of the protagonist role he played in the movie "Padman" but also for his identity of being a fitness role model in Bollywood. The combination of stardom and fitness role model backed up with the success of the movie based on the social awareness made this PSA a popular choice at YouTube, even after repeated broadcasting on television (Table 10.1 and Figure 10.1).

TABLE 10.1　　No Smoking and Women's Health

Theme	No Smoking and Women's health
Ad Category	Public service Ad on 'no smoking and women's health'
Medium	Audio-visual ad broadcasted on television and shared at YouTube
Language	Hindi
HashTag	no hastag
Views	46,236
Likes	719
Dislike	36
Celebrity Involvement	Akshay Kumar (Bollywood Actor)
Ad Duration	1:04 minutes
URL	https://www.youtube.com/watch?v=KVhY3WK9zs4

This public service advertisement is another initiative under "National Rural Health Mission" where the two-dimension animation was used to depict the problem arises with overpopulation and uncontrolled birth-rate and compared with a small and healthy family. The 60 seconds video showed both the adverse side of the life and the problems associated with it along with the solutions for them to bring in harmony and happiness into the family.

FIGURE 10.1　Screenshot of PSA on "no smoking and safe living" endorsed by Akshay Kumar.

Source: https://www.youtube.com/watch?v=7S-PR_TZGmA

The advertising is targeted primarily towards the rural audience where the need of health-related education is greater. The promotion has cleverly linked multiple issues like over population, malnutrition, unhealthy livelihood, women health degradation, condom usage, pregnancy gap, contraceptive usage, copper-T usage, tubectomy, vasectomy, together, and formed a story out of them. The promotional video ends with an appeal through a message of 'All about is to talk mutually about healthy life and health decisions for entire family.'

This beautifully crafted animation makes the depiction of the central theme along with sub-ordinary concepts easier to understand for rural population and implement the same for a better livelihood. While this promotional video covers multiple issues related to family healthcare of rural population, the PSA produced and promoted under National Rural Health Mission' is based on the actual theme of 'small family, happy family' to serve a greater purpose of population control of the entire nation (Table 10.2 and Figure 10.2).

The public service advertisements on "Iodine Deficiency "under the "UNICEF" is a quite long advertisement with a duration of 8 minutes and 17 seconds. The PSA actually an episode of a series called "*Amma Ji Kehti Hain*" where an elderly woman is seen to propagate advices on issues on different health benefits under "Health Phone" series. The Health Phone YouTube channel also hosts a website named healthphone.org promotes multiple issues on health and family welfare ranging from timing birth, safe motherhood, new-born care, HIV, Nutrition, and growth breastfeeding, Immunization, Polio, Hygiene, and sanitation, Diarrhea, malaria, child development and early learning, emergencies: preparedness and response.

TABLE 10.2   Family Planning

Theme	Family Planning
Ad Category	Public service Ad on ' Family Planning'
Medium	Audio-visual ad broadcasted on television and shared at YouTube
Language	Hindi
HASHTAG	None
Views	1893
Likes	05
Dislike	00
Celebrity Involvement	No
Ad Duration	00.60 minutes
URL	https://www.youtube.com/watch?v=7S-PR_TZGmA

FIGURE 10.2   Screenshot of PSA on "family planning and adverse women's health."
Source: https://www.youtube.com/watch?v=SMdgE-cFzgU

This commercial is part of the Health Phone series focuses on encouraging the usage of iodized salt, ensuring physical and cognitive development of a child. The commercial is divided into two parts wherein the first section, the protagonist "Amma Ji" tries to explain the consequences of lees consumption or no consumption of iodine which can disturb the development of the children mental and physical health, while an unborn child can also be affected through the iodine deficiency. The usage of packaged salt has also been encouraged, which is rich in iodine with slightly higher in price but provides multiple health benefits for the entire family (Table 10.3 and Figure 10.3(a–c)).

TABLE 10.3   Iodine Intake

Theme	Iodine Intake
Ad Category	Public service Ad on 'Iodine Intake'
Medium	Audio-visual ad broadcasted on television and shared on YouTube
Language	Hindi
HashTag	None
Views	31,684
Likes	82
Dislike	24
Celebrity Involvement	Raveena Tandon
Ad Duration	08.17 minutes
URL	https://www.youtube.com/watch?v=SMdgE-cFzgU

The second part of this Health Phone series is based on the conversation between the peers where the women are educating their friends about the benefits of using iodized salt. Where the first part of the commercial primarily focuses on the family health development, the second part stresses on the usage of iodine during pregnancy to avoid possible dieses, ensuring healthy development of the child. The second half of the commercial also emphasizes the importance of using iodine as a prevention form Goiter.

The commercial ends with the celebrity "Raveena Tandon" endorsing the benefits of using iodized salt for greater health benefits and also ensuring good health of the family. The PSA is originally produced and promoted for rural health education where the plot was cleverly divided into two different scenarios depicting usual household situation ensuring the delivery of message through a casual learning in the form of elderly advices and an educational setup for women where they can imbibe the knowledge from their peer group. The commercial, though focused on a specific issue, also encourage other prominent issues like woman empowerment and essential of education for women through the subliminal approach.

This is a campaign from the "Ministry of Health and Family Welfare" by the USAID-funded IFPS Technical Assistance Project (ITAP) in 2009–2010 under one integrated campaign on Family Planning. The commercial hosts quite an innovative and rhythmic tagline *'Pati Patni Karein Vichaar,'* *'Swasth Nari Swasth Parivar'* (Inter-spousal interaction leads to a healthy women and family) that not only highlighted the importance of family planning but putting more importance on male's participation in the family decision-making process. The campaign was originally produced and promoted for the male-dominated Indian rural societies where women do not hold the baton of power to take the decisions concerning family health welfare. While previous commercials analyzed for this research stresses on the women education to take on the daily household and hygiene factors, this particular commercial focuses on educating males to take proper care of their family, especially when it come to the family planning.

Another pillar of this commercial lies in the message *'Sahi Waqt Pe'* (at the right time) which encourages the males of the family to maintain the proper gap between pregnancies (a minimum of 3 years) for their spouses, which will ensure the total recovery of the mother leading to a healthy and prosperous family. The messages in the commercial are disguised carefully in the form of protagonist advice which led to a positive action taken up by the antagonist in favor of the family health and welfare (Table 10.4 and Figure 10.3).

This commercial is built upon a plot that is practical and relevant to many of us and has been a great source of agitation for a long period. The commercial implies the importance of growing intimacy between two young adults who are of tender age, prone to misstates that can cause contaminations leading to several health hazards and death.

The commercial was originally created and broadcasted to raise awareness about the human immunodeficiency virus (HIV) among the viewers, focused especially on young adults. The storyline of the advertisement, though looks straightforward but ignites thought-provoking concepts where women are subjected as an inferior gender and let the stronger gender take advantage. It also shows that the women are unable to reject the male favor which are willingly or unwillingly bought to them, but the commercial ends with a strong message encouraging women to take control and reject an advantage with strictness to maintain a healthy life free from sexually transmitted diseases (Table 10.5 and Figure 10.4).

TABLE 10.4   Timing Birth-Right Time

Theme	Timing Birth-'Right Time' campaign
Ad Category	Public service Ad on 'Timing Birth'-'Right Time' Title-'*Sahi Waqt Pe'*
Medium	Audio-visual ad broadcasted on television and shared at YouTube
Language	Hindi
HashTag	None
Views	5,335
Likes	13
Dislike	00
Celebrity Involvement	No
Ad Duration	00.60 minutes
URL	https://www.youtube.com/watch?v=HQI_c09oxgE

FIGURE 10.3   Screenshot of PSA on "*Sahi Waqt Pe,*" 'timing birth-right time.'

Source: https://www.youtube.com/watch?v=ueIgxbgTlt0

TABLE 10.5   HIV Awareness

Theme	HIV Awareness
Ad Category	Public service Ad on 'Timing Birth'-'Right Time' Title-'*Boy Girl*
Medium	Audio-visual ad broadcasted on television and shared at YouTube
Language	Hindi
HashTag	None
Views	27,165
Likes	87
Dislike	01
Celebrity Involvement	No
Ad Duration	00.30 minutes
URL	https://www.youtube.com/watch?v=ueIgxbgTlt0

FIGURE 10.4   Screenshot of PSA on "HIV awareness."

Source: https://www.youtube.com/watch?v=bb-hspoHnis

This PSA became immensely popular with more than half a million views and two thousand four hundred likes. Though the advertisement featured Bollywood celebrities Akshay Kumar and Bhumi Pednekar, the concept of the commercial is plotted in a healthy rural family with a positive mindset, which is so unlikely of Indian rural society.

This advertisement is part of the *"Swachh Bharat Mission"* of the Government of India that was produced and promoted under the "Ministry of Drinking water and Sanitation" with a primary focus of installation and usage of "Twin Pit Toilet" for the dual benefits. The PSA was actually produced to serve the need of rural households while providing a free supply of fertilizer for firming as well as preventing contamination from open excretion. The commercial also approaches the rural people to construct toilets for better sanitation which is a dormant message that ran throughout the advertisement.

The celebrity element in this PSA has definitely helped to pull up the popularity, particularly with Akshay Kumar, who has previously been associated with a PSA concerning women's health and hygiene.

The Actor has already made a film on household sanitation named "Toilet: Ek Prem Katha" and another film on women's health and hygiene named "PadMan," which acclaimed a reputation for the actor where he can be identified as a celebrity symbolizes heath and sanitation (Table 10.6 and Figure 10.5).

TABLE 10.6   Twin Pit Toilet

Theme	Twin Pit Toilets
Ad Category	Public service Ad on Twin pit toilet
Medium	Audio-visual ad broadcasted on television and shared at YouTube
Language	Hindi
HashTag	None
Views	515,679
Likes	2,400
Dislike	193
Celebrity Involvement	Akshay Kumar, Bhumi Pednekar
Ad Duration	00:60 minutes
URL	https://www.youtube.com/watch?v=bb-hspoHnis

This PSA is a part of the "Nirmal Bharat Abhiyan" commercial campaigns that focuses on creating awareness among the rural societies of India on proper sanitation and the installation of an approved waste disposal system. The ground plot for the commercial is based on a typical rural wedding scenario where brides are not expected to uncover their faces in the presence of other men, which is otherwise considered inauspicious and tabooed. But when it comes to sanitization, there is no toilet available for use which runs the risk of exposure and can cause serious bacterial contamination.

FIGURE 10.5   Screenshot of PSA on "twin pit toilets."

Source: https://www.youtube.com/watch?v=oBKeZmJeoy4

Bollywood celebrity Vidya Balan has always been associated with public service advertisements on multiple occasions and for this commercial acted as a protagonist who would take the bold steps to demand for what is right and healthy. The advertisement also strengthens the women's authority to bring positive changes in their family and health.

The commercial tried to focus on the current socio-cultural structure of the rural societies and emphasizes on bringing necessary and positive changes in sanitation and waste disposal systems to prevent unwanted contamination and diseases (Table 10.7 and Figure 10.6).

"Swachh Bharat Abhiyan" or "Swachh Bharat Mission" is an initiative of the Government of India launched on October 2, 2014, divided into two different sub-missions, "Swachh Bharat Mission (Gramin)" and "Swachh Bharat Mission (Urban)." The aim of both missions is to ensure total sanitation throughout the nation.

TABLE 10.7 Total Sanitation – "Shauchalay"

Theme	Total Sanitation – *"Shauchalay"*
Ad Category	Public service Ad on Total Sanitation – *"shauchalay"*
Medium	Audio-visual ad broadcasted on television and shared at YouTube
Language	Hindi
HashTag	None
Views	65,311
Likes	129
Dislike	15
Celebrity Involvement	Vidya Balan
Ad Duration	00.40 minutes
URL	https://www.youtube.com/watch?v=oBKeZmJeoy4

FIGURE 10.6 Screenshot of PSA on total sanitation – *"Shauchalay."*

Source: https://www.youtube.com/watch?v=oBKeZmJeoy4

This particular commercial is actually a part of the "Swachh Bharat Mission (Urban)" to raise the awareness among urban population to maintain a healthy environment while keeping their surroundings clean. The plot of the commercial is based on a typical urban society where a "Safai Wala" took the responsibility to invoke the moralism among the people and make them aware of their responsibilities toward the society to keep it clean through conscious choice (Table 10.8 and Figure 10.7(a–c)).

TABLE 10.8   Total Sanitation – "Shauchalay"

Theme	Cleanliness – "Swachh Bharat Abhiyan"
Ad Category	Public service Ad on "Swachh Bharat Abhiyan"
Medium	Audio-visual ad broadcasted on television and shared at YouTube
Language	Hindi
HashTag	#SwachhBharat
Views	1,55,326
Likes	8,200
Dislike	82
Celebrity Involvement	None
Ad Duration	02.51 minutes
URL	https://www.youtube.com/watch?v=EZsMO2SljgM

The message came through letters with a sender named "Bharat" to strike their conscious and eventually succeeded in the mission where "Bharat" represents the dormant consciousness among the people that needs to be awakened in order to understand and act in favor of the greater good (Figures 10.7b and 10.7c).

The commercial invites people's participation in order to create a cleaner nation and maintain the same. The approach of the commercial is dramatical and emotional, but they wanted to create a long-lasting emotional effect on the views to make them understand their duty towards their nation and society.

This is another public service advertisement from the "Health Phone" series and a part of a popular series called "Amma Ji Kehti Hain," where an elderly woman is in constant search for ways to educate the rural people on different health benefits, eradicating unscientific, orthodox, and unapproved systems. The commercial encourages people to choose 'institutional delivery' for their unborn children to avoid putting the lives of mothers and children at risk. It also highlights other important benefits that can be provided by authorized institutes during and after the child delivery. According to the report published by H. Pletcher, the infant mortality rate in India in 2018 was 30 for every 1,000 live birth, where it was predicted to come down to 8 per 1,000 live birth by 2100 (Plecher, 2020). On the other hand, another research conducted at an Indian hospital shows that the maternal mortality rate in India is 4.21 for every 1000 live births compared

FIGURE 10.7 Screenshot of PSA on cleanliness – "Swachh Bharat Abhiyan."

Source: https://www.youtube.com/watch?v=EZsMO2SljgM

to 4 for every 1000 live births in Northern Europe, while most frequent causes of death include "hemorrhage, infections, hypertensive disorders, ruptured uterus, hepatitis, and anemia" (Table 10.9 (Prakash, 1991)).

TABLE 10.9   Institutional Delivery

Theme	Institutional Delivery
Ad Category	Public service Ad on 'Institutional delivery'
Medium	Audio-visual ad broadcasted on television and shared at YouTube
Language	Hindi
HashTag	None
Views	66, 742
Likes	127
Dislike	34
Celebrity Involvement	Raveena Tandon
Ad Duration	09.11 minutes
URL:	https://www.youtube.com/watch?v=vFzYaf-rbsw

Bollywood celebrity Raveena Tandon has been associated with the "HealthPhone" series to spread awareness among the mass on the multiple health issues and also urged for institutional birth explaining multiple benefits. This commercial shows a rare circumstance where the woman stood against the orthodox tradition and demanded for institutional birth for her unborn child that indicates the raising awareness among the rural women on health and family welfare.

This is another PSA that emphasizes on the children health and development. Though the advertisement is structured to showcase the rural scenario but this concern is equally important and relevant for urban household and people.

The commercial shows the negligence of the parents and immediate family towards the infant while the first 1000 days, including nine months in the mother's womb are very crucial for the physical and cognitive development of the children. The association of Bollywood celebrity Amrita Rao in this ad was more like a family member with a strong sense of children health who provides valuable advice to the family on the children health and development. This commercial also emphasizes on family bonding, which is an essential parameter for child development at a tender age. Unlike other PSAs, this has also created an emotional periphery where a viewer can relate similar circumstances in their own family and institutionalize the changes for better health and family welfare (Table 10.10 and Figure 10.8).

TABLE 10.10   Total Sanitation – *"Shauchalay"*

Theme	First 1000 Days of a Child
Ad Category	Public service Ad on First 1000 days of a child
Medium	Audio-Visual ad broadcasted on Television and shared at YouTube
Language	Hindi
HashTag	None
Views	27,344
Likes	888
Dislike	13
Celebrity Involvement	Amrita Rao
Ad Duration	04.46 Minutes
URL	https://www.youtube.com/watch?v=-zsNDfML5zM&t=181s

FIGURE 10.8   Screenshot of PSA on "first 1000 days of a child."

Source: https://www.youtube.com/watch?v=-zsNDfML5zM&t=181s

10.12 DISCUSSIONS

The main aim of health-related messages through every media (we can say convergent media) is to inform, educate, or moreover to have some behavioral changes. So the content and context play a significant role in encouraging viewers to alter their bad habits and could certainly adapt to cleanliness, health, and hygiene and proper sanitation. Generally, the notion is to comment and criticize the policy formulation, schemes, and programs for the people by the government. But the problem lays their effective means adaptation of behavioral change, to reach the intended public. For this digital medium is very effective because it allow individual to Omnipotent content consumer. The messages which were propagated for television and can still have access by the consumers. In this present study, it has been found that the public service advertisements were revisited, consumed, viewed in a larger scale across the scattered geographical arena.

10.13 LIMITATIONS OF THE STUDY

The qualitative research methodology which has been taken here divulges only the strength of the content of the messages but not include the effect or impact on the public. The study also be short of with ample literature on this domain, especially on the rural area's perspective of PSA on health and hygiene. There is also lack of enough data from government websites related to research in respect to health with PSA of in rural India scenario.

10.14 CONCLUSIONS

The positive depiction of public service advertisements through digital media regarding health, hygiene, and sanitation are oftentimes heavily scrutinized by the public. Given the current public service accountability to the target group embedded with digital media content, service providers (both government and private) may experience strenuous pressure to produce higher results with fewer resources. Though these public service advertisements meant for only Television medium but in order to determine digital media through various means orient the viewpoint of future health care providers through PSA possibly will adhere to. The results of the study indicate that the public can relearn and relook the older content with innovative presentation through digital mode. Health care providers through PSA may hold patient care in high regard and could possibly adopt online interactions. However, the results of the study also show that future health care activities through PSA within the gamut of virtual world with various means may continue for effective communication approach, ethics, system, and legal approve to guide their actions and activities in portraying the health, hygiene, and wellbeing content to reach the scrupulous target group or society as a whole.

10.15 FUTURE DIRECTIONS FOR FURTHER RESEARCH

This present study has its limitation to various themes related to public service advertisements and its intended messages for health and hygiene from a rural Indian perspective. Further research could be taken into consideration in the adaptation of various analyzes of involving the individual's perception and the modification of Knowledge-Attitude and Practice. This study can further approach through a mixed methodology for effective means of information as factor analysis.

KEYWORDS

- digital medium
- health belief model
- human immunodeficiency virus
- IFPS technical assistance project
- Indian Public Service Advertisements
- public service

REFERENCES

Bansal, R., John, S., & Ling, P. M., (2005). Cigarette advertising in Mumbai, India: Targeting different socioeconomic groups, women, and youth. *Tobacco Control, 14*(3), 201–206.
CCP, J. H., (2011). *INDIA Family Planning: Birth Spacing "Right Time" Campaign*. Retrieved from: https://www.youtube.com/watch?v=HQI_c09oxgE (accessed on 24 February 2021).

Ciochetto, L., (2004). Advertising and globalization in India. *Media Asia, 31*(3), 157–169. doi: https://doi.org/10.1080/01296612.2004.11726750.

Clasen, T., Boisson, S., Routray, P., Torondel, B., Bell, M., Cumming, O., & Ray, S., (2014). Effectiveness of a rural sanitation program on diarrhea, soil-transmitted helminth infection, and child malnutrition in Odisha, India: A cluster-randomized trial. *The Lancet Global Health, 2*(11), e645–e653.

Darwaza Band Ad for Twin Pit Toilets, (2018). Retrieved from: https://www.youtube.com/watch?v=bb-hspoHnis (accessed on 24 February 2021).

E-Times, (n.d.). Retrieved from: https://timesofindia.indiatimes.com/life-style/health-fitness/health-news/only-18-women-in-india-have-access-to-sanitary-hygiene-in-india/articleshow/64931350.cms (accessed on 24 February 2021).

Gerhard, J. H., William J. McEwen, & Sharon A. Coyne (1973). Public service advertising on television. *Journal of Broadcasting and Electronic Media*, 387–404. doi: https://doi.org/10.1080/08838157309363703.

Health Phone, (2013). *Health Phone: Institutional Delivery: All Births Should Take Place in a Hospital-Skilled Attendant.* Retrieved from: https://www.youtube.com/watch?v=vFzYaf-rbsw (accessed on 24 February 2021).

Health Phone, (2013). *Health Phone: Iodine Deficiency: Iodized Salt Ensures the Proper Mental and Cognitive Development.* Retrieved from: https://www.youtube.com/watch?v=SMdgE-cFzgU (accessed on 24 February 2021).

Hopkins, J., (2011). *INDIA Family Planning: Birth Spacing "Right Time" Campaign.* Retrieved from: https://www.youtube.com/watch?v=HQI_c09oxgE (accessed on 24 February 2021).

Hueso, A., & Bell, B., (2013). An untold story of policy failure: The total sanitation Campaign in India. *Water Policy, 15*(6), 1001–1017.

India HIV/AIDS: HIV Awareness: Boy-Girl, (2011). Retrieved from: https://www.youtube.com/watch?v=ueIgxbgTlt0 (accessed on 24 February 2021).

India, P. I. B., (2019). *Importance of First 1000 Days of a Child.* Retrieved from: https://www.youtube.com/watch?v=-zsNDfML5zM&t=181s (accessed on 24 February 2021).

Krishna, P. S., & Anurag, S., (2017). Public service advertising in India: An evaluation through literature. *International Journal of Marketing and Financial Management, 5*(3), 53–64. ISSN: 2348 –3954 (online) ISSN: 2349 –2546 (print).

Lynn, J. R., (1974). Effects of persuasive appeals in public service advertising. *Journalism Quarterly, 51*(4), 622–630.

Nagendra, A., & Agrawal, S., (2011). Advertisement claims grow taller! A study of ethics in advertising by FMCG companies in India. *International Proceedings of Economics Development and Research, 2*, 47–50.

Nouria, B., & Judith Green (2020). *Qualitative Research Methodology.* Retrieved from: fieldresearch.msf.org: https://fieldresearch.msf.org/bitstream/handle/10144/84230/Qualitative%20research%20methodology.pdf?sequence=1&isAllowed=y (accessed on 24 February 2021).

O'Barr, W. M., (2006). Public service advertising. *Advertising Educational Foundation, 7*(2). doi: 10.1353/asr.2006.0027.

O'Barr, W. M., (2008). Advertising in India. *Advertising and Society Review, 9*(3), 1–33.

Plecher, H., (2020). *Infant Mortality Rate in India 2018.* Statista. Retrieved from: https://www.statista.com/statistics/806931/infant-mortality-in-india/ (accessed on 24 February 2021).

Prakash. A., S. S., (1991). Maternal mortality in India: Current status and strategies for reduction. *Indian Pediatr, 28*(12), 1395–400.

Raza, H., (2018). *Padman | No Smoking | Safe Living | No to Tobacco| Akshay Kumar | New Bollywood Movies|*. Retrieved from: https://www.youtube.com/watch?v=8b2FUJbUSu8 (accessed on 24 February 2021).

Sinha, D. N., (2005). Gutka advertisement and smokeless tobacco use by adolescents in Sikkim, India. *Indian J. Community Med., 30*(1), 18–20.

Swachh Bharat, (2017). Retrieved from: https://www.youtube.com/watch?v=EZsMO2SljgM (accessed on 24 February 2021).

Tamhankar, A. J., Nachimuthu, R., Singh, R., Harindran, J., Meghwanshi, G. K., Kannan, R., & Sahoo, K. C., (2019). Characteristics of a nationwide voluntary antibiotic resistance awareness campaign in India; future paths and pointers for resource limited settings/ low- and middle-income countries. *International Journal of Environmental Research and Public Health, 16*(24), 5141.

Total Sanitation, (2013). Retrieved from: https://www.youtube.com/watch?v=oBKeZmJeoy4 (accessed on 24 February 2021).

Turk, T., Murukutla, N., Gupta, S., Kaur, J., Mullin, S., Saradhi, R., & Chaturvedi, P., (2012). Using a smokeless tobacco control mass media campaign and other synergistic elements to address social inequalities in India. *Cancer Causes and Control, 23*(1), 81–90.

USAID India, (2010). *Song 60 sec*. Retrieved from: https://www.youtube.com/watch?v=7S-PR_TZGmA (accessed on 24 February 2021).

CHAPTER 11

Technology Usage and Loneliness Among Older Adults

TRISHA BAKSHI

PhD Research Scholar, Department of Sociology, Vidyasagar University, West Bengal, India, Phone: 9088735571, E-mail: trishabksh@gmail.com

ABSTRACT

Research shows that the use of technological interventions and the internet by older adults have a positive impact on not only the physical but also the psychological condition of the elderly population. Since older adults constitute the digitally marginalized section of society; little research has been conducted so far on the impact and effectiveness of various technologies in reducing loneliness among them. This study undertakes a systematic review of existing literature of empirical studies conducted on the role of technology in reducing feelings of social isolation and ways of effectuating digital inclusion of the seniors. For this purpose, both online and offline studies on the mentioned area of enquiry were considered. Following inclusion/exclusion criteria of considering only those studies written in English that provided empirical evidence of the role of specific technologies in reducing loneliness among those aged 50 years or above, a total of 26 studies conducted during 1985 to 2018 were screened out from approximately 1000 studies pertaining to the theme. Among all the available technological interventions the categories like Information and Communication Technologies (ICTs), social media, telecare system, and assistive robots were found to be most frequently applied to mitigate feelings of hopelessness and alienation among the aged. Since the aged are a heterogeneous group who widely vary in their preferences and capabilities, evaluating the effectiveness of such technologies in improving the emotional well-being among the aged, become quite challenging for the research undertaken in that area. However, findings suggest that it is necessary to adopt a holistic view of the elderly user's situation, focusing on the specific contexts in which they adopt or reject certain technologies. This calls for more research work to be undertaken to identify the barriers the older adults face so that the role of new technologies to improve the overall quality of their lives can be effectively evaluated.

11.1   INTRODUCTION

History has recorded no society without the existence of old people, but they previously constituted a very small percentage of the total population in any given time or place (Achenbaum, 2005). With the advent of medical science resulting in low fertility, low mortality, and improved longevity of human life, the number of elderly (60 years +) has increased to a considerable extent. Old people have a distinct place in the society as long as they can do things like their younger counterparts, and failing to do so, they simply disappear. Not only biological but also psychological aging affect cognitive functional ability among the aged. The deleterious effect of loneliness and social isolation on the physical and mental health outcomes as well as on the overall quality of life of the elderly has been recognized by researchers, health practitioners and social workers working in that field (Perissinotto et al., 2012; Ezra and Leitsch, 2010; Heide et al., 2012). Loneliness, a widely prevalent social phenomenon among the gray population, calls not only for the necessity of adopting technological interventions for effectively reducing the burden of elderly health care on the socio-political and economic systems, but also for promoting well-being among those elderly who wish to remain active and functionally independent in their advanced years (Dixit and Goyal, 2008; Ezra and Leitsch, 2010; Khosravi et al., 2016; Broekens, Heerink, and Rosendal, 2009).

Loneliness, the subjective experience of social isolation (measured by the number of social contacts and the level of social engagement), estrangement or companionless, is an unpleasant feeling that arises from a mismatch between the quality and quantity of social relations one has and the relationships one desires to have (Perlman and Peplau, 1982 as cited in Peplau and Goldston, 1982; Fokkema and Knipscheer, 2007; Perissinotto et al., 2012). Relationships when lacking intimacy, sincerity, and emotiveness (Weiss, 1973 as cited in Sar et al., 2012) generate feelings of loneliness, which motivates people to establish new social connections

(Luhmann et al., 2014). Sar et al. (2012) points out that older adults experience two types of loneliness: social and emotional (DiTommaso and Spinner, 1997), the latter being more intensely experienced by the aged. Lack of social integration due to low communication with friends cause social loneliness, while emotional loneliness is related to lacking an intimate relationship in life like having no partner or living alone (Fokkema and Knipscheer, 2007).

There exists a negative relationship between age and the size of one's social network, closeness to other members and the existence of non-primary social ties (Cornwell et al., 2008 as cited in Toepoel, 2013). Since having a partner and a large number of friends or relatives with a high frequency of contact with them reduces loneliness, the feeling aggravates as one's intimate social circle shrinks with age. Also, it is noteworthy to mention here that the perceived quality of family relationship plays a more important role in predicting loneliness than the size of the family, which is why disturbed family relationships often perpetuate feelings of loneliness among the aged (Ezra and Leitsch, 2010). Among the aged population, two domains of the social network-" the descriptive characteristics of the social network" and "the subjective evaluations of the social network"-act as determinants of loneliness as suggested by de Jong (1987). The size of one's social network and frequency of contact form the objective aspect of social contacts representing "the descriptive characteristics of the social network" while the "subjective evaluations of the social network" is all about the quality of social bonds measured through social support received and gratification obtained out of interpersonal relationships (de Jong Gierveld, 1987 as cited in Ezra and Leitsch, 2010).

The predominance of computers and other forms of technology necessitates the use of technology by older adults; pressing for a need to focus our attention on the relationship between the use of technological interventions and loneliness among the elderly. As people are living longer and growing lonelier (due to illness, retirement, loss of friends, or migration of children to distant places for jobs), it is essential to recognize the significance of the role played by technologies in expanding social contact (Khosravi et al., 2016), in reducing communication gap (Cotton et al., 2011) in assisting with daily activities, and in enhancing social inclusion because the information and communication technology (ICT) based modern society is moving most of its services into the Internet (Quico, 2008, as cited in Mikkola and Halonen, 2011). Though the use of technological interventions and the internet by older adults have a positive impact both on the physical and psychological condition of older adults, little research has been conducted so far to evaluate the effectiveness of various technologies in reducing loneliness among them. Also, the existing literature provides controversial, inconsistent, and inconclusive results about the relations. Some studies have reported the positive contribution of various technologies interventions in reducing social isolation (Khosravi et al., 2016; Nowland et al., 2018), alongside highlighting the importance of computer engagement in alleviating loneliness (Blazun et al., 2012; Carpenter and Buday, 2007) and the role of internet in enhancing social support among the seniors (Blit-Cohen and Litwin, 2004; Cotton, 2009; McMellon and Schiffman, 2002; White et al., 1999; Xie, 2007, as cited in Cotton et al., 2012; Sar et al., 2012; Sum et al., 2008; Heo et al., 2015; Chopik, 2016). Other studies have, on the other hand, highlighted the negative effects of internet use on the psychosocial well-being of the elderly (e.g., Marche, 2012, as cited in Nowland et al., 2018; Kraut et al., 1998; Nie and Erbring, 2000, as cited in Cotton et al., 2012). The gap in the existing literature pertaining to the concerned theme calls for a systematic overview of empirical data of various studies undertaken to evaluate the usefulness of technological interventions in alleviating loneliness among the older population and makes this study a useful one.

11.1.1   AIMS OF THE PRESENT STUDY

The aim of the present study is first, to identify various technological interventions designed to mitigate feelings of hopelessness and alienation among the aged; second to evaluate the effectiveness of such technologies in reducing loneliness; and third to identify the challenges the seniors face in adopting the technologies that prevent them from being socially included in the present digital society.

Against this backdrop, the systematic review of the literature undertaken posed the following questions:

1. What technological interventions are designed to alleviate loneliness among older adults?
2. How and to what extent do such technologies help the elderly in overcoming feelings of social isolation?
3. What are the obstacles they face while trying to interact with new technological interventions?

The chapter is structured as follows: it introduces the readers to the idea of loneliness and social isolation widely prevalent among the gray population. The next section discusses the methods chosen for the review undertaken, which is followed by a description of the results obtained and consequent discussion or elaboration on the findings and finally suggests practice implementation and design recommendation through which older adults could make better use of the available technologies for improving the overall quality of their lives.

11.2   METHOD

This study provides a comprehensive review of the literature to identify and evaluate the trends in the existing literature to answer the above-stated research questions, as shown in Figure 11.1. In order to do so, an extensive search of both online and offline studies on the mentioned area of inquiry was undertaken.

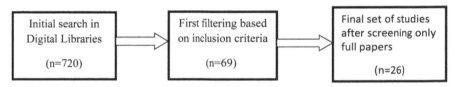

FIGURE 11.1   Flow diagram outlining the review process.

11.3   SEARCH STRATEGY

A systematic search across disciplines was undertaken to look for empirical studies conducted between 1985 and 2018. The databases consulted were: ScienceDirect, Scopus, PubMed, IEEE, and Medline. Keeping in mind the objectives of the study, only those articles that reported the role of specific technologies in reducing loneliness among those aged 50 years or older and the barriers they encounter in adopting such technologies were considered. By locating and identifying relevant articles, using search keywords (e.g., "older adults," "elderly," "aged," "seniors," "gray population," "silver surfers," "loneliness," "social isolation," "depression," "technology," "adoption," "internet," "social media," "computer," "social networks,"

"ICT," "telecare," chat rooms, "barriers"), a total of 26 studies were screened out.

11.3.1 *INCLUSION AND EXCLUSION CRITERIA*

The chapter followed the inclusion criteria of considering: (a) only those studies that provided empirical evidence of the role of specific technologies in reducing loneliness; (b) studies written/published in English; (c) included qualitative, quantitative or both types of studies; (d) individuals studied were 50 years or older or had a mean age of 50 when studied as groups. The exclusion criteria involved excluding: (a) review papers, conceptual articles, letters, unpublished work, editorials; (b) empirical studies involving individuals/groups other than old people; (c) studies in languages other than English.

11.4 RESULTS

As shown in Figure 11.2, most of the studies were carried out in the United States of America (N= 13, 50%). The rest were conducted in Netherlands (N= 5, 19%), and other countries (N= 8, 31%). An extensive study of the existing literature reveals the trend of a steady increase in the number of studies undertaken to identify the role and usefulness of various technologies in reducing loneliness among seniors. Also, researchers have increasingly concerned themselves more with the interconnection between physical and psychological well-being of the aged and the potential barriers they faced in adopting information and communication technologies. The reason for this rise in scholarly interest can be located in two major demographic trends, first, the unprecedented growth of the aging of the aged population, second, the rapid spread of technological innovations.

11.5 IMPACT OF TECHNOLOGICAL INTERVENTION ON OLDER ADULTS' LONELINESS

Modern-day technological advancements have opened up new opportunities for independent and dignified living among the elderly. But there is no consensus among researchers over which technologies, to what extent, have been instrumental in guaranteeing overall well-being among the gray section of the population. This is also true for researches specifically investigating the role of technological interventions on older adults' feeling of loneliness in a world where much of our social relationships or ties have moved to a digital domain. In such a situation, it becomes difficult to ascertain whether a technology acts as a tool to reduce loneliness by enhancing social relationship or it simply adds to one's feeling of isolation by replacing one's more intimate offline relationships with more superficial online social networks.

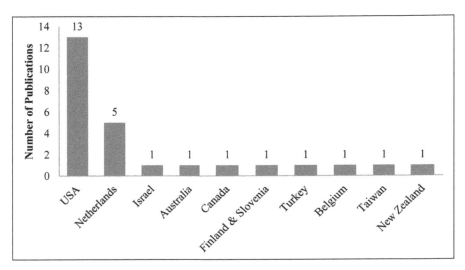

FIGURE 11.2   Country-wise distribution of publication.

However, popular literature is replete with studies that highlight only on how specific technology holds the promise of increasing the physical as well as emotional well-being of older people not only making goods and services available to them at their doorstep but also enabling them to stay connected with their near and dear ones. The dearth of studies assessing the effectiveness of various technologies calls for a systematic review. Among all the available studies dealing with the relationship between technology use and the quality of life and technology, 26 studies were selected for consideration, through a systematic review of the relevant literature, followed by assigning labels or a suitable technology name.

The technologies identified through a study of the existing literature brought to light the following interventions shown in Figure 11.3 that play a role in mitigating loneliness among the aged: e-health applications/ telemedicine/"telecare," personal reminder information and social management systems, peer-led chat rooms/ online forums (to discuss on health and fitness related topics with peers and health experts) online communication technologies like e-mail/video-conference, social media/ social networking sites (SNSs), general "ICT," robotics, and video-games. Out of those available technological interventions, the present study considers the role of 4 main technologies, namely, information and communication technologies (ICTs), social media, telecare/telehealth services, and robotics, in reducing loneliness among the elderly. Most of the studies used the University of California Los Angeles (UCLA) Loneliness Scale; while few studies used various other scales like de Jong Gierveld to measure loneliness.

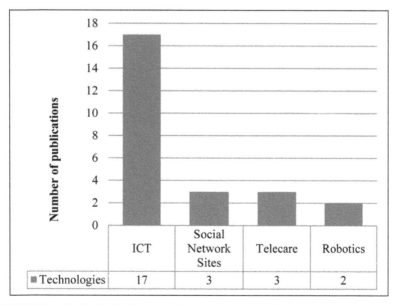

FIGURE 11.3   Technological interventions found across selected papers.

11.5.1   INFORMATION AND COMMUNICATION TECHNOLOGIES (ICTS)

Old age brings with it a number of physical declines, chronic illness, bereavement, retirement, or reduced income, thereby jeopardizing a person's mental well-being. Out of a range of available technological interventions aimed at mitigating loneliness among the aged, voluminous works have focused on the role of Information and Communication Technologies (ICTs) in this regard. Using the internet on a regular basis is linked with reduction in loneliness and depressive symptoms (Cotten et al., 2014), especially among chronically ill and physically handicapped older adults (Fokkema and Knipscheer, 2007). Internet use is associated with perceptions of greater social support and life satisfaction (Chopik, 2016), enables empowerment through better financial decision-making (James, Boyle, Yu, and Bennett, 2013), helps regain control over life and promotes emotional well-being by making communication easy and affordable (Shapira, Barak, and Gal, 2007; Pew Internet and American Life, 2004). Similarly, computer-proficiency can prove beneficial for elderly residents in institutional care, compared to those living in home settings (Blazun, Saranto, and Rissanen, 2012), since frequent use of ICTs (internet) as a communicative tool reduce loneliness by helping to maintain and develop social networks, making socializing possible through internet and computer (Cotten, Anderson, McCullough, 2013; Sum et al., 2008; Erickson and Johnson, 2011).

A few other studies have, however, suggested no relationship between social connectedness through internet and feelings of social isolation among the elderly (Loges and Jung, 2001, as cited in Cotten, Anderson, and McCullough, 2013; Sleger, Van, Boxtel, and Jolles, 2008). Others like Turkle (2012) as cited in Nowland, Necka, and Cacioppo, 2017; and Nimrod (2011), as cited in as cited in Cotten, Anderson, and McCullough (2013), suggested that online relationships are superficial compared to offline relationships because the former often lack in intimacy and lead to heightened feelings of loneliness among the older adults when their expectations of engaging in meaningful relationships are not met. Three of the studies considered for review point in the same direction in demonstrating no significant reduction in loneliness through the adopting of ICTs like the internet and the computer. Through his cross-sectional study conducted to explain the relationship between leisure activities and social connectedness among the elderly Dutch population, Toepoel (2013) found no association between social connectedness and passive leisure activities like watching television, listening to the radio and spending time behind the computer screen, but witnessed an inverse association between engaging in offline social relationships and feelings of social isolation among the older adults.

White et al. (2010) conducted a randomized controlled trial consisting of 39 participants in the intervention group and 45 participants in the control group to investigate the psychosocial effect of internet training provided over a period of two weeks to older adults having a mean age of 72. Despite the intervention and training offered, the scores, recorded on UCLA Loneliness Sale and modified CES-D scale, reflected no statistically significant differences in changes in degrees of loneliness in the intervention and control group of older adults. Still, others like Carpenter and Buday (2007) through their a cross-sectional study, suggested that it is difficult to ascertain whether computer use fosters greater social connectedness or having a larger social network motivates greater use of computers by older adults. However, among all the studies considered for this review, the majority reported the effectiveness of ICTs in reducing loneliness among the adults. This holds true for all the studies employing quasi-experimental method. Only one of the surveys using cross-sectional data and two of the randomized controlled trial studies indicated no significant reduction in levels of loneliness through ICT intervention (see Table 11.1).

11.5.2   SOCIAL NETWORKING SITE (SNS) TECHNOLOGY

In recent years, social media has become an integral part of the everyday lives of millions of people, including the older population. Social media plays an important role in enhancing social connectedness, especially among the aged who, due to their mobility impairments, may miss out on social events, and consequentially, the opportunity to socialize with friends and family (Bell et al., 2013; Hutto et al., 2014). Seen in this light, social media does not replace, but augments traditional modes of communication like talking over the phone or face-to-face (Hutto et al., 2014). Numerous investigations into the usage pattern of social networking site (SNS) technology by the younger population has been carried out by researchers, but little research has focused on social media use by the older population.

Older adults often experience loneliness due to their reduced scope for social connectedness. This feeling is more prominent in rural older adults as compared to their urban counterparts, but the former can overcome barriers of social connectivity in rural areas through the use of social networking site (SNS) technology (Findlay and Nies, 2017). Studies that compared older Facebook users to non-users, indicated that due to higher levels of social connectedness, the former perceived themselves to be

TABLE 11.1 ICT Interventions

Authors	Year	Participants (Age/ Mage and SD)	Sample Size	Country	Method	Loneliness Measure	Findings
White et al.	2002	72 (Mean age)	39 (intervention group) 45 (control group)	United States of America	Randomized controlled trial	University of California Los Angeles (UCLA) loneliness scale (Russell et al., 1980; Russell and Daniel, 1996), modified CES-depression scale (Kohout et al., 1993)	Statistically non-significant differences in the change scores of intervention and control groups on the loneliness scale
Fokkema and Knipscheer	2007	66 (Avg)	12	Netherlands	Quasi-experimental study	De Jong-Gierveld and Kamphuis Scale (1985)	Using computer and internet take people's minds off loneliness, specially emotional loneliness
Shapira, Barak, and Gal	2007	70–93	22 (intervention group) 26 (control group)	Israel	Quasi-experimental study	UCLA loneliness scale	Computer and internet use decreases loneliness and increases well-being
Carpenter and Buday	2007	>= 50	324	United States of America	Survey-Cross-sectional	Geriatric depression scale (GDS) (Lesher and Berryhill)	Computer use alleviates loneliness
Weinert, Cudney, and Hill	2008	51 (M age)	189	United States of America	Intervention study	UCLA loneliness scale (Robinson et al., 1991) CES-Depression scale (Devine and Orne, 1985)	Reduction in loneliness and increase in self-efficacy through computer-delivered intervention
Sum et al.	2008	>= 55	222	Australia	Survey-cross-sectional	15-item social and emotional loneliness scale (SELSA)	Internet when used as a communication tool lowers social loneliness
Slegers, Van, Boxtel and Jolles	2008	64–75	123 (intervention group) 68 (control group)	Netherlands	Randomized controlled trial	De Jong-Gierveld and Kamphuis Scale (1986)	No significant change in loneliness between two groups post-training

TABLE 11.1 *(Continued)*

Authors	Year	Participants (Age/ Mage and SD)	Sample Size	Country	Method	Loneliness Measure	Findings
Erickson and Johnson	2011	>= 60	122	Canada	Survey-cross-sectional	20-item UCLA loneliness scale (Russel and Cutrona, 1980)	Inverse relationship between loneliness and internet used as a communicative tool
Blazun, Saranto and Rissanen	2012	M = 72.4 (58 participants) M = 72.9 (45 participants)	58 (baseline) 45 (follow-up study)	Finland, Slovenia	Quasi-experimental study	Cross tabs and Pearson's Chi-square to examine the difference in loneliness level	Level of loneliness decreased significantly after computer training and subsequent ICT use
Cotten et al.	2012	>= 50	7839	United States of America	Survey-cross-sectional	Center for Epidemiologic Studies Depression Scale (CES-D)	Interest use positively contributes to mental well-being
Cotton et al.	2012	84	70	United States of America	Randomized controlled trial	3-item version of the UCLA loneliness scale	The higher the frequency of going online, the lower the levels of loneliness and social isolation
Sar et al.	2012	>= 55	563	Turkey	Survey-cross-sectional	UCLA loneliness scale short form (ULS8) (Russel and Cutrona, 1980)	Elderly internet users have lower loneliness levels than elderly non-users
Toepel	2013	55–75+	1171 participants (55–64 years), 637 (65–74), 210 aged 75	Netherlands	Survey-cross-sectional	6-item de Jong Gierveld Scale	Social connectedness (explained through leisure activities) was not associated with spending time behind the computer (passive activities)
James et al.	2013	82.2 (mean age; range: 60–101)	661	United States of America	Survey-cross-sectional	Jong Gierveld Scale (de Jong Gierveld, 1987)	The greater the frequency of internet use, the lower the level of loneliness

less lonely (Hutto et al., 2014), scored higher in satisfaction levels with their current social roles, were more confident in using technology (Bell et al., 2013), had higher frequency of SNS use, greater number of social networks established online and invested more time in online activities (Findlay and Nies, 2017). However, in their study on the association between usage of social network sites and loneliness and/or mental health in elderly Dutch population, Aarts, Peek, and Wouters (2014) found the use of social network sites was unrelated to both loneliness and one's mental health since the frequent users, the medium users and the non-users of SNS showed no difference regarding loneliness and mental health. The evidence from studies reviewed in this chapter, however, was mixed when it comes to identifying the role of social media in reducing loneliness. However, most reported that the main purpose of using social networking site (SNS) technology by the older adults was to connect with friends and family rather than participating in various online community activities or seeking information (see Table 11.2).

11.5.3   TELE-MEDICINE/TELE-CARE INTERVENTIONS

Population aging, a widespread phenomenon in the present society, brings with it a number of challenges. As people age, so does the incidents of chronic diseases that require constant care from the family or from health care agencies. This places immense demand on the health care system, the solution of which is possible to be sought through telemedicine and telecare interventions. Shortage of care providers, coupled with lack of adequate care and medical attention, leads to loneliness among the older adults (Broekens, Heerink, and Rosendal, 2009). Since the older adults wish to remain functional, lead a life of self-sufficiency and avoid institutionaliza-tion, receiving adequate care at home is not only preferred but also practical where telecare interventions can be employed to support and benefit both the homebound elderly and their care provider (Heide et al., 2012).

Video conferencing, a computer-mediated communication, when used for medical purposes, provide a cost-effective and convenient way of delivering care, by enabling physicians or providers of care to counsel patients, constantly evaluate the health status of the frail, chronically ill or those older patients lacking in mobility to frequently travel to health care practitioners for regular check-ups (Charness and Czaja, 2005; Tsai and Tsai, 2011).

TABLE 11.2 Social Network Sites Interventions

Authors	Year	Participants (Age/ Mage and SD)	Sample Size	Country	Method	Loneliness Measure	Findings
Bell et al.	2013	52–92 (M age = 71.64)	142	United States of America	Survey-cross sectional	UCLA loneliness scale	No significant difference in loneliness between Facebook users and non-users
Aarts, Peek, and Wouters	2014	>= 60	626	Netherlands	Survey-cross sectional	6-item loneliness scale (de Jong Gierveld and van Tilburg, 2006, 2008)	SNS was unrelated to loneliness and mental health among frequent, medium, and non-users.
Hutto et al.	2015	51–91	268	United States of America	Survey-cross sectional	20-item UCLA loneliness scale	Increase in social satisfaction and decrease in loneliness after using SNSs
Findlay and Nies	2017	>= 65	350	United States of America	Survey-cross sectional	Social connectedness scale-revised	No significant relationship between SNS use and social connectedness or loneliness

Arnaert and Delesie (2007), through their study on home telecare intervention to describe the nature of the relationship between the care and support and health outcomes, reported that the most aged, bereaved elderly living alone, having financial constraints, and using several health and social services showed improvements in levels of loneliness when video telephone intervention was used to connect them with a network of relationships where they felt accepted, had common interests and concerns. This reduction in emotional loneliness was also visible among the less active younger elders having physical and mental health problems or lower life satisfaction following telenursing care. Tsai and Tsai (2011), through their quasi-experiment longitudinal study, reported similar results about the effectiveness of video-conference intervention in reducing perceived loneliness and depressive symptoms among the elderly residents of nursing homes. The aged often experience higher incidents of frailty among, caused due to reduced strength, bodily imbalance, and exhaustion (Ferrucci et al., 2004 as cited in Heide et al., 2012). Cognitive decline and restricted mobility render the elderly population vulnerable to feelings of social isolation and loneliness. Heide et al. (2012) investigated the effectiveness of CareTV video network in homecare organizations in expanding social contacts among the elderly clients through the applications like: alarm service; care service; good morning/good evening (GMGA) service; welfare and housing; family contact. They found that it was possible to enhance feelings of self-sufficiency and decrease loneliness after the elderly clients were exposed to the intervention study using CareTV that effectuates meaningful communication with friends and family through video and voice connection (Table 11.3).

11.5.4 ROBOTIC INTERVENTIONS

The shift in demographics indicating accelerated growth in the proportion of the elderly population across the world demands growing attention on the role of assistive robots designed to enhance physical and psychological well-being among the elderly by assisting them in their daily activities as well as enhancing social interaction with them. Assistive social robots can be of two types-service type robots (that assist the aged in routine work) and companion robots (that improve physical and mental outcomes in the aged by providing companionship, decrease in loneliness and increase in social connections) (Broekens, Heerink, and Rosendal, 2009). Pet robots,

TABLE 11.3 Tele-Care Interventions

Authors	Year	Participants (Age/Mage and SD)	Sample Size	Country	Method	Loneliness Measure	Findings
Arnaert and Delesie	2007	>= 60	71	Belgium	Intervention Study	12 item-de Jong Gierveld and Kamphuis (1985)	Decrease in loneliness level among participants after the study
Tsai and Tsai	2011	73.82 (experimental group) 79.26 (comparison group)	40 (experimental group) 50 (comparison group)	Taiwan	Longitudinal Quasi-experimental study	UCLA Loneliness Scale	Significantly lower mean loneliness and depressive scores of participants in the experimental group compared to the comparison group.
Hiede et al.	2012	73.2 (Avg.)	130	Netherlands	Intervention study	de Jong Gierveld Loneliness Scale	Significant decrease in loneliness between the beginning and end of the study

much like animal-assisted therapy, are functional in reducing loneliness, while conversational agents that offer "talk therapy" provide a sense of social presence and connection with friends and family (Khosravi, Rezvani, and Wiewiora, 2016). Relational agents-computational artifacts designed to establish effective interactions with older users, has no impact on the psychological well-being and do not necessarily reduce loneliness among older adults (Bickmore, Caruso, Gorr, and Heeren, 2005). Other studies have, however, demonstrated a significant decrease in the level of loneliness and overall improvement in mood and quality of life of the elderly through the use of robots (Robinson, MacDonald, Kerse, and Broadbent, 2013). One out of two studies included under this category reported it is possible to decrease feelings of loneliness and social isolation among the older adults through robotic interventions (Table 11.4).

11.6 DISCUSSION

ICTs have touched the lives of the elderly like never before. Immobility, restrictions in functional ability, and loss of autonomy in old age increases the necessity of using the internet as a communicative tool to sustain social ties especially across vast geographical distances (Climo, 2001; Cotten, 2009; McMellon, and Schiffman, 2000; Nahm, and Resnick, 2001; O'Hara, 2004, as cited in Cotten et al., 2012; Fokkema and Knipscheer, 2007; Shapira, Barak, and Gal, 2007; Carpenter and Buday, 2007; Weinert, Cudney, and Hill, 2008; Sum et al., 2008; Erickson and Johnson, 2011; Blazun, Saranto, and Rissanen, 2012; Sar et al., 2012; James et al., 2013; Cotton et al., 2013, 2014; Chopik, 2016). The cognitive and physical declines experienced in old age can be mediated by paying careful attention to the manner in which information is presented on the Web sites (or computer monitors). Training older adults in using I-pads reduce social isolation by enhancing meaningful knowledge exchanges or by connecting older adults to online communities (Delello and McWhorter, 2017). However, researchers are divided on the opinion of usefulness of ICTs in mitigating loneliness among the elderly and not every study portrays a positive correlation between the two (White et al., 2002; Slegers, Van, Boxtel, and Jolles, 2008; Toepel, 2013).

The number of older adults embracing social media technology to maintain their social networks has exhibited a rapid growth during recent times (Chopik, 2016). According to Pew Internet and Technology study

TABLE 11.4 Robotics Interventions

Authors	Year	Participants (Age/ Mage and SD)	Sample Size	Country	Method	Loneliness Measure	Findings
Robinson, MacDonald, Kerse and Broadbent	2013	50–100	40 (intervention group = 20 Control group = 20)	New Zealand	Randomized controlled trial	UCLA loneliness scale (version 3) Geriatric depression scale (GDS)	Loneliness significantly decreased over the trial period
Bickmore, Caruso, Gorr and Heeren	2005	62–84	21	The United States of America	Quasi-experimental study	UCLA loneliness scale (Russell, Peplau, and Curtrona, 1980) Satisfaction with life scale (Diener, Emmons, Larsen, and Griffin, 1985)	There were no significant differences in loneliness between relational and control group before or after the intervention.

undertaken in the United States of America, 34% of Americans aged 65 and above reported using SNSs like, Facebook or Twitter (Anderson and Perrin, 2017). Also the assertion that social media plays as important a role in older adults' life to enhance social connectedness, as much as it does in the lives of the younger population is debatable (Bell et al., 2013; Findlay and Nies, 2017; Aarts, Peek, and Wouters, 2014). The target consumers of telecare technologies are often the aged who benefit in a number of ways from availing telecare facilities that provide reassurance and safety, actively involves patients in medical processes makes health-related information readily available to the patients, reduces socio-economic disparity among rural and urban areas (Magdelena, Fedak, and Borkowska, 2015), apart from providing psychological support through online social groups and forming fostering new friendships (Charness and Czaja, 2005). The frontiers of the existing traditional health care systems can be expanded with the use of Tele-care that can serve as an alternative model in providing less expensive care than institutionalized care and prove to be effective in decreasing depressive symptoms and loneliness especially among the chronically ill homebound elderly (Arnaert and Delesie, 2007; Tsai and Tsai, 2011; Hiede et al., 2012). Assistive social robots are also useful to improve physical and mental outcomes in the aged by providing companionship, decreasing loneliness and increasing social connections (Broekens, Heerink, and Rosendal, 2009). Most of the studies in this review evaluated the association between loneliness and technological interventions through Cross-Sectional surveys. Taking up more longitudinal surveys and a greater number of Randomized Control Trials might help future studies to deliver robust findings.

11.7 PRACTICE IMPLEMENTATION AND DESIGN RECOMMENDATIONS

The fastest-growing group of Internet users, the older adults, purchase computers at a higher rate compared to any other age group; a trend that is likely to increase with an increase in the proportion of a tech-savvy generation coupled with a decrease in the cost of ICT (Sum et al., 2009 as cited in Erickson and Johnson, 2011; Morrell and Echt, 2001; Chopik, 2016). Twenty-two percent of Americans aged 65 and overuse the internet, compared to 58% of those aged 50–64 and 75% of those aged

18–49 (Pew Internet and American Life, 2004). Forty-five percent of Canadians aged 65–74 use the internet while 21% of those aged 75 and over are online (Statistics Canada, 2009 as cited in Erickson and Johnson, 2011). Demographic factors also influence the adoption or diffusion of technological innovations. The more educated individuals, better salaried, placed in higher status occupations are quick to adopt new products or services as they can afford to take the chance of experimenting with technologies (Meeks, 1994; Erickson and Johnson, 2011). Using the internet to reduce loneliness specially holds true in case of the more educated older adults for they are often more proficient in English, are better in acquiring computer proficiency and find it easier to communicate or expand social contacts via e-mail (Fokkema and Knipscheer, 2007).

Studies report that though the internet opens up numerous possibilities for the elderly, this segment of the population largely remains excluded from enjoying the fruits of digitalization of services. The rate of adoption or usage of computers among this segment of the population is relatively low, creating a digital divide between the old and the young generation (Norris, 2001, as cited in Millward, 2003) or a digital marginalization or social exclusion of the older adults (Carpenter and Buday, 2007; Hardey and Loader, 2009). This is because there exists an inverse relationship between digital literacy and age when cognitive and physical impairments lead to loss of patience, reduced learning or memory capacity, low typing skills; thereby creating difficulties for them to handle technologies designed for the youth (Carpenter and Buday, 2007; Delello and McWhorter, 2017). The common barriers in technology use by the aged identified by researchers are: feeling too old or lazy to learn due to lack of interest, inappropriately designed technologies, negative attitudes towards "youth" technologies, concerns over privacy issues, lack of confidence, limited knowledge due to absence of prior experience, financial constraint (Joyce et al., 2011; Anderson and Perrin, 2017; Charness and Boot, 2009; Tsai et al., 2017; Morris and Brading, 2007; Paul and Stegbauer, 2005; Vaportzis et al., 2017; Preusse et al., 2017), inaccessibility, lack of proficiency in English and the inability to understand 'confusing technical' language (Thomas and Krishnamurthi, 2017), space constraint in the houses, absence of social support or technical help and ergonomic impediments like too small-sized text font (Carpenter and Buday, 2007). Hence, designing elderly friendly systems or products can help them be included in the present digital society (Charness and Czaja, 2005; Meeks, 1994).

It is to be remembered that the aged are a heterogeneous group, having differential experiences, contexts, and preferences when it comes to using technologies to alleviate loneliness. Designing elderly-friendly technologies, establishing technological infrastructures, training the elderly to maximize utility of available technological components can help diminish problems of loneliness among many, if not all, older adults. The benefits of using the proposed technological interventions can be reaped only through generating greater awareness about the availability, positives, and negatives, and potential of each of the technologies in reducing loneliness and social isolation. Only then it is possible for older adults to make informed choices about the technology appropriate for them. Special attention needs to be given to make the products accessible and available at affordable costs. The government and social support agencies can play an important role in providing financial support to encourage older adults to try new technologies needed to improve the quality of their lives. Future research needs to highlight potential pathways through which loneliness can be mitigated through augmented social connectedness.

KEYWORDS

- **geriatric depression scale**
- **good morning/good evening**
- **information and communication technology**
- **internet**
- **older adults**
- **social isolation**
- **social networking site**

REFERENCES

Aarts, S., Peek, S., & Wouters, E., (2014). The relation between social network usage and loneliness and mental health in community-dwelling older adults. *Internal Journal of Geriatric Psychiatry.* doi: 10.1002/gps.4241.

Achenbaum, W. A., (2005). Ageing and changing: International historical perspectives on ageing. In: Johnson, M. L., Coleman, P. G., Kirkwood, T. B. L., & Bengtson, V. L., (eds.), *The Cambridge Handbook of Age and Ageing* (pp. 21–29). Cambridge University Press.

Anderson, M., & Perrin, A., (2017). *Tech Adoption Climbs Among Older Adults*. Pew Internet and technology. http://www.pewinternet.org/2017/05/17/tech-adoption-climbs-among-older-adults (accessed on 24 February 2021).

Arnaert, A., & Delesie, L., (2007). Effectiveness of video-telephone nursing care for the homebound elderly. *Canadian Journal of Nursing Research, 39*(1), 20–36.

Bakshi, S., & Pathak, P., (2015). Social context and the health status of older adults in India. In: Paltasingh, T., & Tyagi, R., (eds.), *Caring for the Elderly: Social Gerontology in the Indian Context* (pp. 99–119). Sage Publications India Private Limited.

Bell, C., Fausset, C., Farmer, S., Nguyen, J., Harley, L., & Fain, W. B., (2013). Examining social media use among older adults. In: *Proceedings of the 24ᵗʰ ACM Conference on Hypertext and Social Media* (pp. 158–163). ACM.

Bickmore, T. W., Caruso, L., Gorr, K. C., & Heeren, T., (2005). 'It's just like you talk to a friend': Relational agents for older adults. *Interacting with Computers, 17*(6), 711–735. https://doi.org/10.1016/j.intcom.2005.09.002.

Blazun, H., Saranto, K., & Rissanen, S., (2012). Impact of computer training courses on reduction of loneliness of older people in Finland and Slovenia. *Computers in Human Behavior, 28*(4), 1202–1212.

Bradley, N., & Poppen, W., (2003). Assistive technology, computers and the internet may decrease the sense of isolation for homebound elderly and disabled persons. *Technology and Disability, 15*(1), 19–25.

Broekens, J., Heerink, M., & Rosendal, H., (2009). Assistive social robots in elderly care: A review. *Gerontechnology, 8*(2), 94–103. doi: 10.4017/gt.2009.08.02.002.00.

Carpenter, B. D., & Buday, S., (2007). Computer use among older adults in a naturally occurring retirement community. *Computers in Human Behavior, 23*, 3012–3024.

Charness, N., & Boot, W. R., (2009). Ageing and information technology use: Potential and barriers. *Association for Psychological Science, 18*(5), 253–258.

Charness, N., & Czaja, S. J., (2005). Adaptation to new technologies. In: Johnson, M. L., Bengtson, V. L., Coleman, P. G., & Kirkwood, T. B. L., (eds.), *The Cambridge Handbook of Age and Ageing* (pp. 662–669). Cambridge University Press.

Chopik, W. J., (2016). The benefits of social technology use among older adults are mediated by reduced loneliness. *Cyberpsychology, Behavior, and Social Networking, 19*(9), 551–556. doi: 10.1089/cyber.2016.0151.

Cotten, S. R., Anderson, W. A., & McCullough, B. M., (2013). Impact of Internet use on loneliness and contact with others among older adults: Cross-sectional analysis. *Journal of Medical Internet Research, 15*(2), e 39.

Cotten, S. R., Ford, G., Ford, S., & Hale, T. M., (2014). Internet use and depression among retired older adults in the United States: A longitudinal analysis. *The Journals of Gerontology Series B: Psychological Sciences and Social Sciences, 69*(5), 763–771.

Cotten, S. R., Ford, J., Ford, S., & Hale, T. M., (2012). Internet use and depression among older adults. *Computers in Human Behavior, 28*(2), 496–499.

Cotton, S. R., Goldner, M., Hale, T. M., & Drentes, P., (2011). The importance of type, amount, and timing of internet use for understanding psychological distress. *Social Science Quarterly, 92*(1), 119–139.

Delello, J. A., & McWhorter, R. R., (2017). Reducing the digital divide: Connecting older adults to iPad technology. *Journal of Applied Gerontology, 36*(1), 4–28.

Dixit, U., & Goyal, V. C., (2015). Technology support in active ageing. In: Paltasingh, T., & Tyagi, R., (eds.), *Caring for the Elderly: Social Gerontology in the Indian Context* (pp. 245–263). Sage Publications India Private Limited.

Durak, E. S., & Durak, M., (2011). The mediator roles of life satisfaction and self-esteem between the affective components of psychological well-being and the cognitive symptoms of problematic Internet use. *Social Indicators Research, 103*(1), 23–32.

Erickson, J., & Johnson, M., (2011). Internet use and psychological wellness during late adulthood. *Canadian Journal on Ageing, 30*(2), 197–209.

Ezra, S. S., & Leitsch, S. A., (2010). The role of social relationships in predicting loneliness: The national social life, health, and aging project. *Social Work Research, 34*(3), 157–167.

Findlay, A. H., & Nies, M. A., (2017). Understanding social networking use for social connectedness among rural older adults. *Healthy Aging Research, 6, e12,* http://dx.doi.org/10.1097/HXR.0000000000000012.

Fokkema, T., & Knipscheer, K., (2007). Escape loneliness by going digital: A quantitative and qualitative evaluation of a Dutch experiment in using ECT to overcome loneliness among older adults. *Aging and Mental Health, 11*(5), 496–504.

Hardey, M., & Loader, B., (2009). The informatization of welfare: Older people and the role of digital services. *The British Journal of Social Work, 39*(4), 657–669. Retrieved from: http://www.jstor.org/stable/23724322 (accessed on 24 February 2021).

Heide, L. A., Loek, A., Willems, C. G., Speeuwenberg, M. D., Rietman, J., & De Witte, L. P., (2012). Implementation of care TV in care for the elderly: The effects of feelings of loneliness and safety and future challenges. *Technology and Disability, 24*(4), 283–291.

Heo, J., Chun, S., Lee, S., Lee, H. K., & Kim, J., (2015). Internet use and well-being in older adults. *Cyberpsychology, Behavior, and Social Networking, 18*(5). doi: 10.1089/cyber.2014.0549.

Hill, W., Weinert, C., & Cudney, S., (2006). Influence of a computer intervention on the psychological status of chronically ill rural women: Preliminary results. *Nursing Research, 55*(1), 34.

Hungelmann, J., Rossi, E. K., Klassen, L., & Stollenwerk, R. N., (1985). Spiritual well-being in older adults: Harmonious interconnectedness. *Journal of Religion and Health, 24*(2), 147–153.

Hutto, C. J., Bell, C., Farmer, S., Fausset, C., Harley, L., Nguyan, J., & Fain, B., (2015). Social media gerontology: Understanding social media usage among older adults. *Web Intelligence, 13*(1), 69–87. doi: 10.3233/web-150310.

James, B. D., Boyle, P. A., Yu, L., & Bennett, D. A., (2013). Internet use and decision making in community-based older adults. *Frontiers in Psychology, 4.*

Joyce, K., Williamson, J., & Mamo, L., (2011). Technology, science, and ageism: An examination of three patterns of discrimination. In: McDonald, L., & Sharma, K. L., (eds.), *Ageism and Elder Abuse* (pp. 30–45). Rawat Publications.

Khosravi, P., Rezvani, A., & Wiewiora, A., (2016). The impact of technology on older adults' social isolation. *Computers in Human Behavior, 63,* 594–603.

Luhmann, M., Schonbrodt, F. D., Hawkley, L. C., & Cacioppo, J. T., (2014). Loneliness and social behaviors in a virtual social environment. *Cognition and Emotion.* http://dx.doi.org/10.1080/02699931.2014.922053.

Magdelena, M., Fedak, B., & Borkowska, U. G., (2015). Use of telemedicine-based care for the aging and elderly: Promises and pitfalls. *Smart Homecare Technology and TeleHealth. 2015.* doi: 10.2147/SHTT.S59498.

Margain, T. H., & Boulton, M., (2005). Sensory impairment. In: Johnson, M. L., Coleman, P. G., Kirkwood, T. B. L., & Bengtson, V. L., (eds.), *The Cambridge Handbook of Age and Ageing* (pp. 121–130). Cambridge University Press.

Meeks, C. B., (1994). Technological change and the elderly. *Advancing the Consumer Interest, 6*(1), 15–20.

Mikkola, K., & Halonen, R., (2011). Nonsense?-ICT perceived by the elderly. In: *European, Mediterranean, and Middle Eastern Conference on Information Systems, 2011.*

Millward, P., (2003). The 'grey digital divide': Perception, exclusion and barriers of access to the internet for older people. *Peer-Reviewed Journal on the Internet, 8*(7) https://doi.org/10.5210/fm.v8i7.1066.

Moore, J. K., (2010). Disability and ageing: The social construction of causality. In: Dannefer, D., & Phillipson, C., (eds.), *The Sage Handbook of Social Gerontology* (pp. 96–110). Sage Publications Ltd.

Morrell, R. W., & Echt, K. V., (2001). Presenting information to older adults. *The Journal of Museum Education Museums and the Aging Revolution, 26*(1), 10–12.

Morris, A., & Brading, H., (2007). E-literacy and the grey digital divide: A review with recommendations. *Journal of Information Literacy, 1*(3). https://www.researchgate.net/publication/273608561_Eliteracy_and_the_grey_digital_divide_A_review_with_recommendations (accessed on 24 February 2021).

Nowland, R., Necka, E. A., & Cacioppo, J. T., (2017). Loneliness and social internet use: Pathways to reconnection in a digital world. *Perspectives on Psychological Science, 13*(1), 70–87. doi: 10.1177/1745691617713052.

Paul, G., & Stegbauer, C., (2005) Is the digital divide between young and elderly people increasing? *Peer-Reviewed Journal on the Internet, 10*(10) doi: 10.5210/fm.v10i10.1286.

Peplau, L. A., & Goldston, S. E., (1982). Preventing the harmful consequences of severe and persistent loneliness: *Proceedings of a Research Planning Workshop.* Held in cooperation with the Department of Psychology, University of California, Los Angeles, National Institute of Mental Health, Rockville, Maryland.

Perissinotto, C., Cenzer, I. S., & Covinsky, K. E., (2012). Loneliness in older persons: A predictor of functional decline and death. *Arch Intern. Med., 172*(14), 1078–1083. doi: 10.1001/archinternmed.2012.1993.

Pew Internet and American Life, (2004). *Older Americans and the Internet.* Available at: https://www.pewresearch.org/internet/2004/03/28/older-americans-and-the-internet/ (accessed on 24 February 2021).

Preusse, K. C., Fausset, C. B., Mitzner, T. L., & Rogers, W. A., (2017). Older adults' acceptance of activity trackers. *Journal of Applied Gerontology, 36*(2), 127–155.

Rao, I., Paltasingh, T., & Tyagi, R., (2015). Older people with disability: Concerns and policies. In: Paltasingh, T., & Tyagi, R., (eds.), *Caring for the Elderly: Social Gerontology in the Indian Context* (pp. 139–156). Sage Publications India Private Limited.

Robinson, H., MacDonald, B., Kerse, N., & Broadbent, E., (2013). The psychosocial effects of a companion robot: A randomized control trial. *Journal of the American Medical Directors Association, 14*(9), 661–667. http://dx.doi.org/10.1016/j.jamda.2013.02.007.

Ryan, T., & Xenos, S., (2011). Who uses Facebook? An investigation into the relationship between the big five, shyness, narcissism, loneliness, and Facebook usage. *Computers in Human Behavior, 27*, 1658–1664.

Sar, A. H., Gokturk, G. Y., Turac, G., & Kazazd, N., (2012). Is the internet use an effective method to cope with elderly loneliness and decrease loneliness symptom? *Procedia-Social and Behavioral Sciences, 55*, 1053–1059. doi: 10.1016/j.sbspro.2012.09.597.

Shapira, N., Barak, A., & Gal, I., (2007). Promoting older adults' well-being through Internet training and use. *Aging and Mental Health, 11*(5), 477–484.

Slegers, K., Van, B. M. P., & Jolles, J., (2008). Effects of computer training and internet usage on the well-being and quality of life of older adults: A randomized, controlled study. *The Journals of Gerontology Series B: Psychological Sciences and Social Sciences, 63*(3), P176–P184.

Sum, S., Mathews, R. M., Hughes, I., & Campbell, A., (2008). Internet use and loneliness in older adults. *CyberPsychology and Behavior, 11*(2) 208–211. doi: 10.1089/cpb.2007.0010.

Thomas, S., & Krishnamurthi, G., (2017). Cashless rural economy: A dream or reality? *Jharkhand Journal of Development and Management Studies, 15*(2), 7269–7281,

Toepoel, V., (2013). Ageing, leisure, and social connectedness: How could leisure help reduce social isolation of older people? *Social Indicators Research, 113*(1), 355–372.

Tsai, H. H., & Tsai, Y. F., (2011). Changes in depressive symptoms, social support, and loneliness over 1 year after a minimum 3-month video-conference program for older nursing home residents. *Journal of Medical Internet Research, 13*(4).

Tsai, H. S., Shillair, R., & Cotton, S. R., (2017). Social Support and "playing around": An examination of how older adults acquire digital literacy with tablet computers. *Journal of Applied Gerontology 36*(1), 29–55. doi: 10.1177/0733464815609440.

Vaportzis, E., Clausen, M. G., & Gow, A. J., (2017). Older adults perceptions of technology and barriers to interacting with tablet computers: A focus group study. *Frontiers in Psychology, 8*. doi: 10.3389/fpsyg.2017.01687.

White, H., McConnell, E., Clipp, E., Branch, L. G., Sloane, R., Pieper, C., et al., (2002). A randomized controlled trial of the psychosocial impact of providing internet training and access to older adults. *Aging and Mental Health, 6*(3), 213–221. https://doi.org/10.1080/13607860220142422.

CHAPTER 12

Technology in Language Classrooms of India: Decoding Digital Learning and Dynamics of Context and Curriculum

DEBANJALI ROY and TANMOY PUTATUNDA

Assistant Professor, School of Languages, KIIT Deemed to be University, Bhubaneswar, Odisha, India

ABSTRACT

Constructivist and task-based theories of language learning foregrounded the generation of knowledge through interactions of individuals with an external socio-cultural milieu, thereby positing language teaching at the very heart of scrutinizing socio-political discourse. With the growth of the internet and digital revolution towards the 1990s, there was a global surge of embedding technology in the educational framework. It led to examination and analysis of hitherto followed classroom pedagogy and its objectives. The twin forces of economic liberalization and globalization forged the structure of present-day ELT in India. With technology foraging into the language curriculum, there was a rapid reconstruction of classroom methodology and concepts associated with a 'classroom.' The urban quarters of the nation were rapidly adapting to online learning using Web 2.0 tools. However, the digital divide of the nation led to the asymmetrical distribution of technological and, therefore educational opportunities to the rural and underprivileged sections of the nation. This chapter attempts to probe into the dynamics of Indian socio-cultural contexts and language education vis-à-vis the proliferation of technology-enhanced language learning (TELL).

Language curriculum, especially, pedagogic principles and classroom methodology, has always been intricately enmeshed in contextual sociopolitical structures and has remained a resulting product of dominant ideologies. With a history of colonial enterprise spanning over two centuries, the contours of English language teaching (ELT) in India too has been sketched by negotiations of socio-cultural and political dynamics that has continued to define the educational matrix of this multicultural, multilingual nation. Alok Mukherjee in *Early English Textbooks and Language Policies in India* (2017) further clarifies the position of an English language classroom as a hegemonic signifier as he notes:

English education did not arise in India due to the interplay of certain abstract or impersonal forces; rather, it happened because of the engagement of individuals and institutions who, to draw on the theoretical concepts promulgated by Pierre Bourdieu, used their social and cultural capitals... English was the 'field,' to use another Bourdeauxian term (Bourdieu, 1984) on which these combatants waged what Antonio Gramsci called a 'war of position' (Gramsci, 1971: p. 108) to establish their 'hegemony' (Mukherjee, 2017: p. 10).

From the conflict between adoption of Eurocentric models of English education and traditional modes in the pre-Independence era through the post-Independence debates regarding construction of an appropriate language curriculum that would address the heterogeneity of linguistic geography of the nation, the journey of ELT in India is a metaphor for the evolution of the nation as it attempts to assert its identity and attain global significance. The economic liberalization in India, by connecting "national economy with world economy as an outcome of new economic policy which has been adopted in 1991" (Meenu, 2013: p. 122) catalyzed globalization and radically transformed the socio-economic scenario of the nation. Due to intersecting globalizing forces and the growth of the internet, there was a proliferation of manifold employment opportunities that necessitated communicative competence in English language and knowledge of digital tools, a combination of which altered the pedagogic fabric of ELT in India. The present chapter aims to study the technological penetration in language classrooms and also seek to unearth the subterranean agents that cause its disproportional dispersal across the country.

Owing to inestimable global digital expansion over the last few decades, the language curriculum has integrated the inexhaustible potential of the internet and digital media, leading to revisions in pedagogic principles, course outcomes, and most significantly, the metamorphosis of the language classroom. Burgeoning technological integration in the learning domain has successfully transfigured the 'nature' of classroom learning by extending its dimensions beyond a spatio-temporally grounded infrastructure. Enlisting the number of ways how "technology-enhanced practices have revolutionized the ways in which we learn and teach languages," Fiona Farr and Liam Murray point out how in the last few years, the space of language teaching has been digitized, resulting in re-evaluation of conventional learning principles and methodologies and the origin of technology-enhanced language learning (TELL) (Farr, 2016: pp. 30, 31). Revision of the traditional language curriculum resulted in designing the course content along constructivist and socio-cultural principles (as proposed by Piaget and Vygotsky) and construction of an outcome-based learning environment that drew from the pedagogic principles of task-based language learning. From defining a task to examining the lacunae in pedagogic principles, Task-based language teaching is one of the most recent modes of language teaching that deals with the integration of digital media in language learning (Ellis, 2003; Samuda and Bygate, 2008). Drawing from Pegrum (2009), Hartmann, and Ditfurth note how, "during the last decade we have moved from a conception of computer literacy to electronic literacy and latterly multi-literacies" that has resulted in "a constant interplay between individual agency and social, economic, historical, and political structures that determine the various discourses and hence, human agency, but which are also changed through human activity." Delineating the collaborative relationship between the individual and learning environment, TBLT in TELL specifies the role of the language teacher as providers of "instructional scaffolds" to the learners (Vygotsky, 1986). This "learner and problem-oriented" approach (Hartman and Ditfurth, 2010: p. 19) has continuously evolved ever since its inception in the 1960s.

Initiated in the language classrooms as video and audio recordings, "the first artificial intelligence program specifically designed for language learning" was developed in 1976 (Todd, 2009: pp. 89, 90). Although computers were being introduced in Western countries, particularly the US, the new media was unable to refurbish the traditional pedagogic practices; "computer applications that were used in the classrooms were copies of approaches that teachers had used, and in some cases, had stopped using over the years" (Pritchard, 2007: p. 2). Tracing the growth of TELL, Ken Beatty records how it was implemented in the institutions of Stanford, Dartmouth, and Essex, where learners' competence in Russian through the

Grammar-Translation method was targeted. The teaching methodology consisted of techniques like oral drills and translation tests that were specifically designed to evaluate the learners' competence in the target language and assess his/her progress (Beatty, 2013: pp. 18–22). Corresponding to the necessity for developing communicative competence among the learners, computer-mediated communication (CMC) ushered in computer-assisted language learning (CALL). The term and nature of the discipline was agreed upon at the TESOL Convention in Toronto (1983; Chapelle, 2001: p. 3). Later, CALL as a discipline, evolved, and proliferated through three major phases, namely, Behaviorist CALL, Communicative CALL and Integrative CALL (Warschauer, 1996; Warschauer and Healey, 1998). Around the 1990s, with the emergence and growth of multimedia and the internet, there was a worldwide attempt to harness its endless potential and language teaching too, attempted to blend the collaborative and task-based learning methods within a technological interface, thereby directing the phase of Integrative CALL. However, only towards the latter half of the 1990s did the internet reach the language classrooms and was identified as a learning resource (Dudeney and Hockly, 2007) referred to in the essay Teacher's Use of Internet Resources for Preparing English Lessons. Liliana Piwasecka). Moving away from traditional Grammar-centered methods of teaching, TELL was causing a shift towards the curriculum being more adaptive, accommodating role-plays which were closer to the learner's practical experience. Such a shift in perspective heralded the wave of harnessing technology in language classrooms to develop what will be later termed as a 'learner-centered' environment (Roy, 2017: p. 45).

However, the creation of a "learner-centered environment" in a technological environment would require a close scrutiny of the learning environment and understanding its possibilities and limitations. The 'techno-space,' notwithstanding its wide penetration and uncharted capabilities, is an unregulated environment for learning by virtue of its vast resource of knowledge. Due to this vastness, it was difficult for curriculum designers, language analysts and facilitators to create a curriculum that would actually integrate technology in the structures of language teaching and hence, long after recognizing the need to embed language teaching methods in technological interface, there were debates regarding the process to do so. Challenging the classification of CALL proposed by Warschauer and Healey, Bax (2003) presented three evolutionary phases of this method, namely: Restricted CALL, Open CALL and Integrated CALL where he observed that as of 2003, we are "using the second approach, Open CALL, but that the aim should be to attain a state of 'normalization' in which the technology is invisible and truly integrated into teachers' everyday practice" (Bax, 2003: 5). Such a statement entails the pedagogical shift towards a learner-centered, constructivist approach where technology will cease to be simply a platform or an interface for language learning but rather be the integral learning environment, an active agent in the teaching-learning scenario. Hailed as the future of educational practices, technology-driven learning is thus, constantly evolving with globally changing socio-cultural scenario. In the present age of globalization and technological penetration of the socio-economic fabric of the society, the need for cultural and linguistic immersion in classrooms have been widely recognized, as a result of which collaborative learning and blended learning methods are being encouraged by educators at almost all levels. Accordingly, CALL has evolved from its initial technological approach to its present negotiation between technological applications and creating a collaborative learning environment-a negotiation that interrogates and locates the learners' needs, pedagogic structures and principles.

With the turn of the millennium, the need for familiarizing the 'context' of learning was recognized, and based on the principles of Situated Learning, 'authentic tasks' and activities were developed for the learners. Based on connecting the original context of the learner with the learning context, which facilitates the learner to respond better and learn faster, learning content was being developed. By this time, the internet and the technology associated with it has already become a familiar 'context' for people worldwide. The advancement and wide availability of technology concurrent with globalizing forces, computers, and other portable gadgets viz., tablets, and mobiles started transforming the learning context by replacing the physical dimension of a classroom with the concept of a space; mostly virtual. Internet, slowly but steadily, started becoming a new site for knowledge creation and dissemination with language teachers gradually overcoming their bias against using the techno-space for learning possibilities. "Flipped classrooms" began reversing the traditional learning methods and took the teaching-learning processes beyond the classroom. Jonathan Bergmann and Aaron Sams, in their *Flip Your Classroom: Reaching Every Student in Every Class Every Day* (2012) argues "Flipping the classroom is more about a mindset: redirecting attention away from the teacher and putting attention on the learner and the learning" and that "basically the concept of a flipped class is this: that which is traditionally done in class is now done at home, and that which is traditionally done as homework is now completed in class." Thus, "flipped classrooms," besides encouraging the students in the language learning process by making the idea of the classroom more flexible in nature, also changes the dynamics and basic structure of a language class. A significant example of technology-assisted flipped classroom is Google Classroom, a virtual interactive space offered by Google, one that has revolutionized the concept of classroom in the digital realm by simulating a classroom environment and replacing its physical structure by a virtual space. This space can be actively used for discussion of the lessons taught, creating modules, submitting assignments, and evaluating them. The teacher can check who has submitted the assignment or monitor the progress of the learner by checking who is still working on it while he/she can provide immediate feedback on the same. The clean and user-friendly interface, great commenting system and accessibility across all devices make it a crucial tool in managing classroom activities on the digital platform, thereby ensuring increased learner participation and interest. In this new classroom setting, the teacher is indeed a facilitator, a moderator who controls the discussions rather than the traditional instructor. With the advent of M-Learning or rather, mobile-assisted language learning (MALL), Collaborative Learning in a digital environment has become easier, and language facilitators are harnessing the technological mobility of the teaching tools available in the digital environment to rethink and revise the language curriculum.

The digital tools that have foraged into the classroom pedagogies in the last few decades are also known as Web 2.0 or second generation of world wide web (WWW). Marking a shift from the traditional classrooms, which depends on lectures, text-books, hand-outs, workbooks, and so on, the interactivity offered by these tools have significantly affected the dynamics of the teaching-learning process by making the classrooms more learner-centric rather than teacher-dominated approach of the traditional classrooms. Following are some of the widely used digital tools employed in language classrooms around the world:

1. **Blendspace:** This is a content creation tool. One of the prime advantages of using Blendspace is that one can save the valuable classroom time for student interaction. It can be used to create lessons in only a few minutes and shared with the students who can use them whenever they find it convenient.

TABLE 11.1 *(Continued)*

Authors	Year	Participants (Age/ Mage and SD)	Sample Size	Country	Method	Loneliness Measure	Findings
Cotton et al.	2013	82.8 (mean age)	205	United States of America	Survey-cross-sectional	3-item version of the UCLA loneliness scale	Internet usage enhances social contact and decrease loneliness
Cotton et al.	2014	>= 50	3075	United States of America	Survey-longitudinal (4 waves of data year 2002–2008)	Center for Epidemiologic Studies Depression Scale (CES-D),	Internet use reduced depression and loneliness, affecting mental health in a positive way
Chopik	2016	>= 50	591	United States of America	Survey-longitudinal	Center for Epidemiologic Studies Depression Scale (CES-D), Satisfaction with life scale	Increase in subjective well-being, health condition and decrease in depressive symptoms through greater social technology use

2. **Padlet:** This is an online "notice board" where students and teachers can collaborate and create a virtual board with multimedia elements. This "digital wall" can also be modified and shared on multiple platforms. By using Padlet, teachers can also encourage students to be more creative.

3. **Scoop.it:** This is a content-creating tool which can also act like a social network. It allows to create a board of curated content. In a language classroom, it can be used in several ways, like creating an online magazine or making classroom projects.

4. **Livebinders:** Through Livebinders, a teacher can create a hub for the resources available on the web across all formats. It also helps to view links almost like pages in a book rather than URLs on a page. It provides the facility to make the page either public or private.

5. **Voxopop:** This is an audio tool that allows its users to record their voice on a given topic. It can be used to create online verbal discussions, thereby maximizing spoken English exercises. A teacher can keep track of the students' progress which may help him/her for assessment. One major advantage of this tool is that it can encourage students who are shy and unwilling to participate in classroom discussions.

6. **Gamification:** There are many game-based learning platforms which use lots of activities and processes to solve problems and, in the process, increase the player's / learner's language skills. Learn-Match, Get Set, Go! Phonics, Mind Snacks, The Language Game are among the widely used language learning gamification tools.

7. **PaperRater:** It is a website which is devoted to the writing skills of the learner. It uses artificial intelligence to check for plagiarism, grammar, punctuation, and spelling, and incorporates automated essay scoring.

However, despite the dazzling brilliance and ubiquity of these above-mentioned digital tools for language learning, the biggest challenge of implementing these tools in a curriculum is, as previously noted, designing the curriculum accordingly. Litchfield, Dyson, Lawrence, and Zmijewska (2007) rightly observed: "A body of knowledge of learning and teaching principles and strategies is urgently needed to inform teachers wishing to utilize innovative mobile technologies and also to inform the development of national policy and pedagogical approaches about emerging mobile devices" (Litchfield et al., 2007: p. 591). Digital divide, causing lack of technological infrastructure and the language trainer's limited grip over technology may create obstacles in such learning process. The planning regarding the use of digital tools also must align with the curriculum. The resources and infrastructure required for the digital resources can also be expensive; hence, additional efforts and improvisation may be required in order to make these materials available and effective for learners with disabilities. But most importantly, teachers should be aware of the proper and effective ways of integrating the digital tools in the classroom. Dooly remarks, "if we are truly interested in preparing our students to be responsible citizens in an increasingly technologically advanced society, then our way of teaching our students must reflect this" (Dooly, 2008: p. 23).

TELL in India was almost always viewed as an adjunct, "a support system to regular classroom teaching" (Usha, 2013: p. 270). One of the main reasons behind the lack of integrating technological tools in language classrooms was the digital divide across the nation, arising as an offshoot of the economic divide in the nation. Besides the inaccessibility of digital platforms in some parts of the country, especially rural, another factor that barred the digital tools in educational usage was the bias among the teachers and curriculum designers who had no appropriate model that would curate an effective language curriculum out of technology and can be successfully implemented in pan-Indian context. This remark corroborates with Rodger's Diffusion theory where he reflects on the uncertainty and anxiety generated "in the minds of potentials adopters" by a "technological innovation" (Rodgers, 1983: p. 13). Rodgers associates the 'diffusion' of 'innovations' as "a kind of *social change,* defined as the process by which alteration occurs in the structure and function of a social system. When new ideas are invented, diffused, and are adopted or rejected, leading to certain consequences, social change occurs" (Rodgers, 1983, p.6).

Globalization in India paved the way for diverse employment opportunities; these new sectors required a new set of skills, mainly, spoken, and communicative competence. Accordingly, functional learning techniques were being incorporated in the language curriculum that focused on the use of the target language (L_T) as an authentic input. It was also around this time that using digital platforms in classrooms, particularly language classrooms were being discussed. However, the idea of using digital tools in classrooms at that time were limited to using pre-recorded audio-visual samples; it took another decade for the Digital revolution to happen where pedagogic principles would be scrutinized and the desperate need for updating the curriculum would be envisaged. The turn of the millennium and subsequent proliferation of digital tools in language teaching worldwide had a significant impact on the Indian education system as well. Smart and digital classrooms were envisaged as the future of learning both by administrators who recognized the potential of technology-enhanced education system in updating the national status in the global sphere as well as language facilitators who could upgrade the learning process by instilling "metacognitive" awareness among the learners. The Position Paper of National Focus Group on Teaching of English (NCERT, 2006) recognizes an "input rich environment" as an essential factor for language learning, and hints at the creation of such an environment where a learner will have access to a repertoire of knowledge and will possess the set of skills that would enable him/her to process the knowledge and harness it for practical, functional purposes.

In the last 5 years, however, there has been a marked change in the approach and perspectives regarding technology-enabled language teaching in India, especially at the urban quarters. With the shift from teacher-centered education to student-centered learning, the teachers became facilitators in the process of learning and not merely a singular source of information. Simultaneously, classrooms were no longer limited to their infrastructural existence but became identified as sites for knowledge creation and platforms for individual and ubiquitous learning. In the last 5 years, technology has unfurled its infinite possibilities and accessed the lower rungs of the society. The aggressive expansion of internet services in India made it the fastest-growing market for digital consumption; by the year 2018, there were "560 million internet subscribers" in the country (Kaka, 2019: p. 1). By this time, the administrators, curriculum designers, facilitators were taking active steps in promoting digital learning. The Ministry of Human Resource Development, India has created an integrated platform and portal for readily available online courses (NPTEL-SWAYAM) to encourage ubiquitous and synchronous learning among learners and teachers. Digital tools are now used by teachers in classrooms to integrate constructivist and interaction-based approaches of learning, from the junior school levels to graduate and post-graduate courses of study. Learning applications developed by companies like BYJU'S are emerging as parallel learning platforms beside school classrooms where a learner can access and download learning contents in technological devices (desktop, laptop, mobiles, tablets) and progress through the learning process in a similar way as they progress through mobile and computer games. The contents are simple, easy to understand, and require active engagement of the learners with the learning process. By virtue of familiarity of the learning context (the digital platform), the learning process being based on self-learning and the learner having full autonomy over the space (vast learning environment having access to unlimited knowledge), pace (of the learning) and way (without the intervention of a teacher, since in these learning applications, contents are digitally designed and most often, a digitally created voice explains concepts and ideas for the learner to understand), the learner is way more motivated to learn in this technology-enhanced learning environment than a traditional teacher-centered classroom. Interestingly, most teachers at present, are recommending the use of digital tools to their students (especially in higher levels, graduate, and postgraduate courses of study) and themselves using web tools in their classes. To ensure maximum student engagement, teachers use virtual class lecture simulations (in spaces like Google Doc, Padlet), conduct face-to-face interactions beyond the class hours (through video conferencing apps like Skype, Zoom) and use platforms and web applications like Google Classroom, Dot Storming and ArcGis for classroom activities. These applications are free to use, available in user-friendly platforms, and most significantly, they reduce the learners' anxieties as the learners engage in a learning environment through a platform that they are proficient in.

Language teaching through technology, though not developed to its full potential, is steadily gaining ground in India. One of the major reasons why the growth and proliferation of TELL in India is delayed and slow-paced is because of the language teaching history in the nation. India has a long history of teacher-centered education system where the 'guru' is unanimously considered as the seat of truth, a signifier of finality and authority, and the learning environment, the classroom bears the same hallmark of sanctity. Such a tradition has further complicated the technological intervention in classrooms; the scope of digital tools are often not accepted by the learners because of their bias towards traditional teaching methodology and often not recognized by the teachers who, having been educated in the traditional modes of learning, are skeptical about adopting technologies in the curriculum. Besides skepticism and bias towards integrating technology in teaching, the other challenge that Indian language teachers were facing was addressing functional skills of language in the curriculum and developing a teaching methodology that significantly draws from constructivist principles and situated learning. Meanwhile, institutes, and organizations like British Council, India were attempting to develop language learning platforms and courses where the learners could approach the skills of language learning in the form of micro-units. In the last 3 years, there has been an unprecedented growth in language learners willing and preferring the integration of technology in their learning environment as validated by the extensive enrolment of language learners in online courses and e-learning platforms. As of 2016, "India after US, is dominating the global growth in enrolment" (in Massive Open Online Courses) (Chauhan, 2017: p. 111), indicating the readiness of learners to pursue learning in techno-space. Some digital tools used exclusively for language teaching and learning are applications like DuoLingo, Memrise, Babbel, LinguaLift, and HelloTalk. These application software (apps) are available in free and paid versions, can be easily downloaded in smartphones, desktops/laptops, and tablets, and are used by language teachers and learners in the classrooms and beyond. The learners use these apps to learn their desired language skill at his/her desired pace and mode. As recorded in *The Economic Times*, the online language learning app, DuoLingo "has seen a 13-fold increase in active users in India after introducing an option last year to learn English from Hindi" (Shankar, 2017). This learning platform offers a set of lessons categorized under various skill-sets, for example, listening exercises that involve flashcards and oral drills. One of the significant features of this digital tool is that it allows the users to trace not only his/her own progress but also compare it with other users using the same platform. This feature helps to keep the learner motivated in the learning process and feel actively engaged. The app Memrise is very similar to Duolingo as it helps increase the vocabulary and grammar of the learner. It uses the technique of repetition and mnemonics to increase the retentive capacity of the learner, and besides memorizing the vocabulary and grammar structures, the learner starts to associate the vocabulary with situations creatively. LinguaLift is a language app that requires the intervention of a professional tutor to help with developing linguistic competence in English. This app categorizes its learning modules into progressive levels of language learning. Besides English, this app also targets competence in other languages like French, Japanese, Spanish, and Russian. Babbel uses MCQs, listening exercises and other self-evaluative techniques that help a learner to assess his/ her own competence. HelloTalk is a fun way of learning real-time conversation; this app focuses on developing communicative competence in the learners by engaging them in a collaborative language learning setup that resembles a WhatsApp chatbox. The rationale behind this approach is providing the learners a familiar platform of learning – a platform that they usually do not associate with educational curriculum. This is, in fact, the main aim of employment of digital tools in modern-day classrooms-to decrease learning anxiety by simulating the learning environment with one they usually associate with games, social networking, and other spaces that they are comfortable in. Thus incorporation of digital tools in contemporary classrooms is an extension of, or rather, a culmination of reconstructing the idea of a classroom that is no longer an infrastructural component of the educational curriculum, no longer simply a site for learning but rather a flexible, malleable psycho-geographic space that actively takes part in the learning process.

However, while analyzing TELL in the Indian context, the questions that remain unanswered are the ones that interrogate the success of 'virtual classrooms' in a nation grappling with economic concerns, leading to a digital divide. Besides access and availability of technological services, pedagogic principles and adequate teacher training are also major factors that inhibit language learning in a technologically mediated environment. In India, technology has widely been associated with Western intervention in the traditional, national core values, and hence, most often, technology-driven learning is seen as a replacement of the 'body' of the teacher with an artificial, mechanical system. Besides the dilemma regarding accepting the virtual space of learning, lack of technological infrastructure and production of learning content acts as the biggest impediment in appropriating technology in the language classrooms (Chauhan, 2017: pp. 119, 120). Creating an effective curriculum is also a challenge since the language learning models that are followed in other nations cannot be adopted and implemented in the ELT classrooms of India owing to its heterogeneous demography and the diversity in learning needs. Data from surveys conducted to assess digital penetration in India shows that learning institutes located in cities and developed suburbs have already integrated technology in their language classrooms or are moving towards digitizing the classrooms; however, in the villages, there has been significantly low digital penetration. The irony is, although in the last 3 years, there has been a revolution in access to internet services across the nation, with most people living in the rural areas having access to mobile phones and internet services too, utilizing the digital domain for language learning and other educational purposes is not only beyond the imagination of the users but also teachers and educators who consider mobile phones and such technological tools as distractions and detrimental to the learning process. The present picture of TELL in India thus narrates not only the dilemma regarding the adoption of language learning in a technological interface but also throws light on the subterranean sociopolitical and cultural issues that mediate education in the nation.

KEYWORDS

- **computer-assisted language learning**
- **computer-mediated communication**
- **curriculum**
- **digital tools**
- **English language teaching**
- **mobile-assisted language learning**

REFERENCES

Bax, S., (2003). CALL-past, present and future. *System, 31*(1), 13–28. https://doi.org/10.1016/s0346-251x(02)00071-4.

Beatty, K., (2013). *Teaching and Researching: Computer-Assisted Language Learning.* Routledge.

Bergmann, J., & Sams, A., (2012). *Flip Your Classroom: Reach Every Student in Every Class Every Day.* International Society for Technology in Education.

Chapelle, C., (2001). *Computer Applications in Second Language Acquisition.* Cambridge University Press.

Chauhan, J., (2017). An overview of MOOC in India. *International Journal of Computer Trends and Technology, 49*(2), 111–120. Retrieved from: https://doi.org/10.14445/22312803/ijctt-v49p117.

Dooly, M., (2008). *Telecollaborative Language Learning: A Guidebook to Moderating Intercultural Collaboration Online.* Peter Lang.

Dudeney, G., & Hockly, N., (2007). *How to Teach English with Technology.* Pearson Education Limited.

Elis, R., (2003). *Task-Based Language Learning and Teaching.* Oxford University Press.

Farr, F., & Murray, L., (2016). *The Routledge Handbook of Language Learning and Technology.* Routledge.

Kaka, N., Madgavkar, A., Kshirsagar, A., Gupta, R., Manyika, J., Bahl, K., & Gupta, S., (2019). *Digital India: Technology to Transform a Connected Nation.* McKinsey Global Institute. Retrieved from: https://www.mckinsey.com/~/media/McKinsey/Business%20Functions/McKinsey%20Digital/Our%20Insights/Digital%20India%20Technology%20to%20transform%20a%20connected%20nation/Digital-India-technology-to-transform-a-connected-nation-Executive-Summary.ashx (accessed on 24 February 2021).

Litchfield, A., Dyson, L., Lawrence, E., & Zmijewska, A., (2007). Directions for m-learning research to enhance active learning. In: Atkinson, R. J., McBeath, C., Soong, S. K. A., & Cheers, C., (eds.), *ICT: Providing Choices for Learners and Learning. Proceedings Ascilite Singapore 2007.* Centre for Educational Development, Nanyang Technological University, Singapore. Retrieved from: https://www.ascilite.org/conferences/singapore07/procs/litchfield.pdf (accessed on 24 February 2021).

Meenu, (2013). Impact of globalization and liberalization on Indian administration. *International Journal of Marketing, Financial Services and Management Research, 2*(9), 120–125. http://indianresearchjournals.com/pdf/IJMFSMR/2013/September/13.pdf (accessed on 24 February 2021).

Mukherjee, A., (2017). Early English textbooks and language policies in India. In: Sridhar, M., & Sunita, M., (eds.), *Language Policy and Education in India: Documents, Contexts and Debates.* Routledge.

Muller-Hartmann, A., & Schocker-v, D. M., (2010) Research on the use of technology in task-based language teaching. In: Michael, T., & Hayo, R., (eds.), *Task-Based Language Learning and Teaching with Technology.* Continuum International Publishing Group.

Pegrum, M., (2009). *From Blogs to Bombs: The Future of Digital Technologies in Education.* University of Western Australia Press.

Pritchard, A., (2007). *Effective Teaching with Internet Technologies: Pedagogy and Practice.* SAGE.

Rodgers, E. M., (1983). *Diffusion of Innovations.* The Free Press.

Roy, D., (2017). Learning 'via' media to learning 'with' media: Evolving trends in computer-assisted language learning. In: Sumit, N., & Leena, S. B., (eds.), *Proceedings of National Conference on ELT for Management and Technology: Recent Trends (NCEMT 2017)* (pp. 43–50). Kolkata: Ideal International E-Publication Pvt. Ltd.

Samuda, V., & Bygate, M., (2008). *Tasks in Second Language Learning.* Palgrave Macmillan.

Shankar, S., (2017). *India is the Biggest Emerging Market for Language Learning App Duolingo.* The Economic Times.

Todd, R. W., (2009). Computer-assisted language learning: Its Future. In: Vyas, M. A., & Patel, Y. L., (eds.), *Teaching English as a Second Language: A New Pedagogy for a New Century* (pp. 89–99). Phi Learning Pvt. Ltd.

Usha, B. A., (2013). *Computer-Assisted Language Learning (CALL) Materials for Indian Students: A Study [Doctoral Dissertation].* https://shodhganga.inflibnet.ac.in/handle/10603/8539 (accessed on 24 February 2021).

Vygotsky, L., (1986). *Thought and Language.* The MIT Press.

CHAPTER 13

Electronic Customer Relationship Management (eCRM)

DEBASTUTI DASGUPTA[1] and ALOK KUMAR SAHAI[2]

[1]Assistant Professor, Department of Journalism and Mass Communication. Asutosh College, Kolkata, West Bengal, India

[2]Associate Professor, Faculty of Management Studies, Sri University, Cuttack, Odisha, India

ABSTRACT

Customer relationship management (CRM) has come of age with computerized information systems. Manufacturers and service providers are striving to provide better service to customers and satisfy them profitably. With an increasing share of e-commerce in business, the electronic CRM (eCRM) uses IT to reach and serve the desirable customers in order to increase the value of the relationship. eCRM enables companies to manage customer relationships in real-time. Technology-based eCRM enables companies like Amazon to understand the various microsegments of customers, predict their long-term worth to the company and serve them better and faster. eCRM is a business process of acquiring, retaining, and growing profitable customers. Two main types of eCRM can be identified; operational and analytical. Operations eCRM involves actual contact with the customer through electronic means such as the internet. Analytical eCRM processes the information collected by operational eCRM. Fourth-generation mobile networks have exponentially increased the usefulness of operational and analytical eCRM.

In the last decade, social media have taken the frontstage as the dominant force in the way people interact with each other. Consumers have started sharing data using social media applications such as Facebook,

Twitter, Snapchat and have migrated from basic web-based interactions to social media interactions on their mobile phones. Firms have been quick to join the social media bandwagon causing a metamorphosis of eCRM into social CRM (sCRM). Facebook, with close to 2.5 billion users, and WhatsApp with approximately 1.7 billion users have access to a wealth of customer information such as name, location, preferences, education, language, friends, images, likes, shares, and events, which are key in predictive analysis of customer demand.

The sCRM and awareness of the potentials of social media in customer facing processes has taken center stage in CRM. Firms are convinced of the added value of sCRM for themselves and their customers. sCRM, however, is not without its shortcomings. Data security and winning the trust of the customers is important as far as the data security and integrity is concerned. The potential of sCRM is immense, provided the customers can be won over in parting with their personal information, which can be used as tags in predictive analysis of consumer behavior leading to mutual profitability.

The information has always been the lifeblood of the marketplaces. Computerized information systems of the last half-century have enabled new organizational forms, with the constellations of firms delivering their products as a virtual company, and with process specialists, such as DHL, FedEx, emerging to serve across industries and across countries. Most products in today's marketplaces are either information-based, or are a part of a package involving a physical good, information, and information-based service. Examples would be a customized computer system delivered by Dell, an electronic airline ticket priced by a yield-management system, or an online shopping portal that uses predictive analytics to show the content of choice of the customer. The augmented product is far more responsive to the marketplace and to the customer than in the past. The worldwide web (WWW) driving this transformation today is certainly not the culmination of the change process. It is as certainly a major technological discontinuity, opening the world to transformative technologies. With multiple options available to the customers in market economies, the competition for best customers becomes an engine of economic growth. The competition for customers occurs at the firm level and the firms need to focus all their activities on profitably serving their customers. This means, in turn, being able to continually identify, reach, and satisfy the customers with long-term profitability.

CRM is the strategy with precisely that aim. A multifaceted effort, CRM has been defined in many ways. CRM can be seen as a business strategy to acquire and manage relationships with customers in order to maximize the long-term value of these relationships. Basically, the firm implementing CRM aims to increase the loyalty of profitable customers and to increase the profitability and satisfaction of loyal customers. This is the point of view of the owner firm. From the customer's perspective, an effective CRM program means that the firm satisfies the customer more completely than any competing firm could do. This generates customer loyalty. Indeed, the fundamental premise of CRM is a high level of financial return on customer loyalty. Customer equity is a crucial endowment of a firm (Rust, Zeithaml, and Lemon, 2000). Selecting and acquiring customers based on their lifetime value results in higher profits than seeking out customers based on other criteria (Venkatesan and Kumar, 2004). Metrics are available to actually calculate this return (Pfeifer and Farris, 2004). CRM is a significant development in the shift of the business and marketing orientation from the product focus to the customer focus. The immediately obvious aspects of CRM have then to be these: an integrated view of the customer and the customer's dealings with the firm; the primacy of the long, relational attitude toward the customer over the short-sighted, transactional view; increasingly more refined individualized approach to a customer over the span of the relationship; knowledge of the projected value of the existing customers to the firm over the long term; and a large degree of knowledge of non-customers and of what separates some of them from becoming desirable customers. This brief analysis of CRM tells us that the strategy is impossible without advanced and integrated information systems, centering on data warehouses for the longitudinal analysis of the total view of the customers and on integrated databases for the delivery of service to them. This is, of course, not enough. The organizational transformation into customer-focused culture, customer-oriented business processes, the customer-centric performance metrics, new incentive systems deriving from creating lasting customer relationships, are all necessary components of CRM. Such companies as Indigo Airlines come to mind. Indeed, relationship marketing, the underlying premise of CRM, cannot be effective without an appropriate use of information technology (IT) (Zineldin, 2000). Today, customers are reached via multiple channels, integrating the Internet-based touchpoints of the web and email, delivered also over mobile devices, with the direct marketing and brick-and-mortar-based sales. It is necessary to sustain consistent, unified interaction with the customer across all the touchpoints, from the web to the store, and across all the company's units interacting with the customer, from sales to service (Pan and Lee, 2003). Moreover, integrated collaboration with channel partners such as distributors and retailers is necessary for a producer. Each interaction with the customer, be it a sale or a well-handled customer complaint, ought to have a positive effect on the relationship. As e-commerce becomes increasingly embedded in the physical world, we can no longer treat the internet-based touchpoints in isolation (Zwass, 2002). Hence, electronic CRM (eCRM) has come to signify the use of IT to reach and serve the desirable customers, as well as to increase their value to the vendor over the relationship's time. eCRM enables the company to manage customer relationships in real-time, bringing to bear the necessary information to all the events in this relation-ship. Examples of success abound. Thus, Dell manages the demand for its customized products in real-time, by modifying the offer terms across the customer touchpoints based on the current availability of the components. eCRM mobilizes the collective knowledge of the firm's employees, making it available to a marketing consultant visiting the client's office, and brings out the collective knowledge of a virtual company, making it available to the client of financial services. Amazon captures customer loyalty in its online shopping platforms through the pervasive use of data mining. The technology enables the company to get to understand the various microsegments of its customers, predict their long-term worth to the online shopping site, and devise comprehensive incentives for the customers to indeed increase that worth. Amazon is also using IT to measure their employees service performance based on extensive customer-oriented metrics. eCRM can provide informational dashboards that allow tracking the effects of various CRM initiatives weekly or even daily, as needed. eCRM is being deployed in the consumer-oriented (B2C) and in the business-to-business (B2B) commerce. As one example from the B2C commerce, CRM needs to provide profitably the special levels of service for the special customers, as the credit cards and airlines do it, with several levels of special treatment. Several models of co-production may be supported, with the customers taking an increasingly more active role in shaping products (Klein et al., 2005). Customer participation in the product life cycle ranges from co-innovation in the product development to joint personalization and configuration during the acquisition, on to the feedback during the ongoing product support. The customer is a crucial element in a firm's innovation, since as the users of the vendor's products, both consumers and firms are increasingly able to adapt the information-containing products to new contexts (von Hippel, 2005). In B2B commerce, CRM needs to ensure an integrated global view of the customer to the seller firm, and a uniform product or service where needed and country-specific where desired service to the customer are needed. With an effective eCRM, it should be possible to expand the existing relationships and pursue—profitably—a greater share of the customer's business (Anderson and Narus, 2003). eCRM is becoming a part of a Sense-and-Respond organization, with an IT-enabled capability of adaptation to a rapidly changing business environment (Kapoor et al., 2005). The company has to be classified by the customer on the basis of ease of doing business with. Kalakota and Robinson (2003) have identified the eCRM supported functions into these heads: target (market planning), engage (market), transact, retain (deploying analytics), and service (assist throughout product's lifetime). In various instances, the vendor also helps the customers to retire the product. eCRM delivers results only after a purposive, comprehensive, and painstaking process of organizational change, as part of the overall CRM. Indeed, too few companies are paying enough attention to the organizational challenges inherent in any CRM initiative (Agarwal et al., 2005), with the resulting disappointments. A facile comparison between the direct cost of the customer order taken by a qualified individual and that of the customer being sent into an interactive voice response system motivates CRM implementations doomed to fail. The firm will not learn from the interaction with the customer and, in fact, the customer will likely look for another vendor. The customer expects access to the vendor at any time in the form preferred by the customer. Moreover, it is productive access that the customer expects, where the counterpart on the firm's side is fully informed and empowered to assist. Zuboff (2002) postulate that a solution to the customer's problem goes beyond the corporate boundaries, with collaborative eCRM gaining in importance. If the customer contacts a product or service firm, the customer partnerships need to come into play seamlessly and be transparent to the customer. The total customer experience is likely to be based on a company's weakest link. Three components of eCRM are identified namely, Analytical based on the big data analysis of large chunks of customer data, frequently involving data mining from data warehouses, Operational or delivering top-notch customer service in an integrated fashion across all touchpoints, and Collaborative or coordinating the activities of all business partners in the delivery of customer service. The leading suppliers of CRM software, such as Siebel Systems, SAP, Oracle, PeopleSoft, and Teradata, continually enhance their enterprise software, for example, by adding new process components. IT implementation has to be accompanied by the appropriate IT management practices, with the greater involvement of IT personnel in corporate CRM policies and practices to make the best use of the investments in IT infrastructure (Karimi et al., 2001). Successful implementations of CRM generally require an incremental approach, yet with great attention paid to the data infrastructure and also to the organizational change processes (Goodhue et al., 2002). IT is an enabler of CRM, but getting closer to customer isn't only about an IT system (Gulati and Oldroyd, 2005). CRM itself is no substitute for a great product and process innovation. Although these facts are known about all the organizational information systems, they should be particularly heeded when deploying IT in dealing with customers in the ever more competitive global marketplace. It is the goal of eCRM to assist the competing firm in acquiring a greater share of customer's perception as well as the market share.

13.1   DEFINING ELECTRONIC CRM (ECRM)

CRM has changed over the years from a customer service business unit loosely linked to marketing to an overactive electronic dynamo attempting to maximize the value of existing customer relationships. Dyché (2002) suggests that CRM is the infrastructure that enables the delineation of an increase in customer value, and the correct means by which to motivate valuable customers to remain loyal and be motivated for repeat purchase. The infrastructure consists of the people and processes that an organization has at its disposal to understand, motivate, and attract its customers. It is the technology that enables the organization to improve customer service, differentiate customers, and deliver a unique customer experience. For example, a large retailer like Wal-Mart, the infrastructure is an enterprise data warehouse (Swift, 2001). This eCRM system enables the company to collect massive amounts of data to manage the ever-changing needs of customers and the marketplace. Coupled with people and processes, it permits the integration of operational data with analytics, modeling, historical data, and predictive knowledge management to give its customers what they need and want at the right time. CRM and eCRM are about firms capturing and keeping customers through the Internet in real-time. CRM is about customers interacting with employees, employees collaborating with suppliers, and every interaction's being an opportunity to maintain and improve a relationship.

eCRM has attracted the attention of e-business managers and academic researchers who are interested in increasing repeat business and customer loyalty. Various researchers have defined the eCRM according to different aspects. eCRM is a business strategy that utilizes the power of technology to tie together all aspects of a company's business with the goal of building long-term customer loyalty (Jukic, Jukic, Meamber, and Nezlek, 2003). Jukic et al. (2003) also stressed that eCRM, in practical terms, is the management of customer interactions at all levels, channels, and media. Hansen (2000) sees eCRM as a process of acquiring, retaining and growing profitable customers. It requires a clear focus on the service attributes that represent value to the customer and that create "loyalty." eCRM involves attracting and keeping economically valuable customers while repelling and eliminating economically unviable ones (Romano and Fjermestad, 2003). Overall in the marketing domain, eCRM is to build and maximize the value of the relationship with the customer and to improve customer retention rates (Jukic et al., 2002; Cho, Im, Hiltz, and Fjermestad, 2002). Issues of eCRM have been developed from relationship marketing, which is to establish, maintain, and enhance relationships with customers and other partners, at a profit, so that the objectives of the parties involved are met (Grönroos, 2000). At the lowest level of a relationship, marketers build a financial bond with customers by using pricing strategies (promotional emailers and price discounts to individual users such as AJIO, Flipkart, and Amazon). At a level-two relationship, marketers stimulate social interaction with customers. Managing online community is one of the strategies for a level-two relationship. For a deeper-level relationship, e-businesses rely on creating structural solutions to customer problems. Offering customization service is a good example of level-three relationship (Strauss, El-Ansary, and Frost, 2003). Among various levels of relationship marketing, online companies have been paying attention to making stronger relationships in order to retain existing or create future customers. For example, customization of online communities has been used to maintain a strong relationship with customers. While the Internet services are getting popular, one of the most important challenges is to achieve customer satisfaction and maintain customer loyalty. Julta, Craig, and Bodorik (2001) note that customer metrics affect eCRM; they include customer retention, satisfaction, acquisition, and profitability. Cho, Im, Hiltz, and Fjermestad (2002) posit that minimizing customer dissatisfaction and complaints is a key to successful eCRM.

13.2 NATURE OF eCRM

The foundation of eCRM is the application of traditional CRM methodologies, techniques, and tools to data garnered via electronic commerce as opposed to traditional channels of distribution. Traditional CRM may be defined as a process that balances the use of corporate resources with the satisfaction of customer needs. Traditional CRM looks at outputs in terms of revenues and profits while taking customer value and motivation into account (Shaw, 1999; Gebert et al., 2003). Information technology (IT) is integral to the successful application of CRM, and the definition of CRM may be extended to incorporate the significance of Internet-based technology in managing customer relationships. Plakoyiannaki and Tzokas (2002) formulate a model of the CRM process that revolves around this extended definition. They define the following tasks for the CRM process:

- Creating a corporate culture conducive to customer orientation, learning, and innovations;
- Making customer value a key component of the corporate strategy and planning process;
- Collecting and transforming customer data to aid strategic and operational decision making;
- Appreciating, identifying, and nurturing knowledge creation, dissemination, and use within the organization;
- Developing clear market segments and customer portfolios;
- Defining, developing, and delivering the value proposition;
- Using campaign and channel management as part of the value proposition;
- Measuring performance at each stage of the process to navigate decision making.

eCRM accomplishes these same tasks with the benefit of electronically gathered information, and in such a way as to tailor the service level specific to each customer (Romano and Fjermestad, 2003). For example, logistical services may be tailored to better meet customer needs in a profitable fashion (Fuller, O'Conor, and Rawlinson, 1993). In their pre-internet article, the authors address the challenges of providing a level of service appropriate to the need of logistically distinct businesses, which serve to cluster customers into categories so that the service creation can be provided most efficiently. Before the Internet days, customers would be segmented by logistics requirements, followed by the establishment of a service standard for each segment, and a reconfiguration of the logistics pipelines so that each segment could be served efficiently, according to its newly identified and specially tailored level of service. Fuller et al. (1993) illustrate this with a telecom equipment manufacturer example. It highlights customers with distinctly different needs, including one who needs components for new system installation to be delivered as a complete order. The telecom manufacturer's use of a series of eight variables for segmenting products may disaggregate its customers into some 384 market buckets. The steps identified previously encompass a vision of the CRM process and represent a foundation on which to define eCRM. Gurau et al. (2003) propose descriptions of the transition from traditional forms of media associated with CRM to eCRM-based ones. eCRM involves the collection and mining of data involving online purchases and relationships. In many ways, it can be thought of as a necessary tool for conducting supply chain management (SCM). eCRM also involves using the knowledge gained to improve customer loyalty, expand sales, and improve customer service. CRM and eCRM represent relationship marketing, in direct contrast to traditional marketing mix approaches known as transaction marketing.

Two main types of eCRM exist: operational and analytical (Dyche, 2001; Fjermestad and Romano, 2003). Operational eCRM involves actual contact with the customer through electronic means such as an online Web form or internet portals. The processing of data collected through operational eCRM is analytical eCRM. This involves many of the same techniques as traditional CRM, such as data mining, to glean valuable information about current and potential customers. By definition, any electronic contact with a customer through which data can be gathered for further analysis can be considered a form of eCRM. eCRM has shown the potential to take a quantum leap forward with the tremendous expansion of wireless networking and mobile telephony across the globe. Fourth-generation cellular networks promise high-speed Internet connections, multimedia messaging, and a host of other services such as location-based value-added services which inform wireless users about goods and services available in their immediate area. Knowing the purchasing habits of customers and their cellular/wireless device numbers/network IDs can only lead to developing a more intimate relationship as they travel about. The ability to integrate location-based information about a company's goods or services with traditional e-CRM principles has the potential to even create a new form of eCRM.

13.3   ONLINE SUPPLY CHAIN AND eCRM

Customer relationship management (CRM) and SCM have been the focus of a great deal of practitioner interest and academic research over the last decade. CRM has allowed companies to spend more of their time and resources on valuable customers that make up the majority of their sales and profits. Customer identification/loyalty and savings cards that are used during retail sales transactions are just one example of the use of CRM that allows companies to tailor their goods/services, marketing, and support appropriately. Such cards are common in consumer goods markets and have made their way into the entertainment service industry as well (Loveman, 2003). SCM has allowed companies to gain efficiencies as well as increased sales through reductions in inventories, lead times, and paperwork processing. The tremendous growth of the Internet has led to the development of online versions of both CRM and SCM. eCRM research is still in its initial stages and has focused primarily on the marketing aspects of online transactions (Romano and Fjermestad, 2003). Likewise, research in online SCM has come about only in recent years. An SCM application is effective, in the most general terms, when it produces efficiencies or increases sales for one or more members of the supply chain. For example, an online transportation exchange is effective when it successfully matches buyers of transportation services with providers in a profitable manner for all involved, including the shipper, the carrier, and the intermediary. An online collaborative forecasting application such as collaborative planning, forecasting, and replenishment (CPFR) (McKaige, 2001; White, 1999) is effective when the cost and the responsiveness of the supply network improve because of the Internet-based collaboration. A useful frame of reference is the set of effectiveness metrics advocated by the supply chain operations reference (SCOR) model: reliability, responsiveness/flexibility, cost, and asset management. These metrics define effectiveness in an operational sense directly to SCM, incorporating both productivity and customer-related concerns. In the context of eCRM, effectiveness or success includes the ability to tailor the goods or services provided throughout the supply chain to the needs of each member using an analysis of ordering and related information. eCRM success may also be measured in a similar fashion with the SCOR model metrics. In the case of SCM, reliability can be defined as the ability to have stable lead times for products or materials managed online. For eCRM, reliability can be defined as the ability to quickly identify and serve valuable customers in various online contexts. The other three metrics apply to both in a similar fashion. In this way, the performance of both SCM and eCRM can be measured in a multidimensional fashion. This is especially important, because the mission, strategy, and objectives of the firms participating in the online initiatives can vary considerably, based on the value of the product offered to customers (Keeney, 1999).

13.4   CUSTOMER SATISFACTION AND eCRM

Electronic commerce relies on customer interactions via a computer and telecommunications infrastructure for the purpose of advertising, promoting, and selling products and services online. Electronic commerce replicates most of the physical activities that take place in the market-place, to the point where increasing use of electronic commerce is shifting companies to new market spaces. The traditional marketplace emphasizes customer satisfaction as a way to earn consumer loyalty and attract new customers. To be successful in a market space, a firm must be responsive to its virtual customers' wants, needs, and desires and manage interactions with them properly in order to arrive at a profitable outcome. Marketing considers that interactions between customers or potential customers and the firm result in best payoffs when: (a) such interactions lead to the sale of a given goods or service; and/or (b) such interactions lead to an increased likelihood that a sale of the same or other goods or services will happen in the near future to the satisfaction of both parties. The customer gains through a satisfying purchase of a product or service and the firm gains by selling this product or service. Increased customer satisfaction will increase the likelihood that the customer will purchase again or induce other potential customers to buy, through either testimonials or word-of-mouth effects.

Under this scenario, moving from the marketplace to the market space poses new challenges to the firm. Many years of experience have enabled them to manage a marketplace, but market space is the result of a burgeoning internet. In addition to the new realities of the market space, the constant development of the Web as a new environment medium opens significant challenges to marketers, which they may not be well prepared to face. The key new element is the dynamic nature of the interactive system used by customers to gain access to a firm's website, and what happens after the website has been reached. Under this scenario, three important questions must be answered: (a) How does a firm attract potential customers to its own website? (b) Once customers enter the firm's website, how can the website convince the customer for the best mutually beneficial outcome? (c) How must the firm adjust its marketing information systems to ensure that proper information and feedback is obtained from market space interactions for better management decision making? These three questions are not independent, i.e., the satisfaction experienced by potential customers reaching a firm's website will depend on the prior experience and expectations that they build along the way. Firm management will not have a clue as to what happened if proper arrangements are not made to capture the customers' satisfaction with the overall process. Because a market space is a unique blend of marketing activities in a virtual interactive electronic environment, the issue of customer satisfaction/dissatisfaction must be measured both from the traditional marketing viewpoint and in terms of the more recent IT views about interactive systems.

13.5   EVOLUTION OF eCRM INTO SOCIAL CRM (sCRM)

In the last decade, social media has been the dominant force in the way people interact with each other. Consumers have started sharing data using social media applications such as Facebook, Twitter, Snapchat and have come off the basic web-based interactions to the social media interactions which are accessible with the mobile devices. Firms have not wasted time in joining the social media bandwagon and eCRM has slowly morphed into social CRM (sCRM). sCRM has cut down the response cycle and the turnaround time of the customer contact.

sCRM means applying social media technologies in the field of CRM. After social media have initially focused on the networking among individuals, many companies now try to be active on social media platforms. Today, well-known brands have attracted a large number of members, which are referred to as 'followers,' 'friends,' or 'fans' depending on the terminology of the respective networks. Although these relationships are rather loose, they represent a potential for CRM since each member has expressed an interest in a certain company and/or brand. This is an opportunity for all CRM processes, which comprise marketing, sales, and customer service or rather after-sales services. Social media contribute an additional interaction channel towards customers with a unique set of features. Compared to existing channels, such as call center, sales office, or e-mail, social media are superior regarding availability, interactivity and reach. In the last years, numerous examples, both positive as well as negative have emerged for sCRM.

In the first place, sCRM denotes the use of social media technologies by companies to interact with potential customers. Initially, social media have been referred to as Web 2.0 technologies, which have become known as a third stage of the internet evolution. The first stage goes back to the birth of the internet in 1962. Distributed transport protocols, such as TCP/IP, enabled a worldwide electronic transfer of data. In 1989, the worldwide web (WWW) was developed, which allowed to publish and organize data more easily on the basis of hypertext pages. The WWW also formed the basis for electronic commerce (e-commerce), initially via companies' web pages and later via catalogs and marketplaces, such as Amazon or eBay. During this second stage, internet presences and transactions have increased exponentially, as illustrated by the number of servers connected to the internet and the development of e-commerce. Today, there are around one billion Internet hosts (ISC, 2019b) and an estimated four billion active internet users worldwide. Since 2001, a third stage has emerged, which describes the rise of Web 2.0 and mobile devices that enable access to the internet from any location.

The third stage adds to the previous stages and enhances the functionality of internet-based services. Similar to the first two stages, the technological innovations led to the creation of new businesses. Players of stage one and two, for example, Amazon, Google, and eBay were complemented by social media companies, which offer services in the social web. The social web is a broad term and covers providers and users of content, services, platforms and technologies, data protection organizations that are involved in interaction by means of digital content. Social media are more specific and include providers of digital platforms based on Web 2.0 technologies as well as a variety of other service providers. Compared to the first two evolution stages, the social web is significantly more dynamic, with the number of worldwide social network users having more than doubled from 1.99 billion in 2010 (Statista, 2017) to 4.38 billion in 2019 (We are Social, 2019). Many social media platforms have appeared since then for different purposes such as blogs, messaging, networking and media sharing. Today, millions of users are active on the dominant platforms. Facebook reports 2.41 billion (Facebook, 2020), Twitter 330 million (Twitter, 2020), WeChat 1082 million (Tencent, 2018), WhatsApp 1.7 billion (Facebook, 2020) and YouTube 1.9 billion (Wojcicki, 2018) monthly users. Over time, the functionalities of the platforms have continuously evolved (e.g., messaging on Facebook, media sharing on LinkedIn or live streaming in Twitter (Kantrowitz, 2017)).

While so-called Web 1.0 technologies from the first and the second internet stage, for example, HTML, HTTP, and TCP/IP focused on publishing and linking electronic content on the internet, Web 2.0 technologies were created for users to interact directly with each other. The dynamics on these web platforms follow some basic principles, whereas users may not only passively read content, but also actively publish and forward this content as well as comment or rather evaluate on it. Depending on the respective social media platform, this occurs in communities, which are either private or public in nature. The former consist of selected users that have connected themselves before as 'fans,' 'followers' or through direct messages, and the latter make content accessible to all social web users.

In addition to stationary devices like desktops, mobile devices enable users to easily connect, create and share user-generated content among each other. This has led to a transparent and broadly accessible representation of communication streams between the involved parties, which comprises content, metadata, and other derived data, in particular the well-known 'likes.' Data and information are often distinguished. Information is inferred from data and gives meaning in a certain application setting. Only then, it becomes information. With these properties, social media have several advantages compared to other customer channels. First, due to their 24/7 availability, they are accessible like webpages for customers and businesses alike. Second, interactions are initiated by persons that not only have an identity ID or name, but a rich and telling profile such as current location, personal interests, network of friends, activities, preferred brands. Third, they combine in one channel features for one-to-one communication, as in direct calls, and broadcasting to millions of users, as in television, at the same time. Fourth, users of social media may enrich the content, e.g., with simple likes that indicate the popularity of content, by commenting or by sharing it within communities. Fifth, automated features such as chatbots allow interactivity together with higher efficiency. The combination of these properties in one channel presents the value of social media for customer interaction. For example, companies may target micro-segments of customers, distribute individualized ads, provide a chatbot in case of basic questions and jump into a bidirectional interaction at any time for a price much lower than in traditional channels such as in TV, newspaper, or sales representatives.

Data in social media platforms may be assessed and extracted in different ways. The basic form is to manually access data from social media platforms and to forward it to other systems, such as sCRM or CRM systems. For example, social media managers may read and answer postings of followers in a social network. In case they identify relevant postings, they may create a sales opportunity in the CRM system. More advanced is an electronic integration between the systems, which provides a basis for automation and handling an increasing number of platforms, profiles and interactions. Social media managers may then see postings in a sCRM tool that has electronically extracted data from the selected platforms in a separate sCRM database. This single point of access allows to browse and to answer postings or to define rules or alerts for specific events. The intermediate sCRM system and database are Electronic access is an important element in sCRM and enables to efficiently address the big data challenge. Table 13.1 shows some examples for electronic access on data from social media platforms, which may prove relevant for CRM. This data is available via so-called application programming interfaces that allow data extraction via electronic interfaces. However, the interfaces as well as the accessible data of the various platforms may change.

New services like selling data for advertising and new data fields such as access to links between users at LinkedIn may appear as restrictions to access data. Consequently, companies that obtain data and services via electronic interfaces or crawlers need to adapt these interfaces regularly. This involves continuous changes regarding the electronic interfaces. Above all, businesses need to realize that the extraction of data is inherently linked with the question of data protection. In particular, privately shared and personal data may only be collected when the necessary permissions are available. Since third parties may also access, process, and distribute user-generated content, an extensive ecosystem of service providers has developed in addition to sCRM tool providers. These service providers offer a variety of services related to sCRM strategies and are based on the creation or processing of user-generated content (Brinker, 2018). For example, market researchers analyze the behavior of users for general trends, marketing agencies share and enrich user-generated content during campaigns, or data analysts predict the sales success of products. Besides services, also providers for data have emerged. Third-party aggregators continuously collect and pre-process public content from social media platforms and provide this content via unified interfaces for other companies. Businesses have the advantage that these service providers handle the electronic integration with the social media platforms and deliver ready-to-use services and insights.

TABLE 13.1　　eCRM Data Available from Four Popular Social Media Platforms

Social Media Platform	Data Available via API
Facebook	Facebook ID, Name, profile link, place of residence, user's description, work, schools attended, gender, time zone, language, friends, timeline entries, images, notes, likes, shares, and events.
Twitter	User ID, tweets, timeline, hashtags, private messages, follower, following, trends, location.
LinkedIn	LinkedIn ID, user/company name, date of birth, profile headline, location, industry sector, position, picture, skills, certifications, courses, contents, links to other users as connections, following, related profile views.
Instagram	User ID, user-specific data, liked content, comments, relationships, followed by content data such as tags, locations, comments, likes.

In the beginnings of the social media era, communication was mainly among individuals and within their personal networks. It was only later that companies have established presences in the social web. Meanwhile, companies with well-known brands were able to attract millions of users. In general, the number of these users and the number of 'likes' indicates a certain affinity to the company or the brand and thus, a willingness in obtaining news or offers. Businesses have slowly developed their social media presence since they became aware that attractive content needs to be provided continuously. Many companies also saw social media as an opportunity to reduce costs in customer acquisition. In fact, social media promise a decrease in this respect with costs between one hundredth to one-tenth for simple campaigns compared to classical channels depending on the industry (Chen and Hitt, 2002). Since social media are primarily an interactive channel, their overall goal is to create and maintain long-term customer relationships to increase customer lifetime value (CLV). Typical CRM areas are to be found in all customer-facing activities, i.e., marketing, sales, and customer service. Typically, the CLV concept assumes a customer life cycle, where companies or their products attract potential customers from the anonymous market. This initiates a relationship, where potential buyers are converted to customers who undertake repeated purchases. The customer life cycle has multiple touchpoints to the three core CRM processes and their sub-processes which are as follows:

1. **Marketing:** Although the marketing of products and services may be influenced by all activities along the customer life cycle, a more precise understanding sees marketing primarily in the early stages of the life cycle. It comprises the initial phases with the sub-processes campaign management and lead management.

2. **Sales:** From a business perspective, the sales process starts with the formulation of a specific offer and includes the purchase transaction itself. The sub-process offers management covers negotiating and arranging activities via one or more interaction channels and ends with closing a contract or sale and the settlement of the transaction with delivery and payment.

3. **Customer Service:** The service process contains interactions between customers and businesses after purchasing and during possessing or using a product. It covers the sub-processes complaint management, activities connected with maintenance or defects (service management), as well as the handling of feedback from customers about the company or its products and services (feedback management). Although revenues are typically associated with the sales process, the service process often yields stable service fees and is vital for customer satisfaction.

sCRM now combines social media and CRM. The concept dates back to the second development stage of the internet before the social web came into being. sCRM solutions have emerged within the third stage around 2007 and brought a new quality to CRM with a stronger and more direct interaction potential with individual customers. By definition, sCRM denotes the use of social media in the relationship of customers with companies. Compared to other terms, such as social networking or social media management, sCRM focuses on applications in the field of CRM and the link to CRM processes and systems.

13.5.1 ELEMENTS OF SOCIAL CRM (sCRM)

Users share content on the social web via social media platforms, which are hosted by one or more platform providers. Individuals as well as companies have presences on these platforms, and this is where they interact with other companies and service providers. sCRM solutions feature five technological elements (Table 13.2), which include social media, analytics, interaction, CRM, and management/integration. The first element refers to establishing a corporate presence on a single or on multiple social media platforms. These platforms offer functionalities that enable the interaction between actors (e.g., employees, customers, partners, traders, fans, sponsors) and the extraction of the raw data for sCRM, such as opinions, experiences, and inquiries. Depending on the operation model (owned, hosted) and the openness of the platform (internal, external, access-restricted), different types of social media platforms may be distinguished. Owned platforms are within the responsibility of the company, while hosted platforms are operated by external platform providers, such as Facebook, Twitter, or YouTube.

Openness refers to community membership, which might be restricted to members of the organization (internal), to registered users outside the company (external access restricted), or to all users without restrictions (external open). A key condition for sCRM is that platform providers define the terms of use. This means that businesses are able to influence these conditions only in the owned model.

The second element refers to analytical functionalities, which use data within the social media platforms to derive insights on customers and/or markets. Most platforms offer members to analyze the activity on their social media presence with tools that are integrated in the platform itself. This comprises data about the interactions of users with content, for example, number of likes, comments, impressions, as well as basic analytical functionalities such as campaign success, target group segmentation.

TABLE 13.2 Elements of Social CRM Solutions

SL. No.	Social CRM Elements	Description
1.	Social media	Social media platforms such as forums, wiki, and communities, enable the distribution and the joint generation of information. The objective is to establish a presence in the social web and networking with potential customers.
2.	Analysis	Analytical techniques allow to monitor, filter, search, aggregate, enrich, transform or create business objects such as lead generation. The objective is to identify relevant content, key players, and services in the social web, impact analyzes of customer-oriented activities and interpretation of social web content.
3.	Interaction	Interaction techniques enable dialogs via publishing and sharing of content such as recommendations to contacts. The objective is to have reactive and proactive communication with the social media users.
4.	CRM	Integration with internal systems that support lead, contact, campaign, and service management. The objective is to create functionalities for operative, analytical and collaborative CRM activities and for using social content such as contact details, postings in CRM activities of analysis.
5.	Management and integration	Establishing an overall perspective on multiple social media and internal activities, such as moderation of multiple presences, cross-platform processes and workflows. The objective is to establish strategic and operative control of social media channels and activities, integration between systems and establishing online capabilities.

Although manual monitoring of social media platforms is possible and yields first insights on activities in the social web, the big data nature of the social web calls for automated extraction and evaluation of user-generated content. Via electronic interfaces offered by many social media platforms, user-generated content may be imported in dedicated software tools, which offer advanced analytical functionalities for monitoring and processing.

The third element comprises functionalities for interaction between companies and social media users. They are important to publish news about the company or its products, to answer individual postings or requests as well as to support a community with additional services such as apps for social media platforms. The social media platforms already provide basic functionalities such as alerts, scheduling functions, and different types of interactions, for example, broadcast, private messages, likes which might be extended by additional software tools. Valuable contributions to the interaction element are recent technologies in the area of conversational interfaces chatbots.

The fourth element is CRM, which provides key functionalities in the CRM design areas namely, operational, analytical, communicative, and collaborative CRM. Operational CRM is responsible for supporting the processes along the customer life cycle and aims at a completing a 360° view on the customer. For example, the interaction with customers via social media may be recorded in their customer profile similar to activities on other channels, such as past requests to the call center or offline branch visits. Analytical CRM links to the analytical element in sCRM and contributes categories and metrics on campaign success, which are helpful in assessing and planning customer-oriented activities. Communicative and collaborative CRM include functionalities to align multiple interaction channels and, thus, to integrate social media in the company's channel mix. User-generated content could, for example, be published on the company website, used in the call center database or displayed in the company's electronic shops. The final element provides functionalities for management and integration. Integration predefines processes or how the company reacts to certain critical situations. Incidents may be forwarded to the respective department, e.g., services, customer intelligence within the company, which again requires an integration with the company's internal systems.

sCRM exploits the potentials of the social web for CRM. It leverages the power of social media in establishing direct relationships with consumers, including potential and existing customers. Similar to the CRM concept, sCRM has implications on a company's strategy, organization and systems:

- Strategically speaking, sCRM enhances existing CRM concepts towards more interactivity and brings businesses closer to their customers.
- Organizationally speaking, sCRM requires new competencies and tasks that are necessary to embed social media into more real-time and networked CRM processes.
- Technologically speaking, sCRM application systems automate many tasks, such as monitoring, interaction and management. They allow to extract large data volumes, to conduct analyzes that shape decision-making as well as to align multiple presences.

Ultimately, sCRM has the potential to positively affect the customer experience and key business metrics. This includes stronger emotional and more interactive relationships with 'fans' or 'followers' due to focused and timely recommendations, sales possibilities and service processes. Instead of aiming at increasing customer retention, the customer perspective emphasizes understanding the customer's problems and her view from outside on the providers of products or services. Social media are centered on customers, and via presences in multiple social media platforms, businesses could stay in contact with them along various touchpoints along the cycle. An sCRM strategy may not only associate different goals with these social media platforms, but also design trajectories between the platforms. A customer-oriented life cycle is more dynamic since social media unlock more touchpoints with customers that are also interactive in nature. The key potentials of this customer-orientation are as follows:

- In the digital economy, critical developments and events are increasingly discussed on platforms where customers interact with each other and with businesses. Tracking these channels is a prerequisite to identify and to react to developments in the market.
- The multiple touchpoints for interaction along the customer life cycle are opportunities to create customer value. Among the examples are individualized offers based on aggregated knowledge (collective intelligence, recommendation engines), enhanced sales experience (group shopping, social shopping), new types of customer service (self-service, service dialog via chats), or innovation management (co-creation, open innovation). On many major social media platforms like Facebook and Instagram, previous interactions of companies with users also influence the firm's visibility on these platforms. For example, Facebook increased the priority of content from individuals compared to companies, so that even the reach of paid content will be limited unless prior relationships (based on regular likes, friendship) to users already exist.
- While analytic methods offer numerous possibilities, their application is not necessarily in the user's interest. Businesses should always be conscious of this, keeping data protection issues transparent and having self-determined users in mind. This includes foreseeing and offering options wherever possible as well as disclosing collected personal data to the respective user.
- Multiple social media presences should be assessed in view of the control of content and contact channels. External platforms secure a high reach of the sCRM approach, especially where there is a risk

of losing control. Owned platforms promise independence, superior analytic possibilities and a more individual treatment of contacts. The challenge here is to transfer contacts from external platforms to internal platforms.

- Following a layered approach, businesses are typically present on different social media platforms. These may be owned or hosted presences as well as open or restricted platforms. It is necessary to coordinate multilingual presences and platforms together with other customer interaction channels in the respective countries, in particular, if businesses operate internationally.

Although the long-term effects of sCRM are not fully known, the available data suggests potentials for all CRM core processes. These effects do not arise automatically from simply establishing a social media presence but are the result of a comprehensive and conscious sCRM perspective that includes the alignment of strategy, organization, and systems.

Ultimately, each sCRM approach needs to match the image of a company. For example, businesses with emotionally strong products may use social media for cooperative marketing activities. While social media show many potentials for CRM processes along the customer life cycle (Stelzner, 2019), many sCRM systems rely on marketing and service. However, new features and alliances such as the cooperation between Instagram and Amazon or Chatbots with AI provide new means for directly supporting the sales process. Building on the idea of shops on Facebook, users will be able to jump into a purchase process from any social media-based touchpoint in their customer journey, which further enhances the link between marketing, sales, and service. For example, social media users may order products while they are reading user-generated content or while they are in activities within their community. This way, firms can more easily address potential buyers through community-specific social media platforms, such as fashion-conscious users of Instagram, tech conscious users in IT forums, or travel conscious users on blogs. However, the basis for realizing such scenarios is an existing integration of social media with CRM-related processes and systems. An important precondition for sCRM is the maturity of the organizational and technical infrastructure: If companies only analyze their presences with the functionalities of a social media platform, it is possible to obtain standardized results (e.g., number of postings, likes). More advanced solutions, including automated text analysis, however, may yield much richer insights into background information and may allow to use data for further purpose. For instance, automated searches for problems and solutions discussed on social platforms offer the possibility to identify recurring service-related questions. An example would be an airline passenger who has left a valuable object on the plane and contacts the airline via a social media service. Via a real-time analytics system, the airline could then identify the problem and notify the operating division or operating service provider at the respective airport. They would be able to locate the object and to inform the passenger directly via social media. Twitter has emerged as a very useful instant service tool in this regard. Very fast turnaround times have been achieved and reported by using the direct messaging in Twitter. Service companies have quick response social media teams which respond quickly to serve the customers. Such quick responses require a high degree of alignment of organizational and technological issues.

13.6 FUTURE TRENDS IN CRM

A framework of integrated sCRM, which includes design elements on three conceptual levels:

1. **Strategy Level:** Depending on a company's sCRM goals, the available strategies differ for each CRM process and lead to various combinations. Mature sCRM solutions illustrate that sCRM may contribute to enhance customer satisfaction and lifetime value in every stage of the life cycle. Besides cross-functional processes, such as product and innovation management, the social media team also conducts campaign, lead, offer and services management via social media.
2. **Process Level:** An integrated scenario includes a coordinated presence on multiple social media platforms, the coordination of customer touchpoints in social media as well as the use of analytical and interaction functions that are linked via management functions with the core CRM processes.
3. **Systems Level:** At the system level are the applications and functionalities that support an integrated sCRM. These include the functionalities of the individual social media platforms, the various application systems, and the interfaces among these components.

Going forward, two main perspectives may be expected for integrated sCRM infrastructures. On the one hand, providers of sCRM systems may consolidate their sCRM functionalities like text mining in their tools. This mainly applies to providers of sCRM system as well as to providers of sCRM tools. On the other hand, more specialized systems may evolve with defined interfaces. While providers of CRM systems have the advantage of direct access to relevant customer and market data and the ability to integrate with both back-end and front-end systems, specialized sCRM tools may develop and implement new functions rapidly without taking comprehensive workflows into account.

To summarize, we can conclude that the emerging field of sCRM and awareness of the potentials of social media in customer-facing processes is going to take center stage in CRM. Based on the observed trends, it can safely be surmised that social media will emerge as an important communication and interaction channel, complementing other channels. The goods and services businesses are slowly rising to the added value of sCRM for themselves and their customers.

A positive and constructive use of sCRM offers valuable advantages in achieving more customer-orientation. Convincing incentives are necessary to persuade users to share their personal data. However, businesses have to ensure that this data is handled with trust and in accordance with data protection laws. Companies need to be aware of the legal conditions regarding the collection, processing, and storage of user-generated content. It may be expected that increased legal certainty together with the growing performance and integration skills of existing and new sCRM systems, will allow businesses to implement more mature sCRM solutions with less financial investment in the future.

KEYWORDS

- **customer relationship management**
- **electronic customer relationship management**
- **predictive analysis**
- **supply chain management**
- **supply chain operation reference**
- **worldwide web**

REFERENCES

Agarwal, A., Harding, D. P., & Schumacher, J. R., (2004). Organizing for CRM. *Mckinsey Quarterly, Issue 3.*

Alt, R., & Reinhold, O., (2012). Social customer relationship management (social CRM): Application and technology. *Business and Information Systems Engineering, 4*(5), 287–291.

Alt, R., & Zimmermann, H. D., (2019). Electronic markets on platform competition. *Electronic Markets, 29*(2), 143–149. https://doi.org/10.1007/s12525-019-00353-y.

Anderson, J. A., & Narus, M., (2003). Selectively pursuing more of your customer's business. *T Sloan Management Review*, 42–49.

Brinker, S., (2018). *Marketing Technology Landscape Super Graphic.* https://chiefmartec.com/2018/04/marketing-technology-landscape-supergraphic-2018/ (accessed on 24 February 2021).

Chen, I. J., & Popovich, K., (2003). Understanding customer relationship management (CRM): People, process and technology. *Business Process Management Journal, 9*(5), 672–688.

Chen, P. Y., & Hitt, L., (2002). Measuring switching costs and the determinants of customer retention in internet-enabled businesses: A study of the online brokerage industry. *Information Systems Research, 13*(3), 255–274.

Cho, Y., Im, I., Fjermestad, J., & Hiltz, R., (2002). An analysis of online customer complaints: Implications for web complaint management. *Proceedings of the 35th Hawaii International Conference on System Sciences.* Hawaii: Big Island.

Davydova, O., (2017). *Twenty-Five Chatbot Platforms: A Comparative Table.* https://chatbotsjournal.com/25-chatbot-platforms-a-comparative-table-aeefc932eaff (accessed on 24 February 2021).

Dyché, J., (2002). *The CRM Handbook.* Boston: Addison-Wesley.

Facebook, (2020). *Number of Monthly Active WhatsApp Users Worldwide from April 2013 to December 2019 (in millions).* https://www.statista.com/statistics/260819/number-of-monthlyactive-WhatsApp-users/ (accessed on 24 February 2021).

Fjermestad, J., & Romano, N. C., (2003). Advances in electronic commerce customer relationship management. *International Journal of Electronic Commerce, 7*(2).

Fjermestad, J., (2002). Advances in electronic commerce customer relationship management. *International Journal of Electronic Commerce.*

Fuller, J., O'Conor, J., & Rawlinson, R., (1993). Tailored logistics: The next advantage. *Harvard Business Review*, 87–98.

Goodhue, D. W., (2002). Realizing business benefits through CRM: Hitting the right target the right way. *MIS Quarterly Executive*, 79–94.

Greenberg, P., (2002). *CRM at the Speed of Light.* New York: McGraw-Hill.

Greenberg, P., (2009). *CRM at the Speed of Light: Social CRM Strategies, Tools, and Techniques for Engaging Your Customers.* New York: The McGraw-Hill Companies.

Greenwald, G., (2013). *XKeyscore: NSA Tool Collects 'Nearly Everything a User Does on the Internet.'* https://www.theguardian.com/world/2013/jul/31/nsa-top-secret-program-online-data (accessed on 24 February 2021).

Grönroos, C., (2000). *Service Management and Marketing: A Customer Relationship Management Approach.* UK: Wiley.

Gulati, R., (2005). The quest for customer focus. *Harvard Business Review*, 92–101.

Gurau, C., Ranchhod, A., & Hackney, R., (2003). Customer-centric strategic planning: Integrating CRM in online business systems. *Information Technology and Management*, 199–214.

Hansen, W., (2000). *Principles of Internet Marketing*. Mason: South-Western College Publishing.

Hippel, V., (2005). *E. Democratizing Innovation*. Cambridge: MIT Press.

ISC, (2019a). *Internet Domain Survey*. https://www.isc.org/net-work/survey/ (accessed on 24 February 2021).

ISC, (2019b). *ISC Distributions by Top-Level Domain Name (by name)*. ftp.isc.org/www/survey/reports/current/byname.txt (accessed on 24 February 2021).

Jukic, N., Jukic, B., Meamber, L., & Nezlek, G., (2003). Implementing polyinstantiation as a strategy of electronic commerce customer relationship management. *International Journal of Electronic Commerce*, 9–30.

Julta, D., Craig, J., & Bodorik, P., (2001). Enabling and measuring electronic customer relationship management readiness. *Proceedings of the 34th Hawaii International Conference on System Sciences* (pp. 533–542). Hawaii.

Kabroviski, R., (2017). *Virtual Reality and the Future of Social Media* http://digitalmar-ketingmagazine.co.uk/social-media-marketing/virtual-reality-and-the-future-of-social-media/4745 (accessed on 24 February 2021).

Kalakota, R., (2003). *Services Blueprint: Roadmap for Execution*. Boston: Services Blueprint: Roadmap for Execution.

Kantrowitz, A., (2017). *Twitter Plans to Broadcast Live Video 24 Hours a Day*. https://www.buzzfeed.com/alexkantrowitz/twitter-wants-to-stream-live-video-programming-247?utm_term=.vd8wvw1MO#.rjm6W678l (accessed on 24 February 2021).

Kapoor, S. B., (2005). A technical framework for sense-and-respond business management. *IBM Systems Journal*, 5–24.

Karimi, J. S., (2001). Impact of information technology management practices on customer service. *Journal of Management Information Systems*, 125–158.

Keeney, R., (1999). The value of internet commerce to the customer. *Management Science*, 533–542.

Klein, S. K., (2006). Extending customer's roles in e-commerce-promises, challenges, and some findings. In: Shaw, M. J., (ed.), *Electronic Commerce and Digital Economy. Advances in Management Information Systems* (pp. 75–90). Armonk, NY: M.E. Sharpe.

Loveman, G., (2003). Diamonds in the data mine. *Harvard Business Review*, 109–113.

McKaige, W., (2001). Collaborating on the supply chain. *IIE Solutions*, 34–37.

Pan, S. A., (2003). Using e-CRM for a unified view of the customer. *Communications of the ACM*, 95–99.

Parker, G., & Thomas, L., (2012). *Wave 6: The Business of Social-Media Tracker 2012*. http://www.universalmccann.de/wave6/ (accessed on 24 February 2021).

Peppers, D., & Rogers, M., (2004). *Managing Customer Relationships: A Strategic Framework*. Hoboken: Wiley.

Pfeifer, P. A., (2004). The elasticity of customer value to retention: The duration of customer relationship. *Journal of Interactive Marketing*, 20–31.

Plakoyiannaki, E. A., (2002). Customer relationship management: A capabilities portfolio perspective. *Journal of Database Marketing and Customer Strategy Management*, 228–237.

Press Releases Destatis, (2018). *Ninety Percent of Germany's Inhabitants Online.* https://www.destatis.de/EN/PressServices/Press/pr/2018/09/PE18_330_634.html (accessed on 24 February 2021).

Ries, T. E., Bersoff, D. M., Adkins, S., Armstrong, C., & Bruening, J., (2018). *2018 Edelman Trust Barometer.* New York: Edelman.

Romano, N. A., (2003). Electronic commerce customer relationship management: Research agenda. *Information Technology and Management,* 233–258.

Rust, R. Z., (2000). *Driving Customer Equity: How Customer Lifetime Value is Reshaping Corporate Strategy.* New York: Free Press.

Shaw, R., (1999). *Measuring and Valuing Customer Relationships.* London: Business Intelligence Ltd.

Statista, (2017). *Number of Internet Users Worldwide from 2005 to 2017 (in millions).* Available at: https://www.statista.com/statistics/273018/number-of-internet-users-worldwide/ (accessed on 24 February 2021).

Stelzner, M. A., (2019). *Social Media Marketing Industry Report: How Marketers are Using Social Media to Grow Their Businesses.* https://www.socialmediaexaminer.com/social-media-marketing-industry-report-2019/ (accessed on 24 February 2021).

Strauss, J., El-Ansary, A., & Frost, R., (2003). *E-Marketing.* Upper Saddle River, NJ: Prentice-Hall.

Swift, R., (2001). *Accelerating Customer Relationships.* Upper Saddle River, NJ: Prentice-Hall.

Tencent, (2018). *Tencent Announces 2018 Second Quarter and Interims Results.* https://www.prnewswire.com/news-releases/tencent-announces-2018-second-quarter-and-interim-results-300697463.html (accessed on 24 February 2021).

Twitter, (2018). *Number of Monthly Active Twitter Users Worldwide from 1st Quarter 2010 to 3rd Quarter 2018 (in millions).* https://investor.twitterinc.com/static-files/b9402133-be92-4ea4-ac2b-db20be19d1cd (accessed on 24 February 2021).

Venkatesan, R., (2004). A customer lifetime value framework for customer selection and resource allocations strategy. *Journal of Marketing,* 106–125.

We are Social, (2019). *The State of the Internet in 2019.* https://wearesocial.com/blog/2019/01/digital-2019-global-internet-use-accelerates (accessed on 24 February 2021).

Wojcicki, S., (2018). *Mid-Year Update on Our Five Creator Priorities for 2018.* https://blog.youtube/inside-youtube/mid-year-update-on-our-five-creator?m=1 (accessed on 24 February 2021).

Zineldin, M., (2000). Beyond relationship marketing: Technological ship marketing. *Marketing Intelligence and Planning,* 9–23.

Zuboff, S. A., (2002). *The Support Economy.* New York: Viking.

Zwass, V., (2002). The embedding stage of electronic commerce. In: Lowry, J. O. P. B., (ed.), *The E-Business Handbook* (pp. 33–43). Boca Raton: St. Lucie Press.

Index